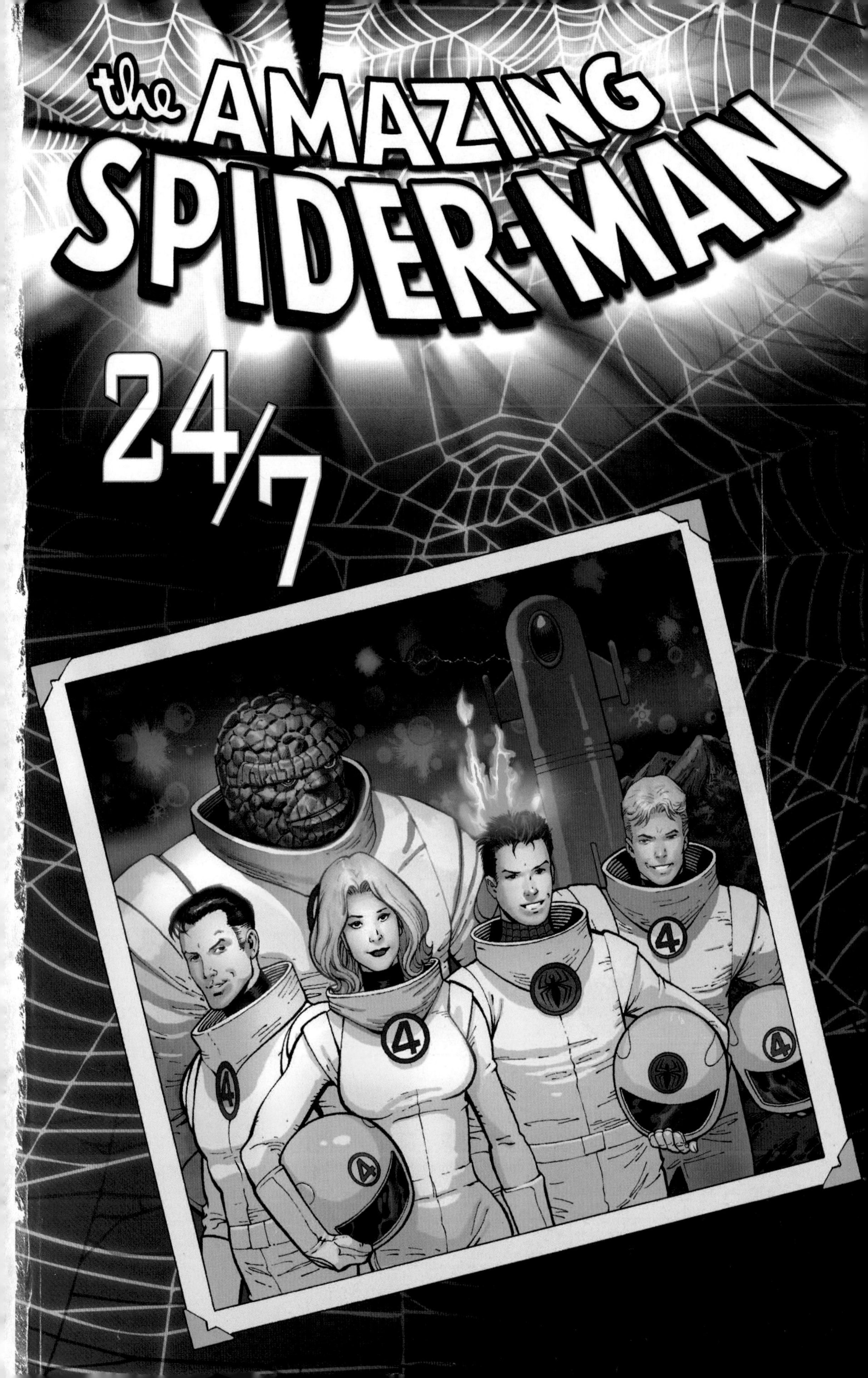
the AMAZING SPIDER-MAN
24/7

the AMAZING SPIDER-MAN
24/7

"LOOSE ENDS"
Writer & Artist: **PHIL JIMENEZ**
Color Artist: **CHRIS CHUCKRY**
Letterer: **VC'S RUS WOOTON**
Cover Art: **TOMM COKER**

ISSUE #289
Writer: **FRED VAN LENTE**
Penciler: **PAULO SIQUEIRA**
Inker: **AMILTON SANTOS**
Color Art: **JEROMY COX**
Letterer: **VC'S CORY PETIT**
Cover: **KLAUS JANSON** WITH **DEAN WHITE**

"BIRTHDAY BOY"
Writer: **ZEB WELLS**
Artist: **PAOLO RIVERA**
Letterer: **VC'S RUS WOOTON**
Cover Art: **STEPHAN ROUX**

ISSUES #590-591
Writer: **DAN SLOTT**
Pencilers: **BARRY KITSON**
WITH **DALE EAGLESHAM**
Inkers: **MARK FARMER**
& **JESSE DELPERDANG**
Color Artists: **DEAN WHITE** WITH **ANDY TROY**
& **CHRIS CHUCKRY**
Letterer: **VC'S JOE CARAMAGNA**
Cover Art: **BARRY KITSON** WITH **JEROMY COX**

ISSUES #592-594
Writer: **MARK WAID**
Pencilers: **MIKE MCKONE**
WITH **BARRY KITSON**
Inkers: **ANDY LANNING**
WITH **MARK MORALES** & **KARL KESEL**
Color Artist: **JEROMY COX**
Letterer: **VC'S JOE CARAMAGNA**
Cover Art: **JOE QUESADA** WITH **DANNY MIKI, TIM
TOWNSEND, RICHARD ISANOVE** & **MORRY HOLLOWELL**

Spidey's Braintrust: **BOB GALE, MARC GUGGENHEIM, JOE KELLY, DAN SLOTT** & **MARK WAID**
Assistant Editor: **THOMAS BRENNAN** • Editor: **STEPHEN WACKER** • Executive Editor: **TOM BREVOORT**

Collection Editor: **JENNIFER GRÜNWALD** • Assistant Editors: **ALEX STARBUCK** & **JOHN DENNING**
Editor, Special Projects: **MARK D. BEAZLEY** • Senior Editor, Special Projects: **JEFF YOUNGQUIST**
Senior Vice President of Sales: **DAVID GABRIEL**

Editor in Chief: **JOE QUESADA** • Publisher: **DAN BUCKLEY** • Executive Producer: **ALAN FINE**

SPIDER-MAN: 24/7. Contains material originally published in magazine form as AMAZING SPIDER-MAN #589-594 and AMAZING SPIDER-MAN: EXTRA! #2-3. First printing 2009. Hardcover ISBN# 978-0-7851-3396-4.
Softcover ISBN# 978-0-7851-3420-6. Published by MARVEL PUBLISHING, INC., a subsidiary of MARVEL ENTERTAINMENT, INC. OFFICE OF PUBLICATION: 417 5th Avenue, New York, NY 10016. Copyright © 2009 Marvel
Characters, Inc. All rights reserved. Hardcover: $24.99 per copy in the U.S. (GST #R127032852). Softcover: $19.99 per copy in the U.S. (GST #R127032852). Canadian Agreement #40668537. All characters featured
in this issue and the distinctive names and likenesses thereof, and all related indicia are trademarks of Marvel Characters, Inc. No similarity between any of the names, characters, persons, and/or institutions in this
magazine with those of any living or dead person or institution is intended, and any such similarity which may exist is purely coincidental. **Printed in the U.S.A.** ALAN FINE, EVP - Office Of The Chief Executive Marvel
Entertainment, Inc. & CMO Marvel Characters B.V.; DAN BUCKLEY, Chief Executive Officer and Publisher - Print, Animation & Digital Media; JIM SOKOLOWSKI, Chief Operating Officer; DAVID GABRIEL, SVP of Publishing
Sales & Circulation; DAVID BOGART, SVP of Business Affairs & Talent Management; MICHAEL PASCIULLO, VP Merchandising & Communications; JIM O'KEEFE, VP of Operations & Logistics; DAN CARR, Executive
Director of Publishing Technology; JUSTIN F. GABRIE, Director of Publishing & Editorial Operations; SUSAN CRESPI, Editorial Operations Manager; ALEX MORALES, Publishing Operations Manager; STAN LEE, Chairman
Emeritus. For information regarding advertising in Marvel Comics or on Marvel.com, please contact Mitch Dane, Advertising Director, at mdane@marvel.com. For Marvel subscription inquiries, please call 800-217-9158.

10 9 8 7 6 5 4 3 2 1

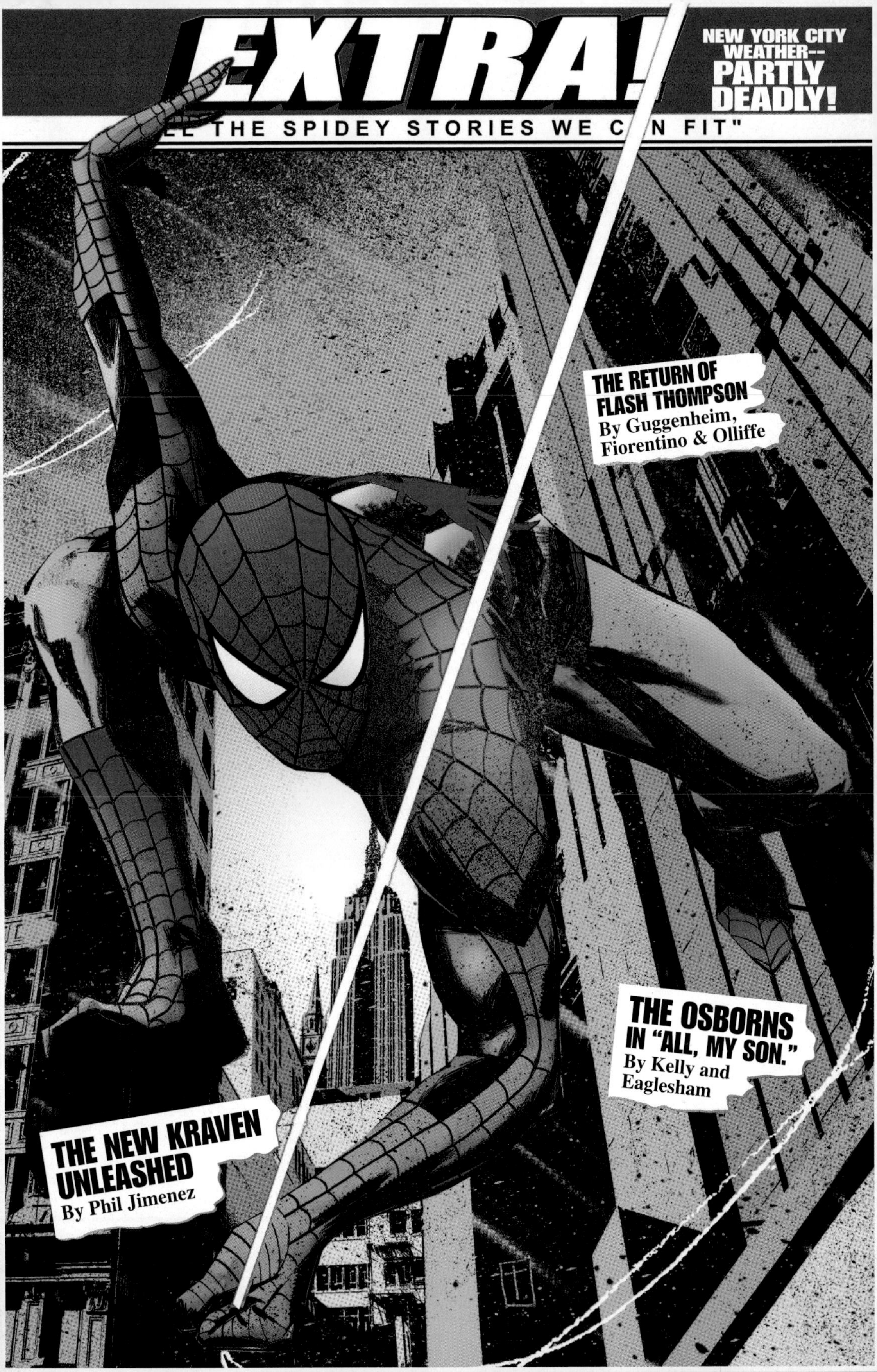
EXTRA!
NEW YORK CITY WEATHER-- PARTLY DEADLY!
THE SPIDEY STORIES WE C N FIT"
THE RETURN OF FLASH THOMPSON
By Guggenheim, Fiorentino & Olliffe
THE OSBORNS IN "ALL, MY SON."
By Kelly and Eaglesham
THE NEW KRAVEN UNLEASHED
By Phil Jimenez

AMAZING SPIDER-MAN: EXTRA! #3 – “LOOSE ENDS”

LOOSE ENDS

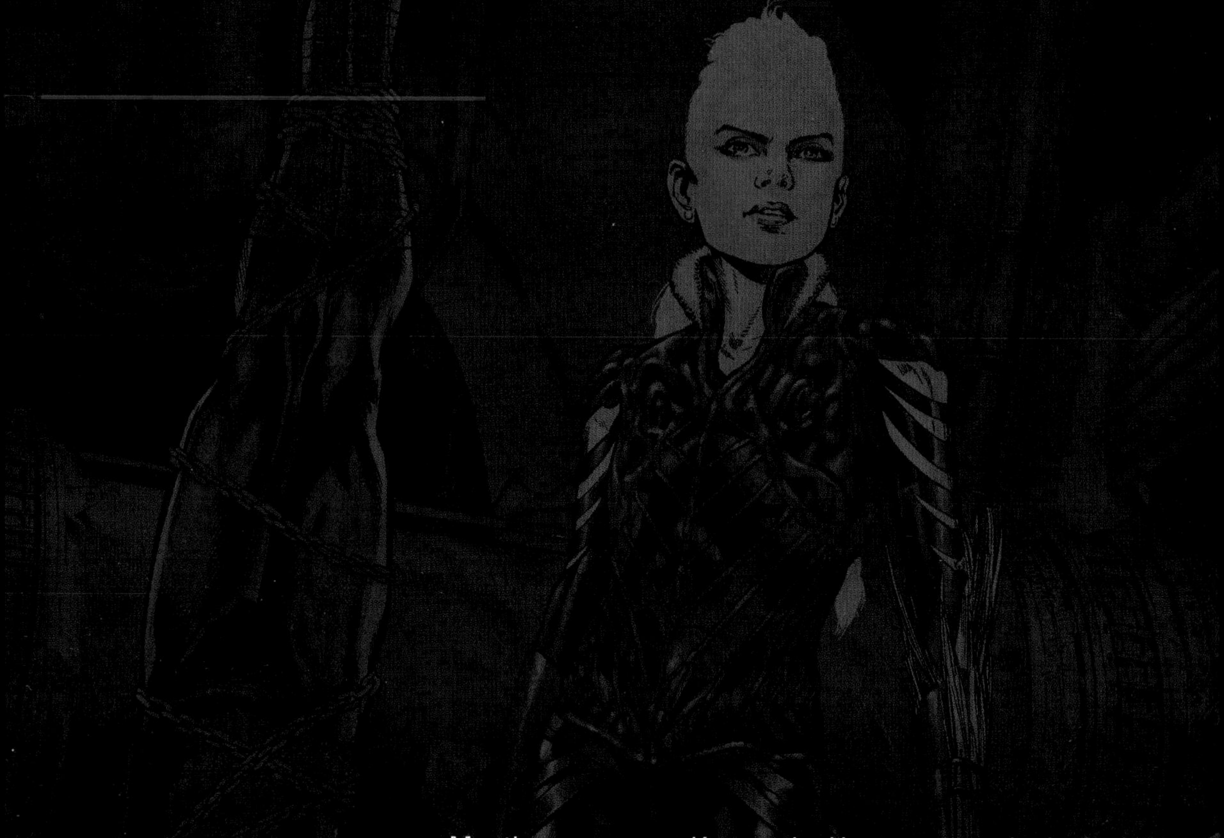

Months ago, a new Kraven the Hunter – seemingly the late Kraven's 12-year-old daughter – stalked Spider-Man, tracing him to his home, apartment of his alter ego, Peter Parker, and Parker's roommate, police officer Vin Gonzales.

The young Ana Kraven deduced Gonzales, not Parker, as Spider-Man's secret identity, systematically destroying his life, wiping out his life savings and getting him suspended from the police force. She then captured Vin and took him to the villainous Vermin's lair in the New York City sewers. There, she pumped Gonzales up with Mutant Growth Hormone and hunted him for sport.

Meanwhile, Peter Parker, borrowing the costume of fellow crime fighter Daredevil to conceal his identity, traced Kraven and Gonzales, rescuing him from certain death and leaving the young Kraven to fight Vermin, who had returned to his home. The young Kraven returned to her mysterious mother with Vermin, now tamed as a prize. Since then she has remained in hiding…

PHIL JIMENEZ
Writer & Artist

CHRIS CHUCKRY
Color Artist

VC'S RUS WOOTON
Letterer

ANTHONY DIAL
Production

TOM BRENNAN
Assistant Editor

STEPHEN WACKER
Editor

TOM BREVOORT
Executive Editor

JOE QUESADA
Editor in Chief

DAN BUCKLEY
Publisher

ALAN FINE
Executive Producer

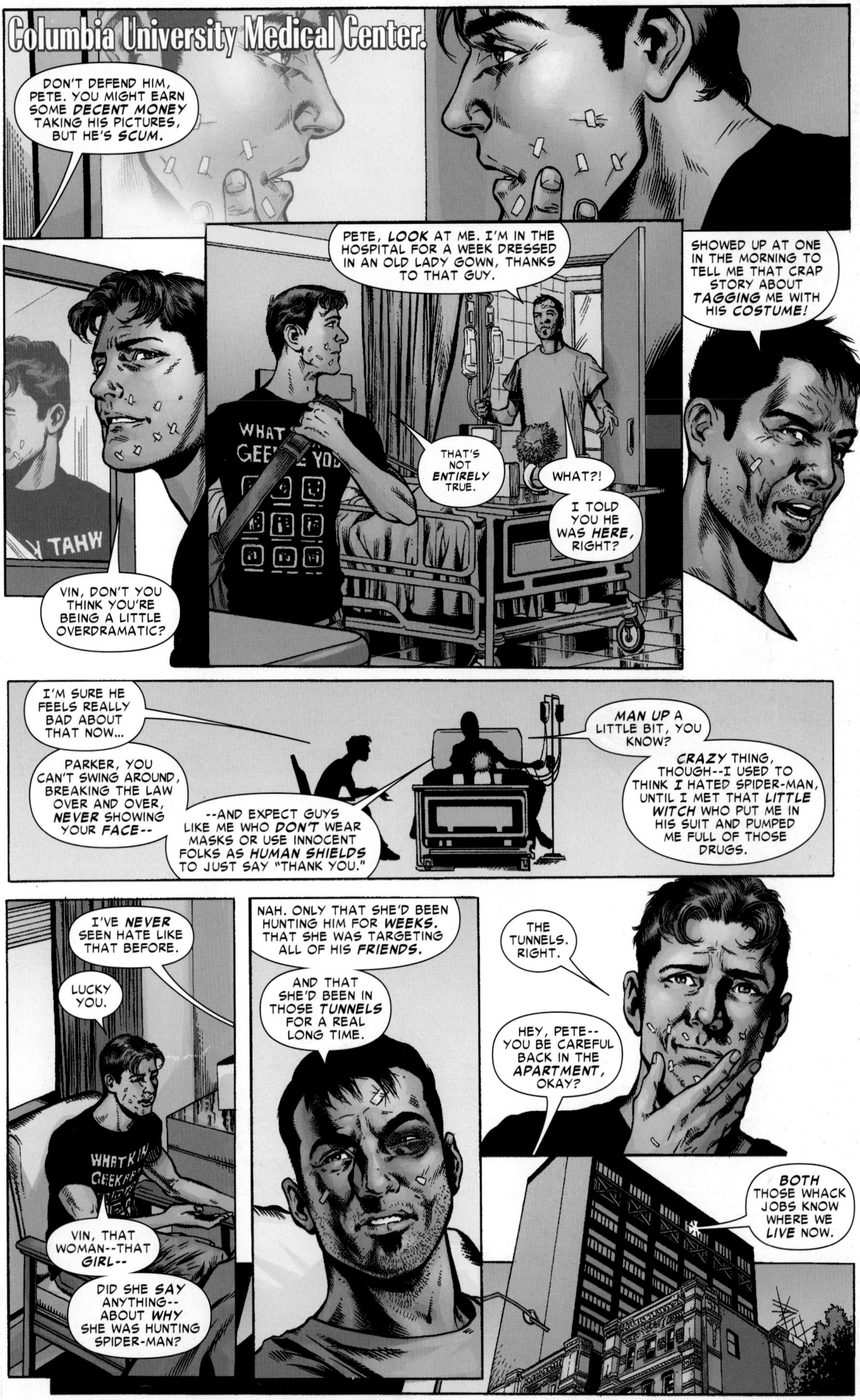
Columbia University Medical Center.
DON'T DEFEND HIM, PETE. YOU MIGHT EARN SOME DECENT MONEY TAKING HIS PICTURES, BUT HE'S SCUM.
PETE, LOOK AT ME. I'M IN THE HOSPITAL FOR A WEEK DRESSED IN AN OLD LADY GOWN, THANKS TO THAT GUY.
SHOWED UP AT ONE IN THE MORNING TO TELL ME THAT CRAP STORY ABOUT TAGGING ME WITH HIS COSTUME!
THAT'S NOT ENTIRELY TRUE.
WHAT?!
I TOLD YOU HE WAS HERE, RIGHT?
VIN, DON'T YOU THINK YOU'RE BEING A LITTLE OVERDRAMATIC?
I'M SURE HE FEELS REALLY BAD ABOUT THAT NOW...
PARKER, YOU CAN'T SWING AROUND, BREAKING THE LAW OVER AND OVER, NEVER SHOWING YOUR FACE--
--AND EXPECT GUYS LIKE ME WHO DON'T WEAR MASKS OR USE INNOCENT FOLKS AS HUMAN SHIELDS TO JUST SAY "THANK YOU."
MAN UP A LITTLE BIT, YOU KNOW?
CRAZY THING, THOUGH--I USED TO THINK I HATED SPIDER-MAN, UNTIL I MET THAT LITTLE WITCH WHO PUT ME IN HIS SUIT AND PUMPED ME FULL OF THOSE DRUGS.
I'VE NEVER SEEN HATE LIKE THAT BEFORE.
LUCKY YOU.
VIN, THAT WOMAN--THAT GIRL--
DID SHE SAY ANYTHING--ABOUT WHY SHE WAS HUNTING SPIDER-MAN?
NAH. ONLY THAT SHE'D BEEN HUNTING HIM FOR WEEKS. THAT SHE WAS TARGETING ALL OF HIS FRIENDS.
AND THAT SHE'D BEEN IN THOSE TUNNELS FOR A REAL LONG TIME.
THE TUNNELS. RIGHT.
HEY, PETE--YOU BE CAREFUL BACK IN THE APARTMENT, OKAY?
BOTH THOSE WHACK JOBS KNOW WHERE WE LIVE NOW.

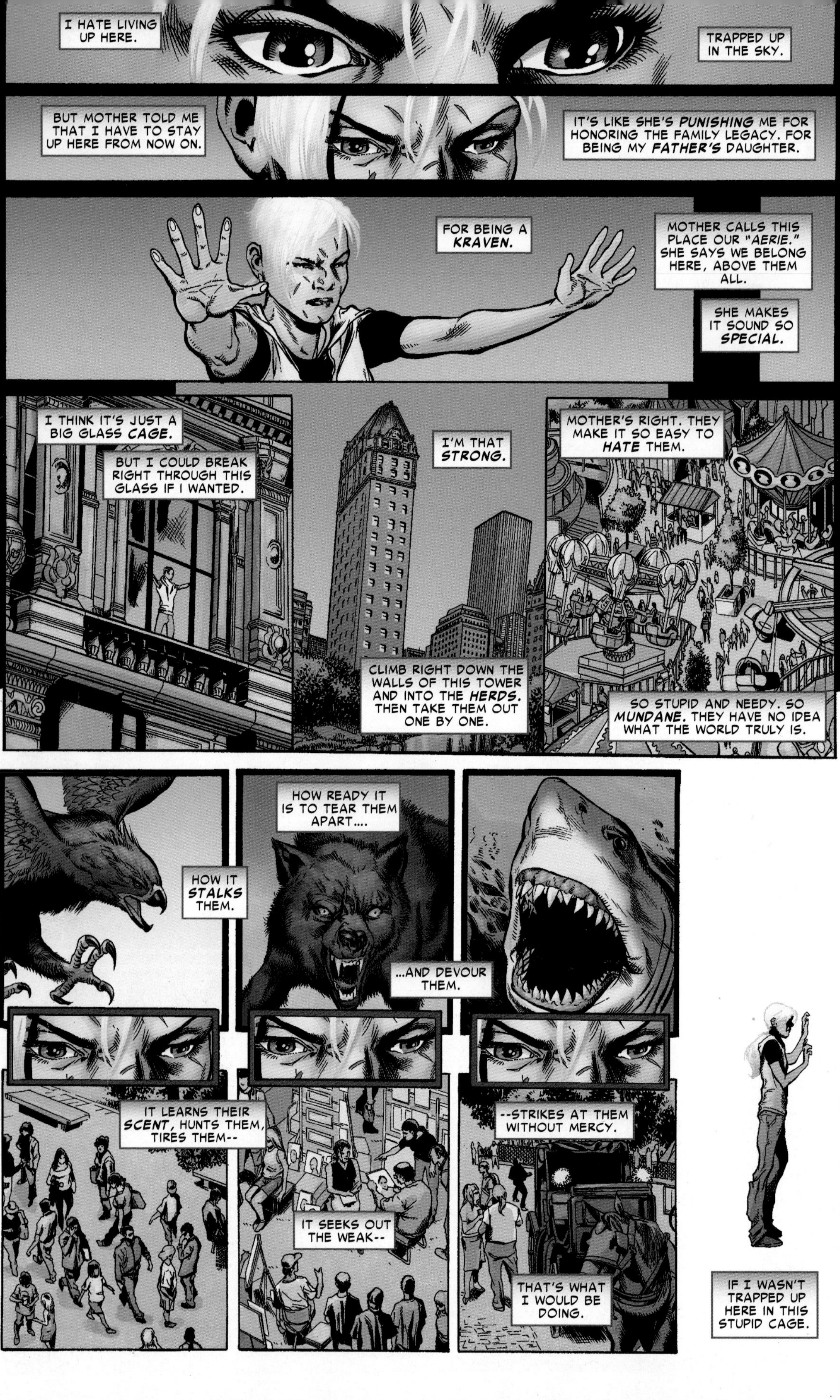
I HATE LIVING UP HERE.
TRAPPED UP IN THE SKY.
BUT MOTHER TOLD ME THAT I HAVE TO STAY UP HERE FROM NOW ON.
IT'S LIKE SHE'S PUNISHING ME FOR HONORING THE FAMILY LEGACY. FOR BEING MY FATHER'S DAUGHTER.
FOR BEING A KRAVEN.
MOTHER CALLS THIS PLACE OUR "AERIE." SHE SAYS WE BELONG HERE, ABOVE THEM ALL.
SHE MAKES IT SOUND SO SPECIAL.
I THINK IT'S JUST A BIG GLASS CAGE.
BUT I COULD BREAK RIGHT THROUGH THIS GLASS IF I WANTED.
I'M THAT STRONG.
CLIMB RIGHT DOWN THE WALLS OF THIS TOWER AND INTO THE HERDS. THEN TAKE THEM OUT ONE BY ONE.
MOTHER'S RIGHT. THEY MAKE IT SO EASY TO HATE THEM.
SO STUPID AND NEEDY. SO MUNDANE. THEY HAVE NO IDEA WHAT THE WORLD TRULY IS.
HOW IT STALKS THEM.
HOW READY IT IS TO TEAR THEM APART....
...AND DEVOUR THEM.
IT LEARNS THEIR SCENT, HUNTS THEM, TIRES THEM--
IT SEEKS OUT THE WEAK--
--STRIKES AT THEM WITHOUT MERCY.
THAT'S WHAT I WOULD BE DOING.
IF I WASN'T TRAPPED UP HERE IN THIS STUPID CAGE.

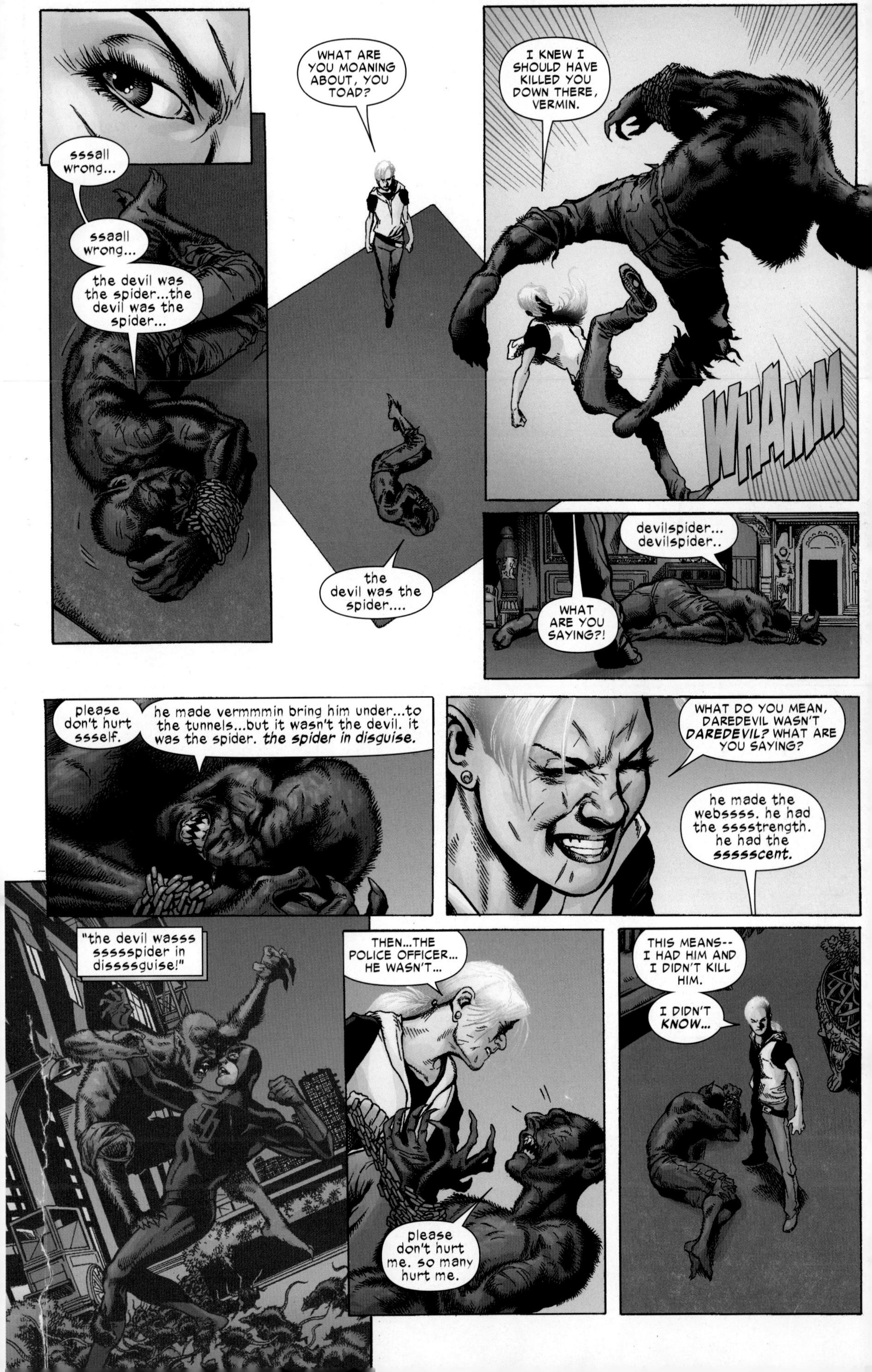
sssall wrong...
ssaall wrong...
the devil was the spider...the devil was the spider...
WHAT ARE YOU MOANING ABOUT, YOU TOAD?
the devil was the spider....
I KNEW I SHOULD HAVE KILLED YOU DOWN THERE, VERMIN.
WHAMM
devilspider... devilspider..
WHAT ARE YOU SAYING?!
please don't hurt ssself.
he made vermmmin bring him under...to the tunnels...but it wasn't the devil. it was the spider. *the spider in disguise.*
WHAT DO YOU MEAN, DAREDEVIL WASN'T *DAREDEVIL?* WHAT ARE YOU SAYING?
he made the webssss. he had the sssstrength. he had the *ssssscent.*
"the devil wasss ssssspider in dissssguise!"
THEN...THE POLICE OFFICER... HE WASN'T...
please don't hurt me. so many hurt me.
THIS MEANS-- I HAD HIM AND I DIDN'T KILL HIM.
I DIDN'T *KNOW...*

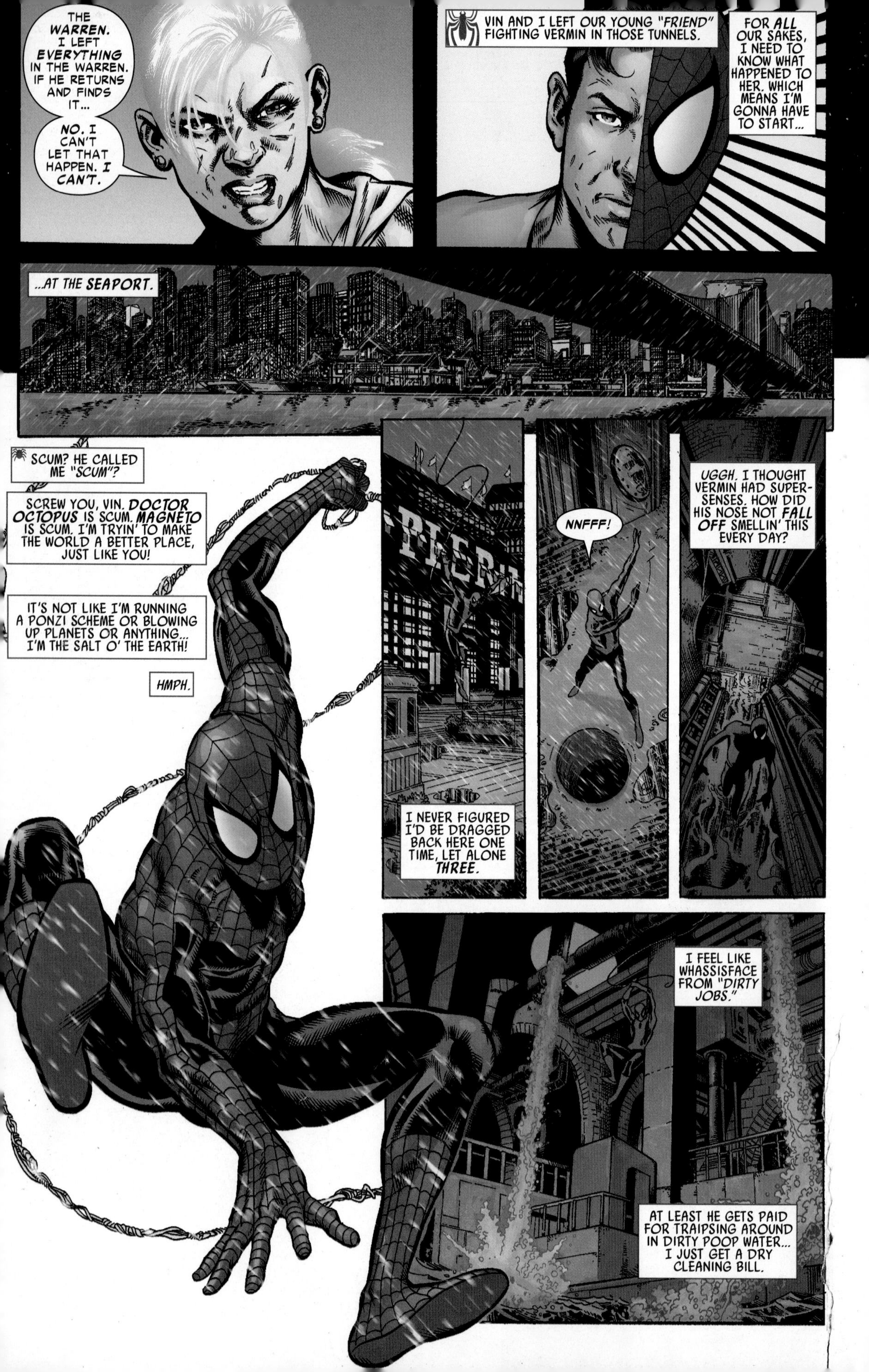
THE WARREN. I LEFT EVERYTHING IN THE WARREN. IF HE RETURNS AND FINDS IT...
NO. I CAN'T LET THAT HAPPEN. I CAN'T.
VIN AND I LEFT OUR YOUNG "FRIEND" FIGHTING VERMIN IN THOSE TUNNELS.
FOR ALL OUR SAKES, I NEED TO KNOW WHAT HAPPENED TO HER. WHICH MEANS I'M GONNA HAVE TO START...
...AT THE SEAPORT.
SCUM? HE CALLED ME "SCUM"?
SCREW YOU, VIN. DOCTOR OCTOPUS IS SCUM. MAGNETO IS SCUM. I'M TRYIN' TO MAKE THE WORLD A BETTER PLACE, JUST LIKE YOU!
IT'S NOT LIKE I'M RUNNING A PONZI SCHEME OR BLOWING UP PLANETS OR ANYTHING... I'M THE SALT O' THE EARTH!
HMPH.
I NEVER FIGURED I'D BE DRAGGED BACK HERE ONE TIME, LET ALONE THREE.
NNFFF!
UGGH. I THOUGHT VERMIN HAD SUPER-SENSES. HOW DID HIS NOSE NOT FALL OFF SMELLIN' THIS EVERY DAY?
I FEEL LIKE WHASSISFACE FROM "DIRTY JOBS."
AT LEAST HE GETS PAID FOR TRAIPSING AROUND IN DIRTY POOP WATER... I JUST GET A DRY CLEANING BILL.

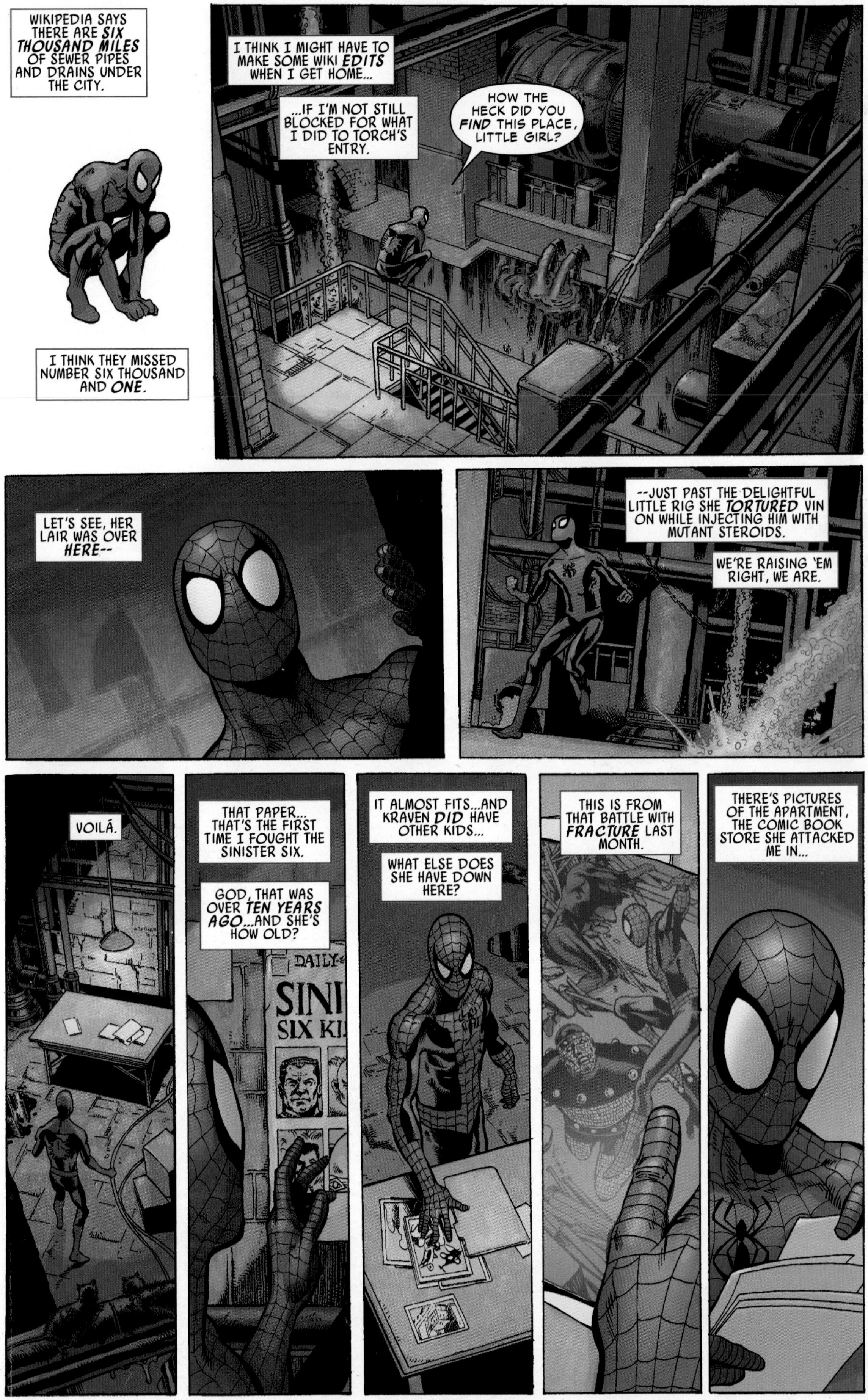

WIKIPEDIA SAYS THERE ARE *SIX THOUSAND MILES* OF SEWER PIPES AND DRAINS UNDER THE CITY.
I THINK THEY MISSED NUMBER SIX THOUSAND AND *ONE.*
I THINK I MIGHT HAVE TO MAKE SOME WIKI *EDITS* WHEN I GET HOME...
...IF I'M NOT STILL BLOCKED FOR WHAT I DID TO TORCH'S ENTRY.
HOW THE HECK DID YOU *FIND* THIS PLACE, LITTLE GIRL?
LET'S SEE, HER LAIR WAS OVER *HERE*--
--JUST PAST THE DELIGHTFUL LITTLE RIG SHE *TORTURED* VIN ON WHILE INJECTING HIM WITH MUTANT STEROIDS.
WE'RE RAISING 'EM RIGHT, WE ARE.
VOILÁ.
THAT PAPER... THAT'S THE FIRST TIME I FOUGHT THE SINISTER SIX.
GOD, THAT WAS OVER *TEN YEARS AGO*...AND SHE'S HOW OLD?
IT ALMOST FITS...AND KRAVEN *DID* HAVE OTHER KIDS...
WHAT ELSE DOES SHE HAVE DOWN HERE?
THIS IS FROM THAT BATTLE WITH *FRACTURE* LAST MONTH.
THERE'S PICTURES OF THE APARTMENT, THE COMIC BOOK STORE SHE ATTACKED ME IN...

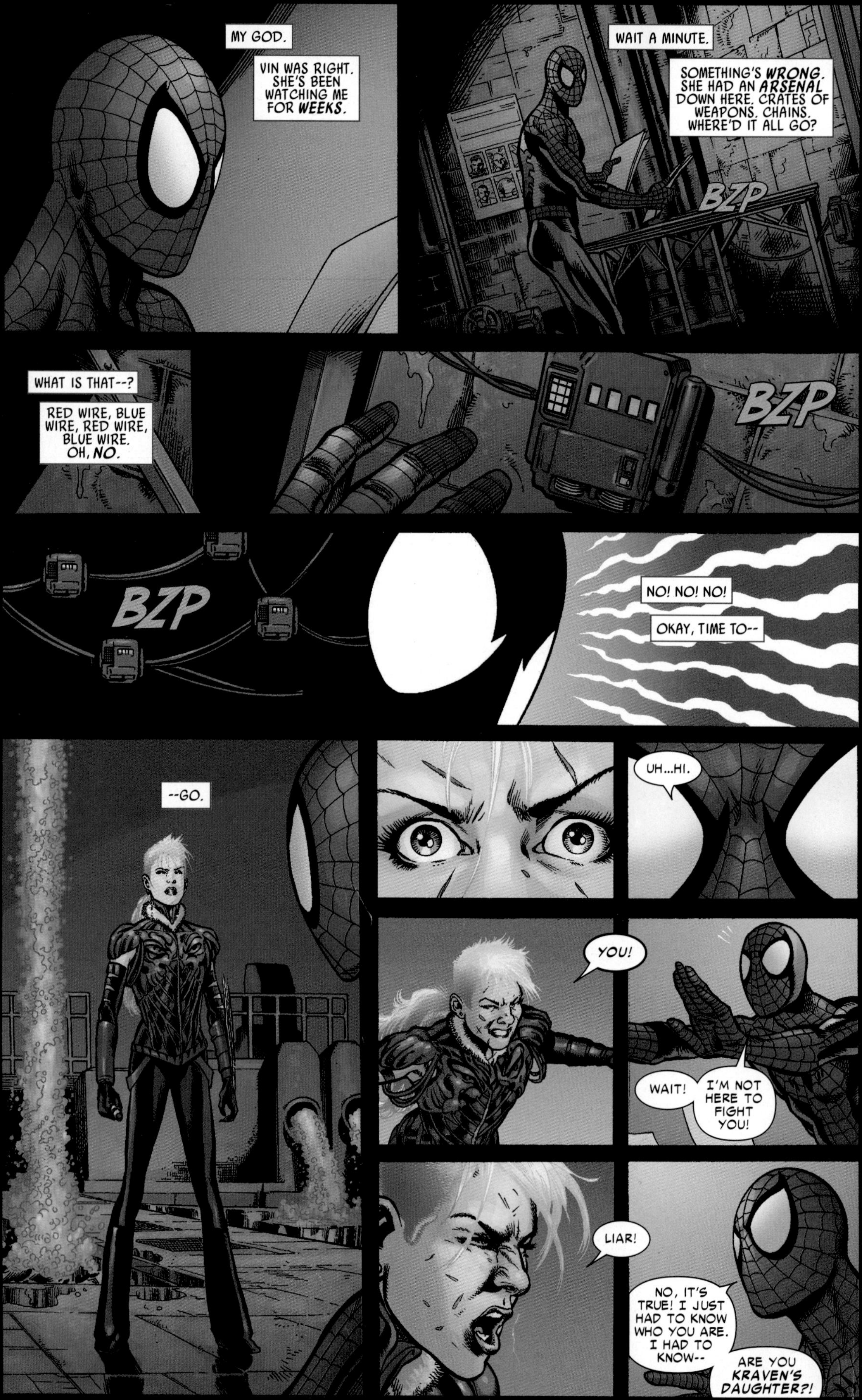
MY GOD.
VIN WAS RIGHT. SHE'S BEEN WATCHING ME FOR WEEKS.
WAIT A MINUTE.
SOMETHING'S WRONG. SHE HAD AN ARSENAL DOWN HERE. CRATES OF WEAPONS. CHAINS. WHERE'D IT ALL GO?
BZP
WHAT IS THAT--?
RED WIRE, BLUE WIRE, RED WIRE, BLUE WIRE. OH, NO.
BZP
BZP
NO! NO! NO!
OKAY, TIME TO--
--GO.
UH...HI.
YOU!
WAIT!
I'M NOT HERE TO FIGHT YOU!
LIAR!
NO, IT'S TRUE! I JUST HAD TO KNOW WHO YOU ARE. I HAD TO KNOW--
ARE YOU KRAVEN'S DAUGHTER?!

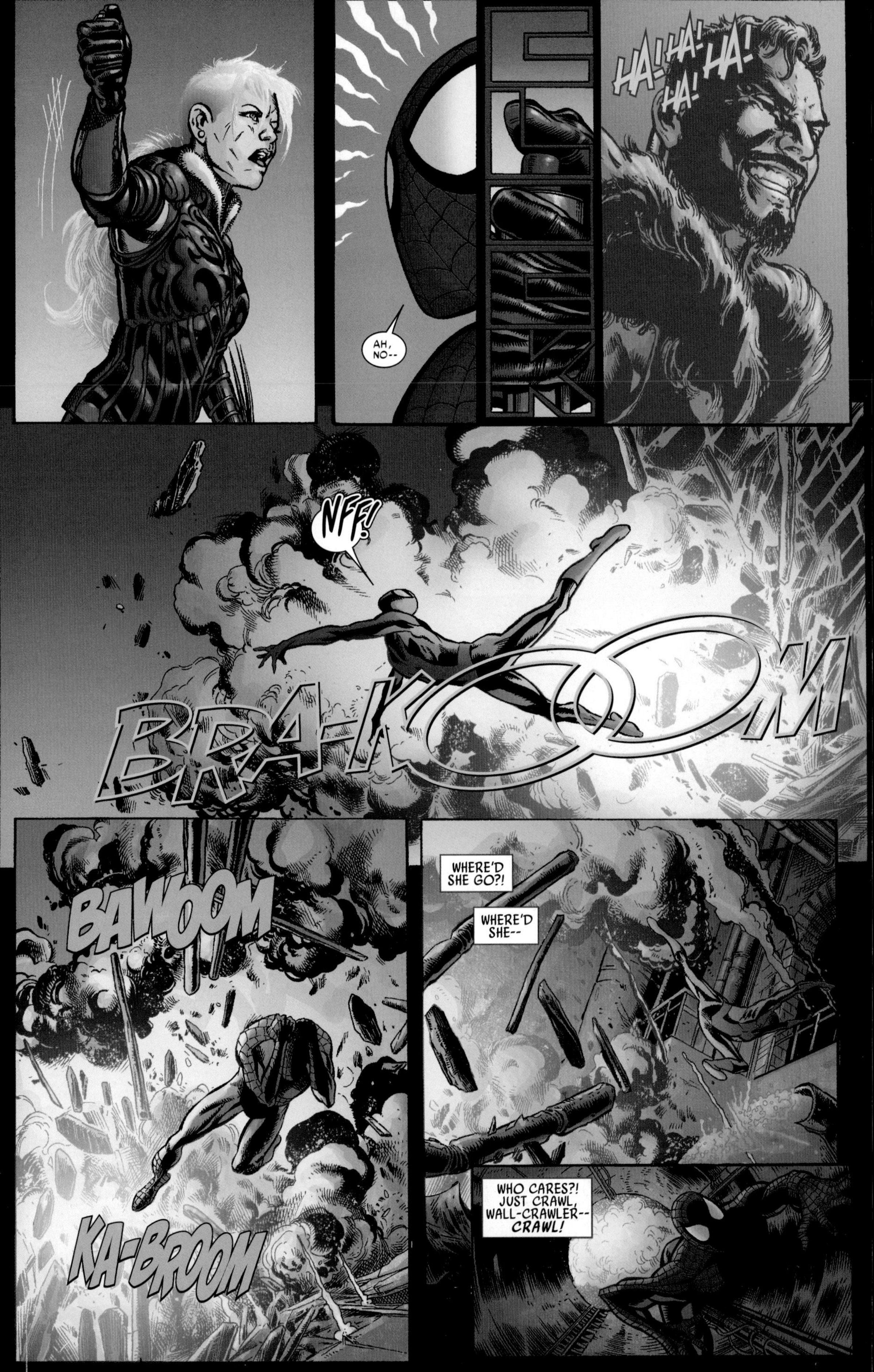
AH, NO--
HA! HA! HA! HA!
NFF!
BRA-KOOM
BAWOOM
KA-BROOM
WHERE'D SHE GO?!
WHERE'D SHE--
WHO CARES?! JUST CRAWL, WALL-CRAWLER-- CRAWL!

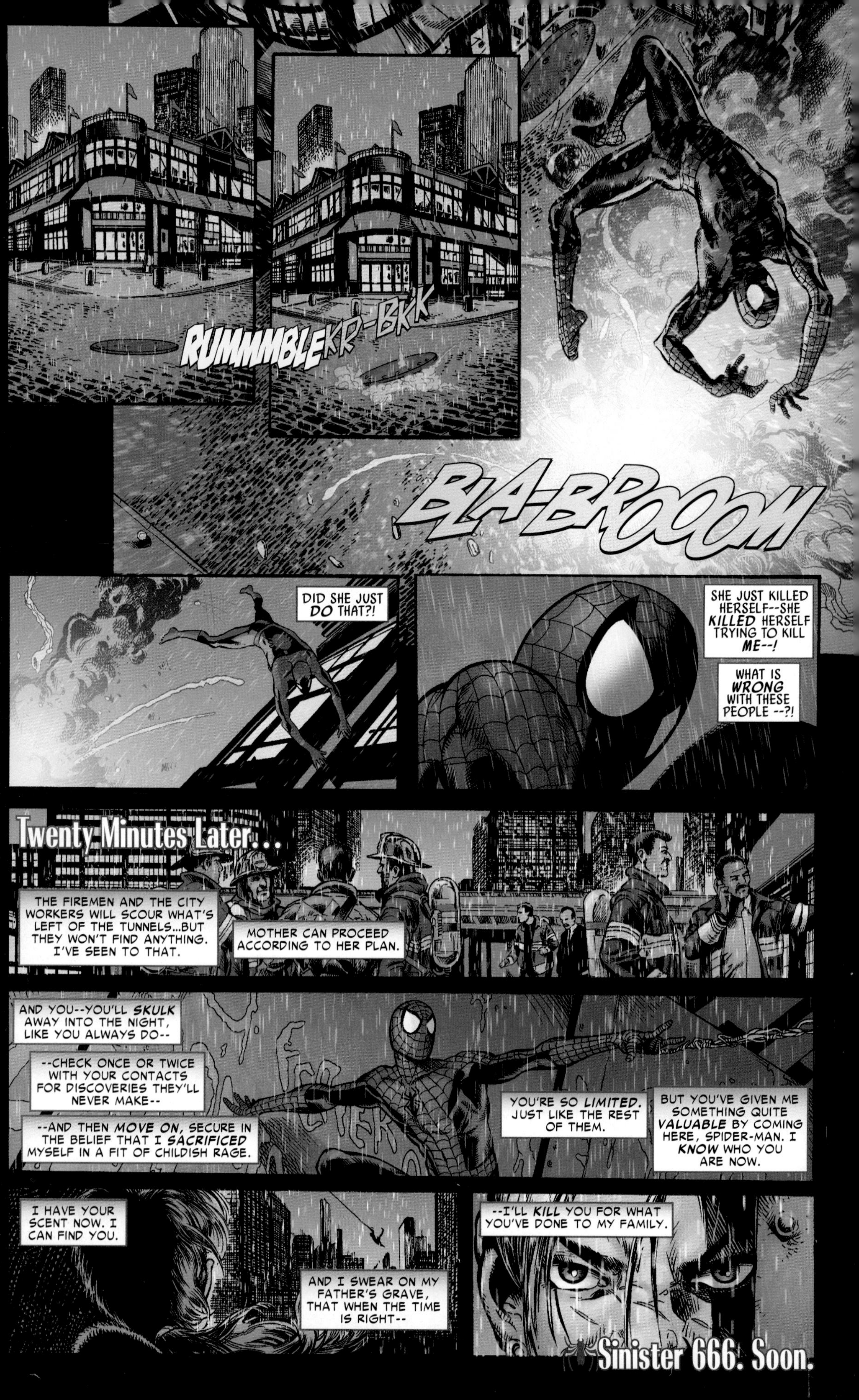
RUMMMBLE
KR-BKK
BLA-BROOOOM
DID SHE JUST DO THAT?!
SHE JUST KILLED HERSELF--SHE KILLED HERSELF TRYING TO KILL ME--!
WHAT IS WRONG WITH THESE PEOPLE --?!
Twenty Minutes Later. . .
THE FIREMEN AND THE CITY WORKERS WILL SCOUR WHAT'S LEFT OF THE TUNNELS...BUT THEY WON'T FIND ANYTHING. I'VE SEEN TO THAT.
MOTHER CAN PROCEED ACCORDING TO HER PLAN.
AND YOU--YOU'LL SKULK AWAY INTO THE NIGHT, LIKE YOU ALWAYS DO--
--CHECK ONCE OR TWICE WITH YOUR CONTACTS FOR DISCOVERIES THEY'LL NEVER MAKE--
--AND THEN MOVE ON, SECURE IN THE BELIEF THAT I SACRIFICED MYSELF IN A FIT OF CHILDISH RAGE.
YOU'RE SO LIMITED. JUST LIKE THE REST OF THEM.
BUT YOU'VE GIVEN ME SOMETHING QUITE VALUABLE BY COMING HERE, SPIDER-MAN. I KNOW WHO YOU ARE NOW.
I HAVE YOUR SCENT NOW. I CAN FIND YOU.
AND I SWEAR ON MY FATHER'S GRAVE, THAT WHEN THE TIME IS RIGHT--
--I'LL KILL YOU FOR WHAT YOU'VE DONE TO MY FAMILY.
Sinister 666. Soon.

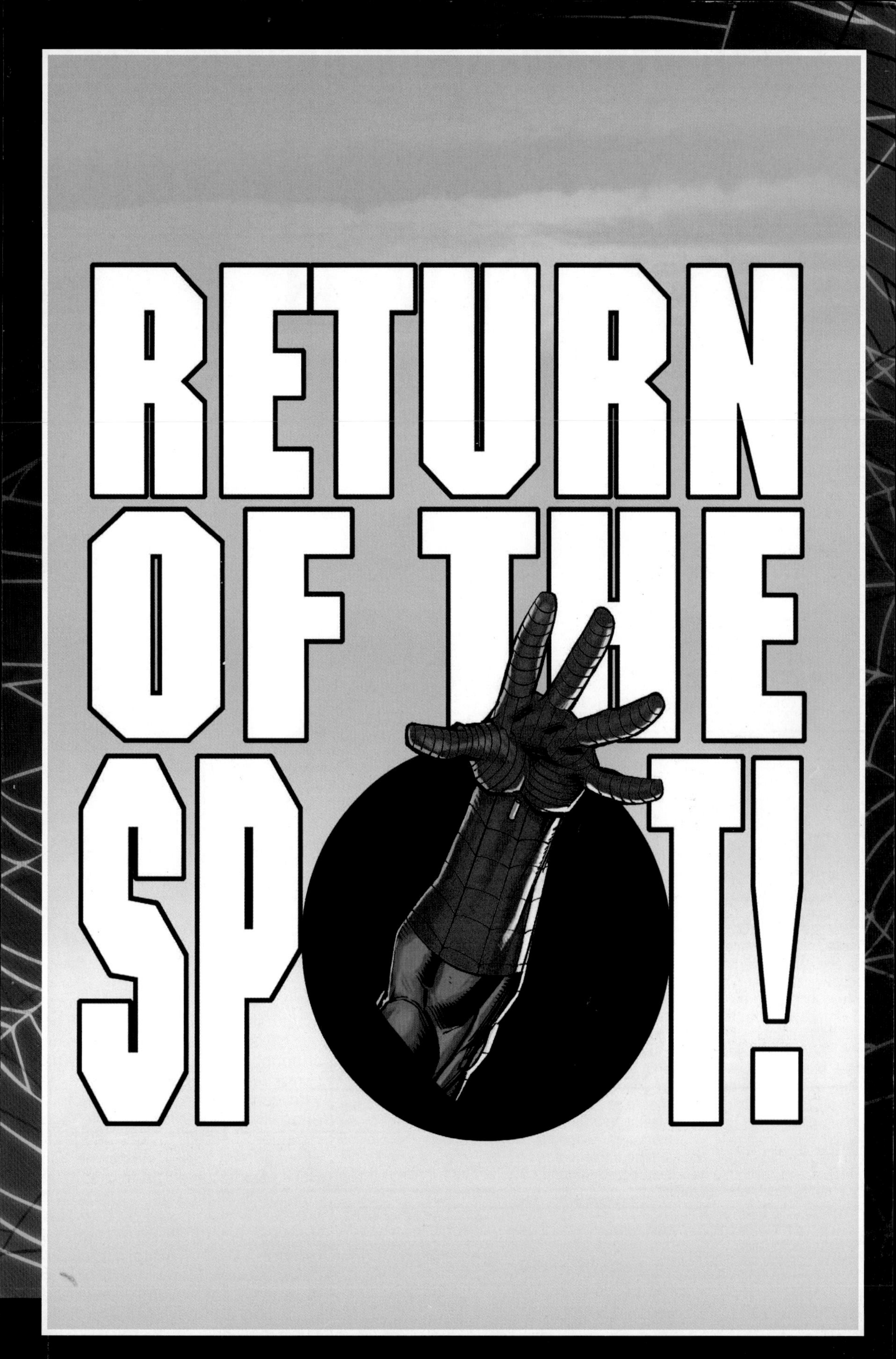
RETURN
OF THE
SP T!

THE DB! FOR EVERY BRAND *NEWS* DAY!

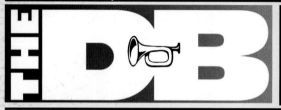

THE DB

MOB VIOLENCE IS UP IN DISGRACED FORMER MAYORAL CANDIDATE BILL HOLLISTER'S HOME BOROUGH OF BROOKLYN. TODAY'S DB POLL SAYS HOLLISTER'S LEADERSHIP SHOULD BE HELD ACCOUNTABLE FOR THE RISE IN CRIME! MORE ON PAGE Y32!

MARCH 25, 2009 • WEDNESDAY

OPEN SPOTS!

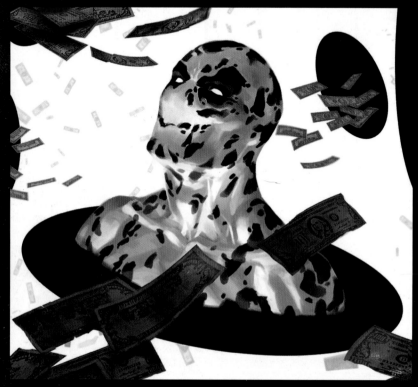

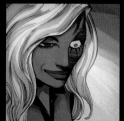

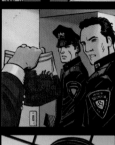

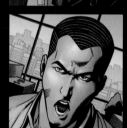

Years ago, Dr. Jonathan Ohnn, a scientist working for the Kingpin, was tasked with repeating the events that created the super hero Cloak in order to access and harness the dimension of darkness. His experiments caused a power surge and blackout in New York City, but the real damage was done when that same power surge bonded him with elements of the dimension of darkness, creating the one man portal conduit known as the Spot, a frequently dispatched enemy of Spider-Man…

Speaking of enemies of Spider-Man, the good news is, Spidey unmasked and busted both Menace and the Spider-Tracer Killer. The bad news? They're both friends of Peter Parker. Menace was secretly Lily Hollister, Harry Osborn's fiancée; and the Spider-Tracer Killer wasn't a killer at all, but a group of cops out to pin unsolvable murders on the web-head. One of those cops? His roommate, Vin Gonzales. Although Gonzales blew the whistle on the conspiracy and arrested the ringleaders, he'll still face jail time for his involvement. With his new friends having gone crazy and to jail respectively, maybe it's time Pete put family first and go visit his Aunt May...

WANTED: A Mayor!

By Betty Brant

With last week's Mayoral madness behind us, who will be our city's next Mayor? A stunning announcement from the Crowne camp says Randall Crowne – who came within a hair of victory after the superhuman Menace revealed herself to be daughter of opponent Bill Hollister – will NOT seek to take part in a special election to fill the post. So who will it be? Names touted by City Hall insiders include Former Damage Control CEO Walter Declun, philanthropist Martin Li, Brooklyn Borough President Jeff Jeffers and crusading attorney Matt Murdock. Even our own publisher, Dexter Bennett, has been suggested by his former protégé, Randall Crowne…(more on page E14)

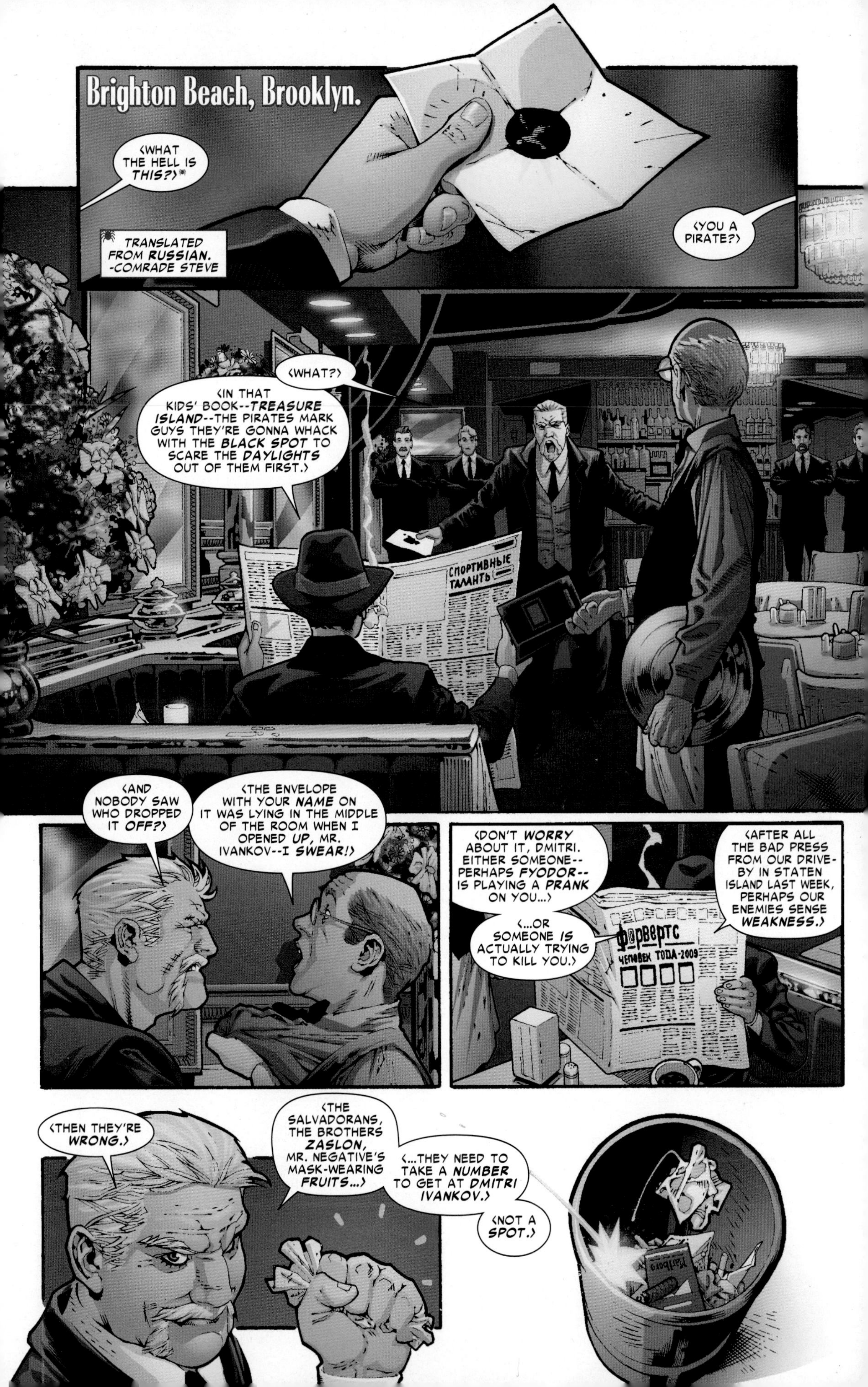
Brighton Beach, Brooklyn.
‹WHAT THE HELL IS THIS?›*
*TRANSLATED FROM RUSSIAN. -COMRADE STEVE
‹YOU A PIRATE?›
‹WHAT?›
‹IN THAT KIDS' BOOK--TREASURE ISLAND--THE PIRATES MARK GUYS THEY'RE GONNA WHACK WITH THE BLACK SPOT TO SCARE THE DAYLIGHTS OUT OF THEM FIRST.›
СПОРТИВНЫЕ ТАЛАНТЬ
‹AND NOBODY SAW WHO DROPPED IT OFF?›
‹THE ENVELOPE WITH YOUR NAME ON IT WAS LYING IN THE MIDDLE OF THE ROOM WHEN I OPENED UP, MR. IVANKOV--I SWEAR!›
‹DON'T WORRY ABOUT IT, DMITRI. EITHER SOMEONE--PERHAPS FYODOR--IS PLAYING A PRANK ON YOU...›
‹...OR SOMEONE IS ACTUALLY TRYING TO KILL YOU.›
‹AFTER ALL THE BAD PRESS FROM OUR DRIVE-BY IN STATEN ISLAND LAST WEEK, PERHAPS OUR ENEMIES SENSE WEAKNESS.›
‹THEN THEY'RE WRONG.›
‹THE SALVADORANS, THE BROTHERS ZASLON, MR. NEGATIVE'S MASK-WEARING FRUITS...›
‹...THEY NEED TO TAKE A NUMBER TO GET AT DMITRI IVANKOV.›
‹NOT A SPOT.›

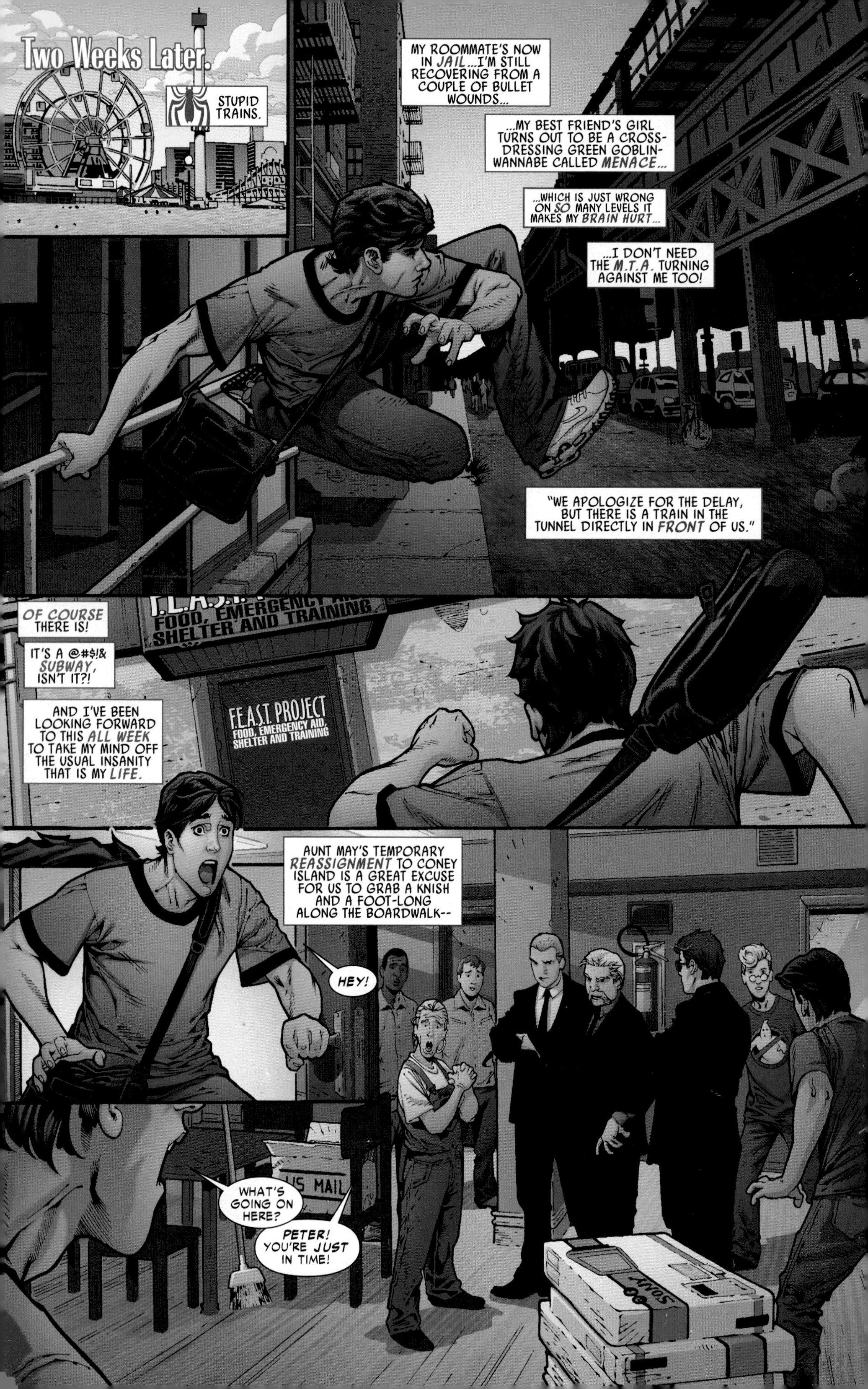
Two Weeks Later.
STUPID TRAINS.
MY ROOMMATE'S NOW IN JAIL...I'M STILL RECOVERING FROM A COUPLE OF BULLET WOUNDS...
...MY BEST FRIEND'S GIRL TURNS OUT TO BE A CROSS-DRESSING GREEN GOBLIN-WANNABE CALLED MENACE...
...WHICH IS JUST WRONG ON SO MANY LEVELS IT MAKES MY BRAIN HURT...
...I DON'T NEED THE M.T.A. TURNING AGAINST ME TOO!
"WE APOLOGIZE FOR THE DELAY, BUT THERE IS A TRAIN IN THE TUNNEL DIRECTLY IN FRONT OF US."
OF COURSE THERE IS!
IT'S A @#$!& SUBWAY, ISN'T IT?!
AND I'VE BEEN LOOKING FORWARD TO THIS ALL WEEK TO TAKE MY MIND OFF THE USUAL INSANITY THAT IS MY LIFE.
F.E.A.S.T. PROJECT
FOOD, EMERGENCY AID, SHELTER AND TRAINING
AUNT MAY'S TEMPORARY REASSIGNMENT TO CONEY ISLAND IS A GREAT EXCUSE FOR US TO GRAB A KNISH AND A FOOT-LONG ALONG THE BOARDWALK--
HEY!
WHAT'S GOING ON HERE?
PETER! YOU'RE JUST IN TIME!
US MAIL

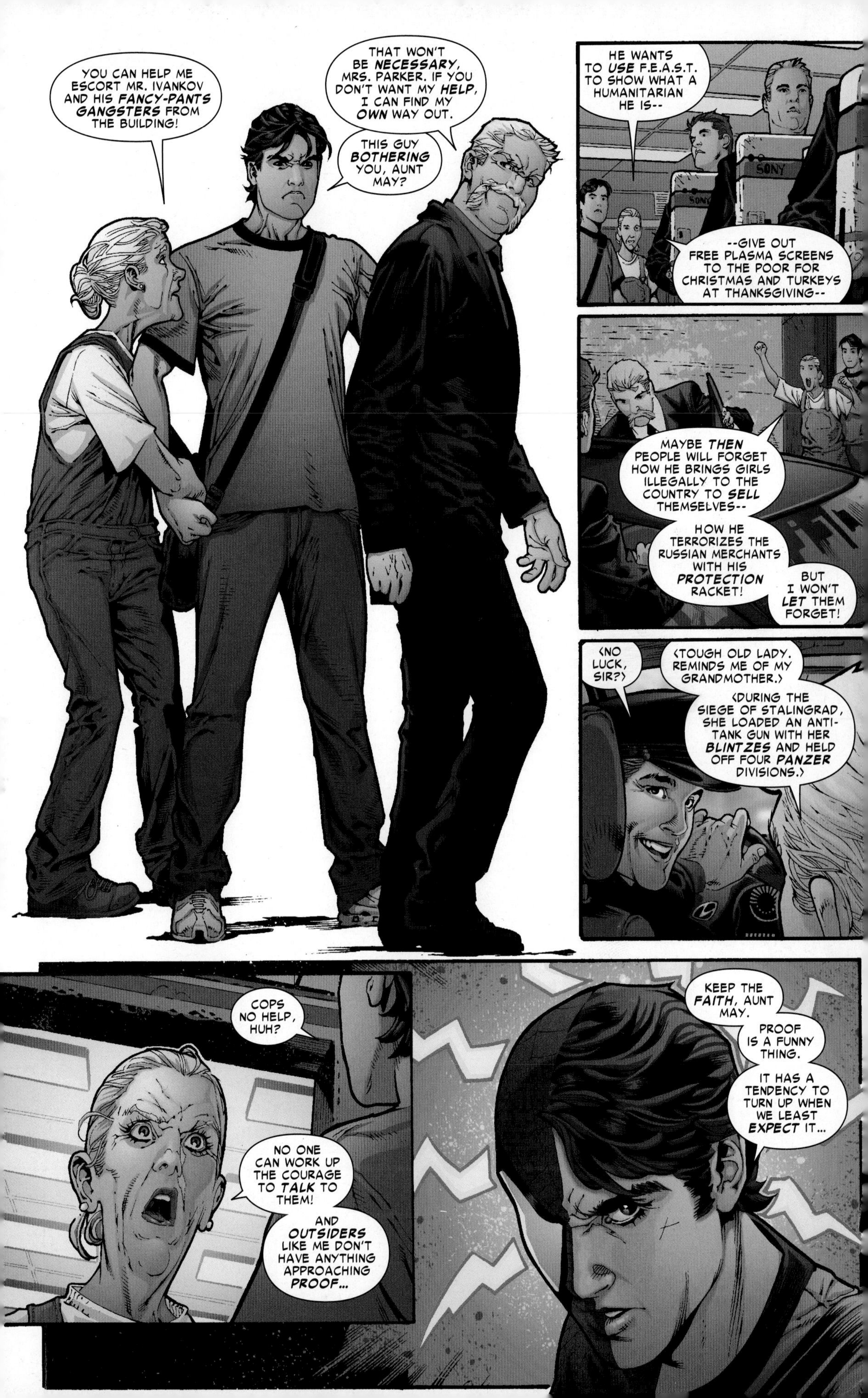

YOU CAN HELP ME ESCORT MR. IVANKOV AND HIS FANCY-PANTS GANGSTERS FROM THE BUILDING!
THAT WON'T BE NECESSARY, MRS. PARKER. IF YOU DON'T WANT MY HELP, I CAN FIND MY OWN WAY OUT.
THIS GUY BOTHERING YOU, AUNT MAY?
HE WANTS TO USE F.E.A.S.T. TO SHOW WHAT A HUMANITARIAN HE IS--
SONY
SONY
--GIVE OUT FREE PLASMA SCREENS TO THE POOR FOR CHRISTMAS AND TURKEYS AT THANKSGIVING--
MAYBE THEN PEOPLE WILL FORGET HOW HE BRINGS GIRLS ILLEGALLY TO THE COUNTRY TO SELL THEMSELVES--
HOW HE TERRORIZES THE RUSSIAN MERCHANTS WITH HIS PROTECTION RACKET!
BUT I WON'T LET THEM FORGET!
<NO LUCK, SIR?>
<TOUGH OLD LADY. REMINDS ME OF MY GRANDMOTHER.>
<DURING THE SIEGE OF STALINGRAD, SHE LOADED AN ANTI-TANK GUN WITH HER BLINTZES AND HELD OFF FOUR PANZER DIVISIONS.>
COPS NO HELP, HUH?
NO ONE CAN WORK UP THE COURAGE TO TALK TO THEM!
AND OUTSIDERS LIKE ME DON'T HAVE ANYTHING APPROACHING PROOF...
KEEP THE FAITH, AUNT MAY.
PROOF IS A FUNNY THING.
IT HAS A TENDENCY TO TURN UP WHEN WE LEAST EXPECT IT...

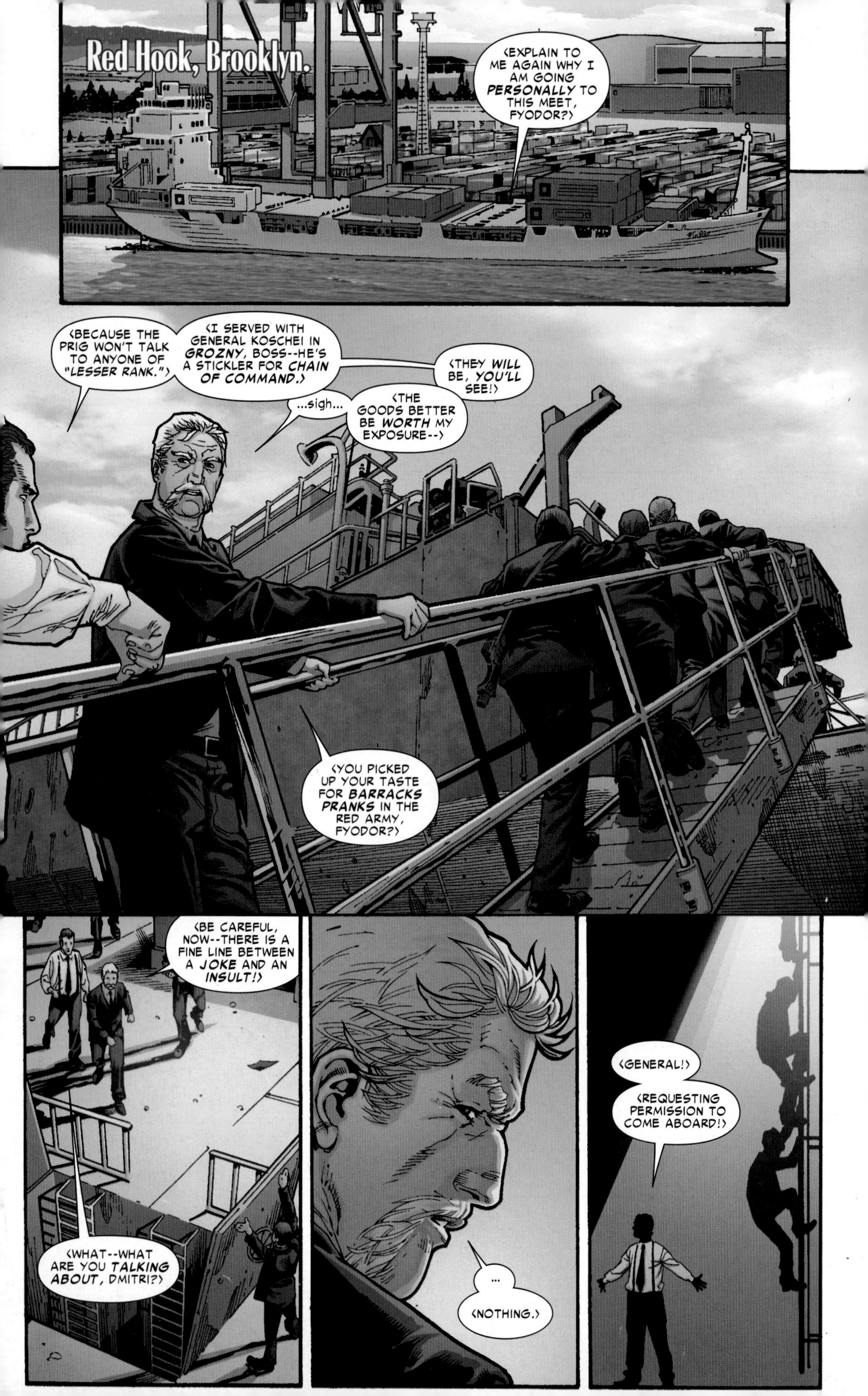
Red Hook, Brooklyn.
‹EXPLAIN TO ME AGAIN WHY I AM GOING PERSONALLY TO THIS MEET, FYODOR?›
‹BECAUSE THE PRIG WON'T TALK TO ANYONE OF "LESSER RANK."›
‹I SERVED WITH GENERAL KOSCHEI IN GROZNY, BOSS--HE'S A STICKLER FOR CHAIN OF COMMAND.›
...sigh...
‹THE GOODS BETTER BE WORTH MY EXPOSURE--›
‹THEY WILL BE, YOU'LL SEE!›
‹YOU PICKED UP YOUR TASTE FOR BARRACKS PRANKS IN THE RED ARMY, FYODOR?›
‹BE CAREFUL, NOW--THERE IS A FINE LINE BETWEEN A JOKE AND AN INSULT!›
‹WHAT--WHAT ARE YOU TALKING ABOUT, DMITRI?›
...
‹NOTHING.›
‹GENERAL!›
‹REQUESTING PERMISSION TO COME ABOARD!›

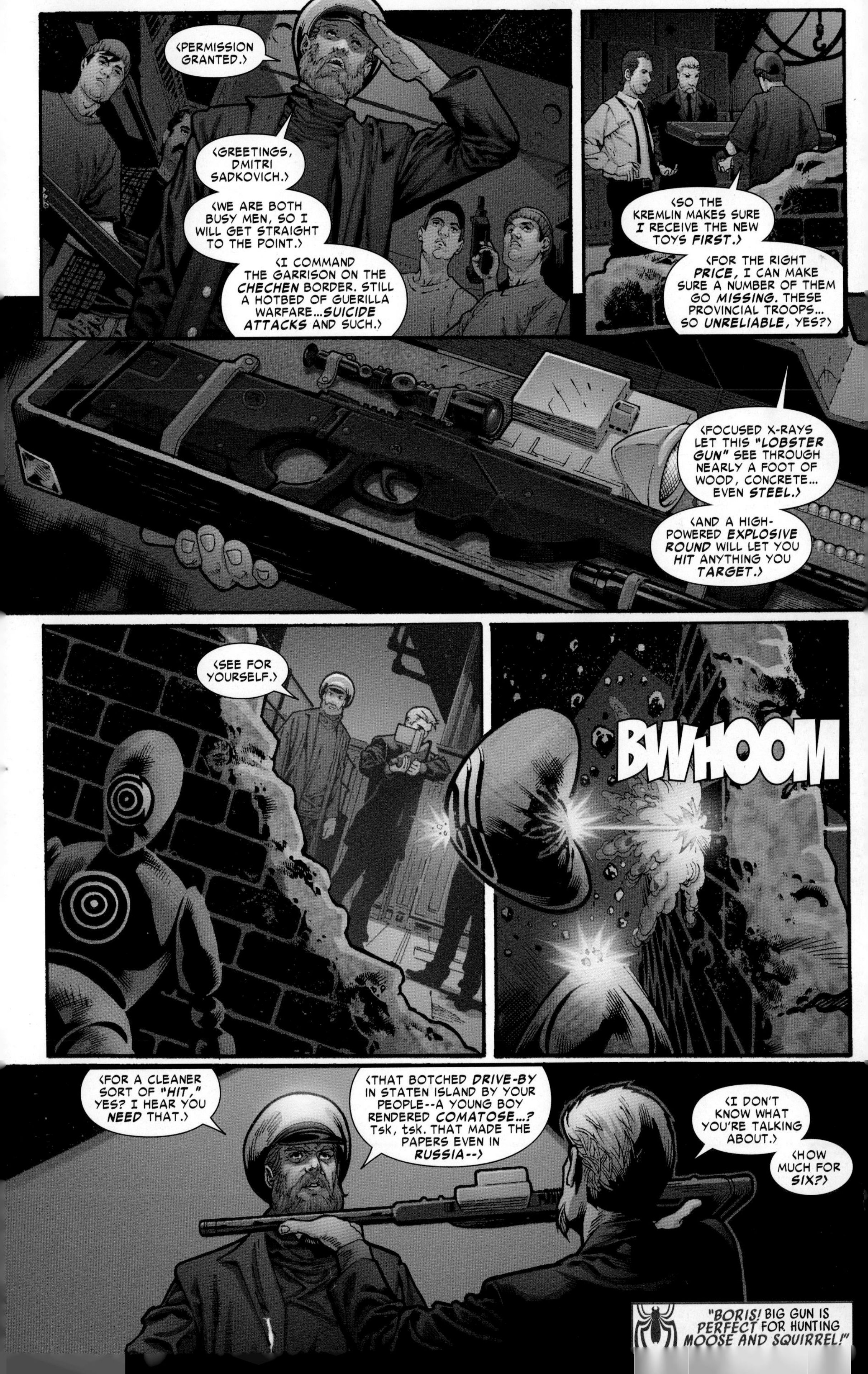

‹PERMISSION GRANTED.›
‹GREETINGS, DMITRI SADKOVICH.›
‹WE ARE BOTH BUSY MEN, SO I WILL GET STRAIGHT TO THE POINT.›
‹I COMMAND THE GARRISON ON THE CHECHEN BORDER. STILL A HOTBED OF GUERILLA WARFARE...SUICIDE ATTACKS AND SUCH.›
‹SO THE KREMLIN MAKES SURE I RECEIVE THE NEW TOYS FIRST.›
‹FOR THE RIGHT PRICE, I CAN MAKE SURE A NUMBER OF THEM GO MISSING. THESE PROVINCIAL TROOPS... SO UNRELIABLE, YES?›
‹FOCUSED X-RAYS LET THIS "LOBSTER GUN" SEE THROUGH NEARLY A FOOT OF WOOD, CONCRETE... EVEN STEEL.›
‹AND A HIGH-POWERED EXPLOSIVE ROUND WILL LET YOU HIT ANYTHING YOU TARGET.›
‹SEE FOR YOURSELF.›
BWHOOM
‹FOR A CLEANER SORT OF "HIT," YES? I HEAR YOU NEED THAT.›
‹THAT BOTCHED DRIVE-BY IN STATEN ISLAND BY YOUR PEOPLE--A YOUNG BOY RENDERED COMATOSE...? Tsk, tsk. THAT MADE THE PAPERS EVEN IN RUSSIA--›
‹I DON'T KNOW WHAT YOU'RE TALKING ABOUT.›
‹HOW MUCH FOR SIX?›
"BORIS! BIG GUN IS PERFECT FOR HUNTING MOOSE AND SQUIRREL!"

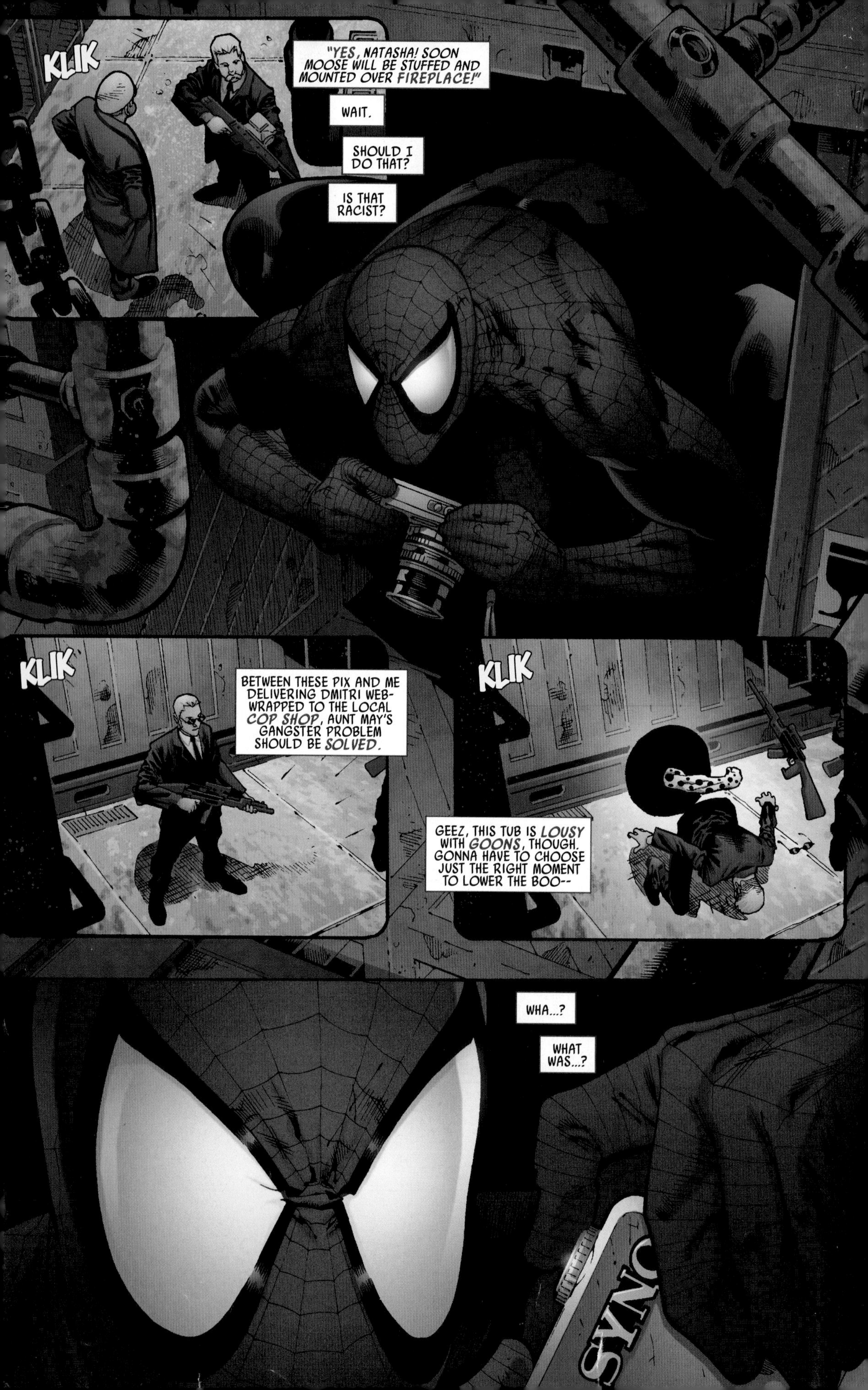
KLIK
"YES, NATASHA! SOON MOOSE WILL BE STUFFED AND MOUNTED OVER FIREPLACE!"
WAIT.
SHOULD I DO THAT?
IS THAT RACIST?
KLIK
BETWEEN THESE PIX AND ME DELIVERING DMITRI WEB-WRAPPED TO THE LOCAL COP SHOP, AUNT MAY'S GANGSTER PROBLEM SHOULD BE SOLVED.
KLIK
GEEZ, THIS TUB IS LOUSY WITH GOONS, THOUGH. GONNA HAVE TO CHOOSE JUST THE RIGHT MOMENT TO LOWER THE BOO--
WHA...?
WHAT WAS...?
SYNC

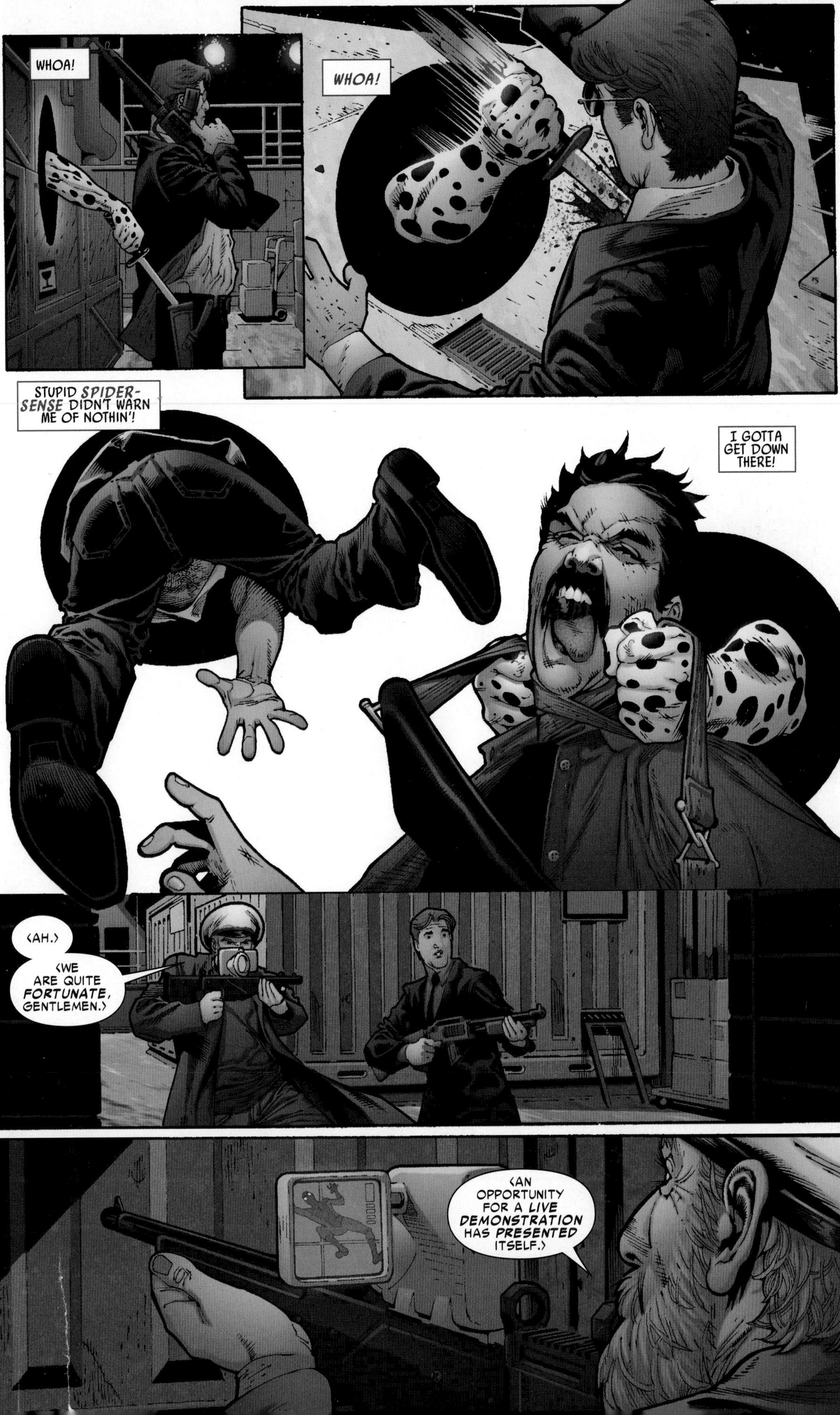
WHOA!
WHOA!
STUPID SPIDER-SENSE DIDN'T WARN ME OF NOTHIN'!
I GOTTA GET DOWN THERE!
‹AH.›
‹WE ARE QUITE FORTUNATE, GENTLEMEN.›
‹AN OPPORTUNITY FOR A LIVE DEMONSTRATION HAS PRESENTED ITSELF.›

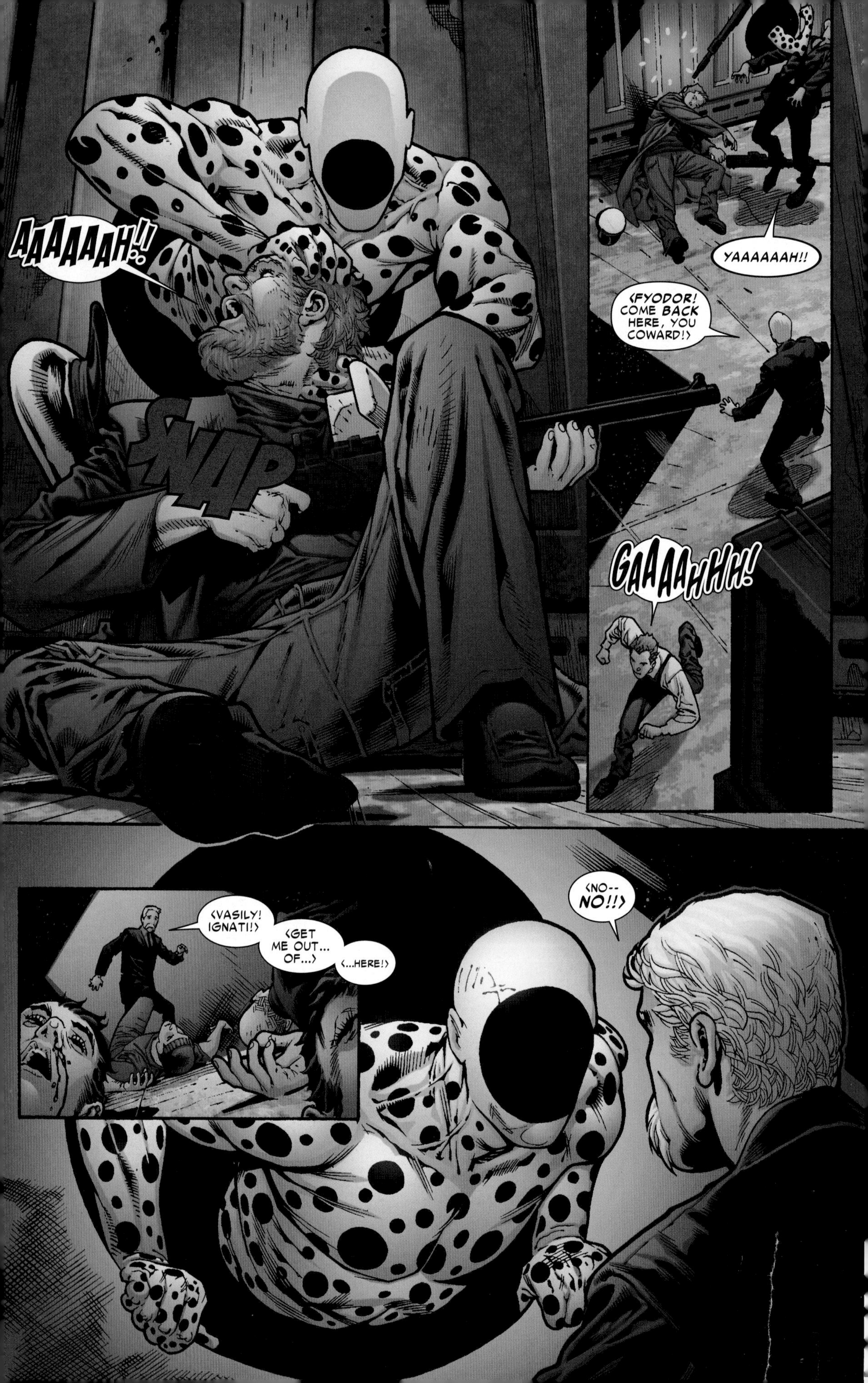
AAAAAAH!!
SNAP
YAAAAAAH!!
‹FYODOR! COME BACK HERE, YOU COWARD!›
GAAAAHHHH!
‹VASILY! IGNATI!›
‹GET ME OUT... OF...›
‹...HERE!›
‹NO-- NO!!›

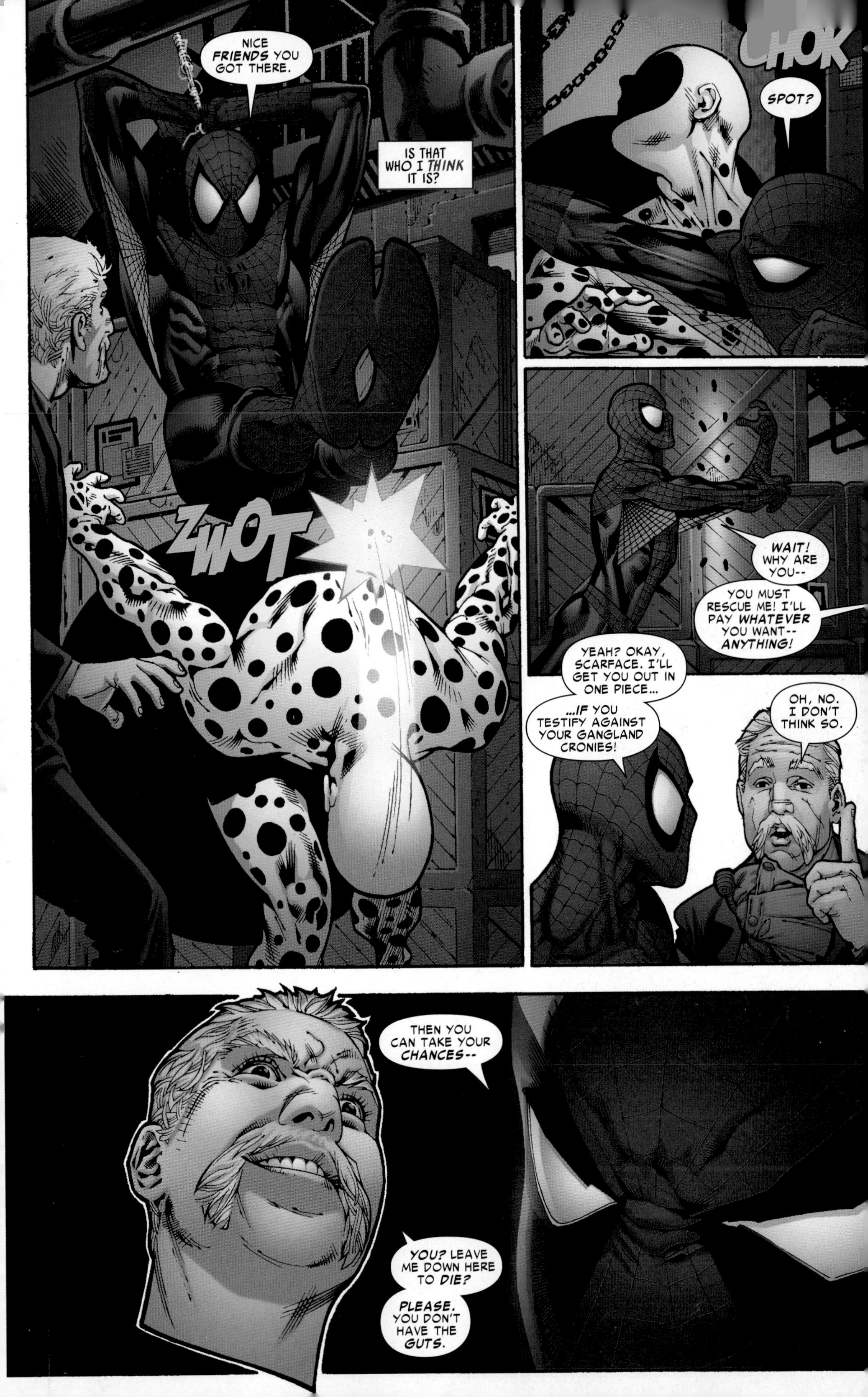
NICE FRIENDS YOU GOT THERE.
IS THAT WHO I THINK IT IS?
ZWOT
CHOK
SPOT?
WAIT! WHY ARE YOU--
YOU MUST RESCUE ME! I'LL PAY WHATEVER YOU WANT-- ANYTHING!
YEAH? OKAY, SCARFACE. I'LL GET YOU OUT IN ONE PIECE...
...IF YOU TESTIFY AGAINST YOUR GANGLAND CRONIES!
OH, NO. I DON'T THINK SO.
THEN YOU CAN TAKE YOUR CHANCES--
YOU? LEAVE ME DOWN HERE TO DIE?
PLEASE. YOU DON'T HAVE THE GUTS.

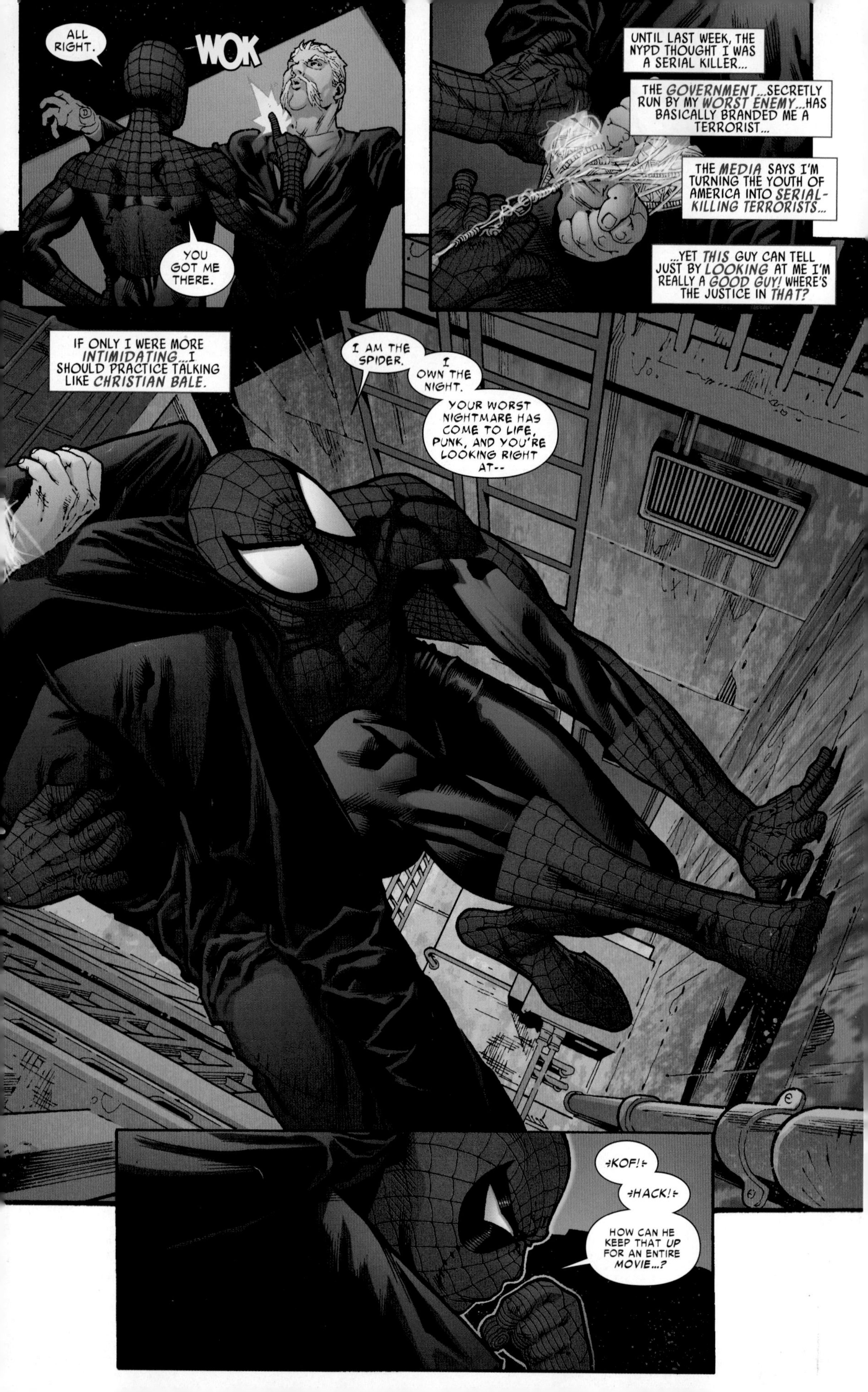
ALL RIGHT.
WOK
YOU GOT ME THERE.
UNTIL LAST WEEK, THE NYPD THOUGHT I WAS A SERIAL KILLER...
THE GOVERNMENT...SECRETLY RUN BY MY WORST ENEMY...HAS BASICALLY BRANDED ME A TERRORIST...
THE MEDIA SAYS I'M TURNING THE YOUTH OF AMERICA INTO SERIAL-KILLING TERRORISTS...
...YET THIS GUY CAN TELL JUST BY LOOKING AT ME I'M REALLY A GOOD GUY! WHERE'S THE JUSTICE IN THAT?
IF ONLY I WERE MORE INTIMIDATING...I SHOULD PRACTICE TALKING LIKE CHRISTIAN BALE.
I AM THE SPIDER.
I OWN THE NIGHT.
YOUR WORST NIGHTMARE HAS COME TO LIFE, PUNK, AND YOU'RE LOOKING RIGHT AT--
KOF!
HACK!
HOW CAN HE KEEP THAT UP FOR AN ENTIRE MOVIE...?

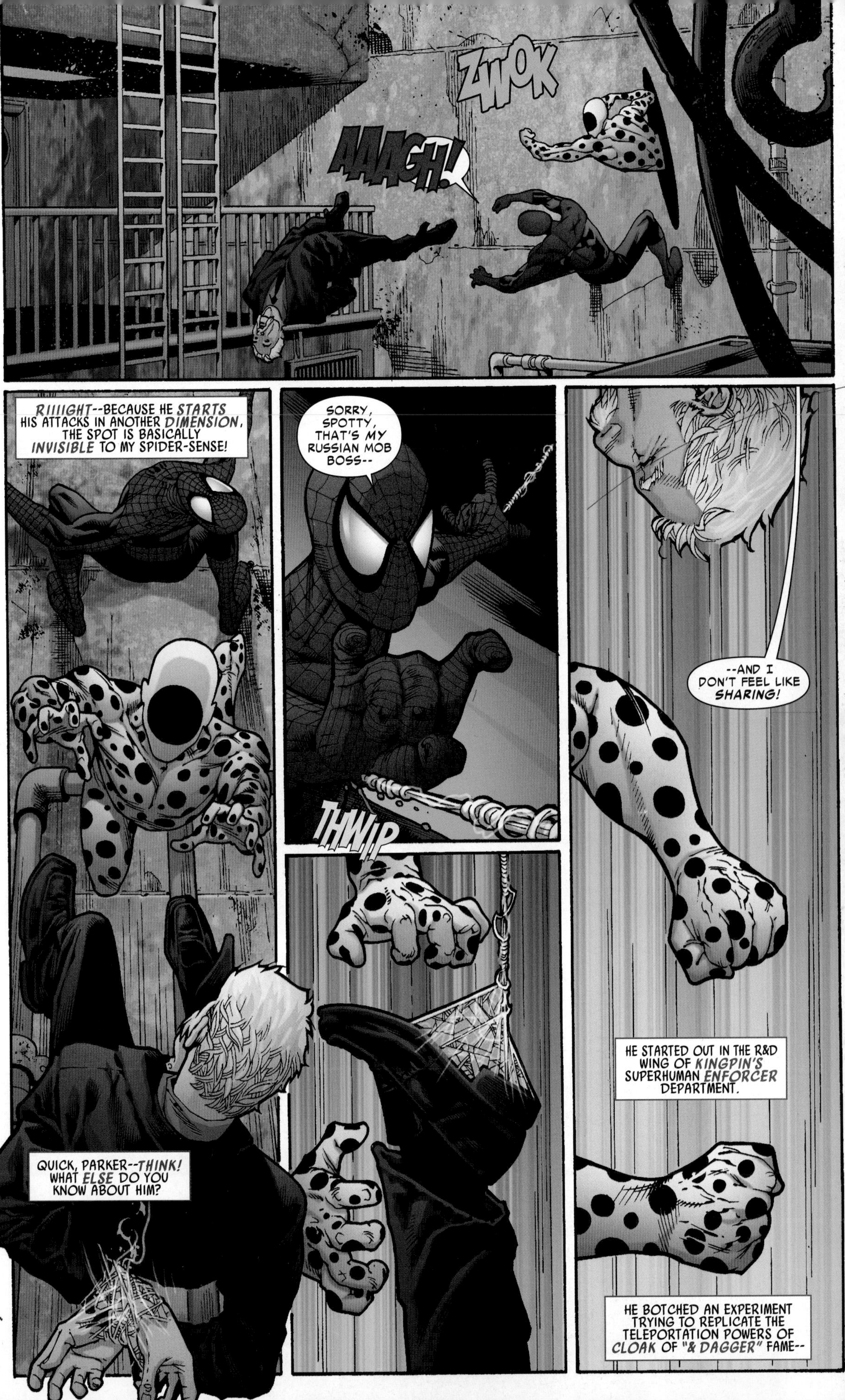

ZWOK
AAAGH!
RIIIIGHT--BECAUSE HE STARTS HIS ATTACKS IN ANOTHER DIMENSION, THE SPOT IS BASICALLY INVISIBLE TO MY SPIDER-SENSE!
SORRY, SPOTTY, THAT'S MY RUSSIAN MOB BOSS--
THWIP
--AND I DON'T FEEL LIKE SHARING!
QUICK, PARKER--THINK! WHAT ELSE DO YOU KNOW ABOUT HIM?
HE STARTED OUT IN THE R&D WING OF KINGPIN'S SUPERHUMAN ENFORCER DEPARTMENT.
HE BOTCHED AN EXPERIMENT TRYING TO REPLICATE THE TELEPORTATION POWERS OF CLOAK OF "& DAGGER" FAME--

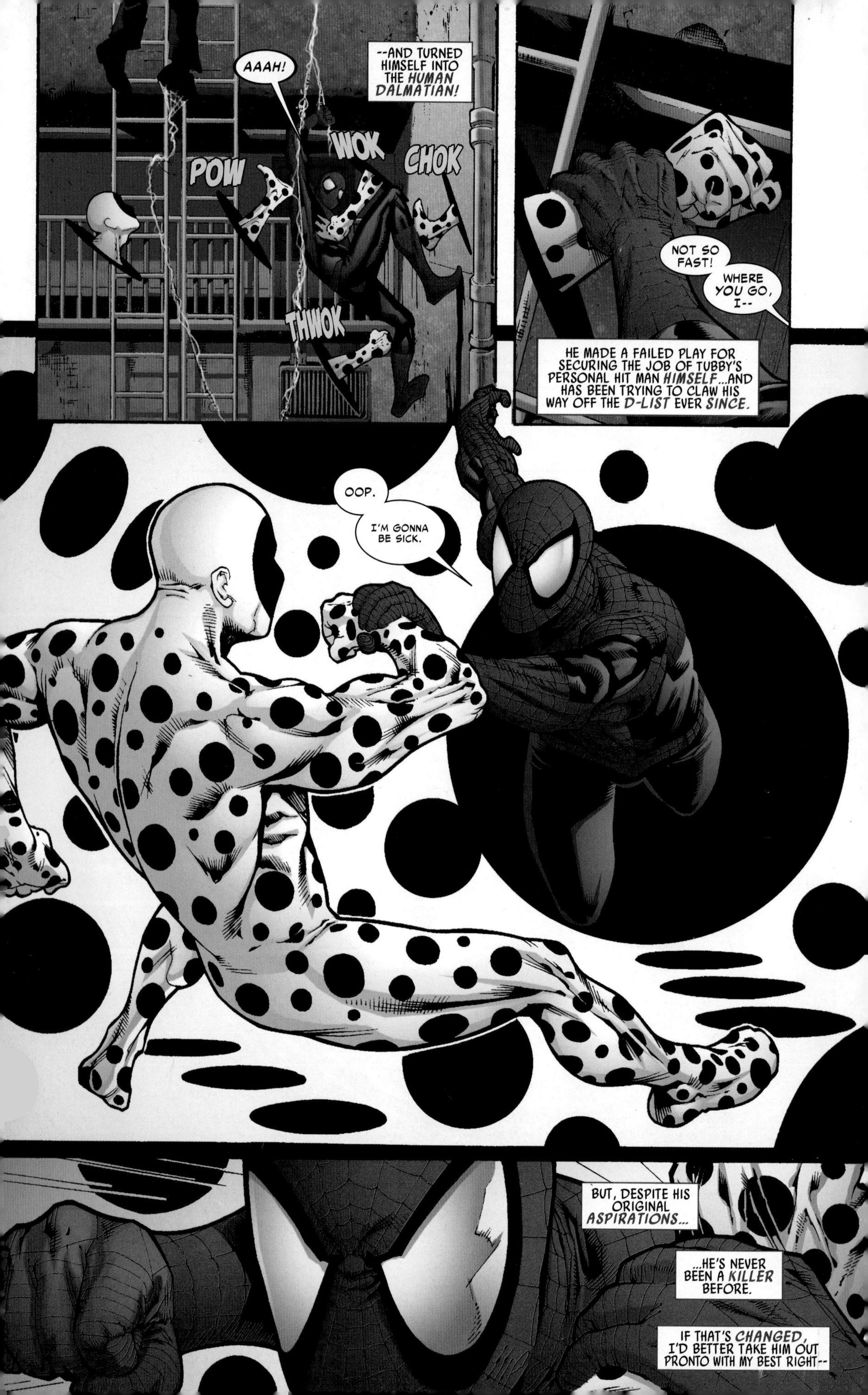

--AND TURNED HIMSELF INTO THE HUMAN DALMATIAN!
AAAH!
POW
WOK
CHOK
THWOK
NOT SO FAST!
WHERE YOU GO, I--
HE MADE A FAILED PLAY FOR SECURING THE JOB OF TUBBY'S PERSONAL HIT MAN HIMSELF...AND HAS BEEN TRYING TO CLAW HIS WAY OFF THE D-LIST EVER SINCE.
OOP.
I'M GONNA BE SICK.
BUT, DESPITE HIS ORIGINAL ASPIRATIONS...
...HE'S NEVER BEEN A KILLER BEFORE.
IF THAT'S CHANGED, I'D BETTER TAKE HIM OUT PRONTO WITH MY BEST RIGHT--

WHAM

OW! SON-OF-AN-OSBORN!

MY DOSE!

HE'S STEPPED UP HIS *GAME*.

OR BEEN PUSHED OVER THE *EDGE*.

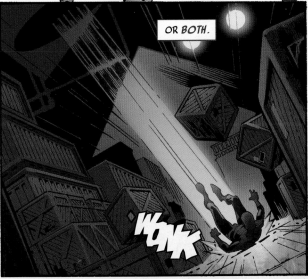

OR *BOTH*.

WONK

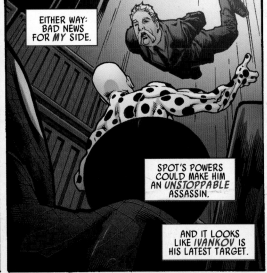

EITHER WAY: BAD NEWS FOR *MY* SIDE.

SPOT'S POWERS COULD MAKE HIM AN *UNSTOPPABLE* ASSASSIN.

AND IT LOOKS LIKE IVANKOV IS HIS LATEST TARGET.

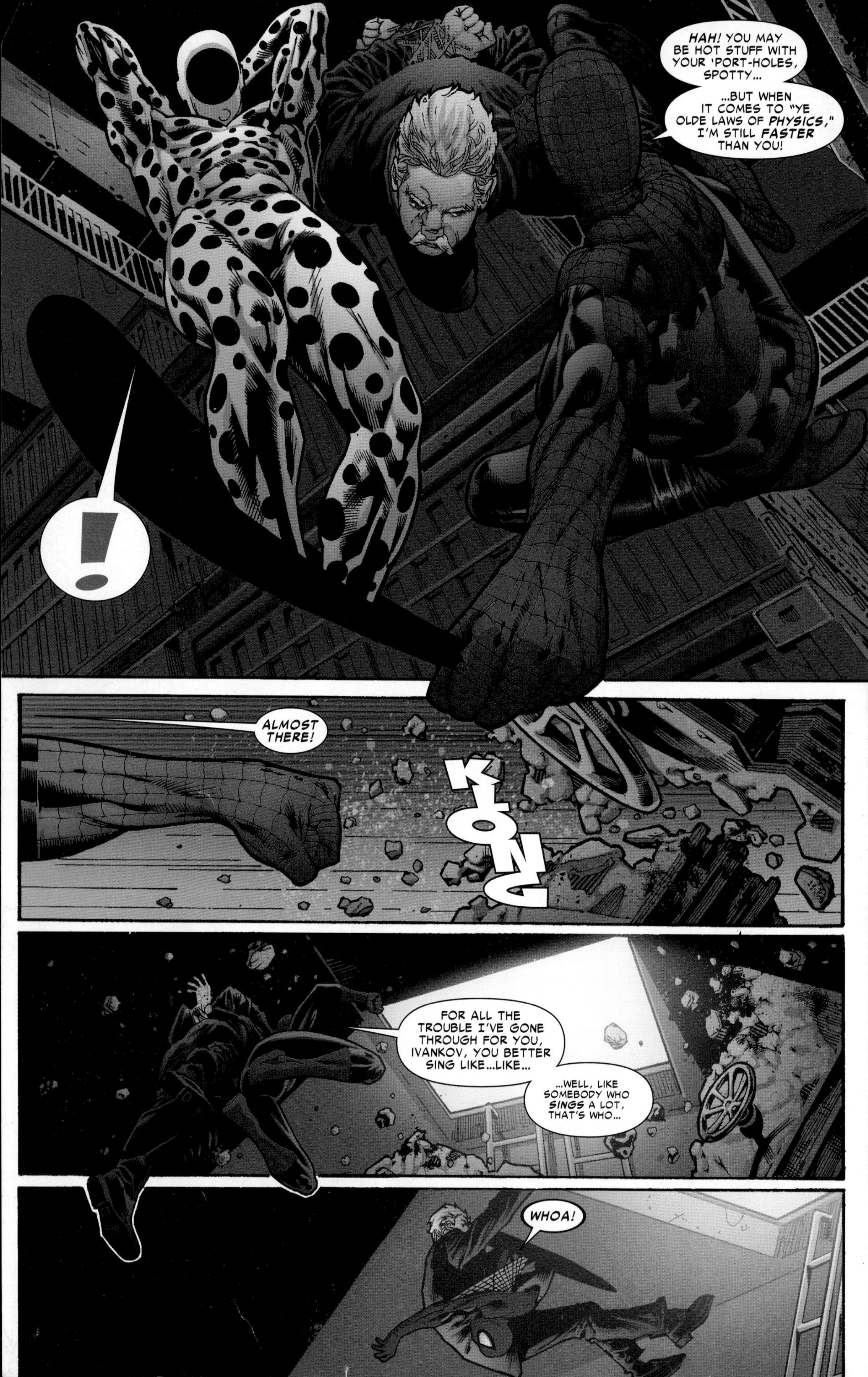
HAH! YOU MAY BE HOT STUFF WITH YOUR 'PORT-HOLES, SPOTTY...
...BUT WHEN IT COMES TO "YE OLDE LAWS OF PHYSICS," I'M STILL FASTER THAN YOU!
!
ALMOST THERE!
KLONG
FOR ALL THE TROUBLE I'VE GONE THROUGH FOR YOU, IVANKOV, YOU BETTER SING LIKE...LIKE...
...WELL, LIKE SOMEBODY WHO SINGS A LOT, THAT'S WHO...
WHOA!

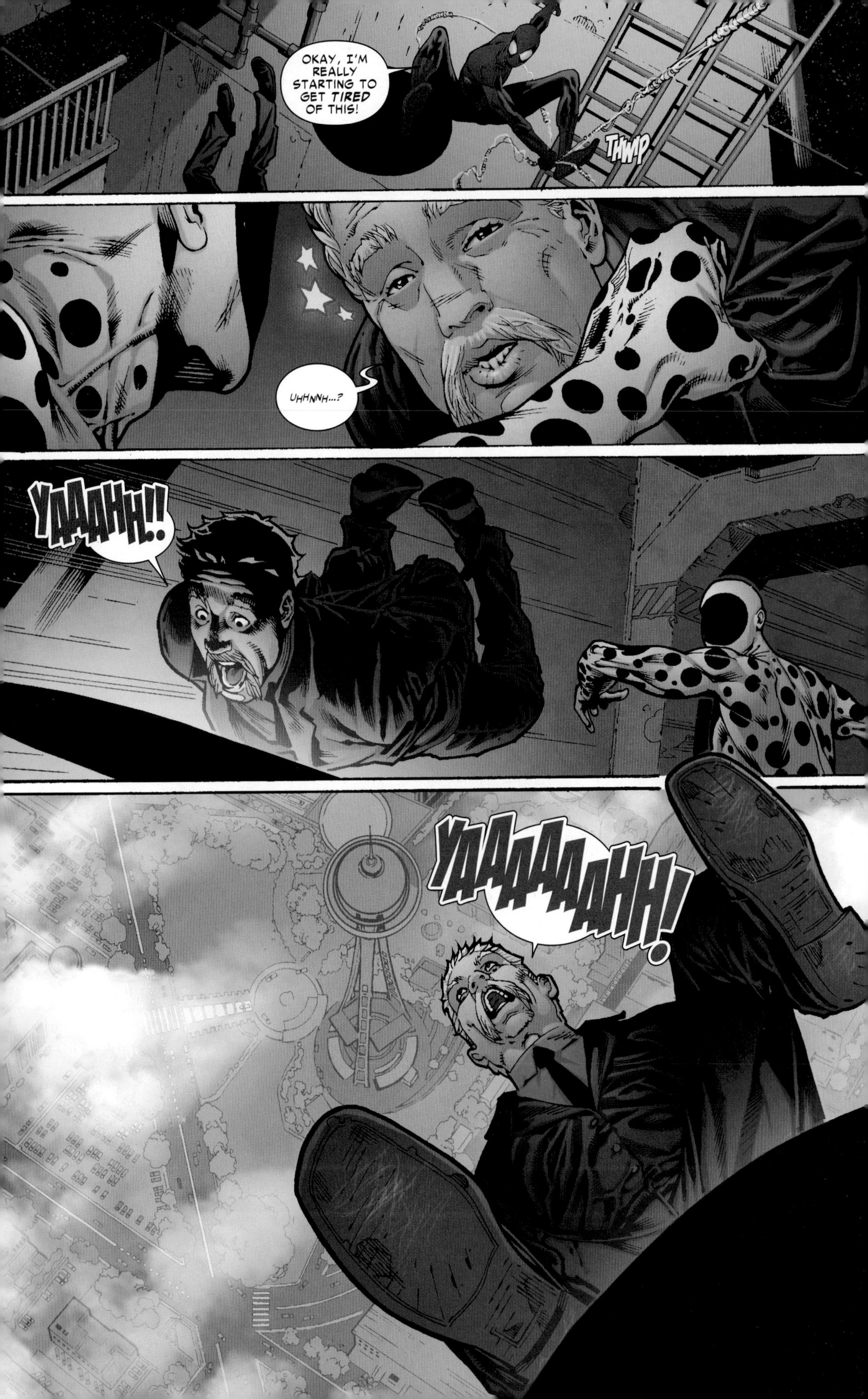
OKAY, I'M REALLY STARTING TO GET TIRED OF THIS!
THWIP
UHHNNH...?
YAAAHH!!
YAAAAAAAHH!

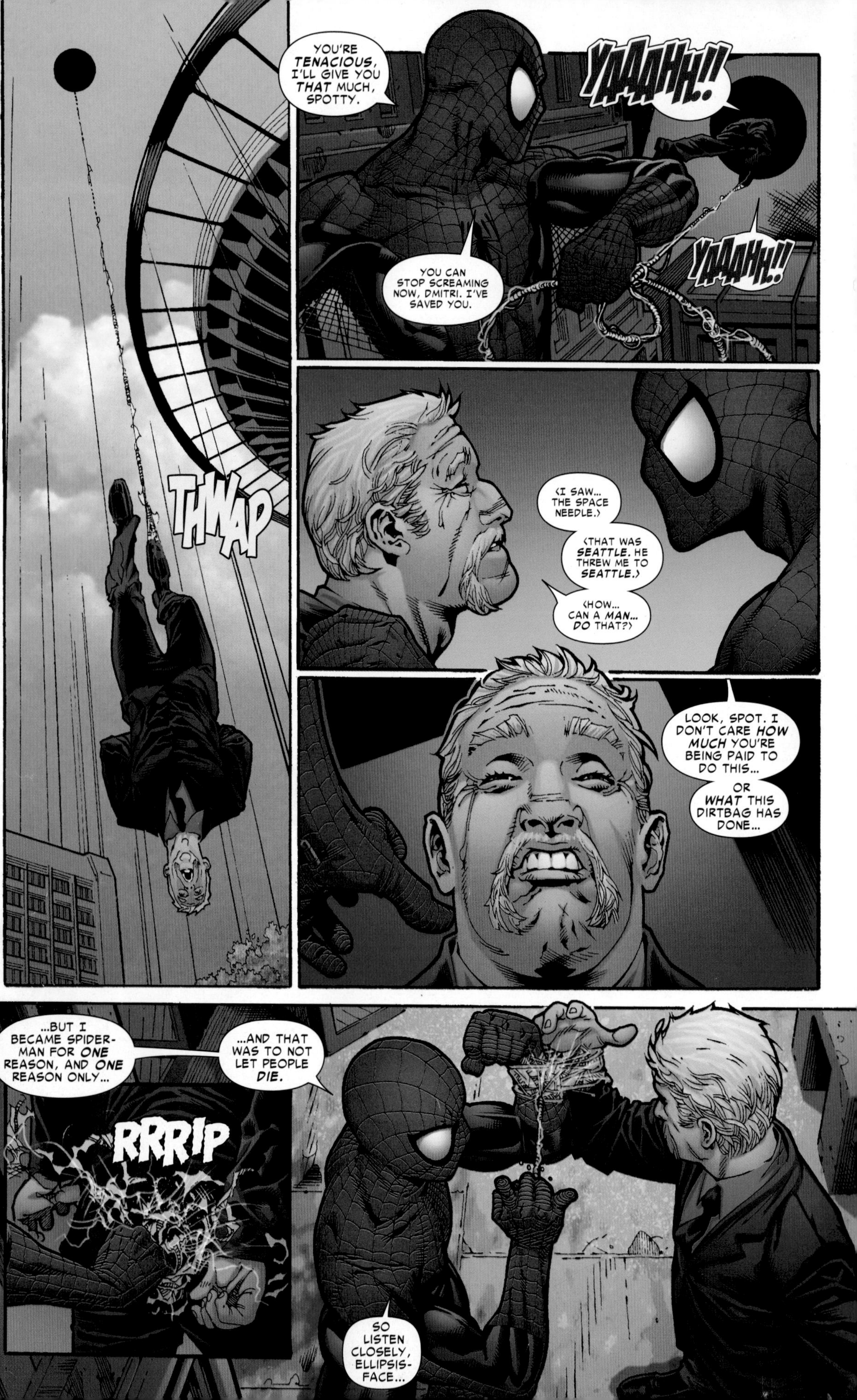
THWAP
YOU'RE TENACIOUS, I'LL GIVE YOU THAT MUCH, SPOTTY.
YAAAHH!!
YAAAHH!!
YOU CAN STOP SCREAMING NOW, DMITRI. I'VE SAVED YOU.
‹I SAW... THE SPACE NEEDLE.›
‹THAT WAS SEATTLE. HE THREW ME TO SEATTLE.›
‹HOW... CAN A MAN... DO THAT?›
LOOK, SPOT. I DON'T CARE HOW MUCH YOU'RE BEING PAID TO DO THIS...
OR WHAT THIS DIRTBAG HAS DONE...
...BUT I BECAME SPIDER-MAN FOR ONE REASON, AND ONE REASON ONLY...
...AND THAT WAS TO NOT LET PEOPLE DIE.
RRRIP
SO LISTEN CLOSELY, ELLIPSIS-FACE...

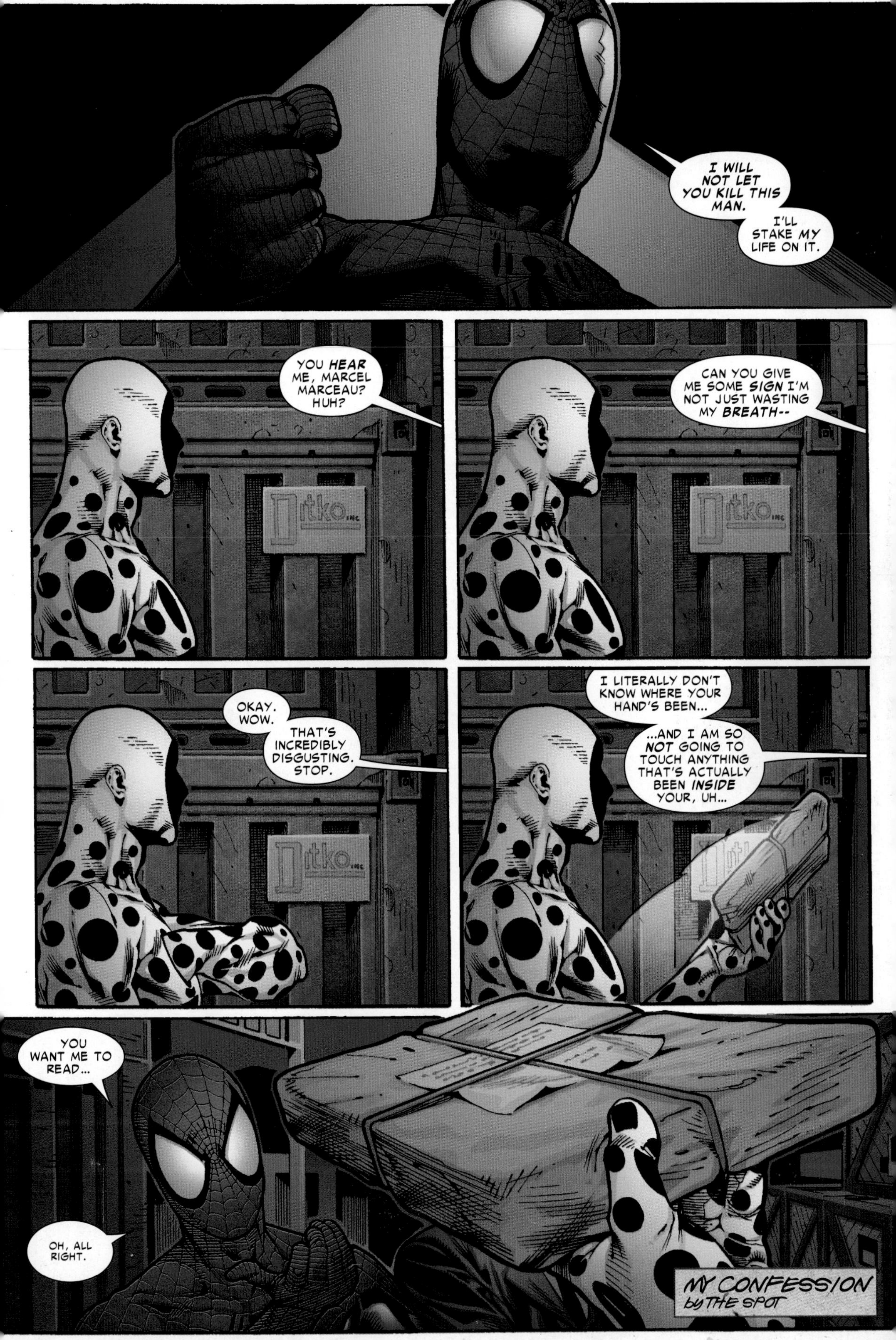
I WILL NOT LET YOU KILL THIS MAN.
I'LL STAKE MY LIFE ON IT.
YOU HEAR ME, MARCEL MARCEAU? HUH?
CAN YOU GIVE ME SOME SIGN I'M NOT JUST WASTING MY BREATH--
Ditko INC
OKAY. WOW.
THAT'S INCREDIBLY DISGUSTING. STOP.
I LITERALLY DON'T KNOW WHERE YOUR HAND'S BEEN...
...AND I AM SO NOT GOING TO TOUCH ANYTHING THAT'S ACTUALLY BEEN INSIDE YOUR, UH...
YOU WANT ME TO READ...
OH, ALL RIGHT.
MY CONFESSION by THE SPOT

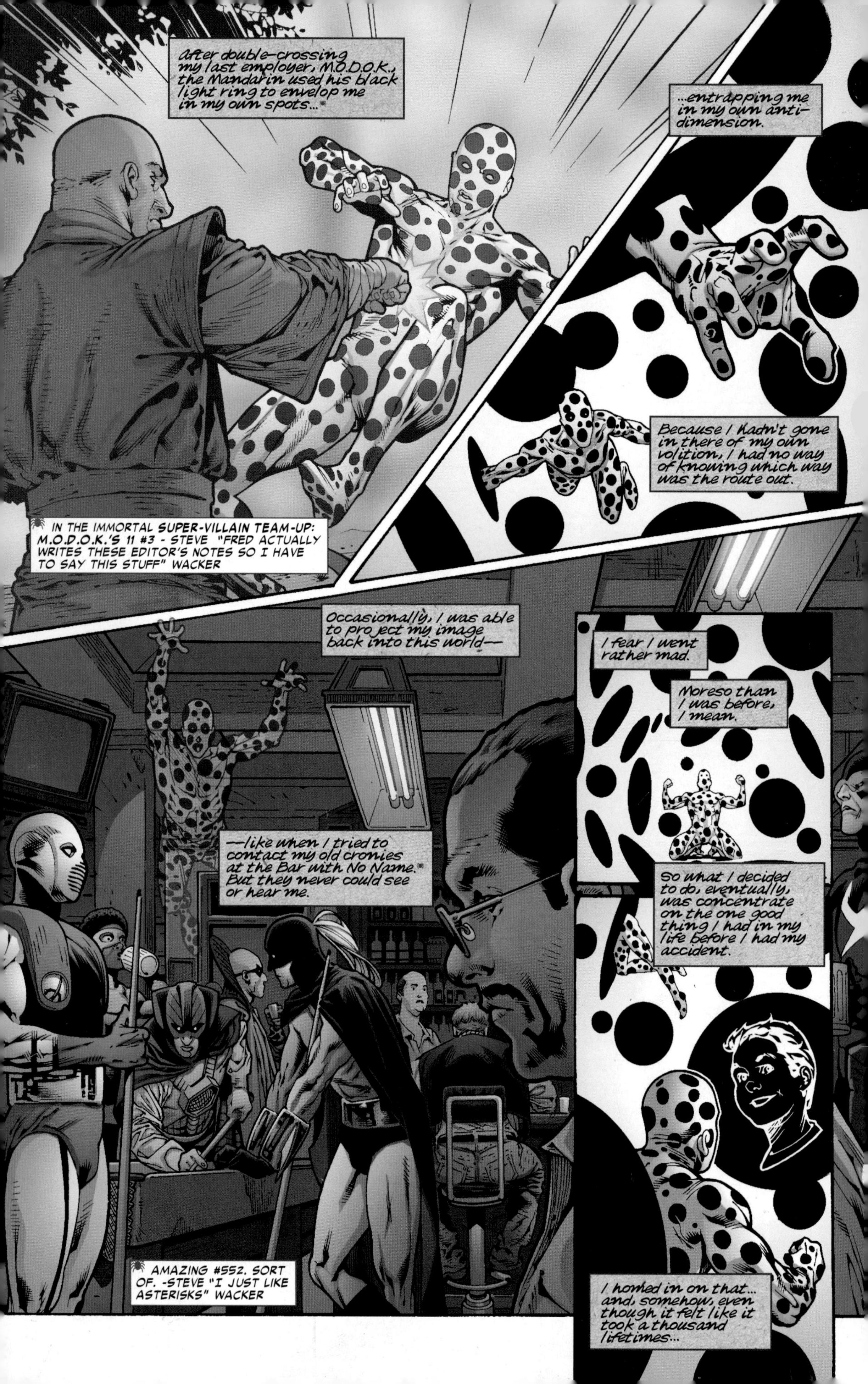
After double-crossing my last employer, M.O.D.O.K., the Mandarin used his black light ring to envelop me in my own spots...*
...entrapping me in my own anti-dimension.
Because I hadn't gone in there of my own volition, I had no way of knowing which way was the route out.
* IN THE IMMORTAL SUPER-VILLAIN TEAM-UP: M.O.D.O.K.'S 11 #3 - STEVE "FRED ACTUALLY WRITES THESE EDITOR'S NOTES SO I HAVE TO SAY THIS STUFF" WACKER
Occasionally, I was able to project my image back into this world—
—like when I tried to contact my old cronies at the Bar with No Name.* But they never could see or hear me.
* AMAZING #552. SORT OF. -STEVE "I JUST LIKE ASTERISKS" WACKER
I fear I went rather mad.
Moreso than I was before, I mean.
So what I decided to do, eventually, was concentrate on the one good thing I had in my life before I had my accident.
I homed in on that... and, somehow, even though it felt like it took a thousand lifetimes...

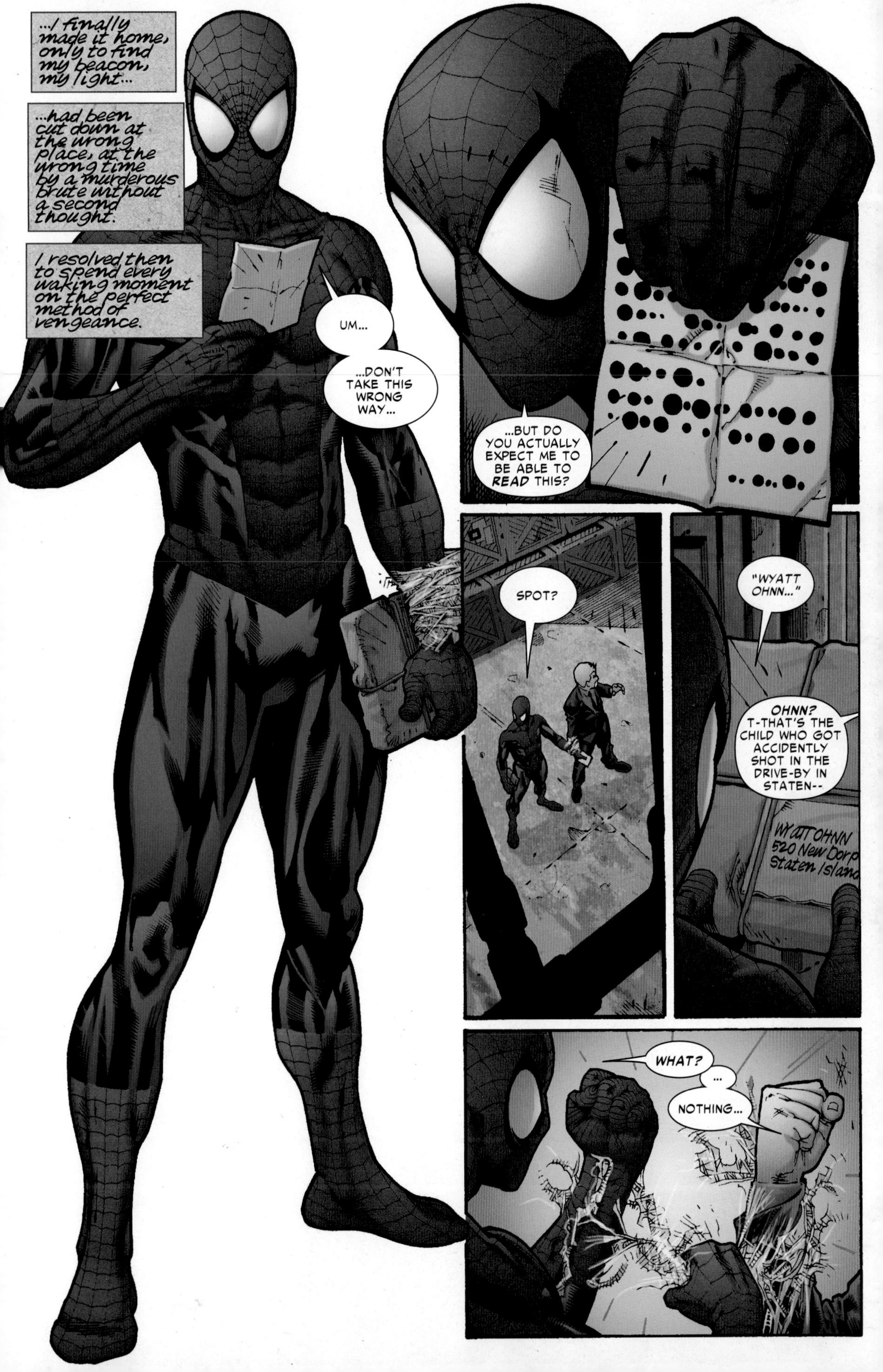
...I finally made it home, only to find my beacon, my light...
...had been cut down at the wrong place, at the wrong time by a murderous brute without a second thought.
I resolved then to spend every waking moment on the perfect method of vengeance.
UM...
...DON'T TAKE THIS WRONG WAY...
...BUT DO YOU ACTUALLY EXPECT ME TO BE ABLE TO READ THIS?
SPOT?
"WYATT OHNN..."
OHNN? T-THAT'S THE CHILD WHO GOT ACCIDENTLY SHOT IN THE DRIVE-BY IN STATEN--
WYATT OHNN
520 New Dorp
Staten Island
WHAT?
...
NOTHING...

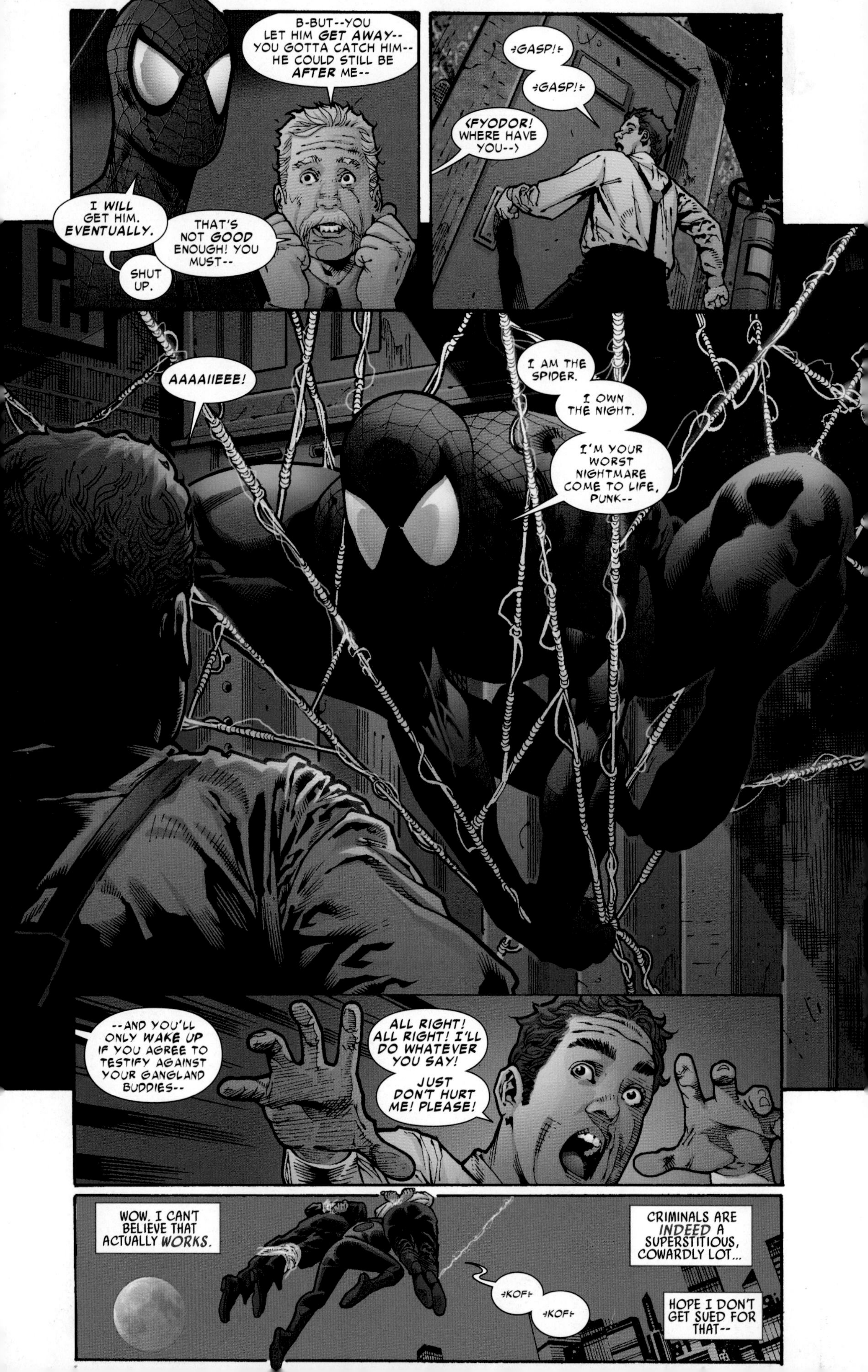
B-BUT--YOU LET HIM GET AWAY--YOU GOTTA CATCH HIM--HE COULD STILL BE AFTER ME--
I WILL GET HIM. EVENTUALLY.
THAT'S NOT GOOD ENOUGH! YOU MUST--
SHUT UP.
GASP!
GASP!
<FYODOR! WHERE HAVE YOU-->
AAAAIIEEE!
I AM THE SPIDER.
I OWN THE NIGHT.
I'M YOUR WORST NIGHTMARE COME TO LIFE, PUNK--
--AND YOU'LL ONLY WAKE UP IF YOU AGREE TO TESTIFY AGAINST YOUR GANGLAND BUDDIES--
ALL RIGHT! ALL RIGHT! I'LL DO WHATEVER YOU SAY!
JUST DON'T HURT ME! PLEASE!
WOW. I CAN'T BELIEVE THAT ACTUALLY WORKS.
KOF
KOF
CRIMINALS ARE INDEED A SUPERSTITIOUS, COWARDLY LOT...
HOPE I DON'T GET SUED FOR THAT--

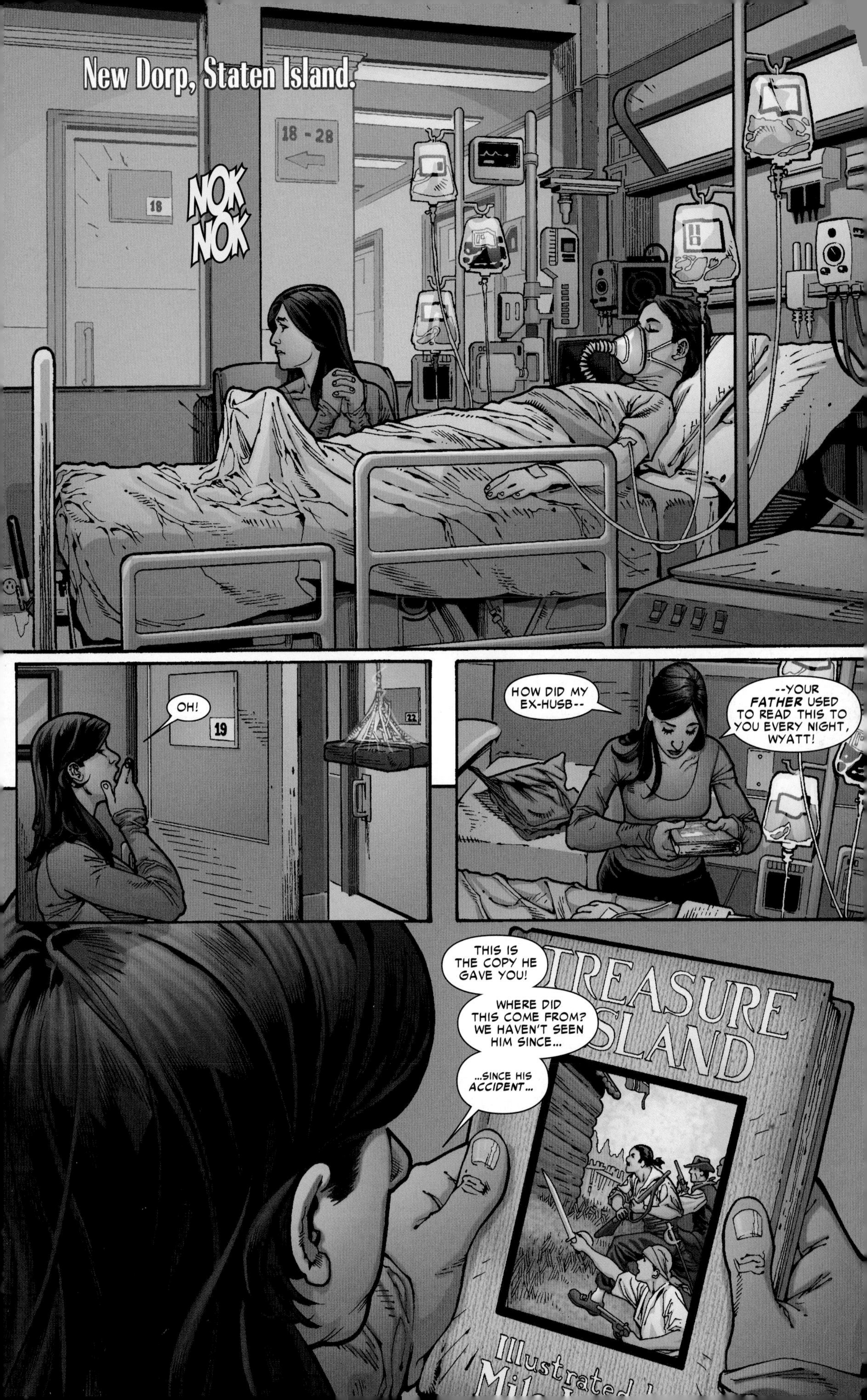
New Dorp, Staten Island.
NOK NOK
OH!
HOW DID MY EX-HUSB--
--YOUR FATHER USED TO READ THIS TO YOU EVERY NIGHT, WYATT!
THIS IS THE COPY HE GAVE YOU!
WHERE DID THIS COME FROM? WE HAVEN'T SEEN HIM SINCE...
...SINCE HIS ACCIDENT...
TREASURE ISLAND

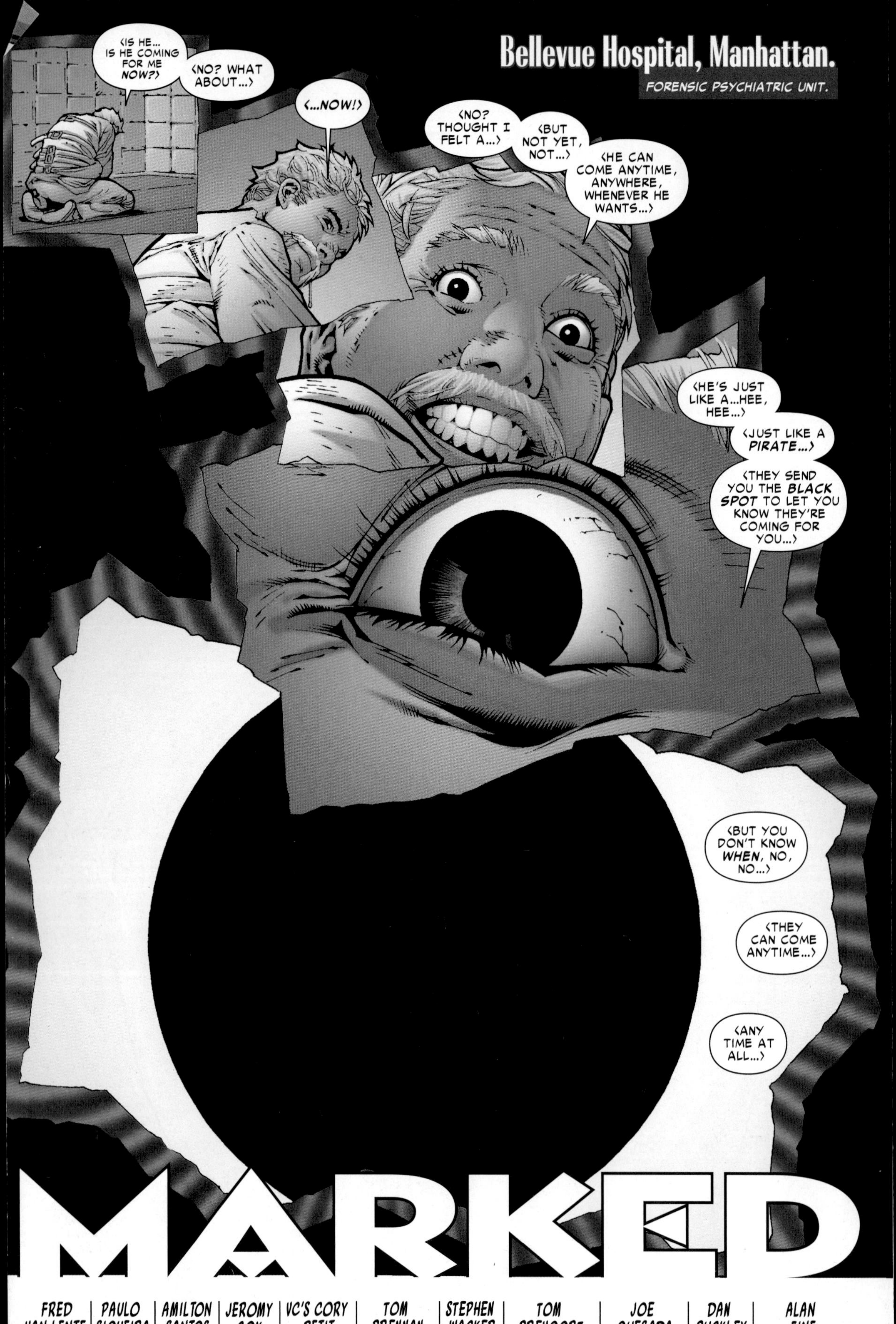
Bellevue Hospital, Manhattan.
FORENSIC PSYCHIATRIC UNIT.
‹IS HE... IS HE COMING FOR ME NOW?›
‹NO? WHAT ABOUT...›
‹...NOW!›
‹NO? THOUGHT I FELT A...›
‹BUT NOT YET, NOT...›
‹HE CAN COME ANYTIME, ANYWHERE, WHENEVER HE WANTS...›
‹HE'S JUST LIKE A...HEE, HEE...›
‹JUST LIKE A PIRATE...›
‹THEY SEND YOU THE BLACK SPOT TO LET YOU KNOW THEY'RE COMING FOR YOU...›
‹BUT YOU DON'T KNOW WHEN, NO, NO...›
‹THEY CAN COME ANYTIME...›
‹ANY TIME AT ALL...›
MARKED

FRED VAN LENTE WRITER | PAULO SIQUEIRA PENCILS | AMILTON SANTOS INKS | JEROMY COX COLORS | VC'S CORY PETIT LETTERS | TOM BRENNAN ASST. EDITOR | STEPHEN WACKER MILGROM-Y | TOM BREVOORT EXECUTIVE EDITOR | JOE QUESADA EDITOR IN CHIEF | DAN BUCKLEY PUBLISHER | ALAN FINE EXEC. PRODUCER

BOB GALE, MARC GUGGENHEIM, JOE KELLY, DAN SLOTT & MARK WAID-WEB-HEADS

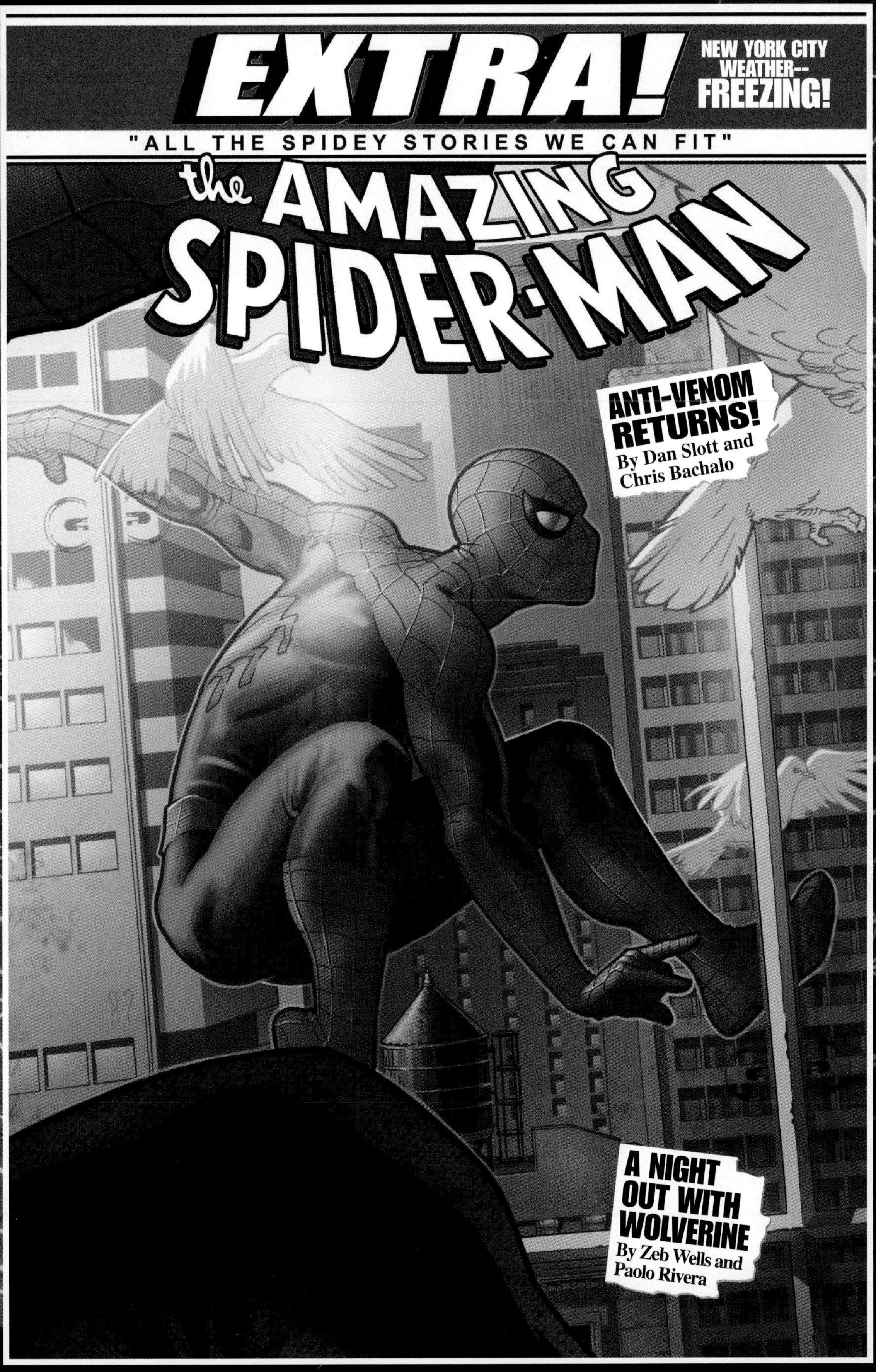

AMAZING SPIDER-MAN: EXTRA! #2 – "BIRTHDAY BOY"

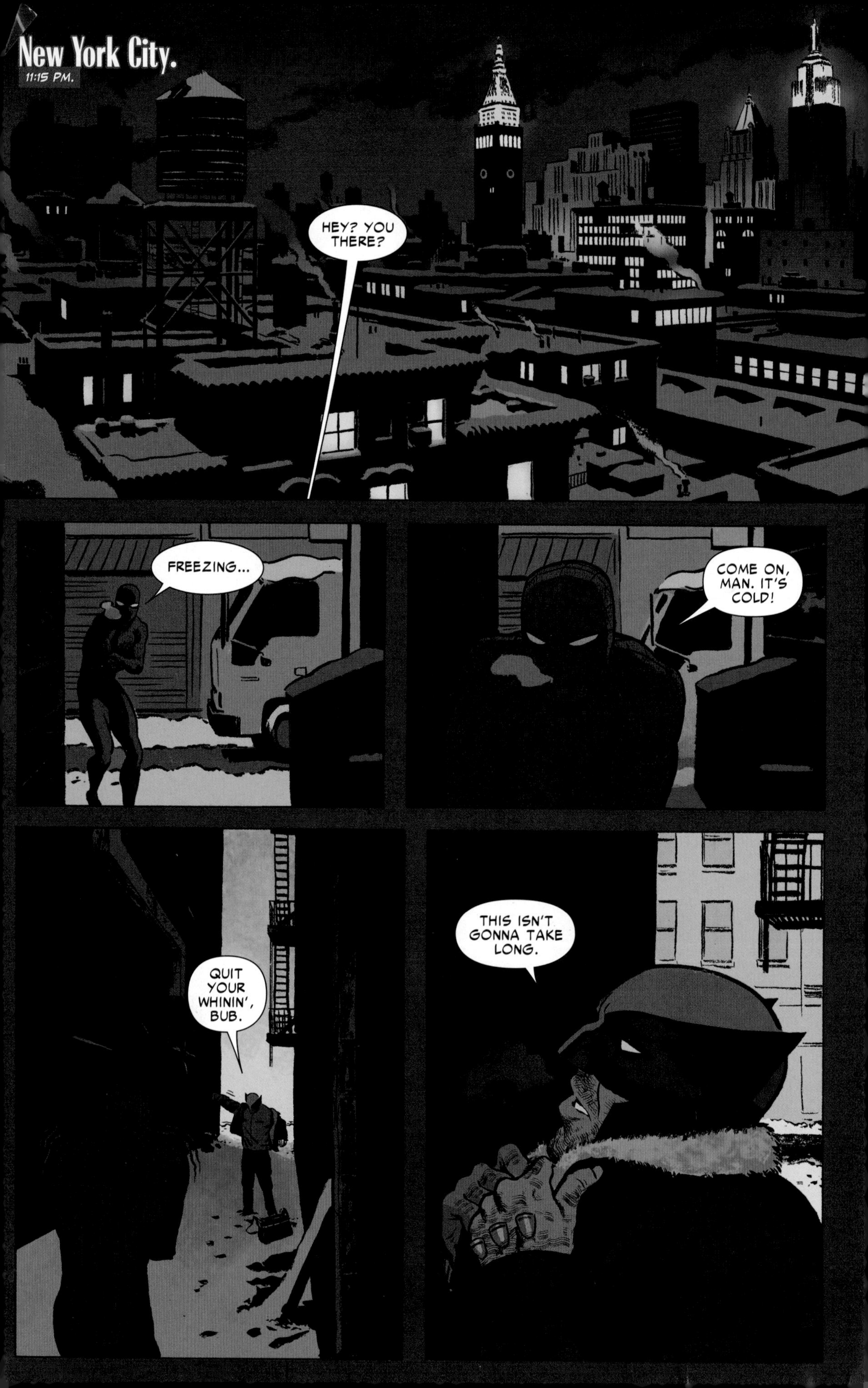
New York City.
11:15 PM.
HEY? YOU THERE?
FREEZING...
COME ON, MAN. IT'S COLD!
QUIT YOUR WHININ', BUB.
THIS ISN'T GONNA TAKE LONG.

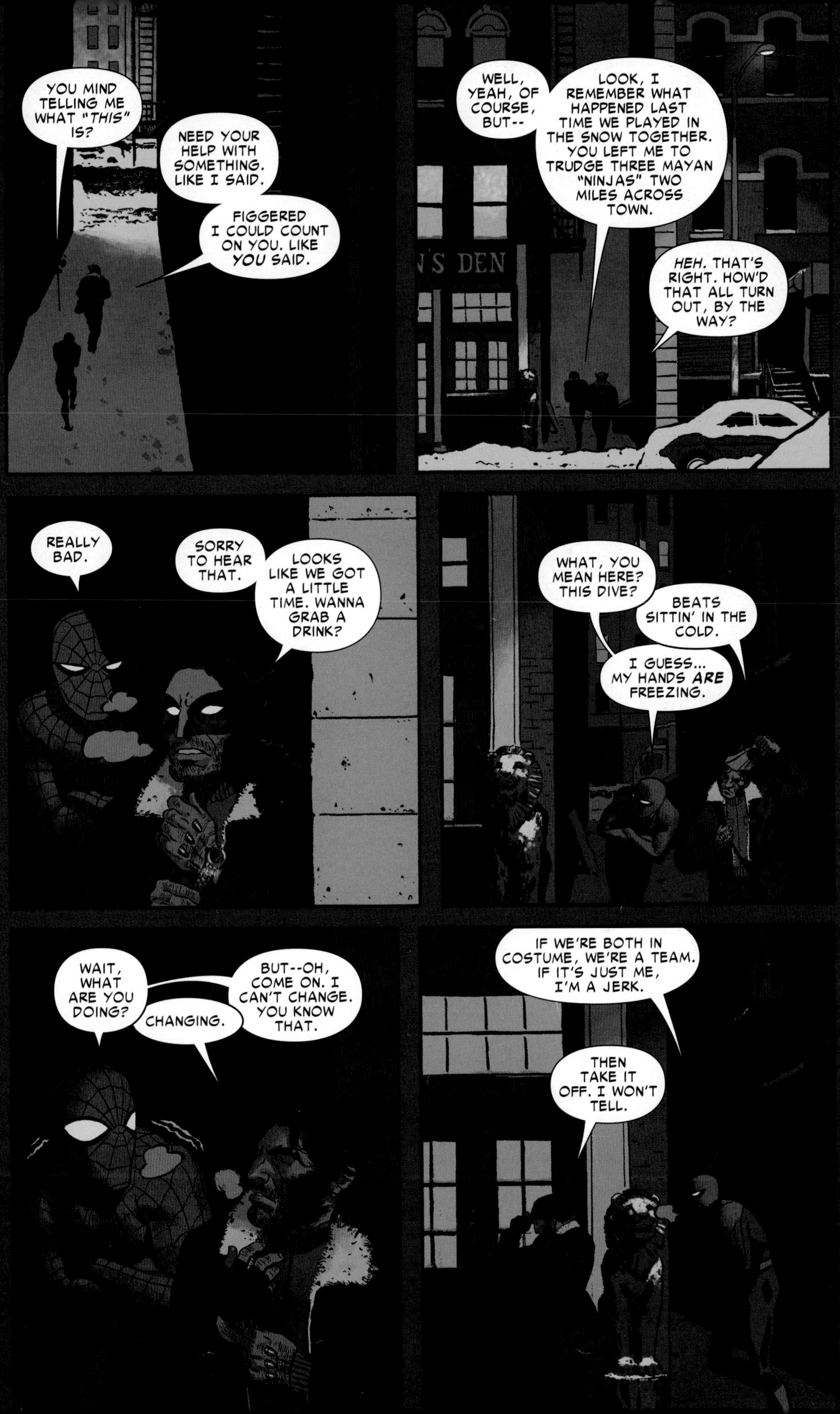
YOU MIND TELLING ME WHAT "*THIS*" IS?
NEED YOUR HELP WITH SOMETHING. LIKE I SAID.
FIGGERED I COULD COUNT ON YOU. LIKE *YOU* SAID.
WELL, YEAH, OF COURSE, BUT--
LOOK, I REMEMBER WHAT HAPPENED LAST TIME WE PLAYED IN THE SNOW TOGETHER. YOU LEFT ME TO TRUDGE THREE MAYAN "NINJAS" TWO MILES ACROSS TOWN.
'S DEN
HEH. THAT'S RIGHT. HOW'D THAT ALL TURN OUT, BY THE WAY?
REALLY BAD.
SORRY TO HEAR THAT.
LOOKS LIKE WE GOT A LITTLE TIME. WANNA GRAB A DRINK?
WHAT, YOU MEAN HERE? THIS DIVE?
BEATS SITTIN' IN THE COLD.
I GUESS... MY HANDS *ARE* FREEZING.
WAIT, WHAT ARE YOU DOING?
CHANGING.
BUT--OH, COME ON. I CAN'T CHANGE. YOU KNOW THAT.
IF WE'RE BOTH IN COSTUME, WE'RE A TEAM. IF IT'S JUST ME, I'M A JERK.
THEN TAKE IT OFF. I WON'T TELL.

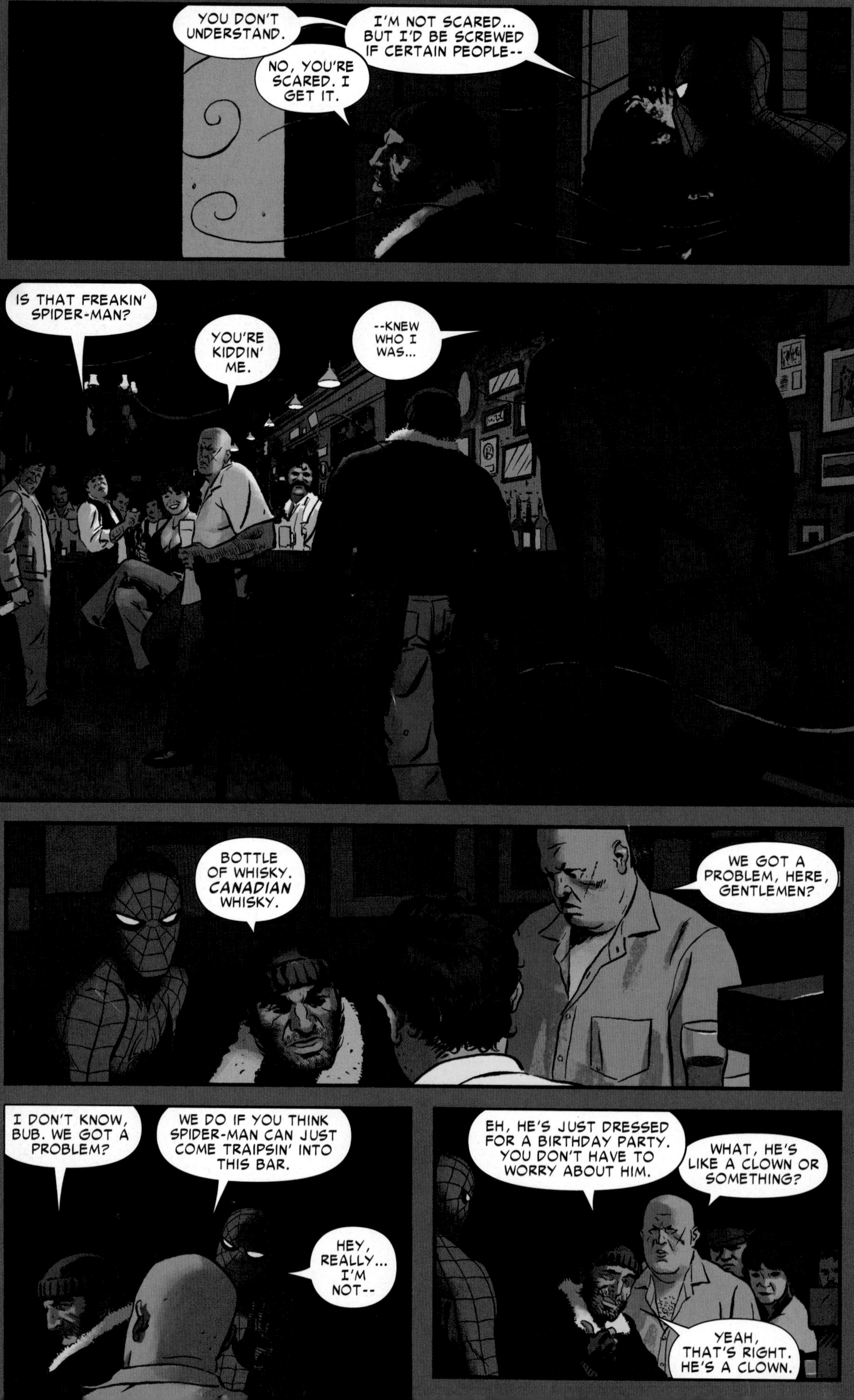
YOU DON'T UNDERSTAND.
NO, YOU'RE SCARED. I GET IT.
I'M NOT SCARED... BUT I'D BE SCREWED IF CERTAIN PEOPLE--
IS THAT FREAKIN' SPIDER-MAN?
YOU'RE KIDDIN' ME.
--KNEW WHO I WAS...
BOTTLE OF WHISKY. *CANADIAN* WHISKY.
WE GOT A PROBLEM, HERE, GENTLEMEN?
I DON'T KNOW, BUB. WE GOT A PROBLEM?
WE DO IF YOU THINK SPIDER-MAN CAN JUST COME TRAIPSIN' INTO THIS BAR.
HEY, REALLY... I'M NOT--
EH, HE'S JUST DRESSED FOR A BIRTHDAY PARTY. YOU DON'T HAVE TO WORRY ABOUT HIM.
WHAT, HE'S LIKE A CLOWN OR SOMETHING?
YEAH, THAT'S RIGHT. HE'S A CLOWN.

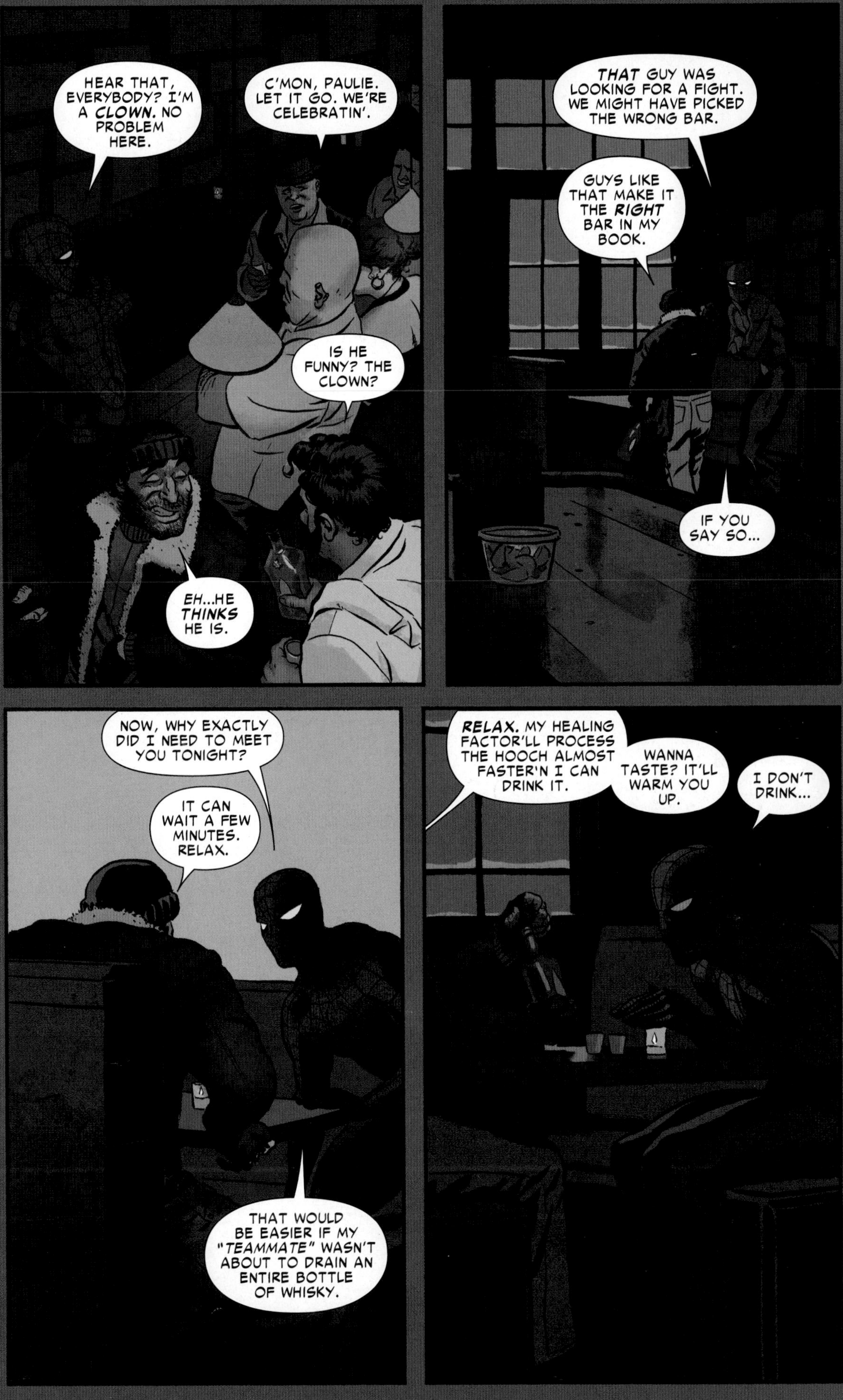
HEAR THAT, EVERYBODY? I'M A CLOWN. NO PROBLEM HERE.
C'MON, PAULIE. LET IT GO. WE'RE CELEBRATIN'.
IS HE FUNNY? THE CLOWN?
EH...HE THINKS HE IS.
THAT GUY WAS LOOKING FOR A FIGHT. WE MIGHT HAVE PICKED THE WRONG BAR.
GUYS LIKE THAT MAKE IT THE RIGHT BAR IN MY BOOK.
IF YOU SAY SO...
NOW, WHY EXACTLY DID I NEED TO MEET YOU TONIGHT?
IT CAN WAIT A FEW MINUTES. RELAX.
THAT WOULD BE EASIER IF MY "TEAMMATE" WASN'T ABOUT TO DRAIN AN ENTIRE BOTTLE OF WHISKY.
RELAX. MY HEALING FACTOR'LL PROCESS THE HOOCH ALMOST FASTER'N I CAN DRINK IT.
WANNA TASTE? IT'LL WARM YOU UP.
I DON'T DRINK...

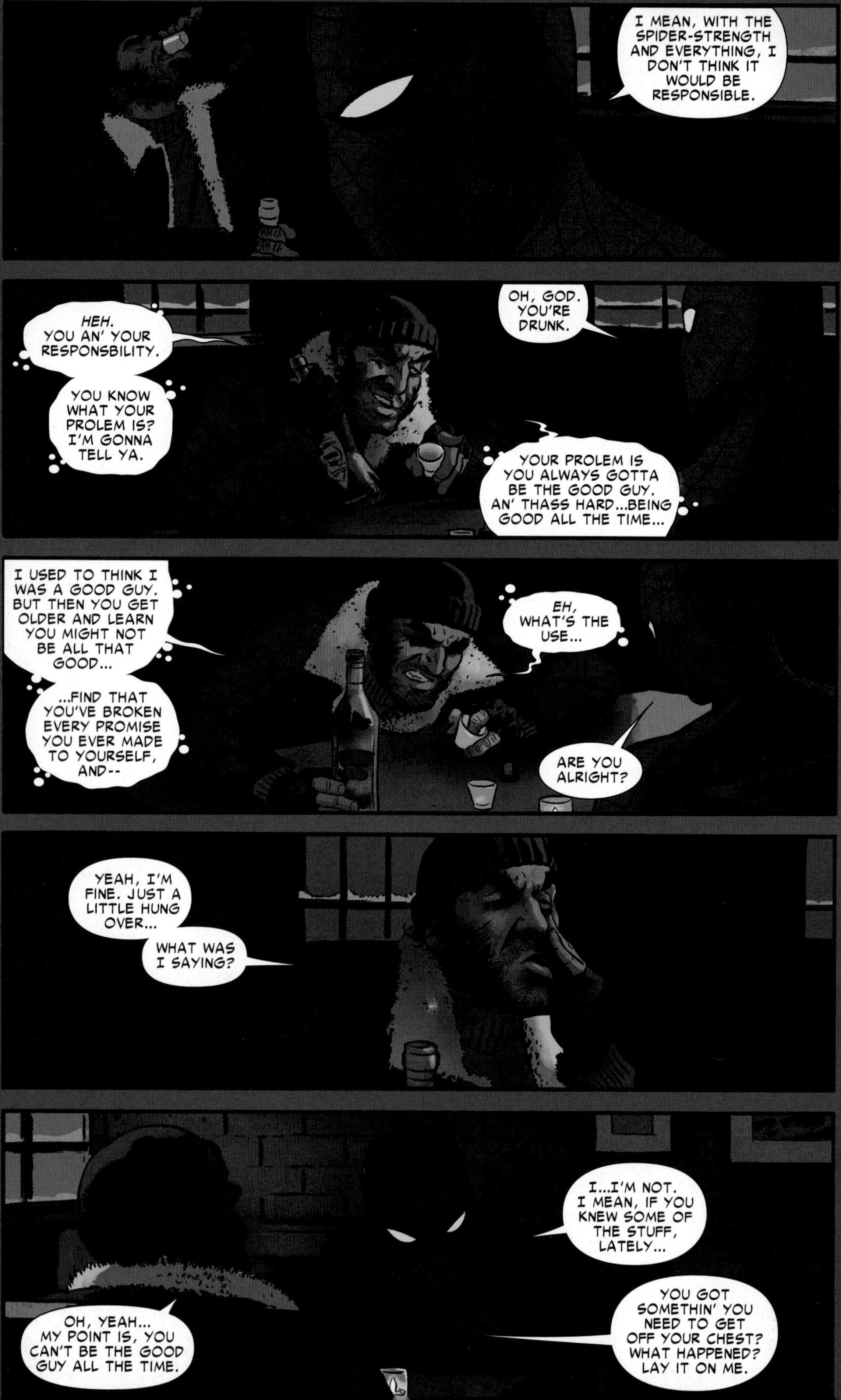
I MEAN, WITH THE SPIDER-STRENGTH AND EVERYTHING, I DON'T THINK IT WOULD BE RESPONSIBLE.
HEH. YOU AN' YOUR RESPONSBILITY.
YOU KNOW WHAT YOUR PROLEM IS? I'M GONNA TELL YA.
OH, GOD. YOU'RE DRUNK.
YOUR PROLEM IS YOU ALWAYS GOTTA BE THE GOOD GUY. AN' THASS HARD...BEING GOOD ALL THE TIME...
I USED TO THINK I WAS A GOOD GUY. BUT THEN YOU GET OLDER AND LEARN YOU MIGHT NOT BE ALL THAT GOOD...
...FIND THAT YOU'VE BROKEN EVERY PROMISE YOU EVER MADE TO YOURSELF, AND--
EH, WHAT'S THE USE...
ARE YOU ALRIGHT?
YEAH, I'M FINE. JUST A LITTLE HUNG OVER...
WHAT WAS I SAYING?
I...I'M NOT. I MEAN, IF YOU KNEW SOME OF THE STUFF, LATELY...
OH, YEAH... MY POINT IS, YOU CAN'T BE THE GOOD GUY ALL THE TIME.
YOU GOT SOMETHIN' YOU NEED TO GET OFF YOUR CHEST? WHAT HAPPENED? LAY IT ON ME.

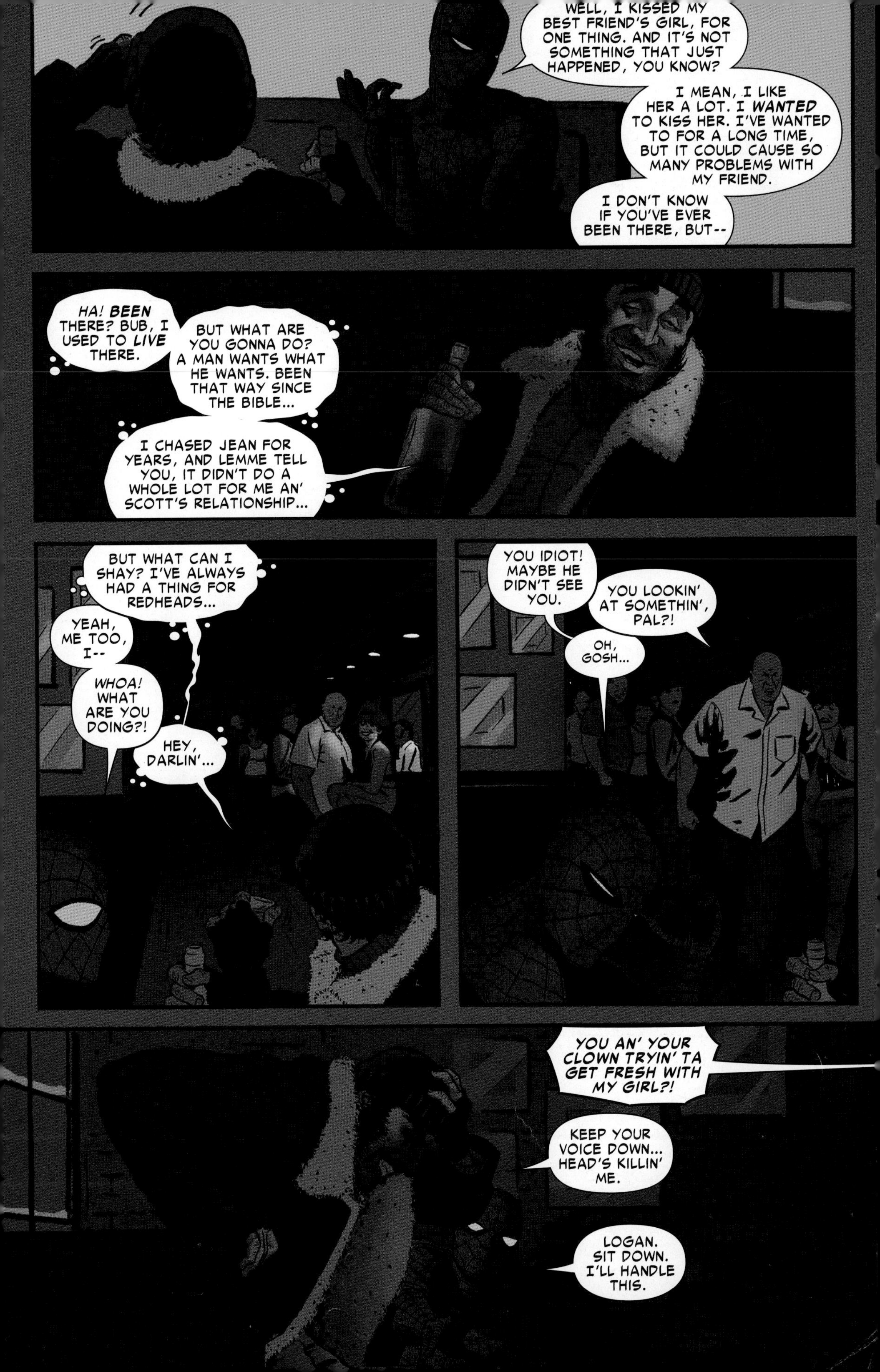
WELL, I KISSED MY BEST FRIEND'S GIRL, FOR ONE THING. AND IT'S NOT SOMETHING THAT JUST HAPPENED, YOU KNOW?
I MEAN, I LIKE HER A LOT. I *WANTED* TO KISS HER. I'VE WANTED TO FOR A LONG TIME, BUT IT COULD CAUSE SO MANY PROBLEMS WITH MY FRIEND.
I DON'T KNOW IF YOU'VE EVER BEEN THERE, BUT--
*HA! **BEEN** THERE? BUB, I USED TO **LIVE** THERE.*
BUT WHAT ARE YOU GONNA DO? A MAN WANTS WHAT HE WANTS. BEEN THAT WAY SINCE THE BIBLE...
I CHASED JEAN FOR YEARS, AND LEMME TELL YOU, IT DIDN'T DO A WHOLE LOT FOR ME AN' SCOTT'S RELATIONSHIP...
BUT WHAT CAN I SHAY? I'VE ALWAYS HAD A THING FOR REDHEADS...
YEAH, ME TOO, I--
WHOA! WHAT ARE YOU DOING?!
HEY, DARLIN'...
YOU IDIOT! MAYBE HE DIDN'T SEE YOU.
YOU LOOKIN' AT SOMETHIN', PAL?!
OH, GOSH...
YOU AN' YOUR CLOWN TRYIN' TA GET FRESH WITH MY GIRL?!
KEEP YOUR VOICE DOWN... HEAD'S KILLIN' ME.
LOGAN. SIT DOWN. I'LL HANDLE THIS.

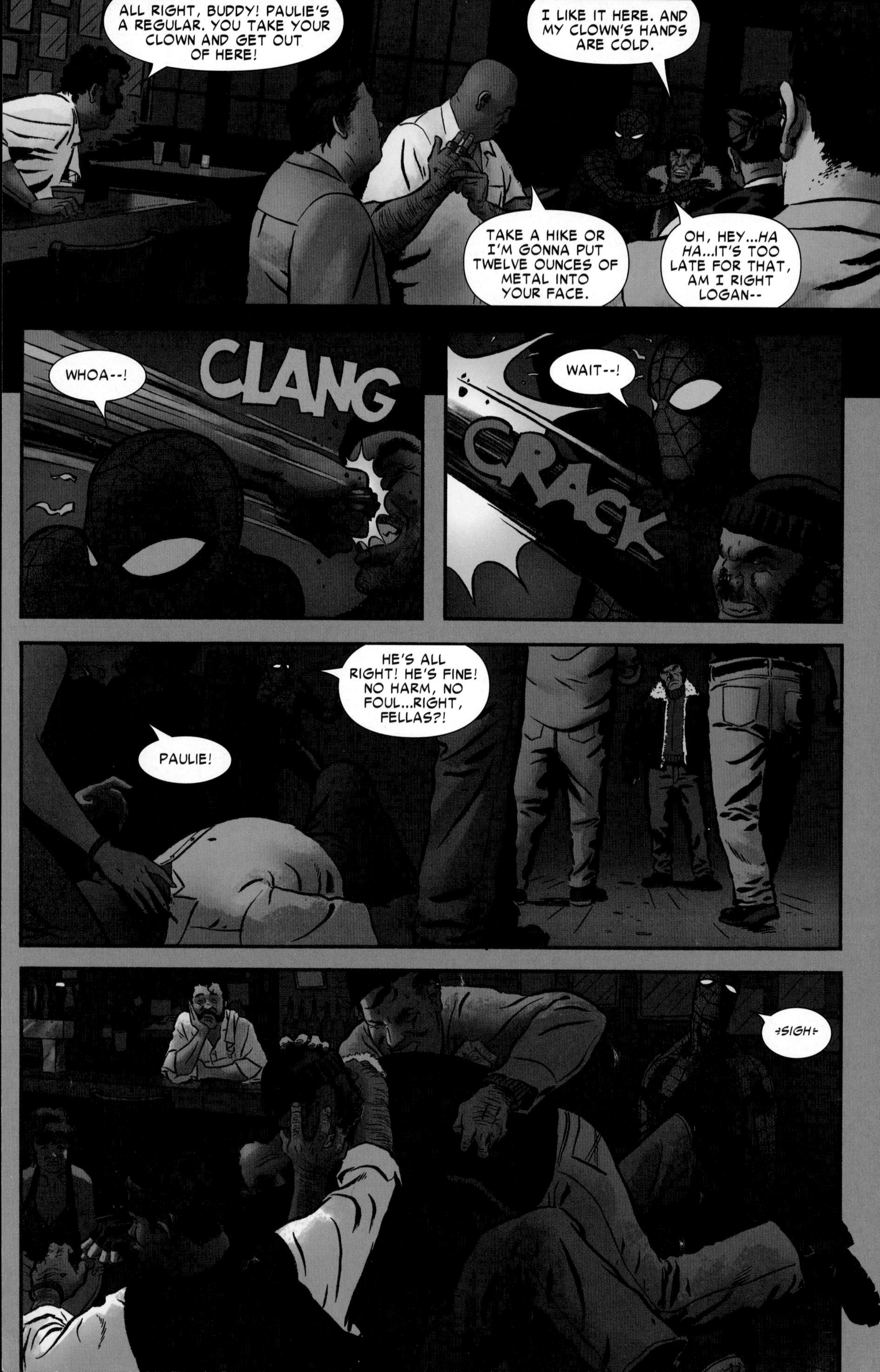
ALL RIGHT, BUDDY! PAULIE'S A REGULAR. YOU TAKE YOUR CLOWN AND GET OUT OF HERE!
I LIKE IT HERE. AND MY CLOWN'S HANDS ARE COLD.
TAKE A HIKE OR I'M GONNA PUT TWELVE OUNCES OF METAL INTO YOUR FACE.
OH, HEY...HA HA...IT'S TOO LATE FOR THAT, AM I RIGHT LOGAN--
WHOA--!
CLANG
WAIT--!
CRACK
HE'S ALL RIGHT! HE'S FINE! NO HARM, NO FOUL...RIGHT, FELLAS?!
PAULIE!
SIGH

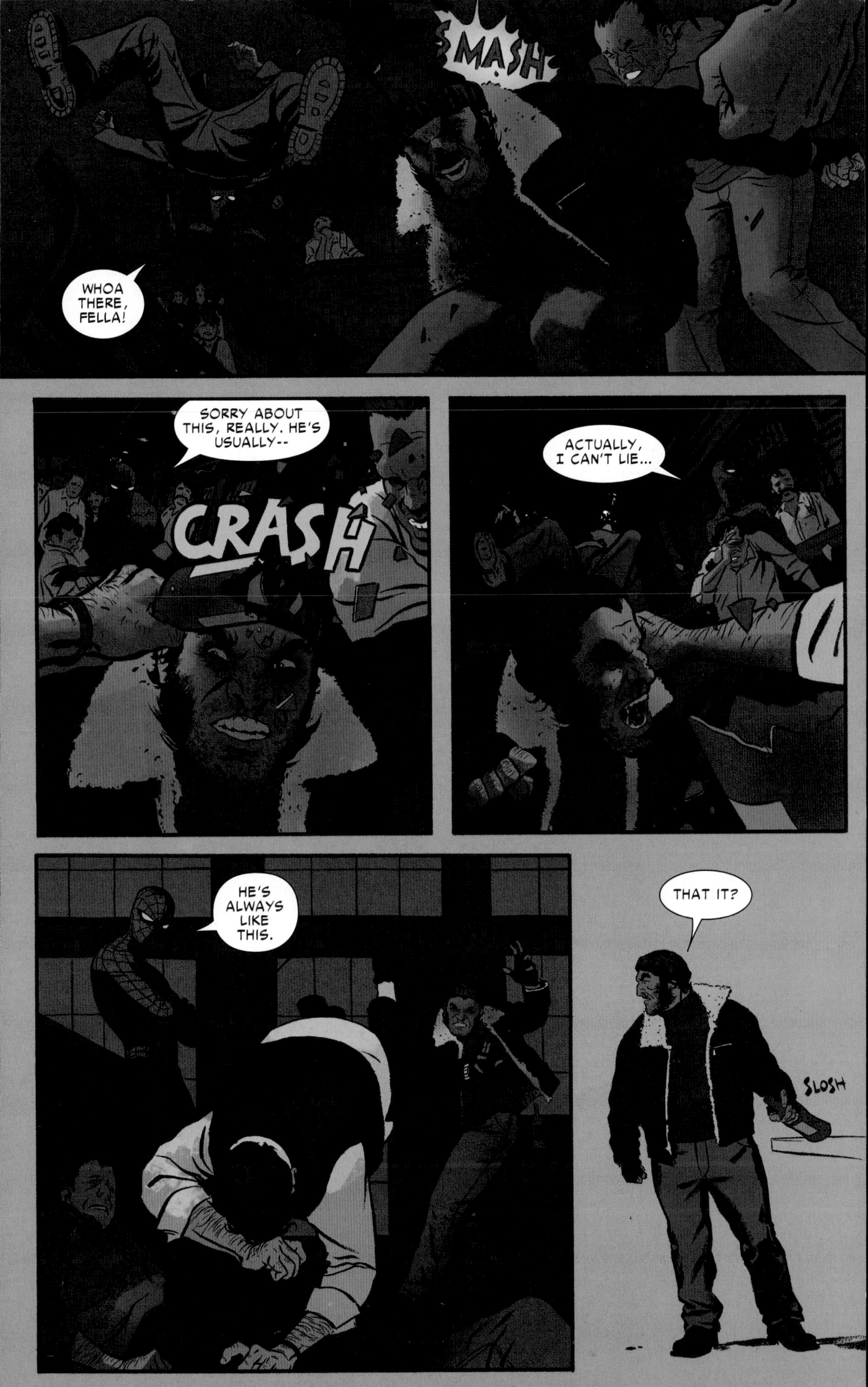
SMASH
WHOA THERE, FELLA!
SORRY ABOUT THIS, REALLY. HE'S USUALLY--
CRASH
ACTUALLY, I CAN'T LIE...
HE'S ALWAYS LIKE THIS.
THAT IT?
SLOSH

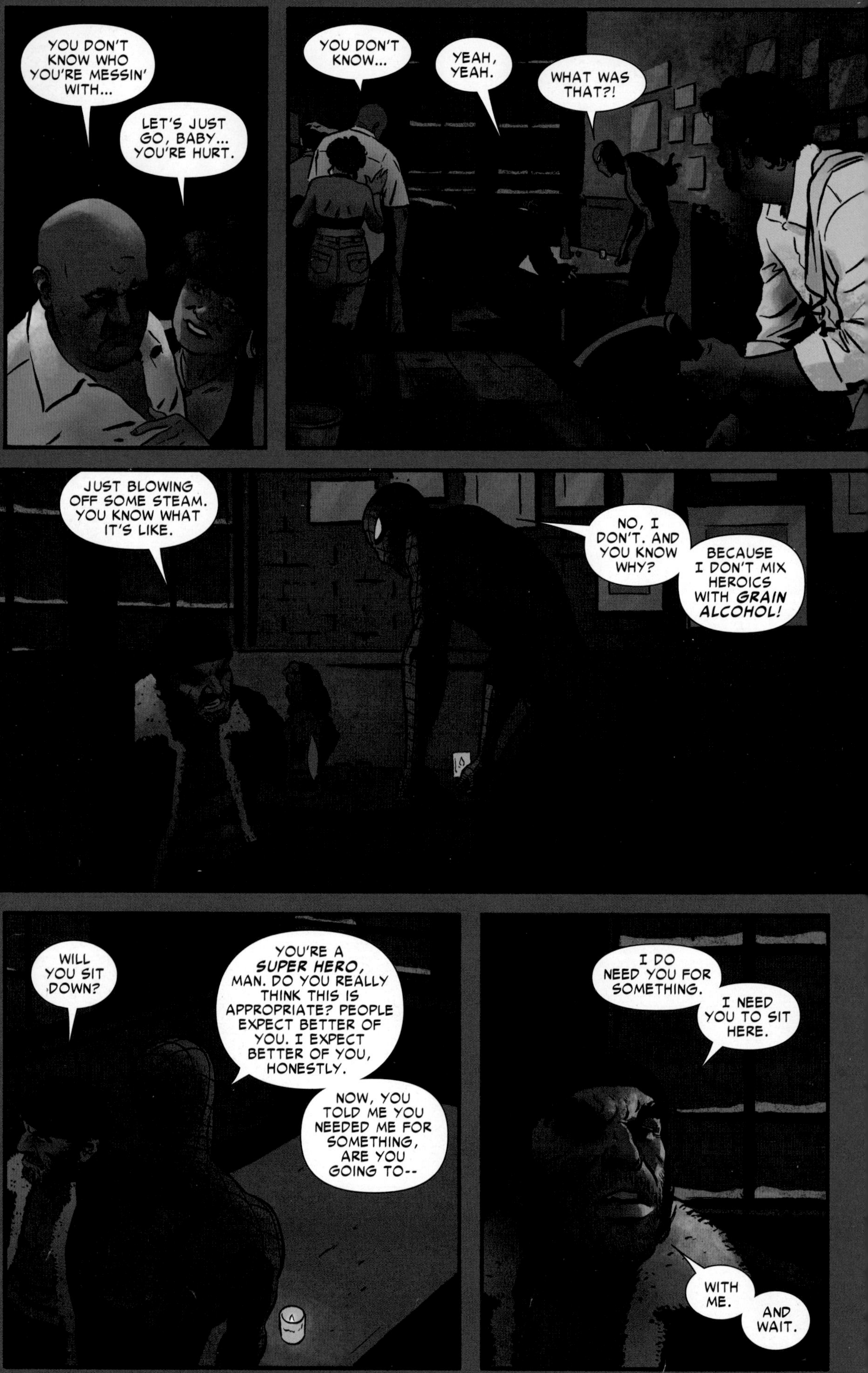
YOU DON'T KNOW WHO YOU'RE MESSIN' WITH...
LET'S JUST GO, BABY... YOU'RE HURT.
YOU DON'T KNOW...
YEAH, YEAH.
WHAT WAS THAT?!
JUST BLOWING OFF SOME STEAM. YOU KNOW WHAT IT'S LIKE.
NO, I DON'T. AND YOU KNOW WHY?
BECAUSE I DON'T MIX HEROICS WITH GRAIN ALCOHOL!
WILL YOU SIT DOWN?
YOU'RE A SUPER HERO, MAN. DO YOU REALLY THINK THIS IS APPROPRIATE? PEOPLE EXPECT BETTER OF YOU. I EXPECT BETTER OF YOU, HONESTLY.
NOW, YOU TOLD ME YOU NEEDED ME FOR SOMETHING, ARE YOU GOING TO--
I DO NEED YOU FOR SOMETHING.
I NEED YOU TO SIT HERE.
WITH ME.
AND WAIT.

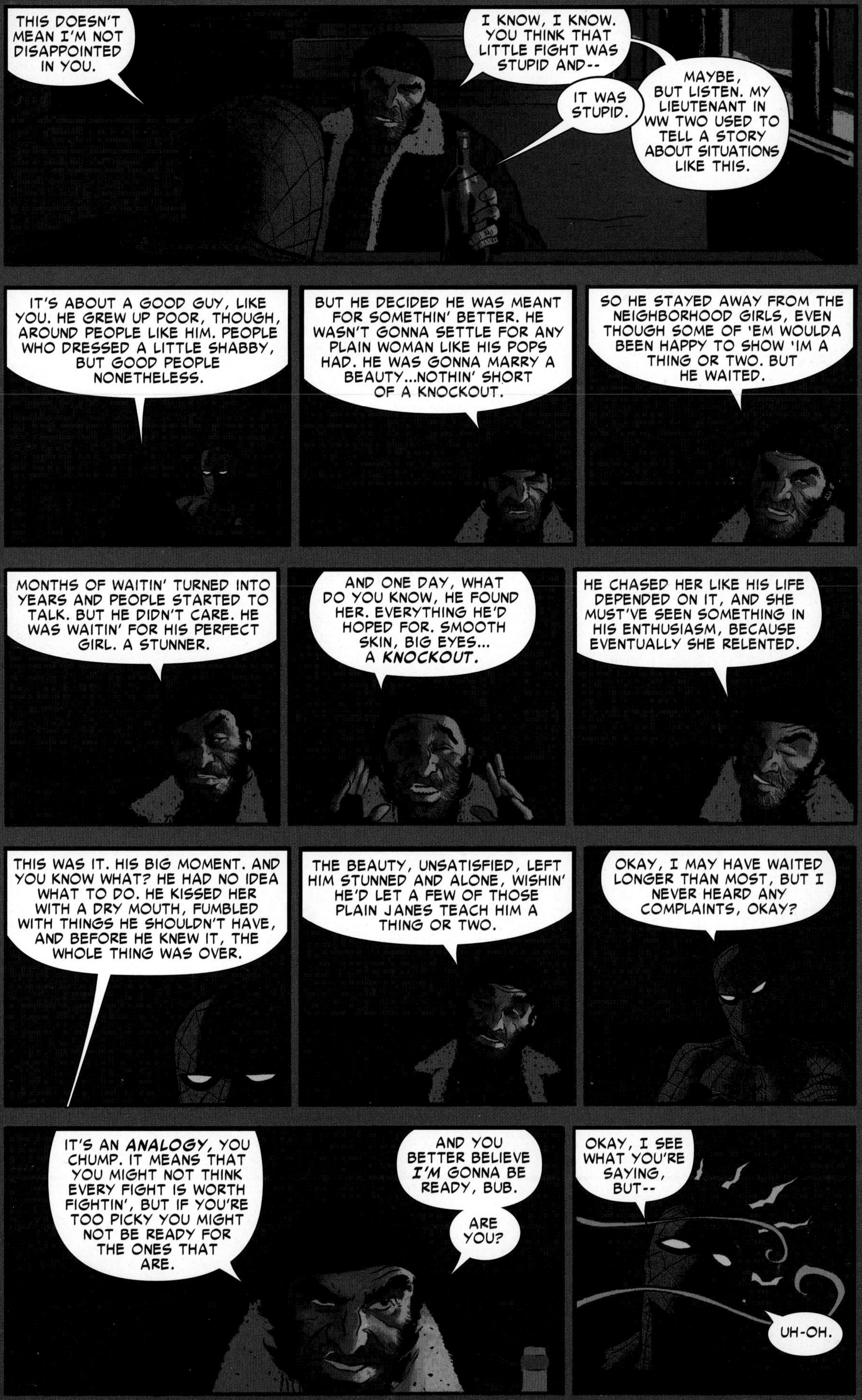
THIS DOESN'T MEAN I'M NOT DISAPPOINTED IN YOU.
I KNOW, I KNOW. YOU THINK THAT LITTLE FIGHT WAS STUPID AND--
IT WAS STUPID.
MAYBE, BUT LISTEN. MY LIEUTENANT IN WW TWO USED TO TELL A STORY ABOUT SITUATIONS LIKE THIS.
IT'S ABOUT A GOOD GUY, LIKE YOU. HE GREW UP POOR, THOUGH, AROUND PEOPLE LIKE HIM. PEOPLE WHO DRESSED A LITTLE SHABBY, BUT GOOD PEOPLE NONETHELESS.
BUT HE DECIDED HE WAS MEANT FOR SOMETHIN' BETTER. HE WASN'T GONNA SETTLE FOR ANY PLAIN WOMAN LIKE HIS POPS HAD. HE WAS GONNA MARRY A BEAUTY...NOTHIN' SHORT OF A KNOCKOUT.
SO HE STAYED AWAY FROM THE NEIGHBORHOOD GIRLS, EVEN THOUGH SOME OF 'EM WOULDA BEEN HAPPY TO SHOW 'IM A THING OR TWO. BUT HE WAITED.
MONTHS OF WAITIN' TURNED INTO YEARS AND PEOPLE STARTED TO TALK. BUT HE DIDN'T CARE. HE WAS WAITIN' FOR HIS PERFECT GIRL. A STUNNER.
AND ONE DAY, WHAT DO YOU KNOW, HE FOUND HER. EVERYTHING HE'D HOPED FOR. SMOOTH SKIN, BIG EYES... A *KNOCKOUT.*
HE CHASED HER LIKE HIS LIFE DEPENDED ON IT, AND SHE MUST'VE SEEN SOMETHING IN HIS ENTHUSIASM, BECAUSE EVENTUALLY SHE RELENTED.
THIS WAS IT. HIS BIG MOMENT. AND YOU KNOW WHAT? HE HAD NO IDEA WHAT TO DO. HE KISSED HER WITH A DRY MOUTH, FUMBLED WITH THINGS HE SHOULDN'T HAVE, AND BEFORE HE KNEW IT, THE WHOLE THING WAS OVER.
THE BEAUTY, UNSATISFIED, LEFT HIM STUNNED AND ALONE, WISHIN' HE'D LET A FEW OF THOSE PLAIN JANES TEACH HIM A THING OR TWO.
OKAY, I MAY HAVE WAITED LONGER THAN MOST, BUT I NEVER HEARD ANY COMPLAINTS, OKAY?
IT'S AN *ANALOGY*, YOU CHUMP. IT MEANS THAT YOU MIGHT NOT THINK EVERY FIGHT IS WORTH FIGHTIN', BUT IF YOU'RE TOO PICKY YOU MIGHT NOT BE READY FOR THE ONES THAT ARE.
AND YOU BETTER BELIEVE *I'M* GONNA BE READY, BUB.
ARE YOU?
OKAY, I SEE WHAT YOU'RE SAYING, BUT--
UH-OH.

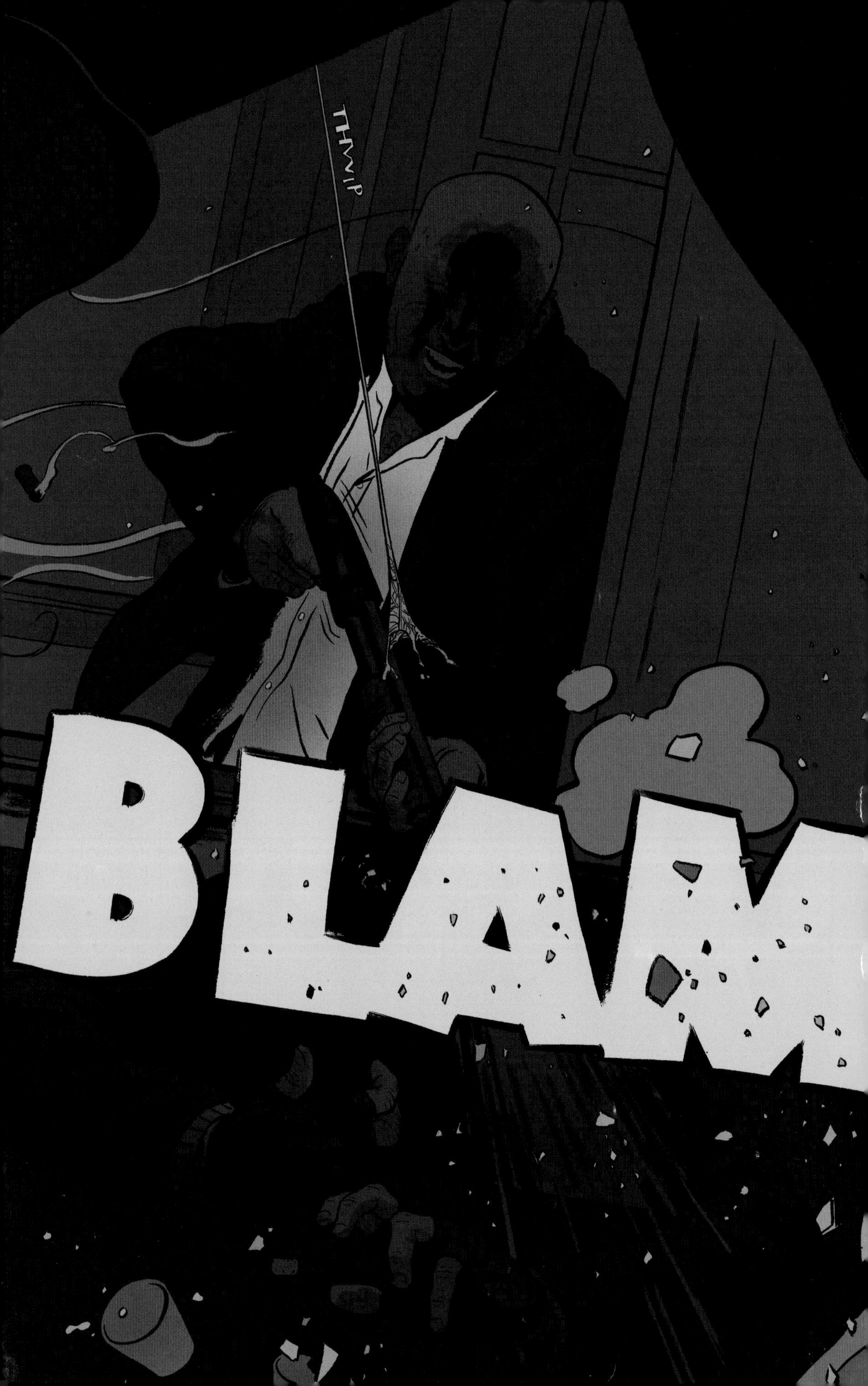
THWIP
BLAM

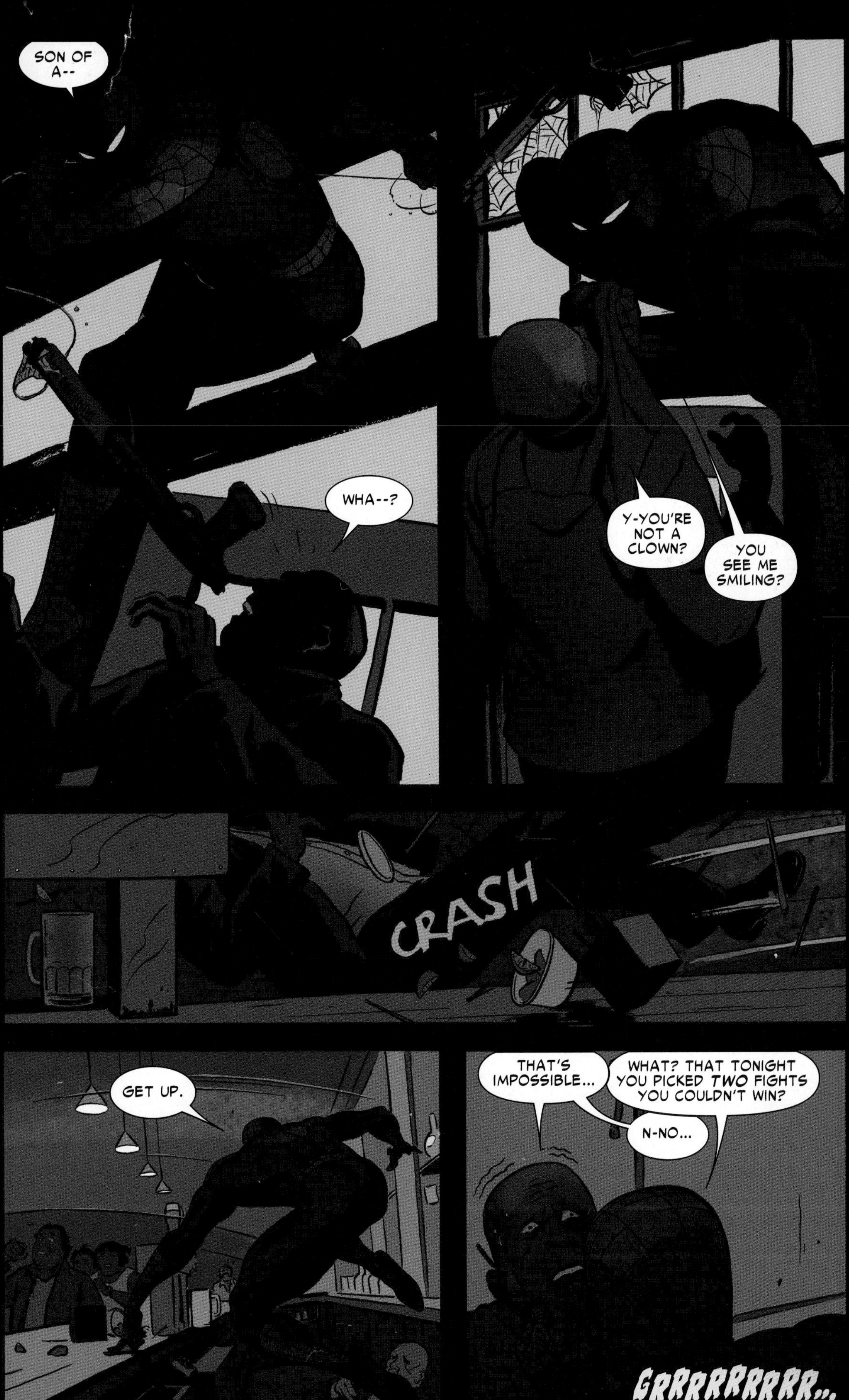
SON OF A--
WHA--?
Y-YOU'RE NOT A CLOWN?
YOU SEE ME SMILING?
CRASH
GET UP.
THAT'S IMPOSSIBLE...
WHAT? THAT TONIGHT YOU PICKED *TWO* FIGHTS YOU COULDN'T WIN?
N-NO...
GRRRRRRRRR...

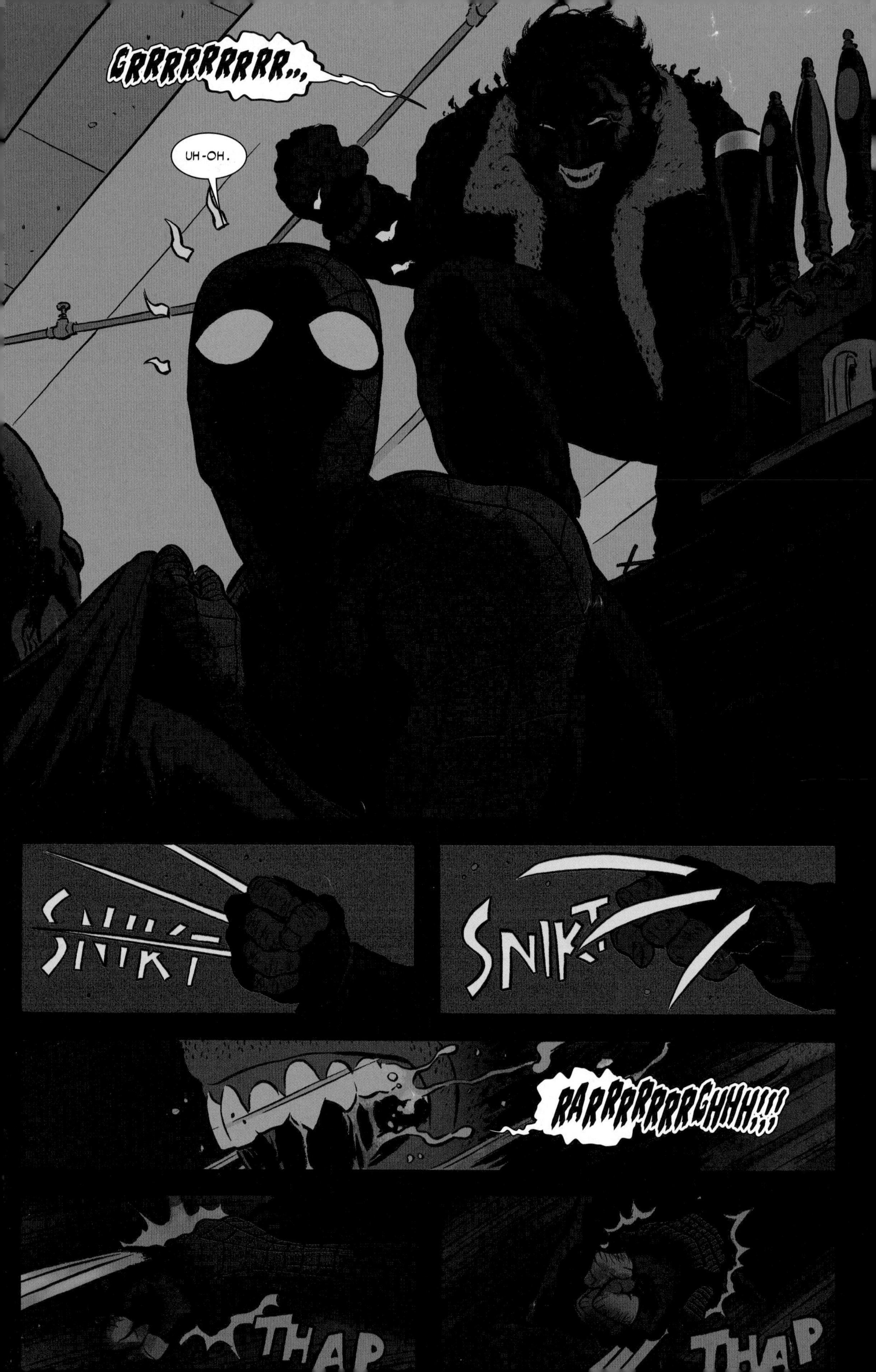
GRRRRRRRRR...
UH-OH.
SNIKT
SNIKT
RARRRRRRRGHHH!!!
THAP
THAP

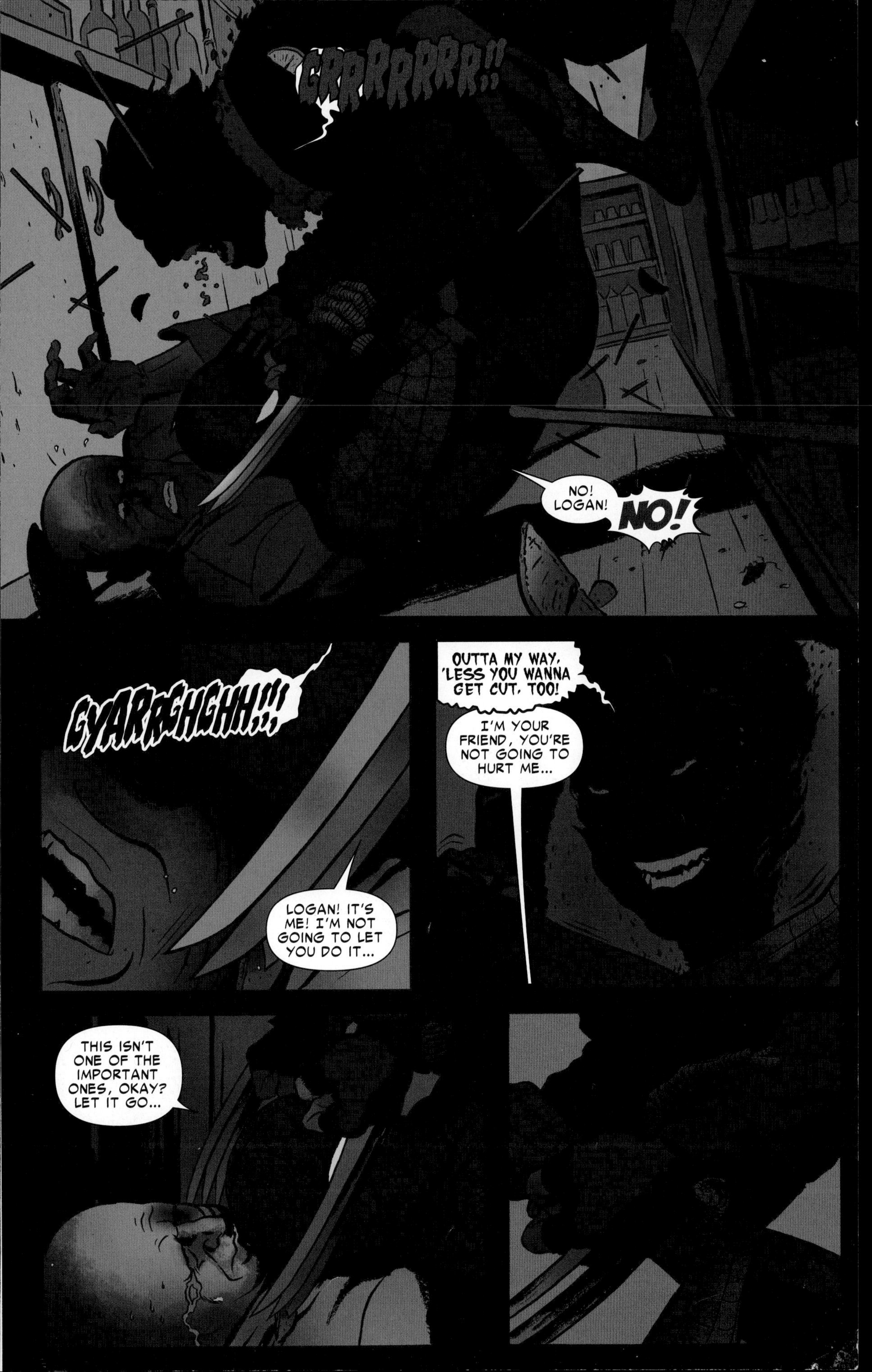
GRRRRRRR!!
NO! LOGAN!
NO!
GYARRGHGHH!!!
LOGAN! IT'S ME! I'M NOT GOING TO LET YOU DO IT...
OUTTA MY WAY, 'LESS YOU WANNA GET CUT, TOO!
I'M YOUR FRIEND, YOU'RE NOT GOING TO HURT ME...
THIS ISN'T ONE OF THE IMPORTANT ONES, OKAY? LET IT GO...

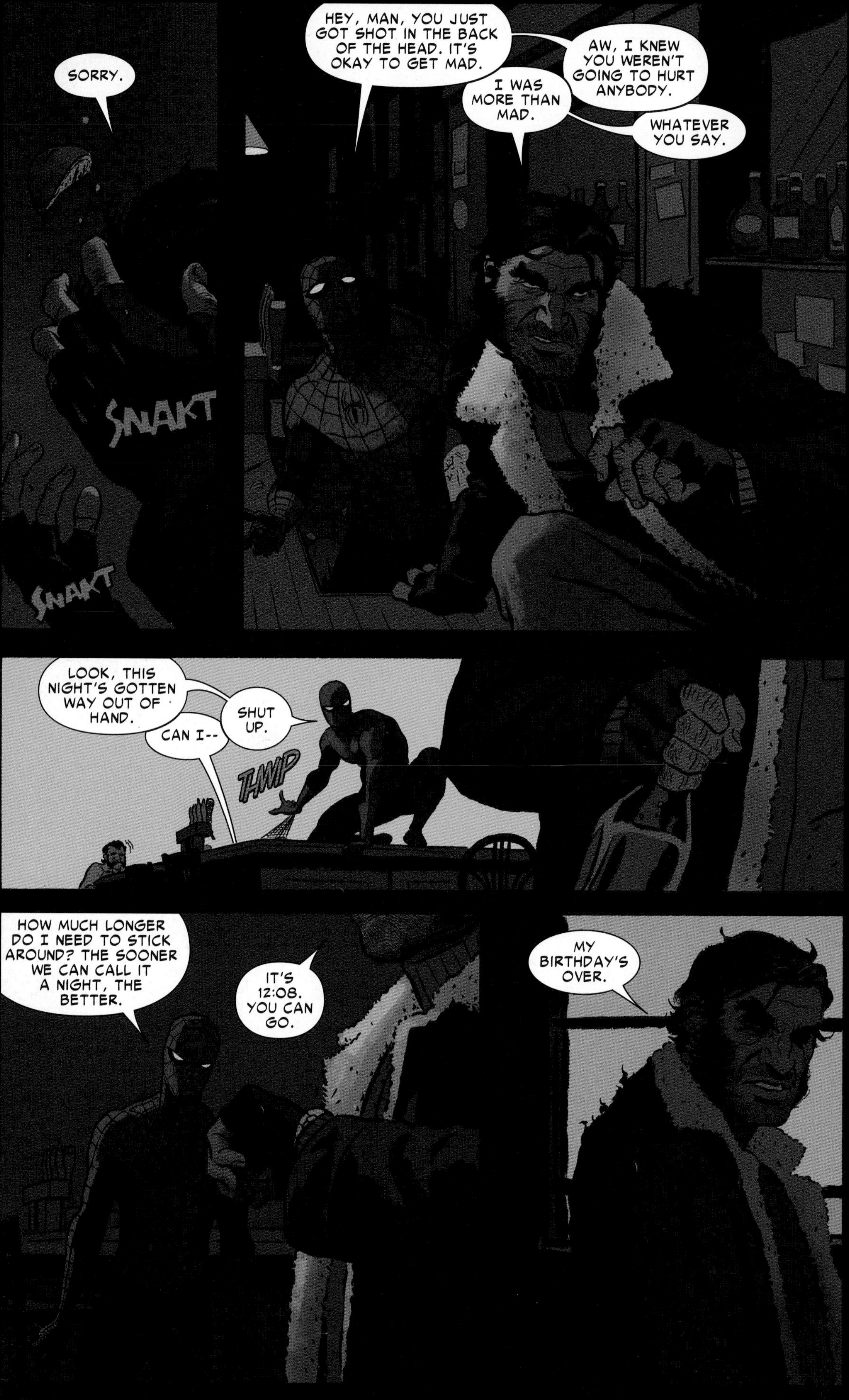
SORRY.
SNAKT
SNAKT
HEY, MAN, YOU JUST GOT SHOT IN THE BACK OF THE HEAD. IT'S OKAY TO GET MAD.
AW, I KNEW YOU WEREN'T GOING TO HURT ANYBODY.
I WAS MORE THAN MAD.
WHATEVER YOU SAY.
LOOK, THIS NIGHT'S GOTTEN WAY OUT OF HAND.
CAN I--
SHUT UP.
THWIP
HOW MUCH LONGER DO I NEED TO STICK AROUND? THE SOONER WE CAN CALL IT A NIGHT, THE BETTER.
IT'S 12:08. YOU CAN GO.
MY BIRTHDAY'S OVER.

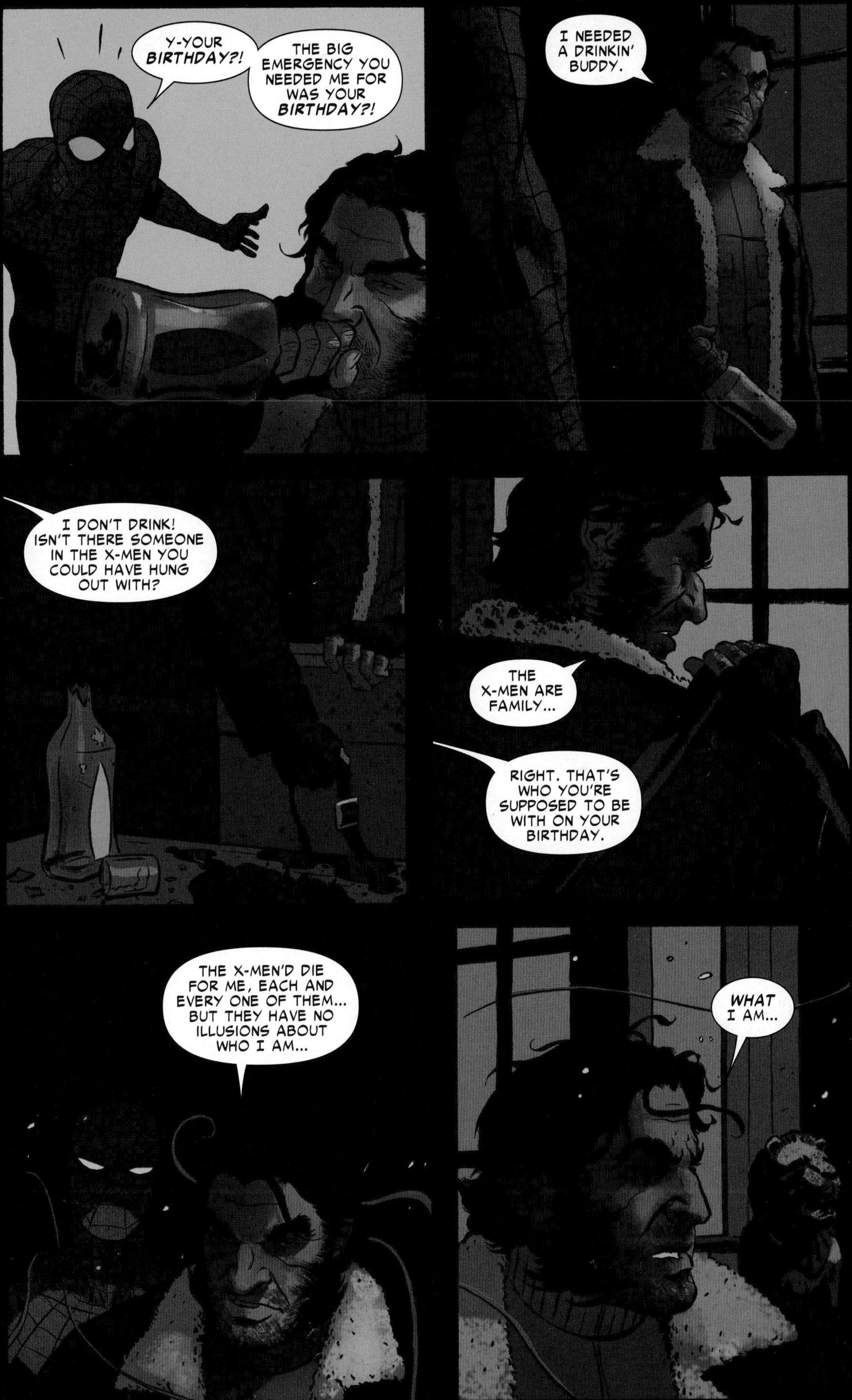

Y-YOUR *BIRTHDAY?!*
THE BIG EMERGENCY YOU NEEDED ME FOR WAS YOUR *BIRTHDAY?!*
I NEEDED A DRINKIN' BUDDY.
I DON'T DRINK! ISN'T THERE SOMEONE IN THE X-MEN YOU COULD HAVE HUNG OUT WITH?
THE X-MEN ARE FAMILY...
RIGHT. THAT'S WHO YOU'RE SUPPOSED TO BE WITH ON YOUR BIRTHDAY.
THE X-MEN'D DIE FOR ME, EACH AND EVERY ONE OF THEM... BUT THEY HAVE NO ILLUSIONS ABOUT WHO I AM...
WHAT I AM...

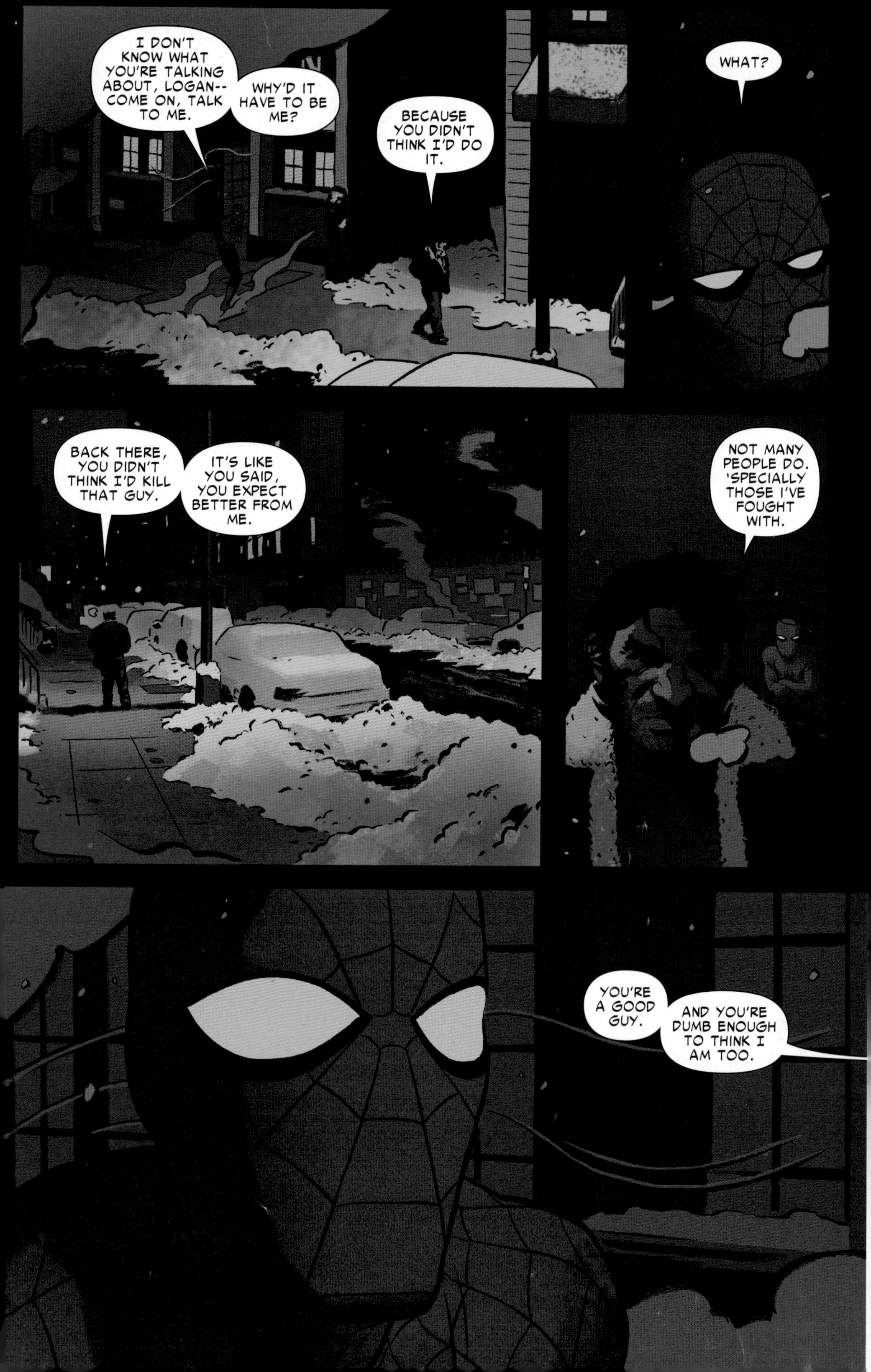
I DON'T KNOW WHAT YOU'RE TALKING ABOUT, LOGAN-- COME ON, TALK TO ME.
WHY'D IT HAVE TO BE ME?
BECAUSE YOU DIDN'T THINK I'D DO IT.
WHAT?
BACK THERE, YOU DIDN'T THINK I'D KILL THAT GUY.
IT'S LIKE YOU SAID, YOU EXPECT BETTER FROM ME.
NOT MANY PEOPLE DO. 'SPECIALLY THOSE I'VE FOUGHT WITH.
YOU'RE A GOOD GUY.
AND YOU'RE DUMB ENOUGH TO THINK I AM TOO.

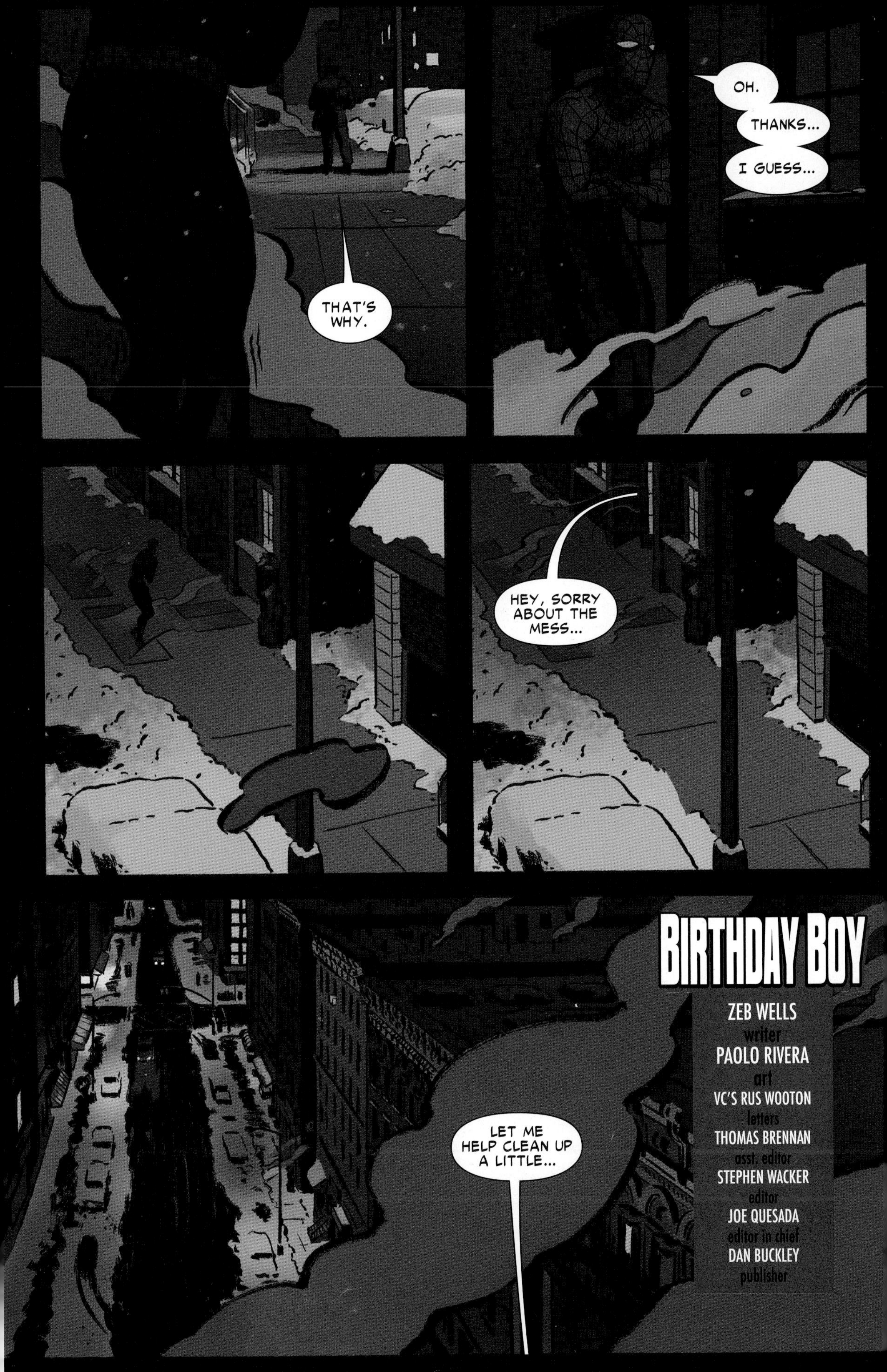
THAT'S WHY.
OH.
THANKS...
I GUESS...
HEY, SORRY ABOUT THE MESS...
BIRTHDAY BOY
ZEB WELLS writer
PAOLO RIVERA art
VC'S RUS WOOTON letters
THOMAS BRENNAN asst. editor
STEPHEN WACKER editor
JOE QUESADA editor in chief
DAN BUCKLEY publisher
LET ME HELP CLEAN UP A LITTLE...

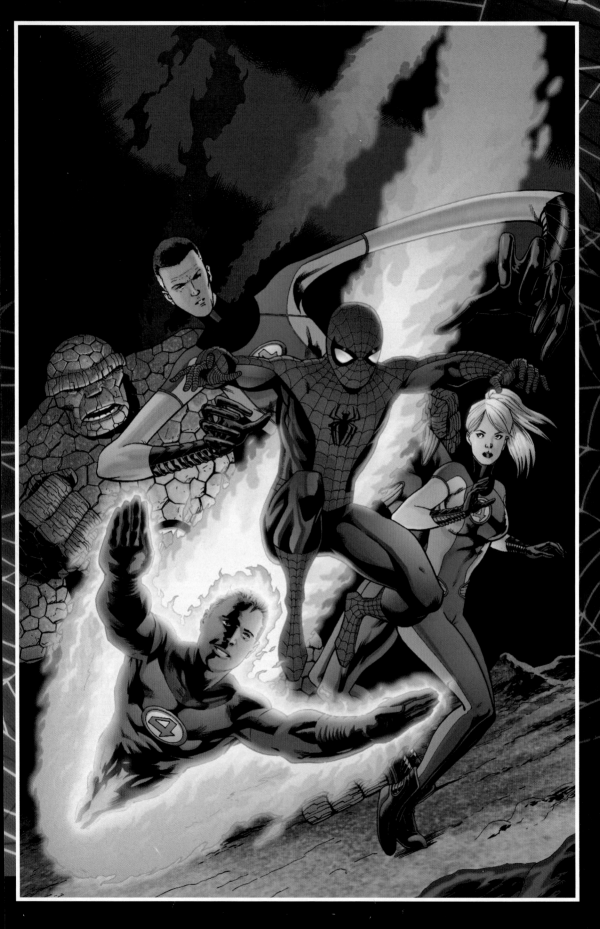

AMAZING SPIDER-MAN #590

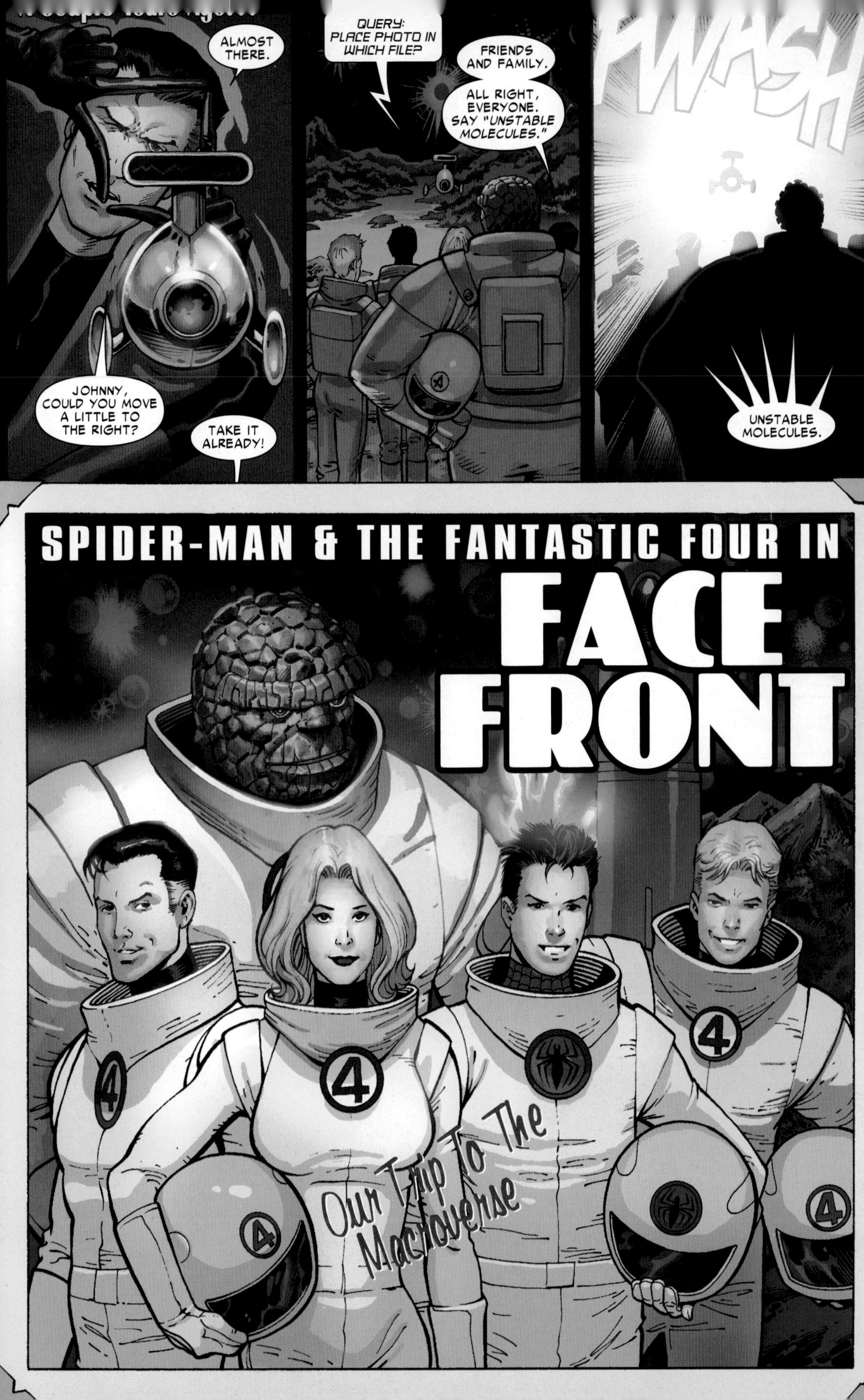
ALMOST THERE.
JOHNNY, COULD YOU MOVE A LITTLE TO THE RIGHT?
TAKE IT ALREADY!
QUERY: PLACE PHOTO IN WHICH FILE?
FRIENDS AND FAMILY.
ALL RIGHT, EVERYONE. SAY "UNSTABLE MOLECULES."
PWASH
UNSTABLE MOLECULES.
SPIDER-MAN & THE FANTASTIC FOUR IN
FACE FRONT
Our Trip To The Macroverse

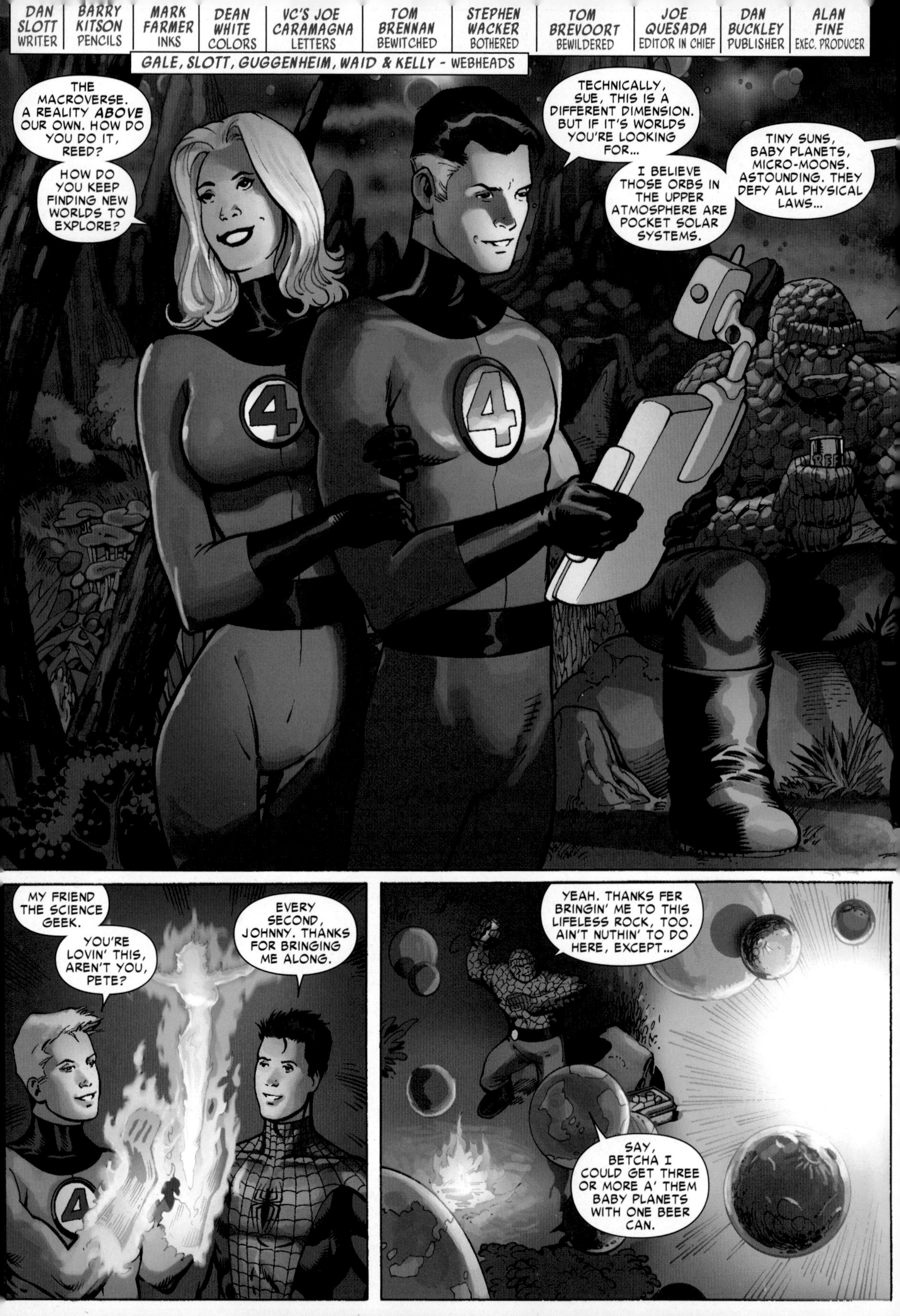
DAN SLOTT WRITER
BARRY KITSON PENCILS
MARK FARMER INKS
DEAN WHITE COLORS
VC'S JOE CARAMAGNA LETTERS
TOM BRENNAN BEWITCHED
STEPHEN WACKER BOTHERED
TOM BREVOORT BEWILDERED
JOE QUESADA EDITOR IN CHIEF
DAN BUCKLEY PUBLISHER
ALAN FINE EXEC. PRODUCER
GALE, SLOTT, GUGGENHEIM, WAID & KELLY - WEBHEADS
THE MACROVERSE. A REALITY ABOVE OUR OWN. HOW DO YOU DO IT, REED?
HOW DO YOU KEEP FINDING NEW WORLDS TO EXPLORE?
TECHNICALLY, SUE, THIS IS A DIFFERENT DIMENSION. BUT IF IT'S WORLDS YOU'RE LOOKING FOR...
I BELIEVE THOSE ORBS IN THE UPPER ATMOSPHERE ARE POCKET SOLAR SYSTEMS.
TINY SUNS, BABY PLANETS, MICRO-MOONS. ASTOUNDING. THEY DEFY ALL PHYSICAL LAWS...
MY FRIEND THE SCIENCE GEEK.
YOU'RE LOVIN' THIS, AREN'T YOU, PETE?
EVERY SECOND, JOHNNY. THANKS FOR BRINGING ME ALONG.
YEAH. THANKS FER BRINGIN' ME TO THIS LIFELESS ROCK, TOO. AIN'T NUTHIN' TO DO HERE, EXCEPT...
SAY, BETCHA I COULD GET THREE OR MORE A' THEM BABY PLANETS WITH ONE BEER CAN.

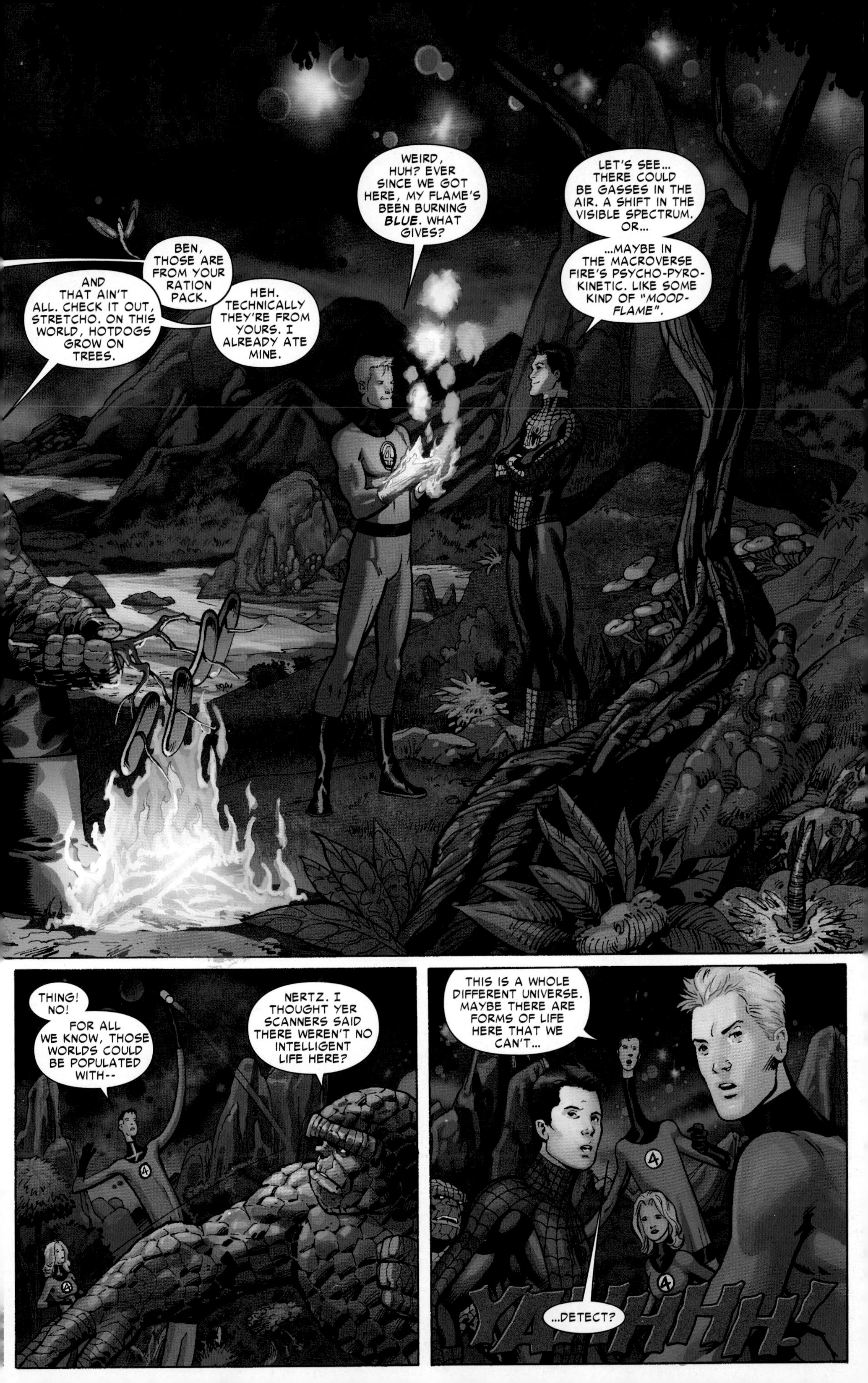
AND THAT AIN'T ALL. CHECK IT OUT, STRETCHO. ON THIS WORLD, HOTDOGS GROW ON TREES.
BEN, THOSE ARE FROM YOUR RATION PACK.
HEH. TECHNICALLY THEY'RE FROM YOURS. I ALREADY ATE MINE.
WEIRD, HUH? EVER SINCE WE GOT HERE, MY FLAME'S BEEN BURNING *BLUE*. WHAT GIVES?
LET'S SEE... THERE COULD BE GASSES IN THE AIR. A SHIFT IN THE VISIBLE SPECTRUM. OR...
...MAYBE IN THE MACROVERSE FIRE'S PSYCHO-PYRO-KINETIC. LIKE SOME KIND OF *"MOOD-FLAME"*.
THING! NO!
FOR ALL WE KNOW, THOSE WORLDS COULD BE POPULATED WITH--
NERTZ. I THOUGHT YER SCANNERS SAID THERE WEREN'T NO INTELLIGENT LIFE HERE?
THIS IS A WHOLE DIFFERENT UNIVERSE. MAYBE THERE ARE FORMS OF LIFE HERE THAT WE CAN'T...
...DETECT?
YAHHHH!

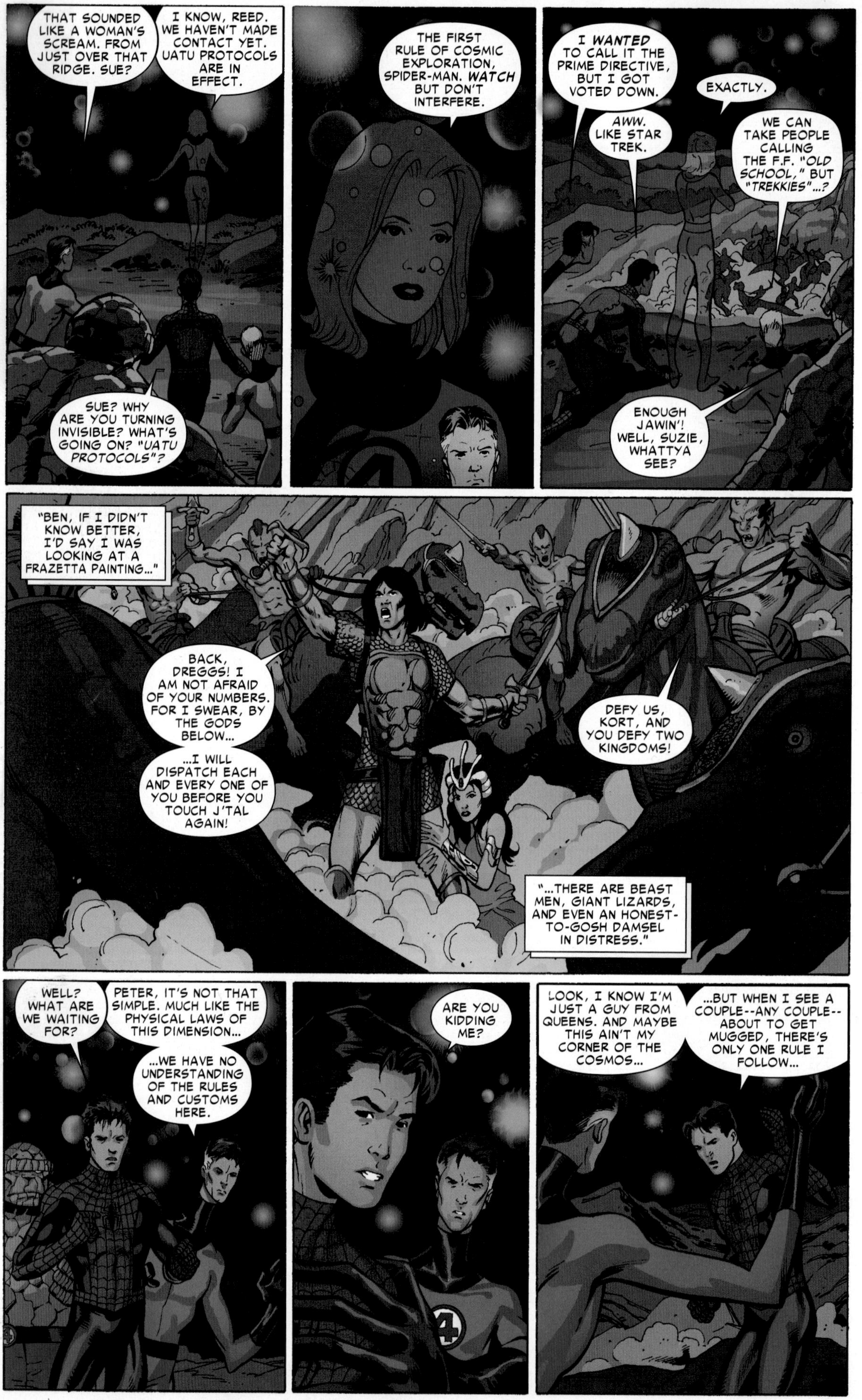
THAT SOUNDED LIKE A WOMAN'S SCREAM. FROM JUST OVER THAT RIDGE. SUE?
I KNOW, REED. WE HAVEN'T MADE CONTACT YET. UATU PROTOCOLS ARE IN EFFECT.
SUE? WHY ARE YOU TURNING INVISIBLE? WHAT'S GOING ON? "UATU PROTOCOLS"?
THE FIRST RULE OF COSMIC EXPLORATION, SPIDER-MAN. WATCH BUT DON'T INTERFERE.
I WANTED TO CALL IT THE PRIME DIRECTIVE, BUT I GOT VOTED DOWN.
AWW. LIKE STAR TREK.
EXACTLY.
WE CAN TAKE PEOPLE CALLING THE F.F. "OLD SCHOOL," BUT "TREKKIES"...?
ENOUGH JAWIN'! WELL, SUZIE, WHATTYA SEE?
"BEN, IF I DIDN'T KNOW BETTER, I'D SAY I WAS LOOKING AT A FRAZETTA PAINTING..."
BACK, DREGGS! I AM NOT AFRAID OF YOUR NUMBERS. FOR I SWEAR, BY THE GODS BELOW...
...I WILL DISPATCH EACH AND EVERY ONE OF YOU BEFORE YOU TOUCH J'TAL AGAIN!
DEFY US, KORT, AND YOU DEFY TWO KINGDOMS!
"...THERE ARE BEAST MEN, GIANT LIZARDS, AND EVEN AN HONEST-TO-GOSH DAMSEL IN DISTRESS."
WELL? WHAT ARE WE WAITING FOR?
PETER, IT'S NOT THAT SIMPLE. MUCH LIKE THE PHYSICAL LAWS OF THIS DIMENSION...
...WE HAVE NO UNDERSTANDING OF THE RULES AND CUSTOMS HERE.
ARE YOU KIDDING ME?
LOOK, I KNOW I'M JUST A GUY FROM QUEENS. AND MAYBE THIS AIN'T MY CORNER OF THE COSMOS...
...BUT WHEN I SEE A COUPLE--ANY COUPLE--ABOUT TO GET MUGGED, THERE'S ONLY ONE RULE I FOLLOW...

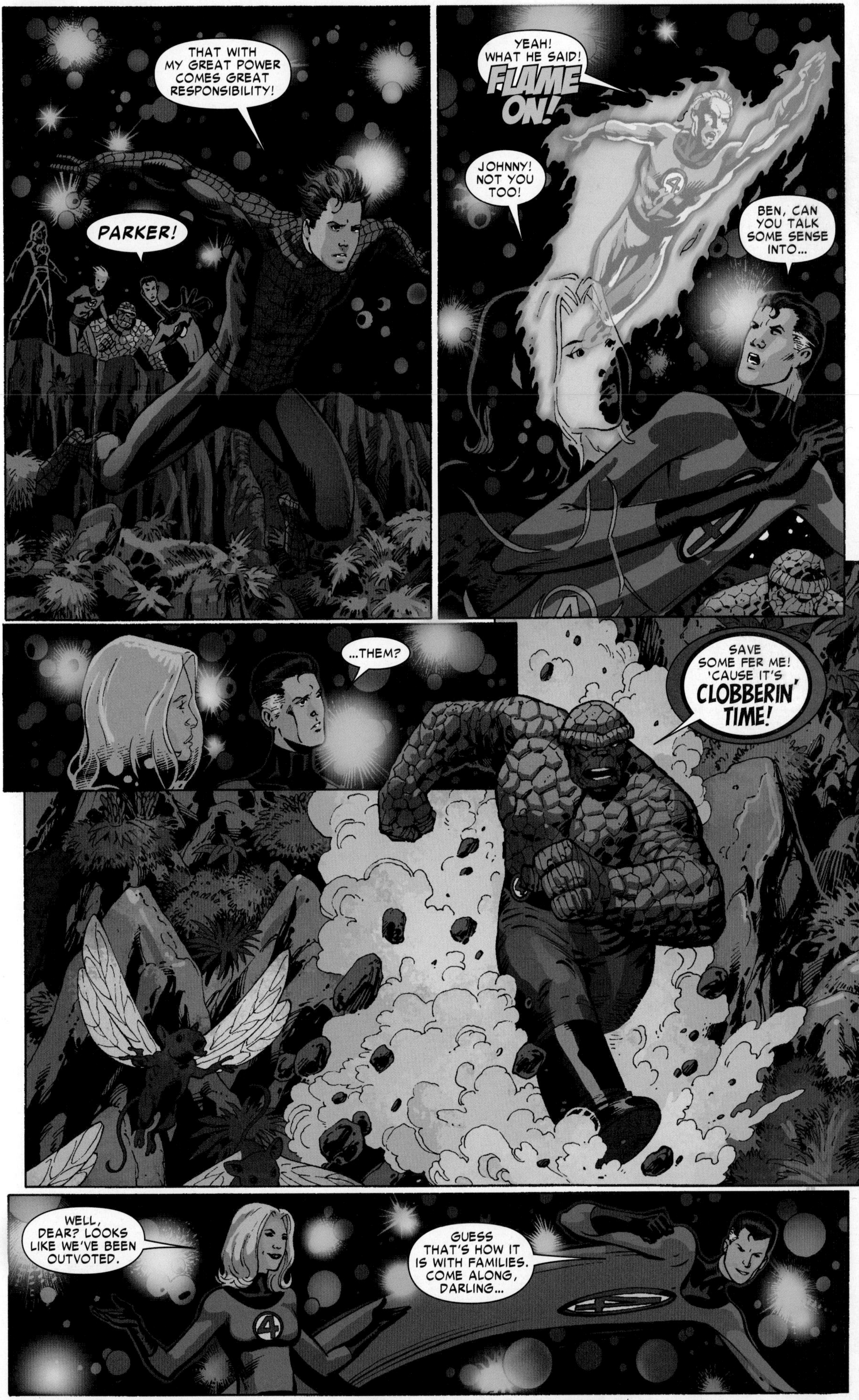
THAT WITH MY GREAT POWER COMES GREAT RESPONSIBILITY!
PARKER!
YEAH! WHAT HE SAID!
FLAME ON!
JOHNNY! NOT YOU TOO!
BEN, CAN YOU TALK SOME SENSE INTO...
...THEM?
SAVE SOME FER ME! 'CAUSE IT'S CLOBBERIN' TIME!
WELL, DEAR? LOOKS LIKE WE'VE BEEN OUTVOTED.
GUESS THAT'S HOW IT IS WITH FAMILIES. COME ALONG, DARLING...

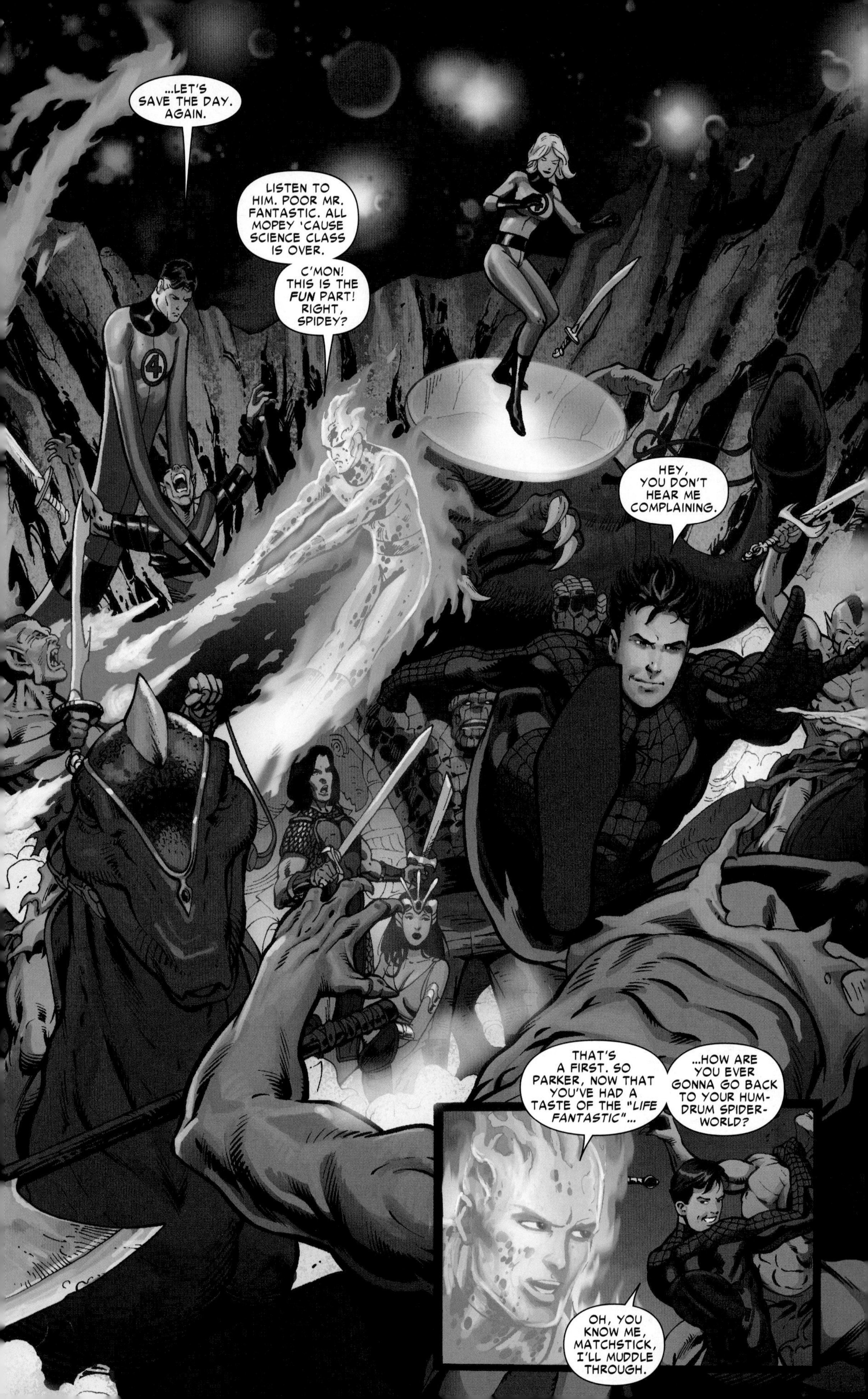
...LET'S SAVE THE DAY. AGAIN.
LISTEN TO HIM. POOR MR. FANTASTIC. ALL MOPEY 'CAUSE SCIENCE CLASS IS OVER.
C'MON! THIS IS THE *FUN* PART! RIGHT, SPIDEY?
HEY, YOU DON'T HEAR ME COMPLAINING.
THAT'S A FIRST. SO PARKER, NOW THAT YOU'VE HAD A TASTE OF THE "*LIFE FANTASTIC*"...
...HOW ARE YOU EVER GONNA GO BACK TO YOUR HUM-DRUM SPIDER-WORLD?
OH, YOU KNOW ME, MATCHSTICK, I'LL MUDDLE THROUGH.

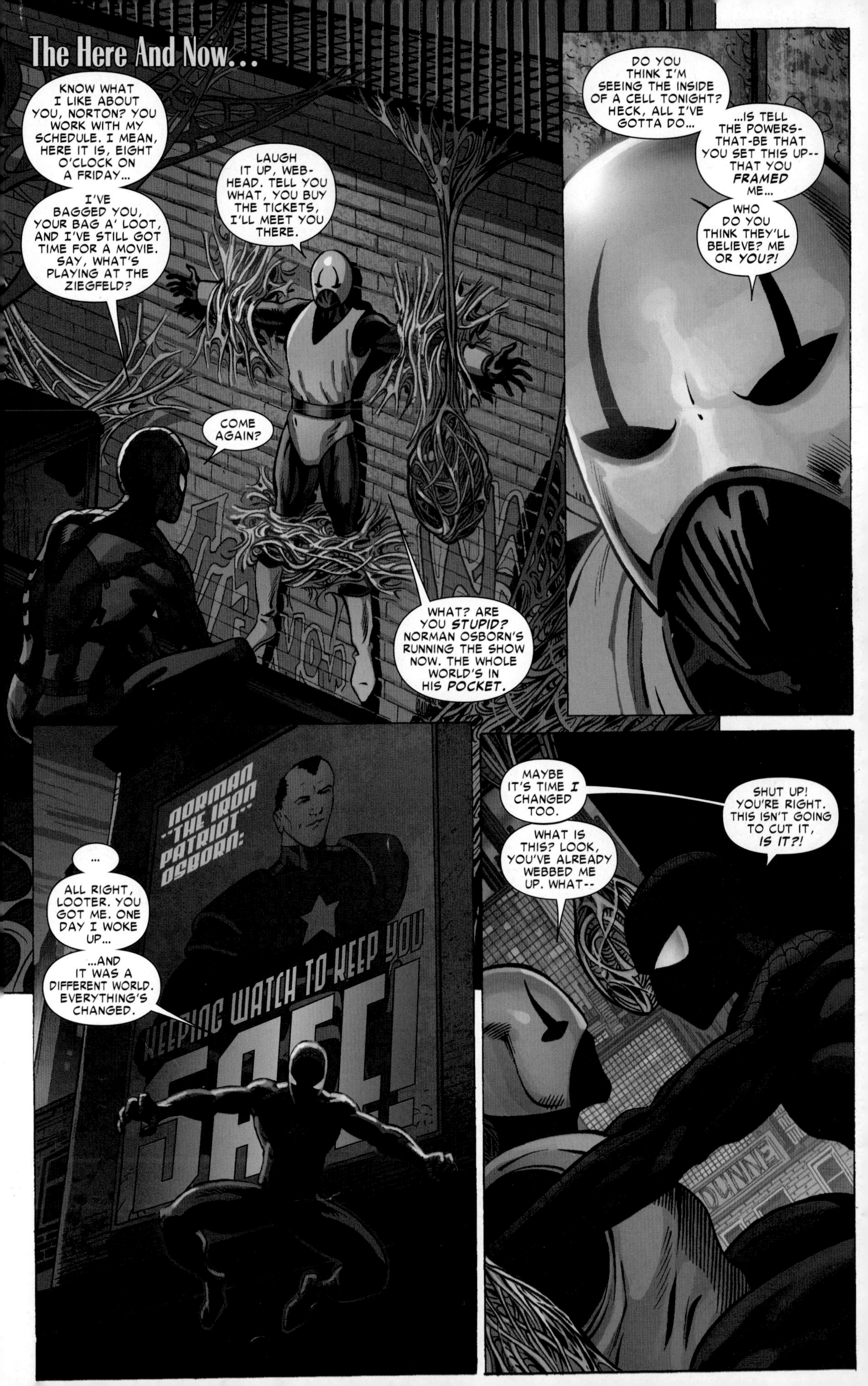
The Here And Now...
KNOW WHAT I LIKE ABOUT YOU, NORTON? YOU WORK WITH MY SCHEDULE. I MEAN, HERE IT IS, EIGHT O'CLOCK ON A FRIDAY...
I'VE BAGGED YOU, YOUR BAG A' LOOT, AND I'VE STILL GOT TIME FOR A MOVIE. SAY, WHAT'S PLAYING AT THE ZIEGFELD?
LAUGH IT UP, WEB-HEAD. TELL YOU WHAT, YOU BUY THE TICKETS, I'LL MEET YOU THERE.
COME AGAIN?
WHAT? ARE YOU STUPID? NORMAN OSBORN'S RUNNING THE SHOW NOW. THE WHOLE WORLD'S IN HIS POCKET.
DO YOU THINK I'M SEEING THE INSIDE OF A CELL TONIGHT? HECK, ALL I'VE GOTTA DO...
...IS TELL THE POWERS-THAT-BE THAT YOU SET THIS UP--THAT YOU FRAMED ME...
WHO DO YOU THINK THEY'LL BELIEVE? ME OR YOU?!
NORMAN "THE IRON PATRIOT" OSBORN:
KEEPING WATCH TO KEEP YOU SAFE!
...
ALL RIGHT, LOOTER. YOU GOT ME. ONE DAY I WOKE UP...
...AND IT WAS A DIFFERENT WORLD. EVERYTHING'S CHANGED.
MAYBE IT'S TIME I CHANGED TOO.
WHAT IS THIS? LOOK, YOU'VE ALREADY WEBBED ME UP. WHAT--
SHUT UP! YOU'RE RIGHT. THIS ISN'T GOING TO CUT IT, IS IT?!
DUNNE

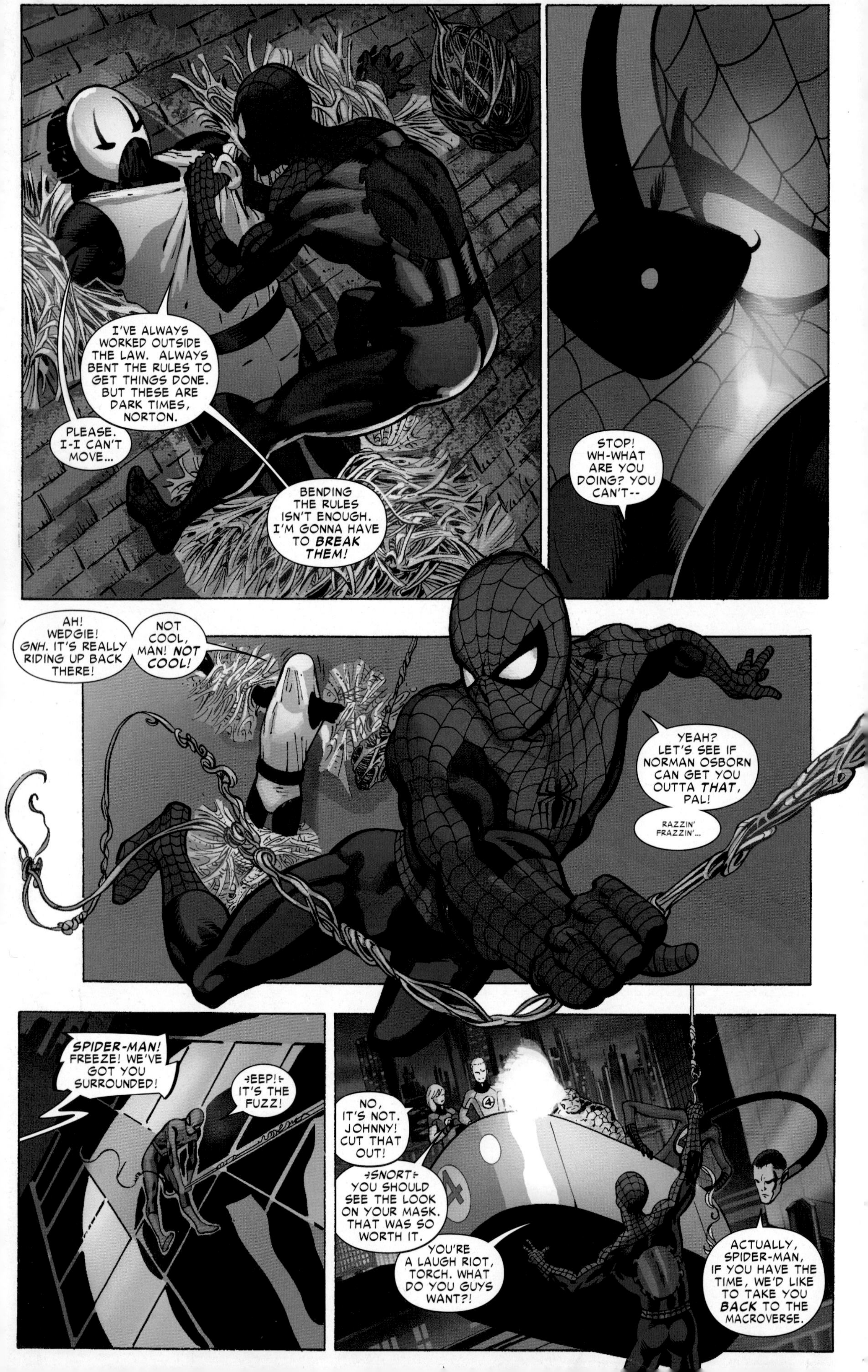
I'VE ALWAYS WORKED OUTSIDE THE LAW. ALWAYS BENT THE RULES TO GET THINGS DONE. BUT THESE ARE DARK TIMES, NORTON.
PLEASE. I-I CAN'T MOVE...
BENDING THE RULES ISN'T ENOUGH. I'M GONNA HAVE TO BREAK THEM!
STOP! WH-WHAT ARE YOU DOING? YOU CAN'T--
AH! WEDGIE! GNH. IT'S REALLY RIDING UP BACK THERE!
NOT COOL, MAN! NOT COOL!
YEAH? LET'S SEE IF NORMAN OSBORN CAN GET YOU OUTTA THAT, PAL!
RAZZIN' FRAZZIN'...
SPIDER-MAN! FREEZE! WE'VE GOT YOU SURROUNDED!
EEP! IT'S THE FUZZ!
NO, IT'S NOT. JOHNNY! CUT THAT OUT!
SNORT YOU SHOULD SEE THE LOOK ON YOUR MASK. THAT WAS SO WORTH IT.
YOU'RE A LAUGH RIOT, TORCH. WHAT DO YOU GUYS WANT?!
ACTUALLY, SPIDER-MAN, IF YOU HAVE THE TIME, WE'D LIKE TO TAKE YOU BACK TO THE MACROVERSE.

WE'VE RECEIVED A DISTRESS SIGNAL OF SORTS, ASKING FOR *BOTH* THE FANTASTIC FOUR AND SPIDER-MAN.

A DISTRESS SIGNAL? THE LAST TIME WE WERE THERE, THEY WEREN'T EVEN WEARING PANTS.

HOW'D THEY PLACE A CALL...DOWN HERE? INTRIGUING, ISN'T IT?

KNOW WHAT'S *MORE* INTRIGUING? NOT THAT OUR HIGH-TECH CELL PHONES WERE *GETTING* CALLS FROM ALIENS...

...IT'S THAT WE COULDN'T MAKE A CALL TO *YOU*. WHY IS THAT?

WHY DO I SUDDENLY *NOT* HAVE YOUR DIGITS? OR A NAME I CAN LOOK UP? IT'S LIKE I USED TO KNOW, BUT--

SHH. ADULTS TALKING. LOOK, I APPRECIATE THE OFFER.

AND AS MUCH AS I'D LOVE TO GET AWAY FROM IT ALL... ESPECIALLY AFTER THE LAST COUPLE OF WEEKS...

...I'VE GOT WORK TO DO, BILLS TO PAY...

OF COURSE. AND FANTASTIC FOUR INCORPORATED IS MORE THAN HAPPY TO COMPENSATE YOU FOR YOUR TIME.

I BELIEVE THIS SHOULD COVER IT.

AWW. AND IT'S MADE OUT TO "CASH". THAT'S LIKE MY MIDDLE NAME.

ACTUALLY, SPIDER-MAN, I FELT THAT WAS BEST.

WE KNOW HOW YOU FEEL ABOUT PROTECTING YOUR TRUE IDENTITY. EVEN FROM US.

THANKS. THAT--MEANS A LOT.

Fantastic Four
4 Freedoms Plaza
New York, NY 100
Pay to the order of *Cash*
Amount $
Memo *Consulting fee*
Check No

YEAH, AUNT MAY. I'LL BE OUT OF TOWN FOR A FEW DAYS.

SORT OF LIKE A CAMPING TRIP. WITH ONE OF MY OLD PROFESSORS AND HIS FAMILY. A KIND OF SCIENCE-CAMPING TRIP.

NO. RENT'S COVERED. ACTUALLY, IT'S *MORE* THAN COVERED.

G & G Realty Group
675 Third Avenue
York, NY 10018

42 USA

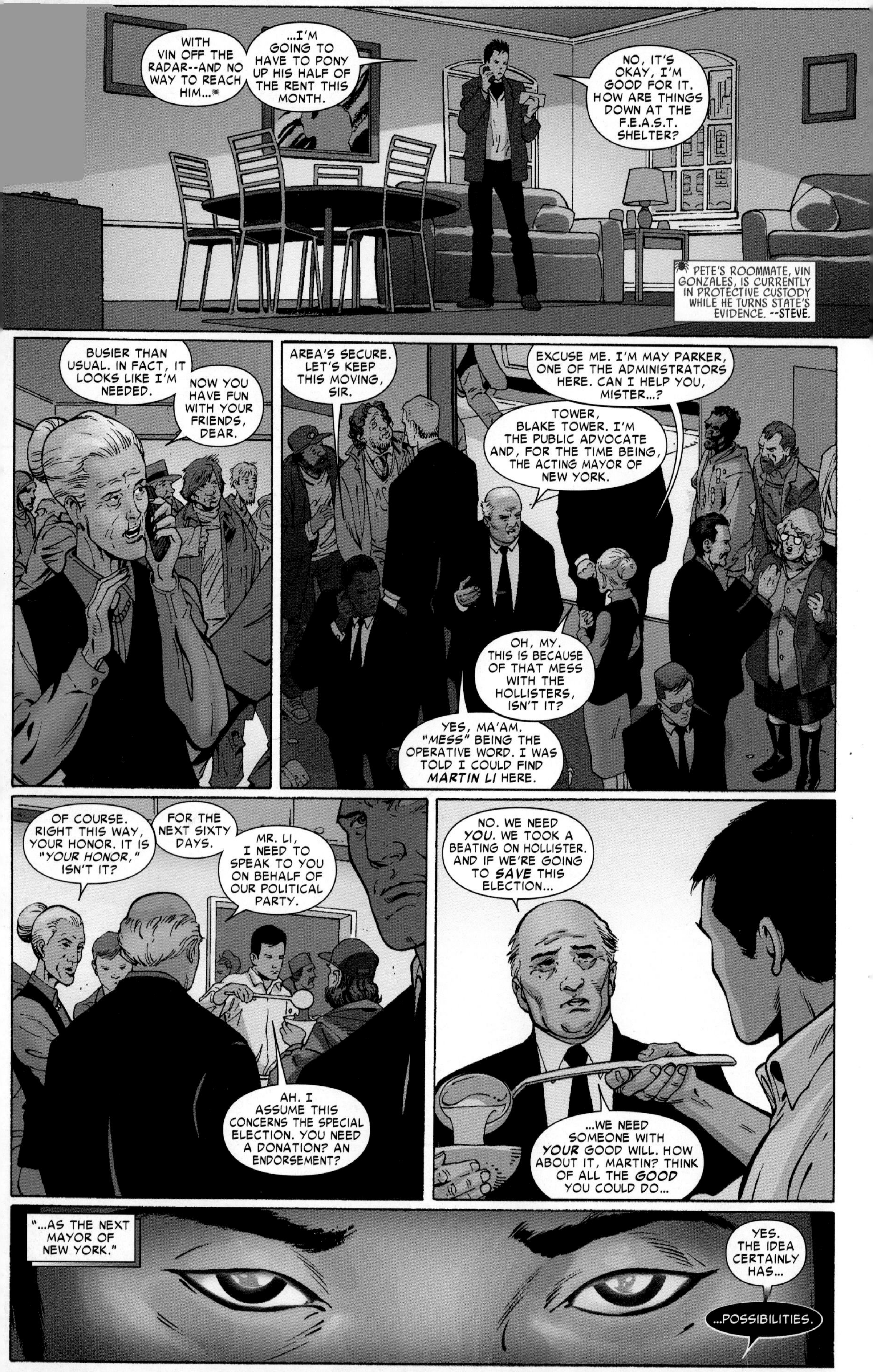
WITH VIN OFF THE RADAR--AND NO WAY TO REACH HIM...
...I'M GOING TO HAVE TO PONY UP HIS HALF OF THE RENT THIS MONTH.
NO, IT'S OKAY, I'M GOOD FOR IT. HOW ARE THINGS DOWN AT THE F.E.A.S.T. SHELTER?
PETE'S ROOMMATE, VIN GONZALES, IS CURRENTLY IN PROTECTIVE CUSTODY WHILE HE TURNS STATE'S EVIDENCE. --STEVE.
BUSIER THAN USUAL. IN FACT, IT LOOKS LIKE I'M NEEDED.
NOW YOU HAVE FUN WITH YOUR FRIENDS, DEAR.
AREA'S SECURE. LET'S KEEP THIS MOVING, SIR.
EXCUSE ME. I'M MAY PARKER, ONE OF THE ADMINISTRATORS HERE. CAN I HELP YOU, MISTER...?
TOWER, BLAKE TOWER. I'M THE PUBLIC ADVOCATE AND, FOR THE TIME BEING, THE ACTING MAYOR OF NEW YORK.
OH, MY. THIS IS BECAUSE OF THAT MESS WITH THE HOLLISTERS, ISN'T IT?
YES, MA'AM. "MESS" BEING THE OPERATIVE WORD. I WAS TOLD I COULD FIND MARTIN LI HERE.
OF COURSE. RIGHT THIS WAY, YOUR HONOR. IT IS "YOUR HONOR," ISN'T IT?
FOR THE NEXT SIXTY DAYS.
MR. LI, I NEED TO SPEAK TO YOU ON BEHALF OF OUR POLITICAL PARTY.
AH. I ASSUME THIS CONCERNS THE SPECIAL ELECTION. YOU NEED A DONATION? AN ENDORSEMENT?
NO. WE NEED YOU. WE TOOK A BEATING ON HOLLISTER. AND IF WE'RE GOING TO SAVE THIS ELECTION...
...WE NEED SOMEONE WITH YOUR GOOD WILL. HOW ABOUT IT, MARTIN? THINK OF ALL THE GOOD YOU COULD DO...
"...AS THE NEXT MAYOR OF NEW YORK."
YES. THE IDEA CERTAINLY HAS...
...POSSIBILITIES.

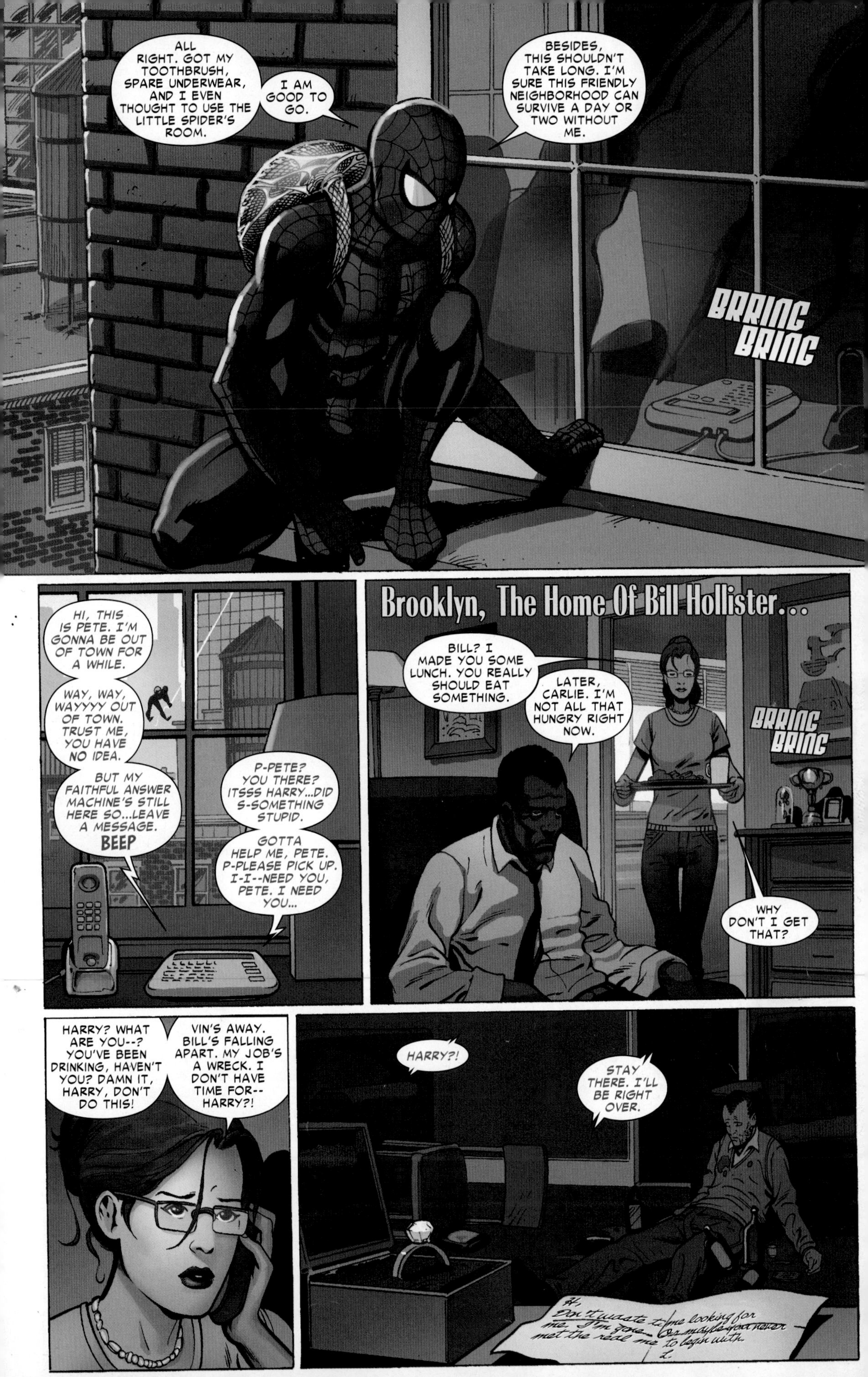
ALL RIGHT. GOT MY TOOTHBRUSH, SPARE UNDERWEAR, AND I EVEN THOUGHT TO USE THE LITTLE SPIDER'S ROOM.
I AM GOOD TO GO.
BESIDES, THIS SHOULDN'T TAKE LONG. I'M SURE THIS FRIENDLY NEIGHBORHOOD CAN SURVIVE A DAY OR TWO WITHOUT ME.
BRRING BRING
HI, THIS IS PETE. I'M GONNA BE OUT OF TOWN FOR A WHILE.
WAY, WAY, WAYYYY OUT OF TOWN. TRUST ME, YOU HAVE NO IDEA.
BUT MY FAITHFUL ANSWER MACHINE'S STILL HERE SO...LEAVE A MESSAGE. BEEP
P-PETE? YOU THERE? ITSSS HARRY...DID S-SOMETHING STUPID.
GOTTA HELP ME, PETE. P-PLEASE PICK UP. I-I--NEED YOU, PETE. I NEED YOU...
Brooklyn, The Home Of Bill Hollister...
BILL? I MADE YOU SOME LUNCH. YOU REALLY SHOULD EAT SOMETHING.
LATER, CARLIE. I'M NOT ALL THAT HUNGRY RIGHT NOW.
BRRING BRING
WHY DON'T I GET THAT?
HARRY? WHAT ARE YOU--? YOU'VE BEEN DRINKING, HAVEN'T YOU? DAMN IT, HARRY, DON'T DO THIS!
VIN'S AWAY. BILL'S FALLING APART. MY JOB'S A WRECK. I DON'T HAVE TIME FOR-- HARRY?!
HARRY?!
STAY THERE. I'LL BE RIGHT OVER.
H,
Don't waste time looking for me. I'm gone... Or maybe you never met the real me to begin with.
L.

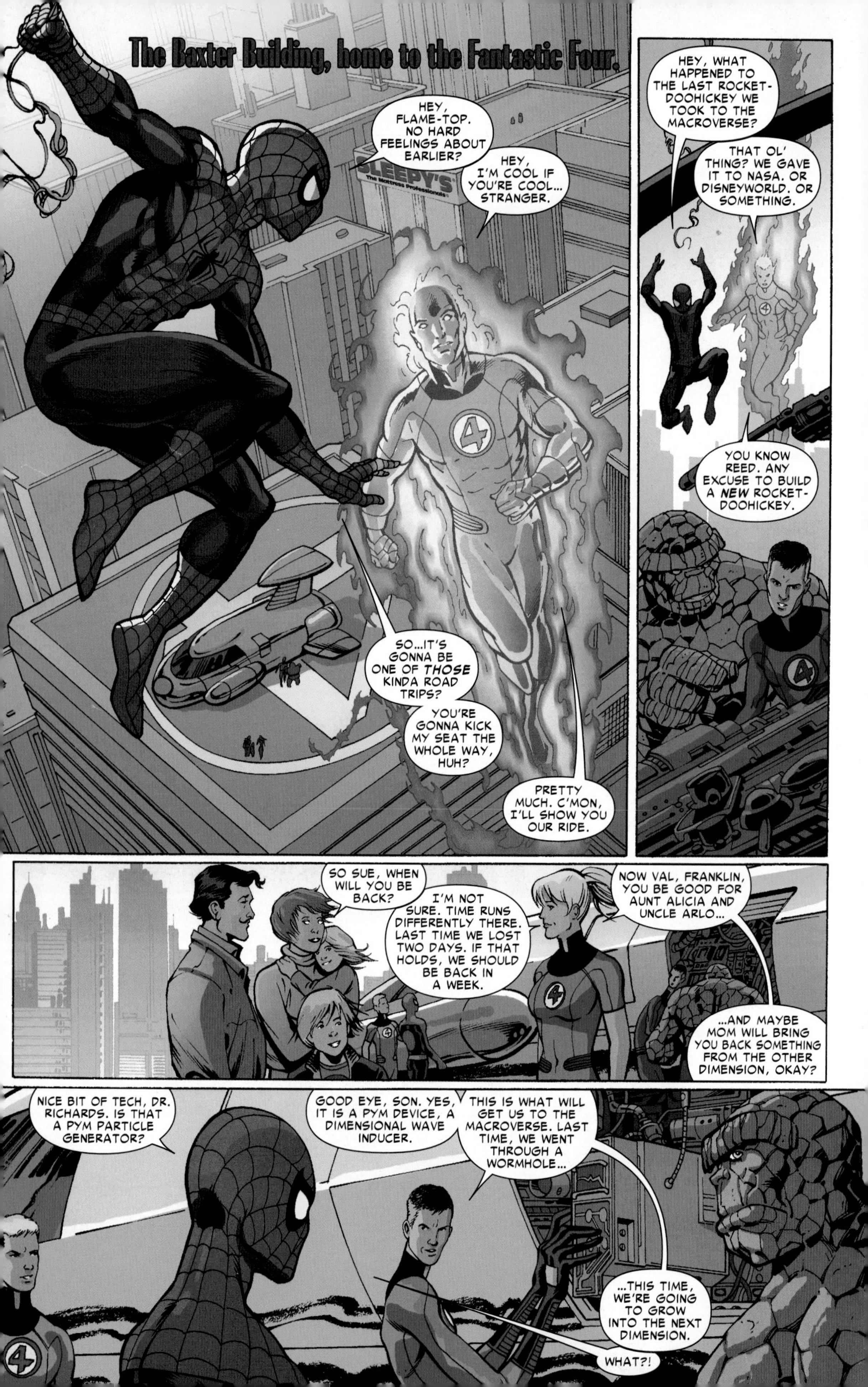

The Baxter Building, home to the Fantastic Four.
HEY, FLAME-TOP. NO HARD FEELINGS ABOUT EARLIER?
HEY, I'M COOL IF YOU'RE COOL... STRANGER.
SLEEPY'S The Mattress Professionals
SO...IT'S GONNA BE ONE OF *THOSE* KINDA ROAD TRIPS?
YOU'RE GONNA KICK MY SEAT THE WHOLE WAY, HUH?
PRETTY MUCH. C'MON, I'LL SHOW YOU OUR RIDE.
HEY, WHAT HAPPENED TO THE LAST ROCKET-DOOHICKEY WE TOOK TO THE MACROVERSE?
THAT OL' THING? WE GAVE IT TO NASA. OR DISNEYWORLD. OR SOMETHING.
YOU KNOW REED. ANY EXCUSE TO BUILD A *NEW* ROCKET-DOOHICKEY.
SO SUE, WHEN WILL YOU BE BACK?
I'M NOT SURE. TIME RUNS DIFFERENTLY THERE. LAST TIME WE LOST TWO DAYS. IF THAT HOLDS, WE SHOULD BE BACK IN A WEEK.
NOW VAL, FRANKLIN, YOU BE GOOD FOR AUNT ALICIA AND UNCLE ARLO...
...AND MAYBE MOM WILL BRING YOU BACK SOMETHING FROM THE OTHER DIMENSION, OKAY?
NICE BIT OF TECH, DR. RICHARDS. IS THAT A PYM PARTICLE GENERATOR?
GOOD EYE, SON. YES, IT IS A PYM DEVICE, A DIMENSIONAL WAVE INDUCER.
THIS IS WHAT WILL GET US TO THE MACROVERSE. LAST TIME, WE WENT THROUGH A WORMHOLE...
...THIS TIME, WE'RE GOING TO GROW INTO THE NEXT DIMENSION.
WHAT?!

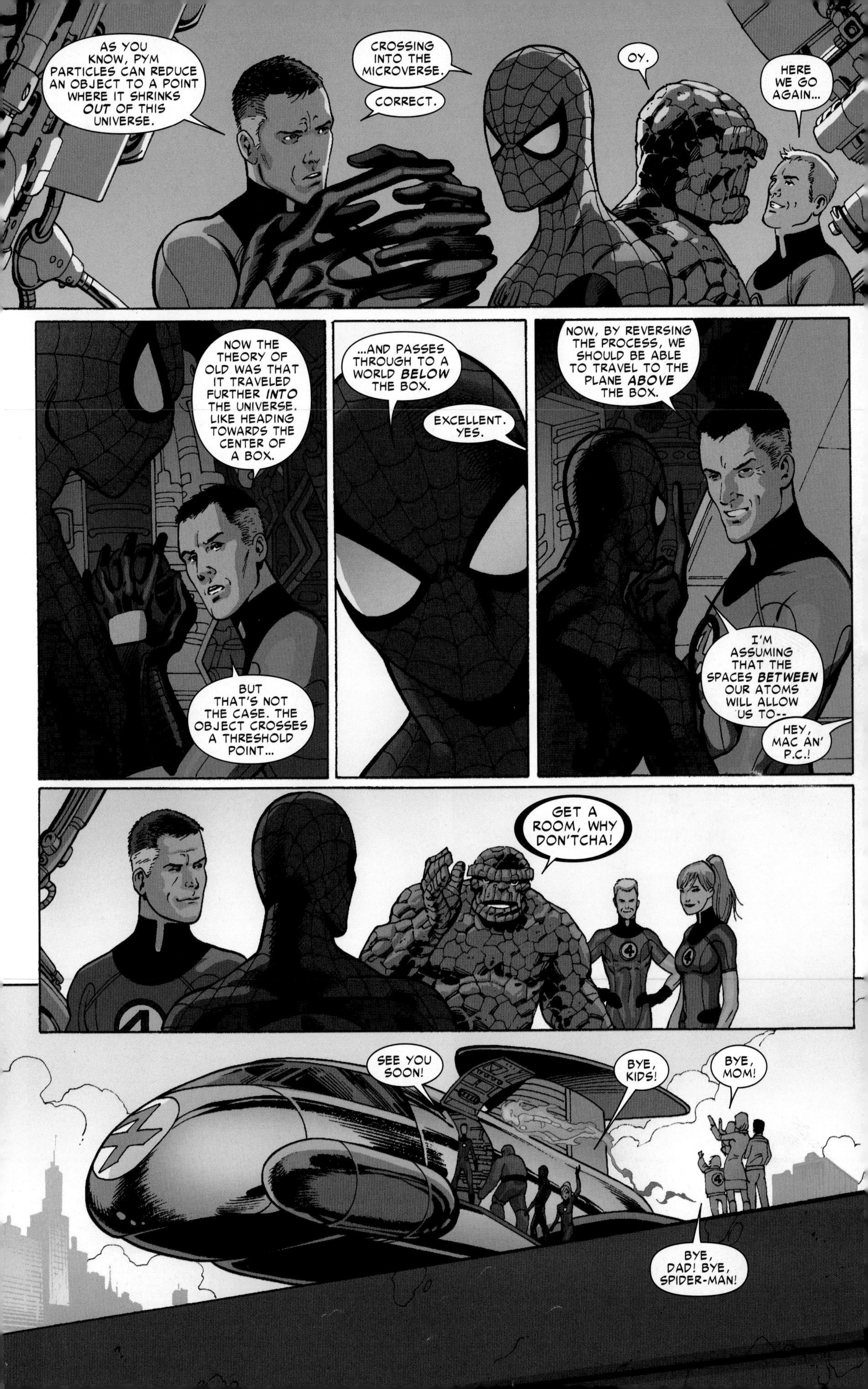
AS YOU KNOW, PYM PARTICLES CAN REDUCE AN OBJECT TO A POINT WHERE IT SHRINKS OUT OF THIS UNIVERSE.
CROSSING INTO THE MICROVERSE.
CORRECT.
OY.
HERE WE GO AGAIN...
NOW THE THEORY OF OLD WAS THAT IT TRAVELED FURTHER INTO THE UNIVERSE. LIKE HEADING TOWARDS THE CENTER OF A BOX.
BUT THAT'S NOT THE CASE. THE OBJECT CROSSES A THRESHOLD POINT...
...AND PASSES THROUGH TO A WORLD BELOW THE BOX.
EXCELLENT. YES.
NOW, BY REVERSING THE PROCESS, WE SHOULD BE ABLE TO TRAVEL TO THE PLANE ABOVE THE BOX.
I'M ASSUMING THAT THE SPACES BETWEEN OUR ATOMS WILL ALLOW US TO--
HEY, MAC AN' P.C.!
GET A ROOM, WHY DON'TCHA!
SEE YOU SOON!
BYE, KIDS!
BYE, MOM!
BYE, DAD! BYE, SPIDER-MAN!

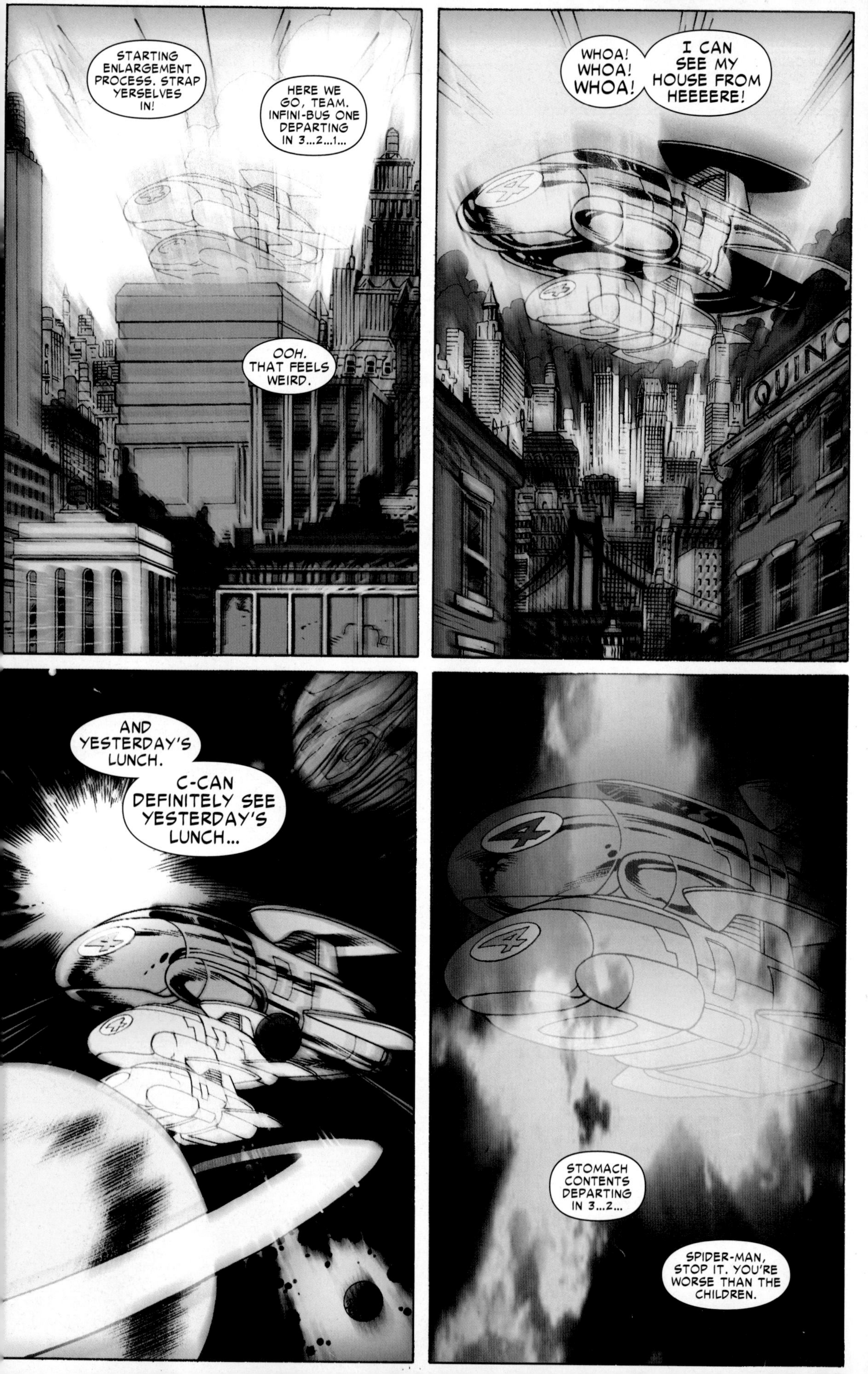
STARTING ENLARGEMENT PROCESS. STRAP YERSELVES IN!
HERE WE GO, TEAM. INFINI-BUS ONE DEPARTING IN 3...2...1...
OOH. THAT FEELS WEIRD.
WHOA! WHOA! WHOA!
I CAN SEE MY HOUSE FROM HEEEERE!
QUINC
AND YESTERDAY'S LUNCH.
C-CAN DEFINITELY SEE YESTERDAY'S LUNCH...
STOMACH CONTENTS DEPARTING IN 3...2...
SPIDER-MAN, STOP IT. YOU'RE WORSE THAN THE CHILDREN.

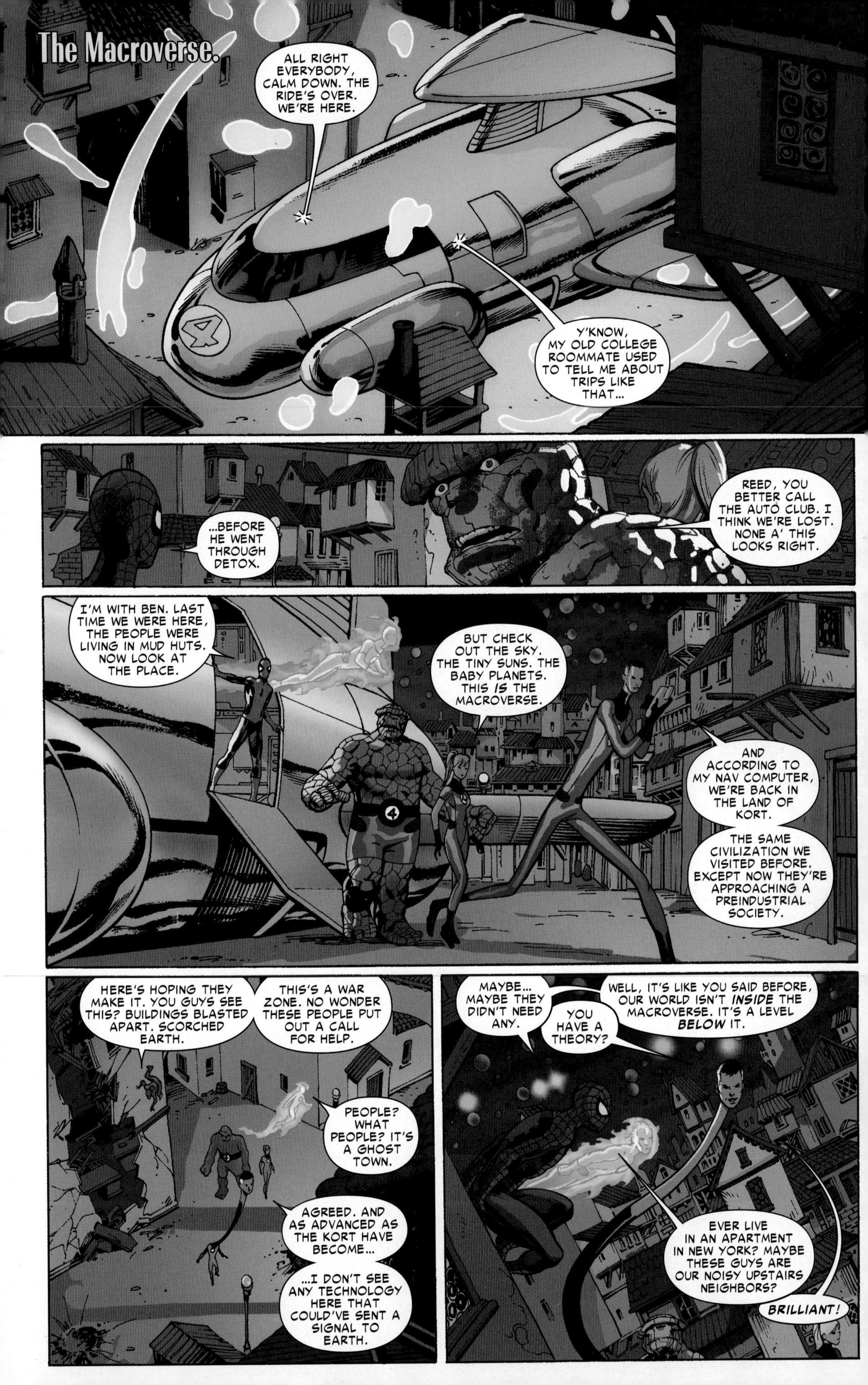
The Macroverse.
ALL RIGHT EVERYBODY, CALM DOWN. THE RIDE'S OVER. WE'RE HERE.
Y'KNOW, MY OLD COLLEGE ROOMMATE USED TO TELL ME ABOUT TRIPS LIKE THAT...
...BEFORE HE WENT THROUGH DETOX.
REED, YOU BETTER CALL THE AUTO CLUB. I THINK WE'RE LOST. NONE A' THIS LOOKS RIGHT.
I'M WITH BEN. LAST TIME WE WERE HERE, THE PEOPLE WERE LIVING IN MUD HUTS. NOW LOOK AT THE PLACE.
BUT CHECK OUT THE SKY. THE TINY SUNS. THE BABY PLANETS. THIS IS THE MACROVERSE.
AND ACCORDING TO MY NAV COMPUTER, WE'RE BACK IN THE LAND OF KORT.
THE SAME CIVILIZATION WE VISITED BEFORE. EXCEPT NOW THEY'RE APPROACHING A PREINDUSTRIAL SOCIETY.
HERE'S HOPING THEY MAKE IT. YOU GUYS SEE THIS? BUILDINGS BLASTED APART. SCORCHED EARTH.
THIS'S A WAR ZONE. NO WONDER THESE PEOPLE PUT OUT A CALL FOR HELP.
PEOPLE? WHAT PEOPLE? IT'S A GHOST TOWN.
AGREED. AND AS ADVANCED AS THE KORT HAVE BECOME...
...I DON'T SEE ANY TECHNOLOGY HERE THAT COULD'VE SENT A SIGNAL TO EARTH.
MAYBE... MAYBE THEY DIDN'T NEED ANY.
YOU HAVE A THEORY?
WELL, IT'S LIKE YOU SAID BEFORE, OUR WORLD ISN'T INSIDE THE MACROVERSE. IT'S A LEVEL BELOW IT.
EVER LIVE IN AN APARTMENT IN NEW YORK? MAYBE THESE GUYS ARE OUR NOISY UPSTAIRS NEIGHBORS?
BRILLIANT!

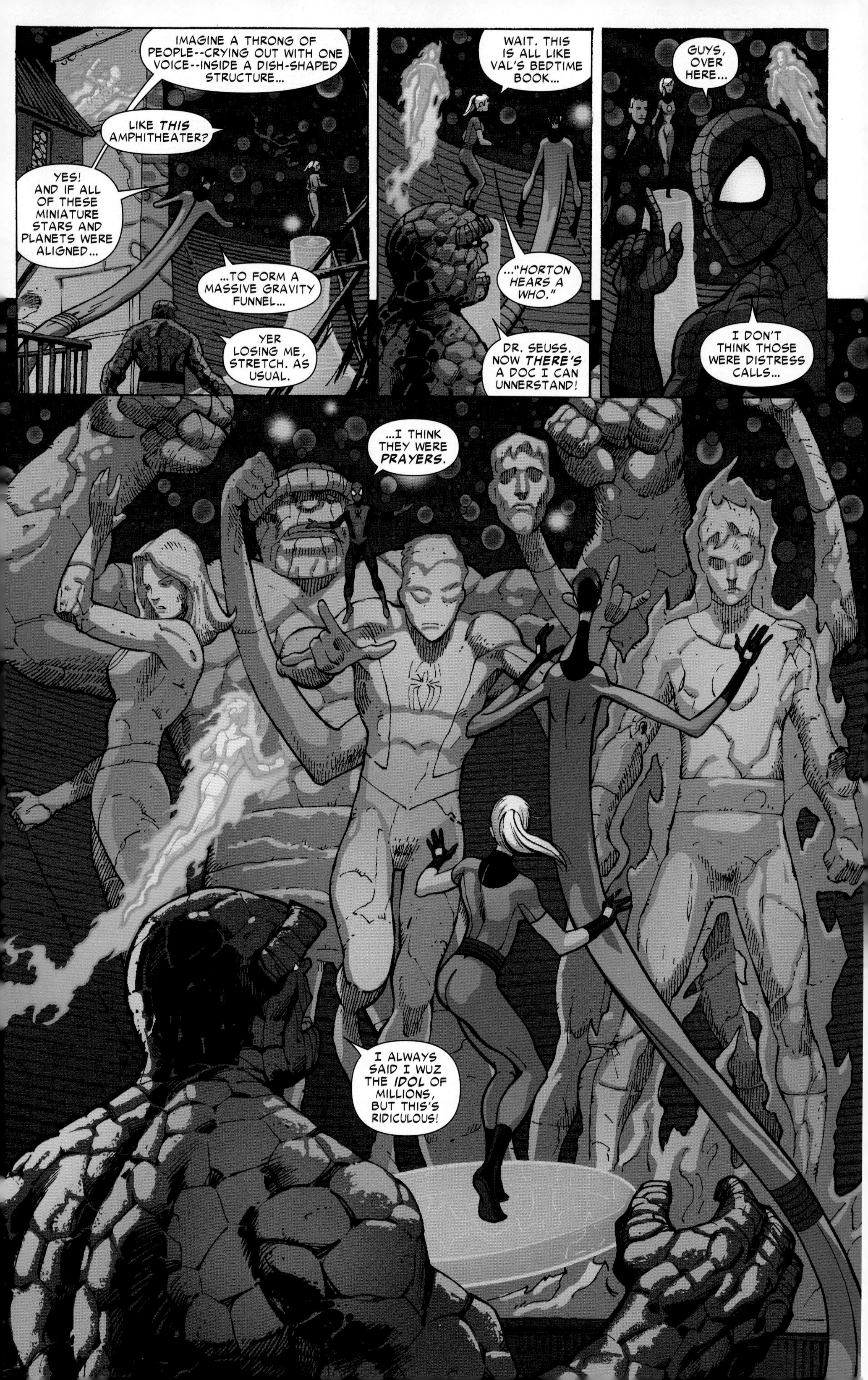
IMAGINE A THRONG OF PEOPLE--CRYING OUT WITH ONE VOICE--INSIDE A DISH-SHAPED STRUCTURE...
LIKE THIS AMPHITHEATER?
YES! AND IF ALL OF THESE MINIATURE STARS AND PLANETS WERE ALIGNED...
...TO FORM A MASSIVE GRAVITY FUNNEL...
YER LOSING ME, STRETCH. AS USUAL.
WAIT. THIS IS ALL LIKE VAL'S BEDTIME BOOK...
..."HORTON HEARS A WHO."
DR. SEUSS. NOW THERE'S A DOC I CAN UNNERSTAND!
GUYS, OVER HERE...
I DON'T THINK THOSE WERE DISTRESS CALLS...
...I THINK THEY WERE PRAYERS.
I ALWAYS SAID I WUZ THE IDOL OF MILLIONS, BUT THIS'S RIDICULOUS!

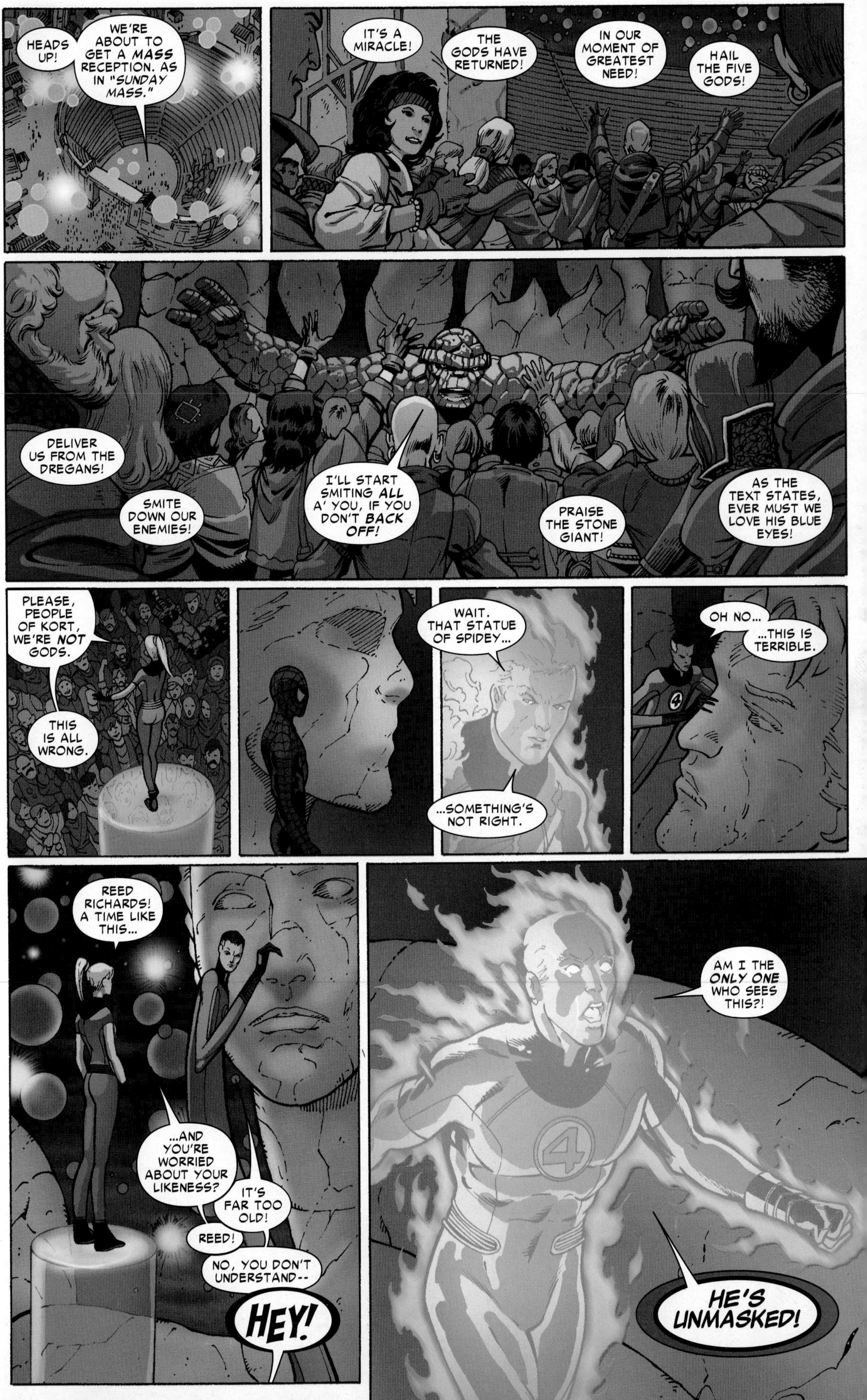
HEADS UP!
WE'RE ABOUT TO GET A MASS RECEPTION. AS IN "SUNDAY MASS."
IT'S A MIRACLE!
THE GODS HAVE RETURNED!
IN OUR MOMENT OF GREATEST NEED!
HAIL THE FIVE GODS!
DELIVER US FROM THE DREGANS!
SMITE DOWN OUR ENEMIES!
I'LL START SMITING ALL A' YOU, IF YOU DON'T BACK OFF!
PRAISE THE STONE GIANT!
AS THE TEXT STATES, EVER MUST WE LOVE HIS BLUE EYES!
PLEASE, PEOPLE OF KORT, WE'RE NOT GODS.
THIS IS ALL WRONG.
WAIT. THAT STATUE OF SPIDEY...
...SOMETHING'S NOT RIGHT.
OH NO...
...THIS IS TERRIBLE.
REED RICHARDS! A TIME LIKE THIS...
...AND YOU'RE WORRIED ABOUT YOUR LIKENESS?
IT'S FAR TOO OLD!
REED!
NO, YOU DON'T UNDERSTAND--
HEY!
AM I THE ONLY ONE WHO SEES THIS?!
HE'S UNMASKED!

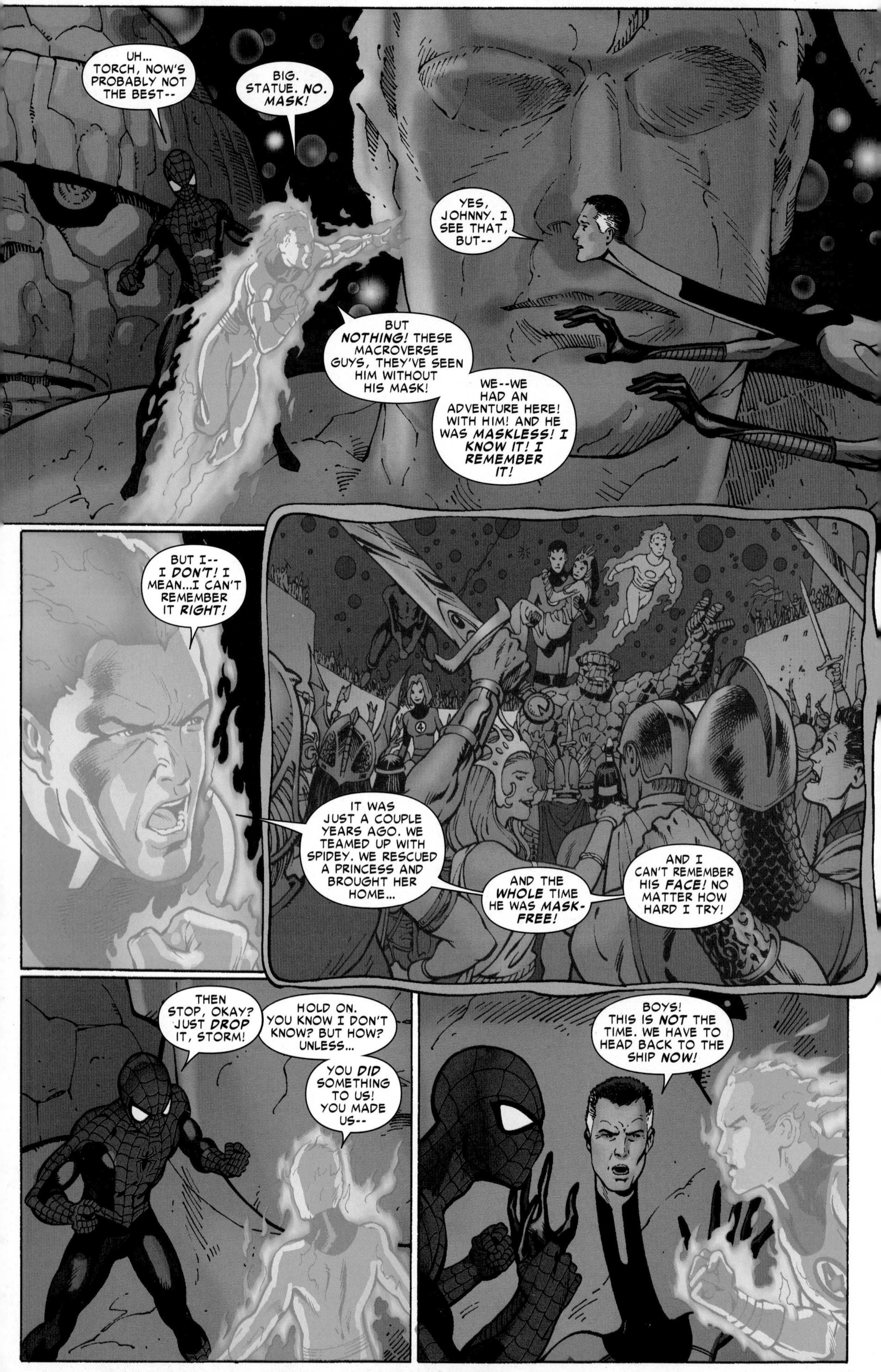
UH... TORCH, NOW'S PROBABLY NOT THE BEST--
BIG. STATUE. NO. MASK!
YES, JOHNNY. I SEE THAT, BUT--
BUT NOTHING! THESE MACROVERSE GUYS, THEY'VE SEEN HIM WITHOUT HIS MASK!
WE--WE HAD AN ADVENTURE HERE! WITH HIM! AND HE WAS MASKLESS! I KNOW IT! I REMEMBER IT!
BUT I-- I DON'T! I MEAN...I CAN'T REMEMBER IT RIGHT!
IT WAS JUST A COUPLE YEARS AGO. WE TEAMED UP WITH SPIDEY. WE RESCUED A PRINCESS AND BROUGHT HER HOME...
AND THE WHOLE TIME HE WAS MASK-FREE!
AND I CAN'T REMEMBER HIS FACE! NO MATTER HOW HARD I TRY!
THEN STOP, OKAY? JUST DROP IT, STORM!
HOLD ON. YOU KNOW I DON'T KNOW? BUT HOW? UNLESS...
YOU DID SOMETHING TO US! YOU MADE US--
BOYS! THIS IS NOT THE TIME. WE HAVE TO HEAD BACK TO THE SHIP NOW!

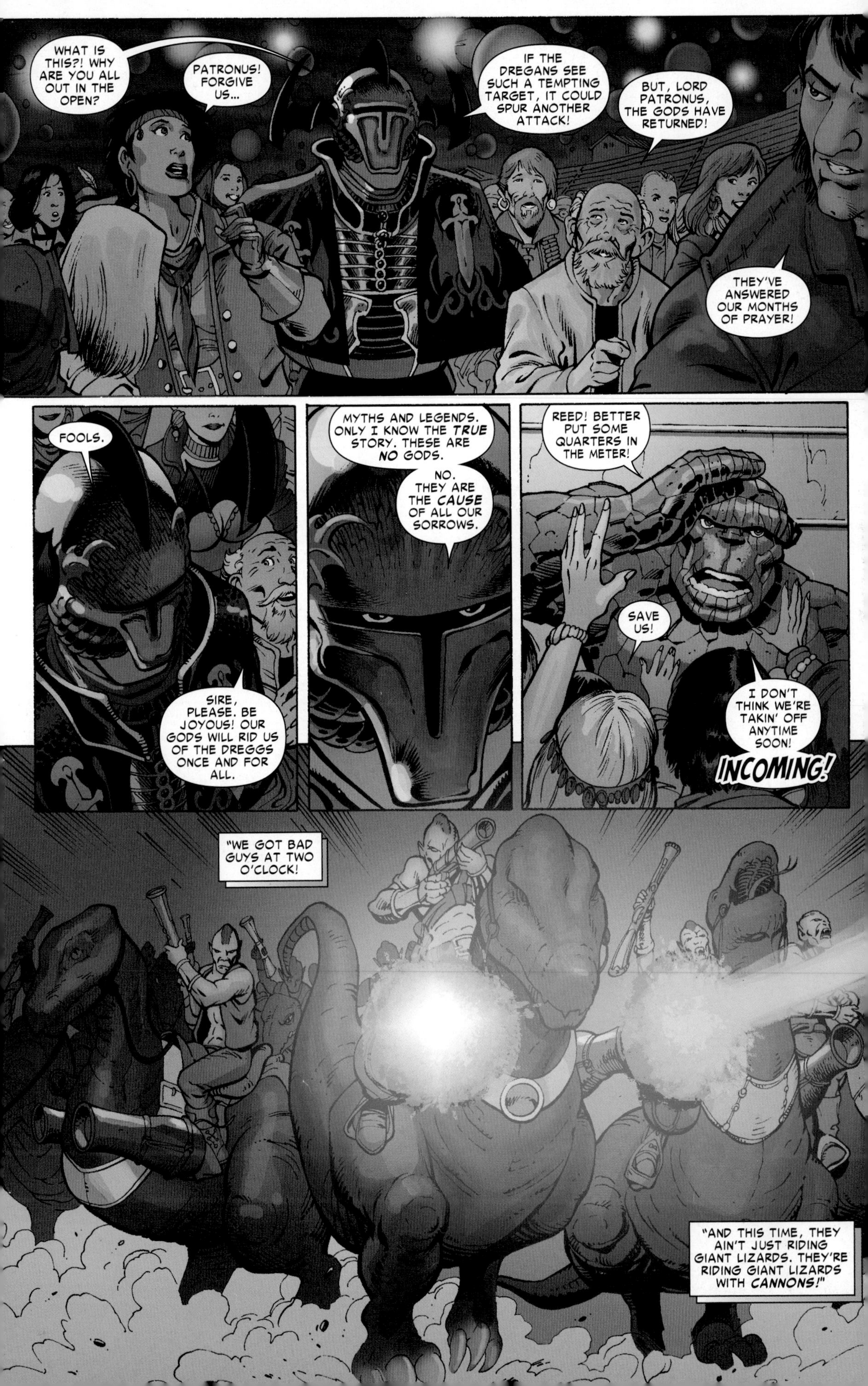

WHAT IS THIS?! WHY ARE YOU ALL OUT IN THE OPEN?
PATRONUS! FORGIVE US...
IF THE DREGANS SEE SUCH A TEMPTING TARGET, IT COULD SPUR ANOTHER ATTACK!
BUT, LORD PATRONUS, THE GODS HAVE RETURNED!
THEY'VE ANSWERED OUR MONTHS OF PRAYER!
FOOLS.
SIRE, PLEASE. BE JOYOUS! OUR GODS WILL RID US OF THE DREGGS ONCE AND FOR ALL.
MYTHS AND LEGENDS. ONLY I KNOW THE TRUE STORY. THESE ARE NO GODS.
NO. THEY ARE THE CAUSE OF ALL OUR SORROWS.
REED! BETTER PUT SOME QUARTERS IN THE METER!
SAVE US!
I DON'T THINK WE'RE TAKIN' OFF ANYTIME SOON!
INCOMING!
"WE GOT BAD GUYS AT TWO O'CLOCK!
"AND THIS TIME, THEY AIN'T JUST RIDING GIANT LIZARDS. THEY'RE RIDING GIANT LIZARDS WITH CANNONS!"

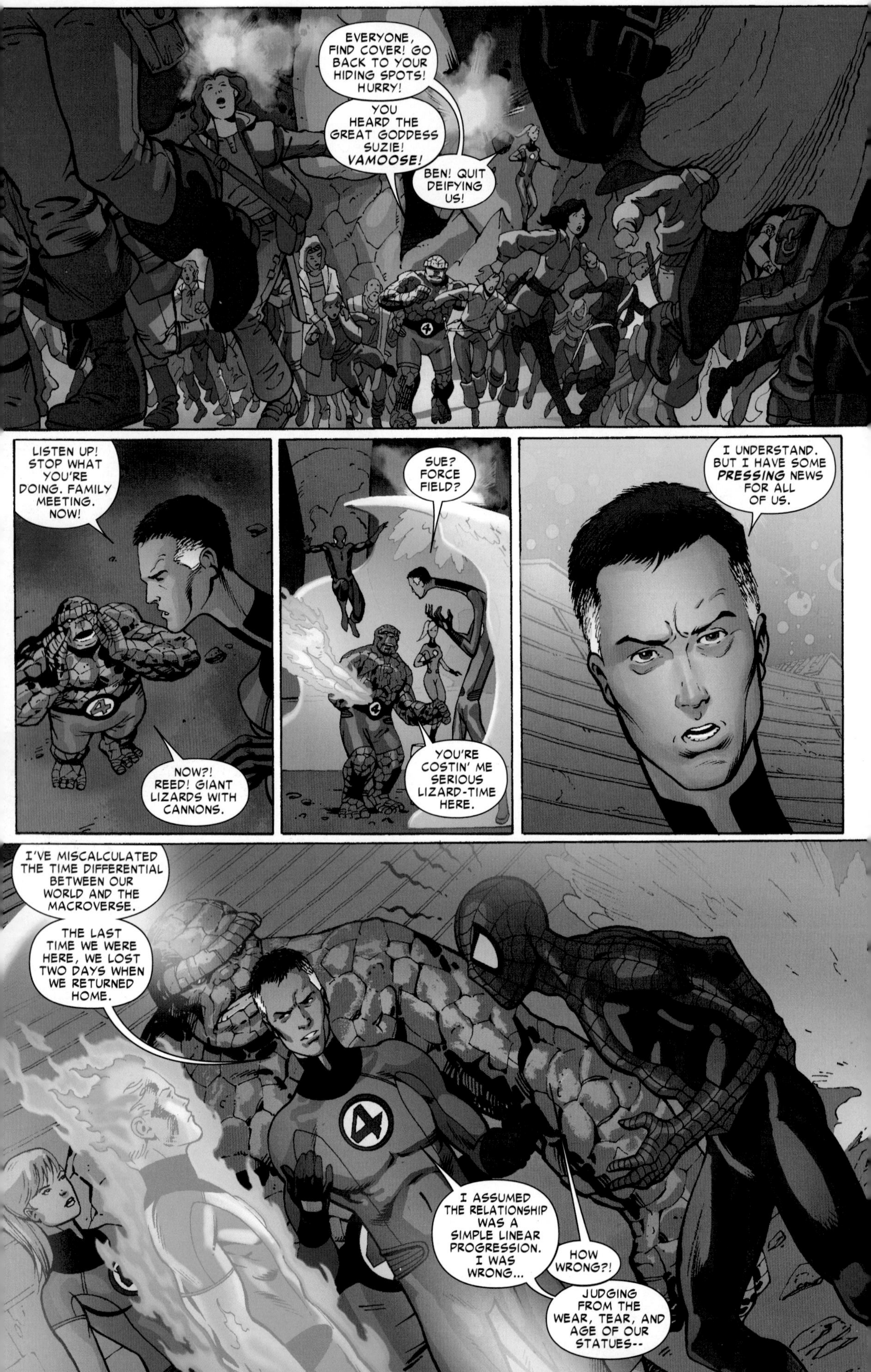

EVERYONE, FIND COVER! GO BACK TO YOUR HIDING SPOTS! HURRY!
YOU HEARD THE GREAT GODDESS SUZIE! VAMOOSE!
BEN! QUIT DEIFYING US!
LISTEN UP! STOP WHAT YOU'RE DOING. FAMILY MEETING. NOW!
NOW?! REED! GIANT LIZARDS WITH CANNONS.
SUE? FORCE FIELD?
YOU'RE COSTIN' ME SERIOUS LIZARD-TIME HERE.
I UNDERSTAND. BUT I HAVE SOME PRESSING NEWS FOR ALL OF US.
I'VE MISCALCULATED THE TIME DIFFERENTIAL BETWEEN OUR WORLD AND THE MACROVERSE.
THE LAST TIME WE WERE HERE, WE LOST TWO DAYS WHEN WE RETURNED HOME.
I ASSUMED THE RELATIONSHIP WAS A SIMPLE LINEAR PROGRESSION. I WAS WRONG...
HOW WRONG?!
JUDGING FROM THE WEAR, TEAR, AND AGE OF OUR STATUES--

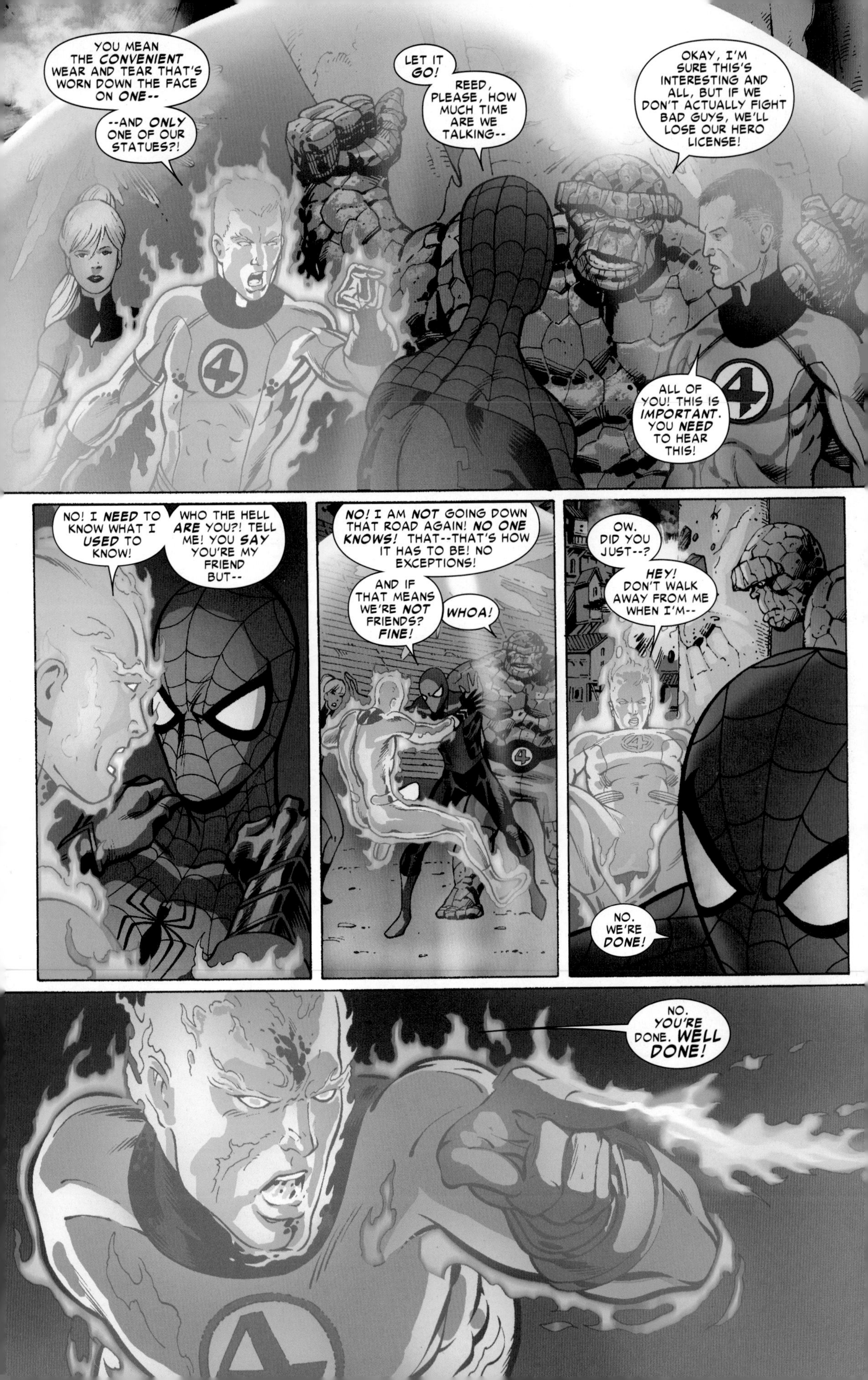
YOU MEAN THE CONVENIENT WEAR AND TEAR THAT'S WORN DOWN THE FACE ON ONE--
--AND ONLY ONE OF OUR STATUES?!
LET IT GO!
REED, PLEASE, HOW MUCH TIME ARE WE TALKING--
OKAY, I'M SURE THIS'S INTERESTING AND ALL, BUT IF WE DON'T ACTUALLY FIGHT BAD GUYS, WE'LL LOSE OUR HERO LICENSE!
ALL OF YOU! THIS IS IMPORTANT. YOU NEED TO HEAR THIS!
NO! I NEED TO KNOW WHAT I USED TO KNOW!
WHO THE HELL ARE YOU?! TELL ME! YOU SAY YOU'RE MY FRIEND BUT--
NO! I AM NOT GOING DOWN THAT ROAD AGAIN! NO ONE KNOWS! THAT--THAT'S HOW IT HAS TO BE! NO EXCEPTIONS!
AND IF THAT MEANS WE'RE NOT FRIENDS? FINE!
WHOA!
OW. DID YOU JUST--?
HEY! DON'T WALK AWAY FROM ME WHEN I'M--
NO. WE'RE DONE!
NO. YOU'RE DONE. WELL DONE!

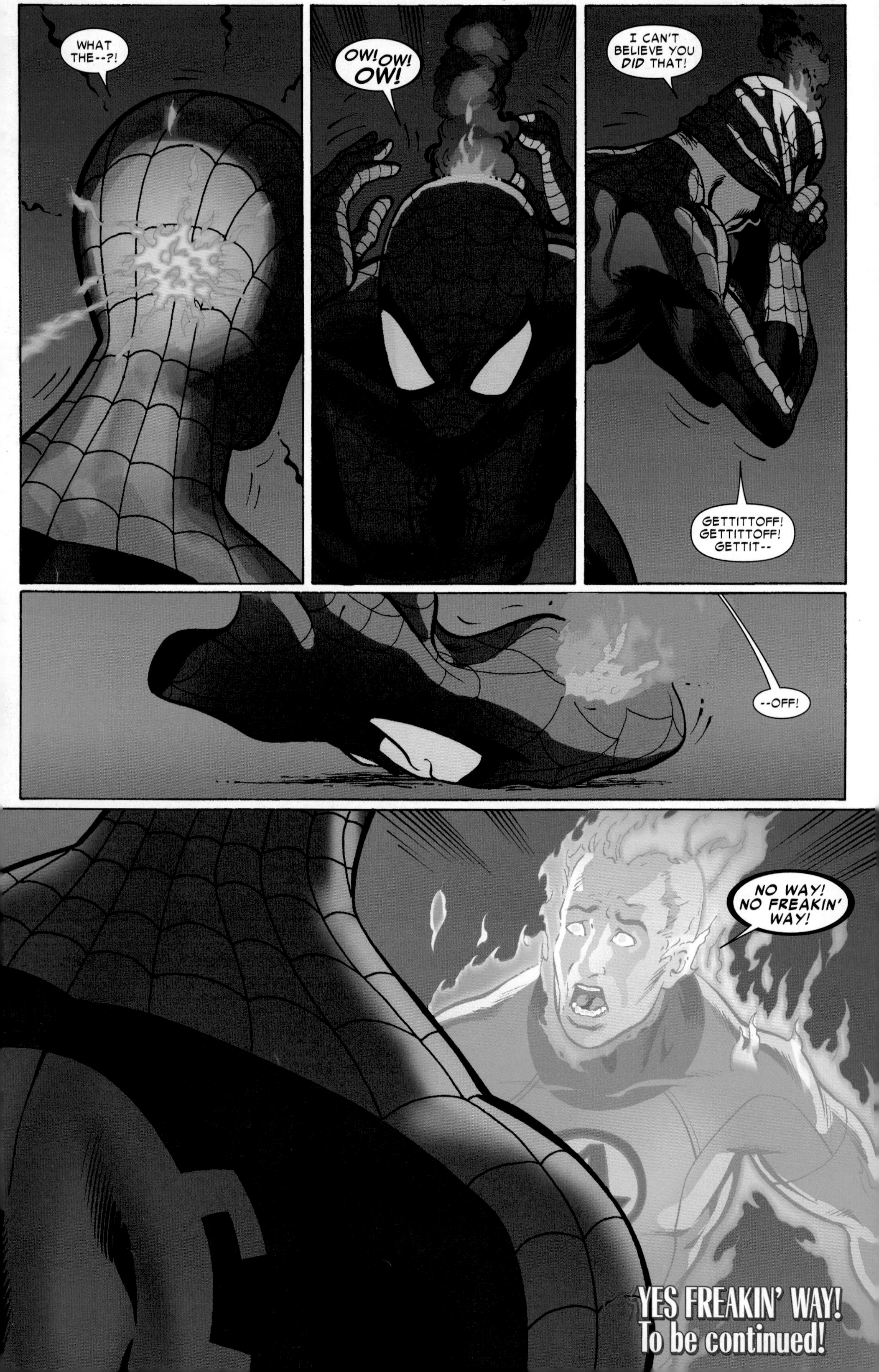
WHAT THE--?!
OW! OW! OW!
I CAN'T BELIEVE YOU *DID* THAT!
GETTITTOFF! GETTITTOFF! GETTIT--
--OFF!
NO WAY! NO FREAKIN' WAY!
YES FREAKIN' WAY!
To be continued!

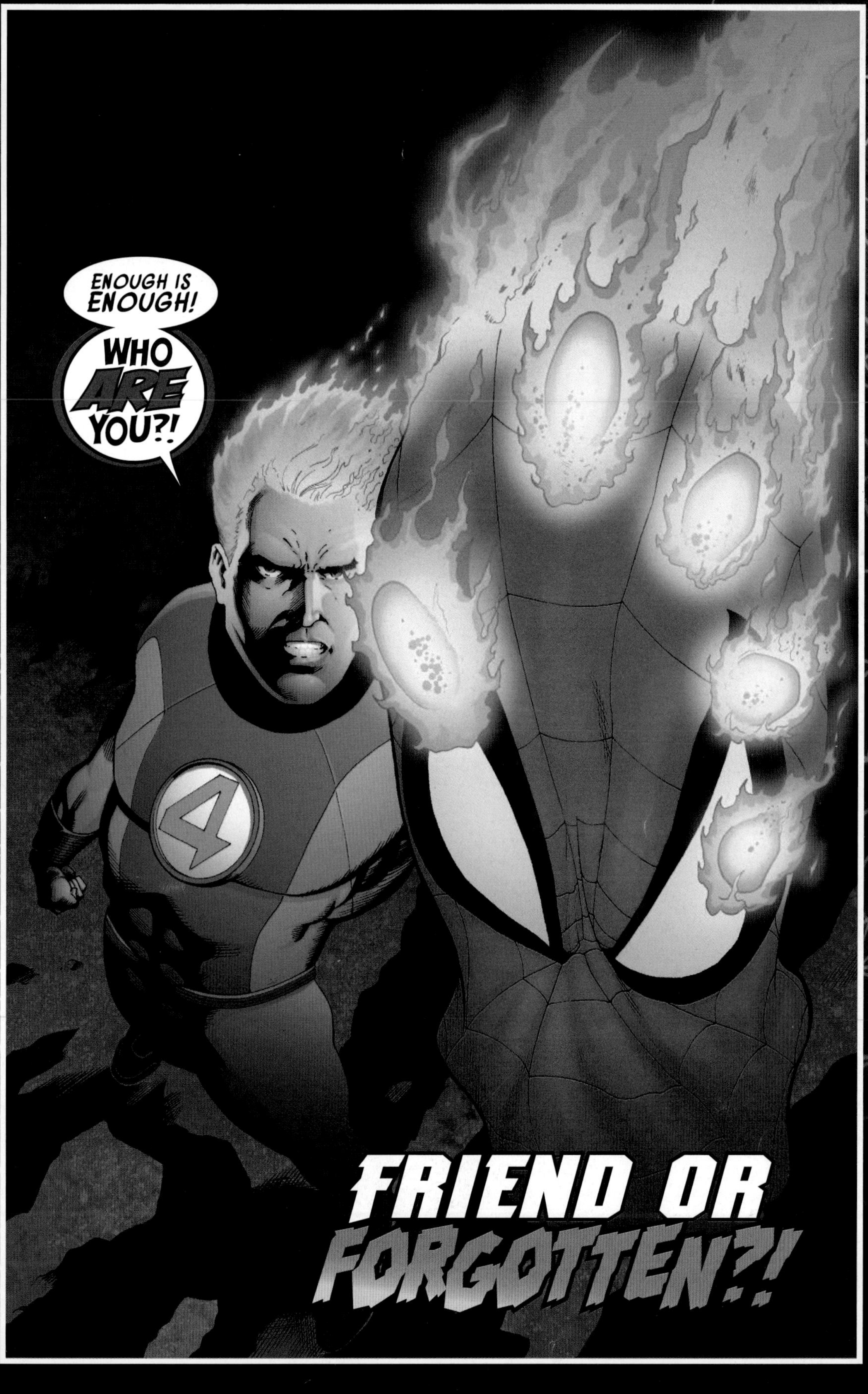
ENOUGH IS ENOUGH!
WHO ARE YOU?!
FRIEND OR FORGOTTEN?!

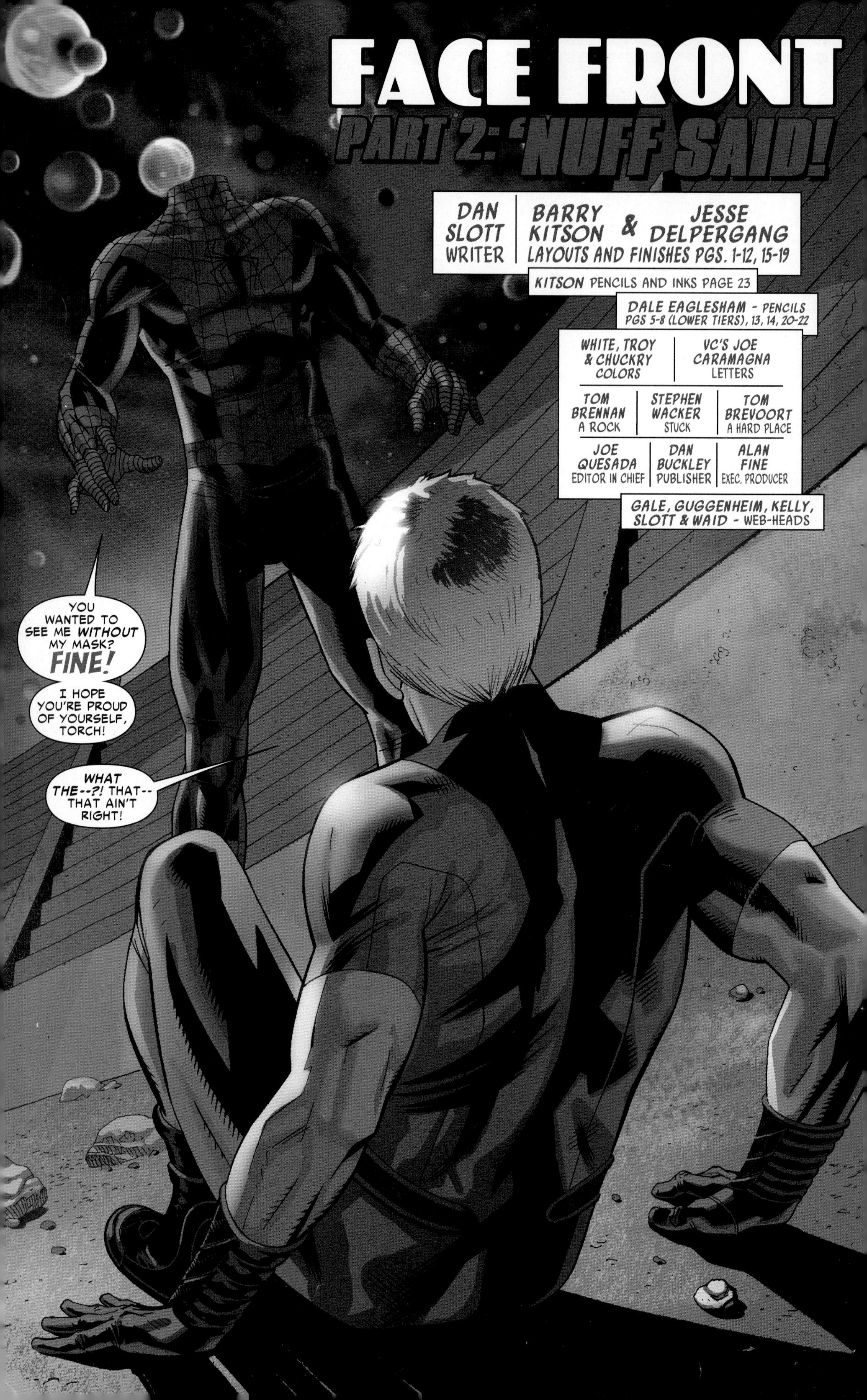
FACE FRONT
PART 2: 'NUFF SAID!
DAN SLOTT WRITER
BARRY KITSON & JESSE DELPERGANG LAYOUTS AND FINISHES PGS. 1-12, 15-19
KITSON PENCILS AND INKS PAGE 23
DALE EAGLESHAM - PENCILS PGS 5-8 (LOWER TIERS), 13, 14, 20-22
WHITE, TROY & CHUCKRY COLORS
VC'S JOE CARAMAGNA LETTERS
TOM BRENNAN A ROCK
STEPHEN WACKER STUCK
TOM BREVOORT A HARD PLACE
JOE QUESADA EDITOR IN CHIEF
DAN BUCKLEY PUBLISHER
ALAN FINE EXEC. PRODUCER
GALE, GUGGENHEIM, KELLY, SLOTT & WAID - WEB-HEADS
YOU WANTED TO SEE ME WITHOUT MY MASK? FINE!
I HOPE YOU'RE PROUD OF YOURSELF, TORCH!
WHAT THE--?! THAT--THAT AIN'T RIGHT!

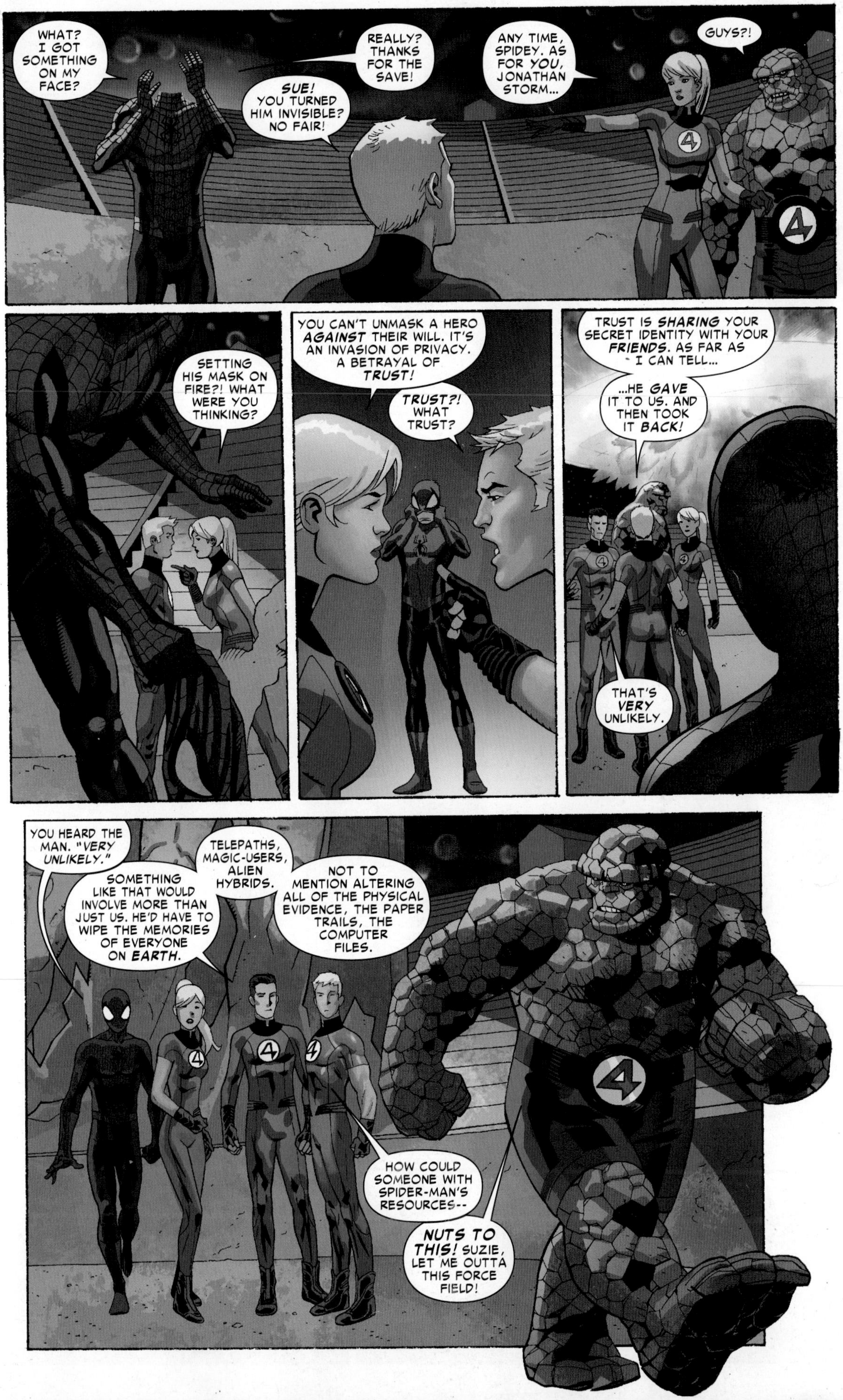
WHAT? I GOT SOMETHING ON MY FACE?
REALLY? THANKS FOR THE SAVE!
SUE! YOU TURNED HIM INVISIBLE? NO FAIR!
ANY TIME, SPIDEY. AS FOR YOU, JONATHAN STORM...
GUYS?!
SETTING HIS MASK ON FIRE?! WHAT WERE YOU THINKING?
YOU CAN'T UNMASK A HERO AGAINST THEIR WILL. IT'S AN INVASION OF PRIVACY. A BETRAYAL OF TRUST!
TRUST?! WHAT TRUST?
TRUST IS SHARING YOUR SECRET IDENTITY WITH YOUR FRIENDS. AS FAR AS I CAN TELL...
...HE GAVE IT TO US. AND THEN TOOK IT BACK!
THAT'S VERY UNLIKELY.
YOU HEARD THE MAN. "VERY UNLIKELY."
SOMETHING LIKE THAT WOULD INVOLVE MORE THAN JUST US. HE'D HAVE TO WIPE THE MEMORIES OF EVERYONE ON EARTH.
TELEPATHS, MAGIC-USERS, ALIEN HYBRIDS.
NOT TO MENTION ALTERING ALL OF THE PHYSICAL EVIDENCE, THE PAPER TRAILS, THE COMPUTER FILES.
HOW COULD SOMEONE WITH SPIDER-MAN'S RESOURCES--
NUTS TO THIS! SUZIE, LET ME OUTTA THIS FORCE FIELD!

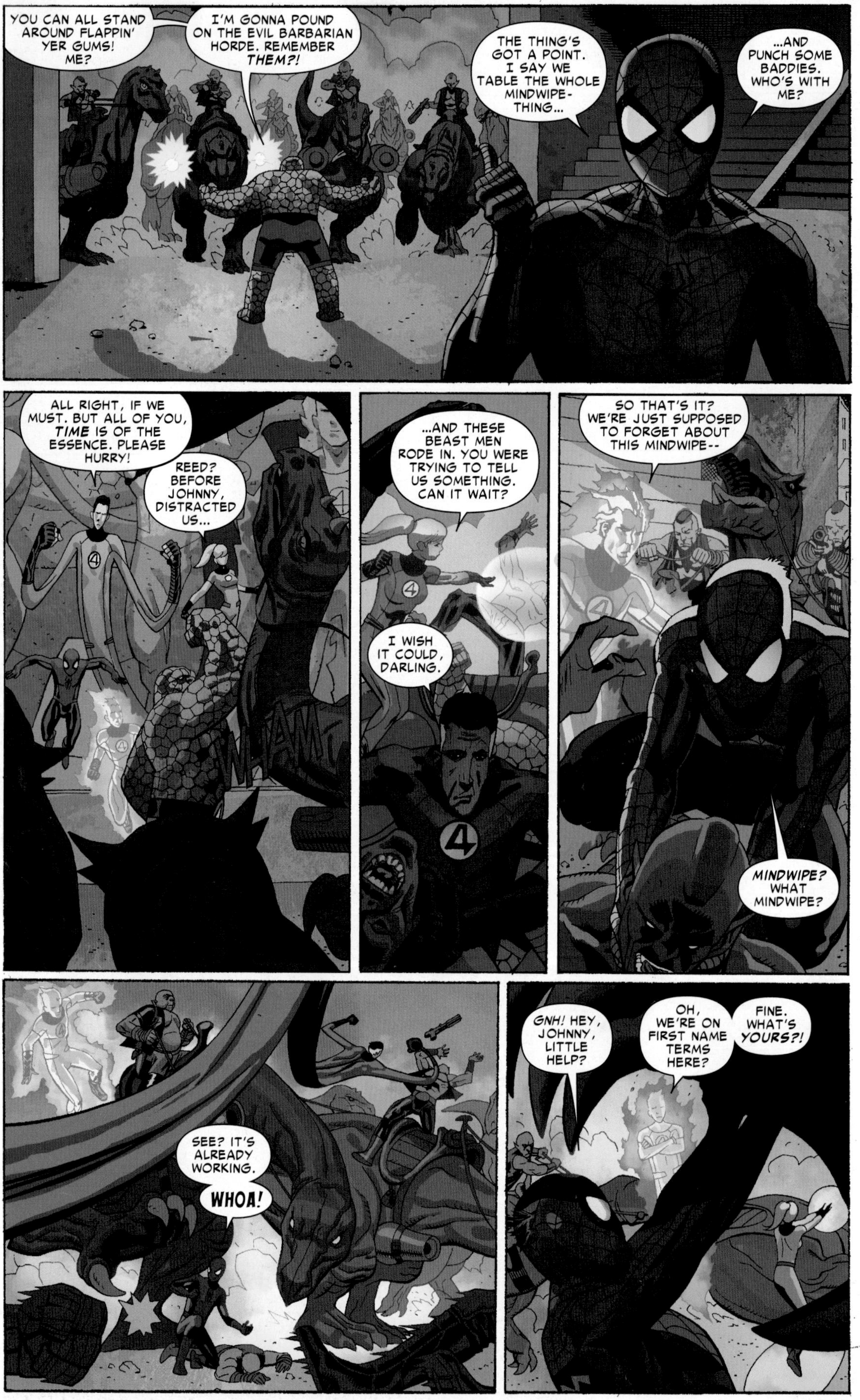
YOU CAN ALL STAND AROUND FLAPPIN' YER GUMS! ME?
I'M GONNA POUND ON THE EVIL BARBARIAN HORDE. REMEMBER THEM?!
THE THING'S GOT A POINT. I SAY WE TABLE THE WHOLE MINDWIPE-THING...
...AND PUNCH SOME BADDIES. WHO'S WITH ME?
ALL RIGHT, IF WE MUST. BUT ALL OF YOU, TIME IS OF THE ESSENCE. PLEASE HURRY!
REED? BEFORE JOHNNY, DISTRACTED US...
WHAM
...AND THESE BEAST MEN RODE IN. YOU WERE TRYING TO TELL US SOMETHING. CAN IT WAIT?
I WISH IT COULD, DARLING.
SO THAT'S IT? WE'RE JUST SUPPOSED TO FORGET ABOUT THIS MINDWIPE--
MINDWIPE? WHAT MINDWIPE?
SEE? IT'S ALREADY WORKING.
WHOA!
GNH! HEY, JOHNNY, LITTLE HELP?
OH, WE'RE ON FIRST NAME TERMS HERE?
FINE. WHAT'S YOURS?!

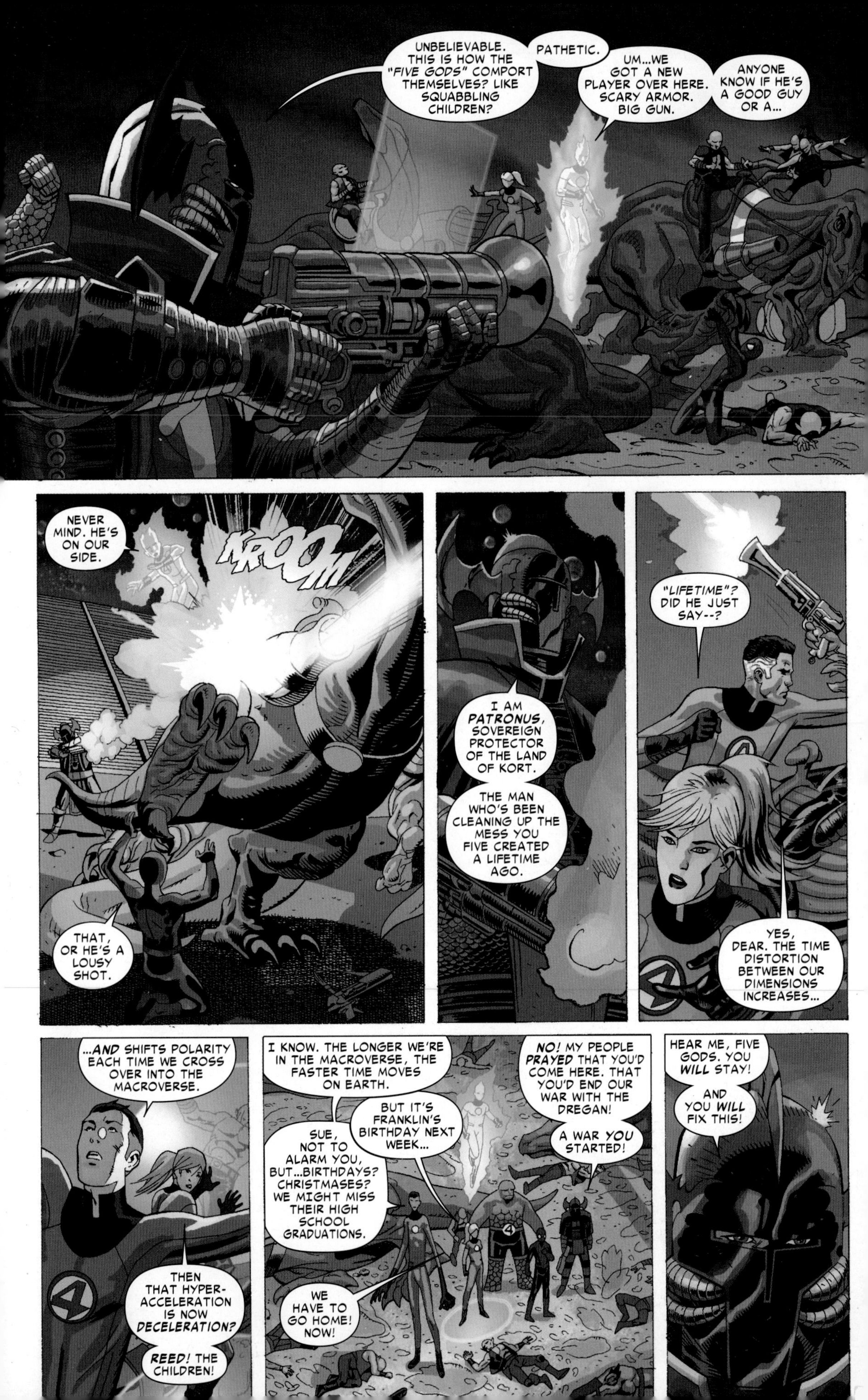
UNBELIEVABLE. THIS IS HOW THE "FIVE GODS" COMPORT THEMSELVES? LIKE SQUABBLING CHILDREN?
PATHETIC.
UM...WE GOT A NEW PLAYER OVER HERE. SCARY ARMOR. BIG GUN.
ANYONE KNOW IF HE'S A GOOD GUY OR A...
NEVER MIND. HE'S ON OUR SIDE.
KROOM
THAT, OR HE'S A LOUSY SHOT.
I AM PATRONUS, SOVEREIGN PROTECTOR OF THE LAND OF KORT.
THE MAN WHO'S BEEN CLEANING UP THE MESS YOU FIVE CREATED A LIFETIME AGO.
"LIFETIME"? DID HE JUST SAY--?
YES, DEAR. THE TIME DISTORTION BETWEEN OUR DIMENSIONS INCREASES...
...AND SHIFTS POLARITY EACH TIME WE CROSS OVER INTO THE MACROVERSE.
THEN THAT HYPER-ACCELERATION IS NOW DECELERATION?
REED! THE CHILDREN!
I KNOW. THE LONGER WE'RE IN THE MACROVERSE, THE FASTER TIME MOVES ON EARTH.
BUT IT'S FRANKLIN'S BIRTHDAY NEXT WEEK...
SUE, NOT TO ALARM YOU, BUT...BIRTHDAYS? CHRISTMASES? WE MIGHT MISS THEIR HIGH SCHOOL GRADUATIONS.
WE HAVE TO GO HOME! NOW!
NO! MY PEOPLE PRAYED THAT YOU'D COME HERE. THAT YOU'D END OUR WAR WITH THE DREGAN!
A WAR YOU STARTED!
HEAR ME, FIVE GODS. YOU WILL STAY!
AND YOU WILL FIX THIS!

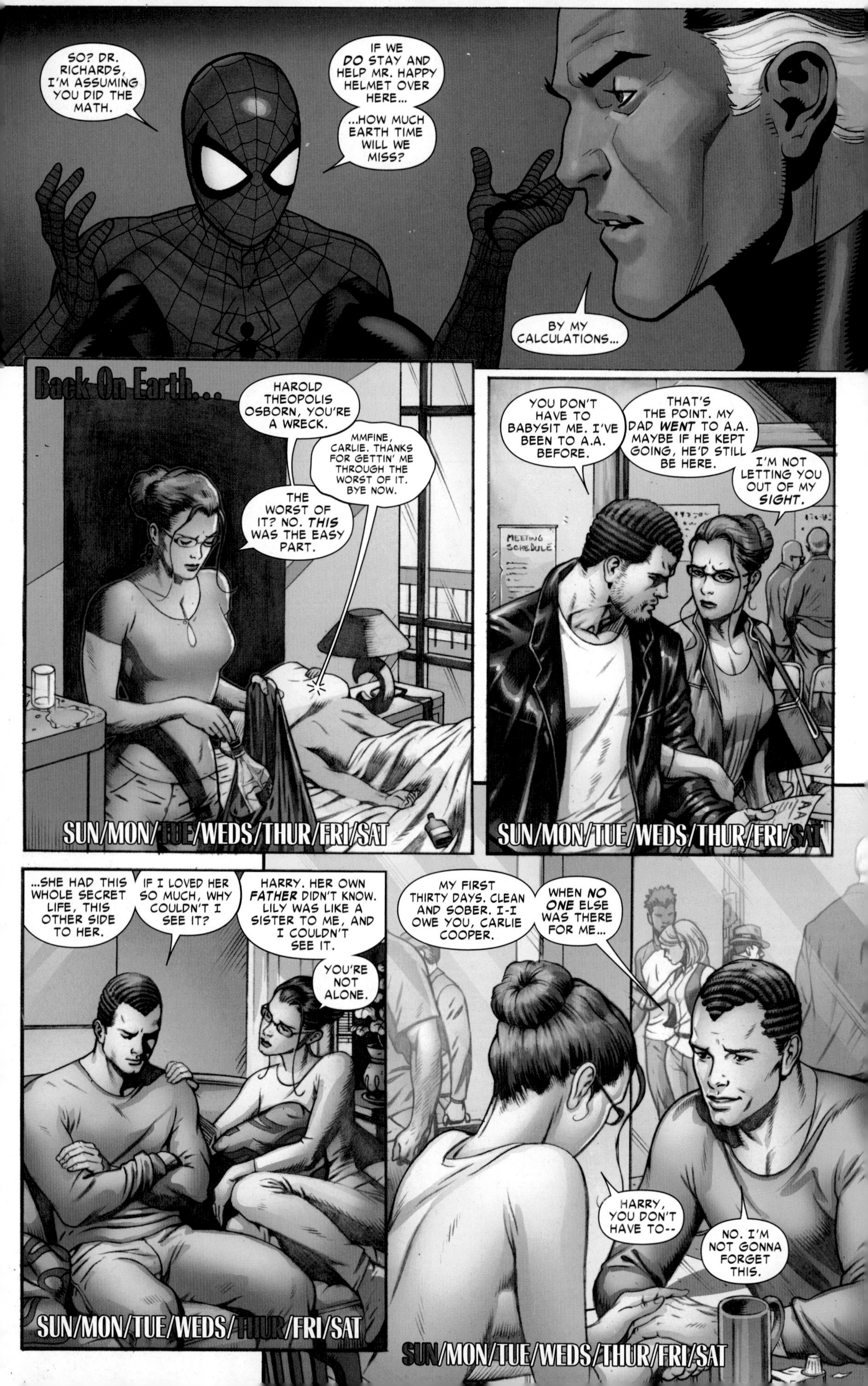
SO? DR. RICHARDS, I'M ASSUMING YOU DID THE MATH.
IF WE DO STAY AND HELP MR. HAPPY HELMET OVER HERE...
...HOW MUCH EARTH TIME WILL WE MISS?
BY MY CALCULATIONS...
Back On Earth...
HAROLD THEOPOLIS OSBORN, YOU'RE A WRECK.
MMFINE, CARLIE. THANKS FOR GETTIN' ME THROUGH THE WORST OF IT. BYE NOW.
THE WORST OF IT? NO. THIS WAS THE EASY PART.
SUN/MON/TUE/WEDS/THUR/FRI/SAT
YOU DON'T HAVE TO BABYSIT ME. I'VE BEEN TO A.A. BEFORE.
THAT'S THE POINT. MY DAD WENT TO A.A. MAYBE IF HE KEPT GOING, HE'D STILL BE HERE.
I'M NOT LETTING YOU OUT OF MY SIGHT.
MEETING SCHEDULE
SUN/MON/TUE/WEDS/THUR/FRI/SAT
...SHE HAD THIS WHOLE SECRET LIFE, THIS OTHER SIDE TO HER.
IF I LOVED HER SO MUCH, WHY COULDN'T I SEE IT?
HARRY. HER OWN FATHER DIDN'T KNOW. LILY WAS LIKE A SISTER TO ME, AND I COULDN'T SEE IT.
YOU'RE NOT ALONE.
SUN/MON/TUE/WEDS/THUR/FRI/SAT
MY FIRST THIRTY DAYS. CLEAN AND SOBER. I-I OWE YOU, CARLIE COOPER.
WHEN NO ONE ELSE WAS THERE FOR ME...
HARRY, YOU DON'T HAVE TO--
NO. I'M NOT GONNA FORGET THIS.
SUN/MON/TUE/WEDS/THUR/FRI/SAT

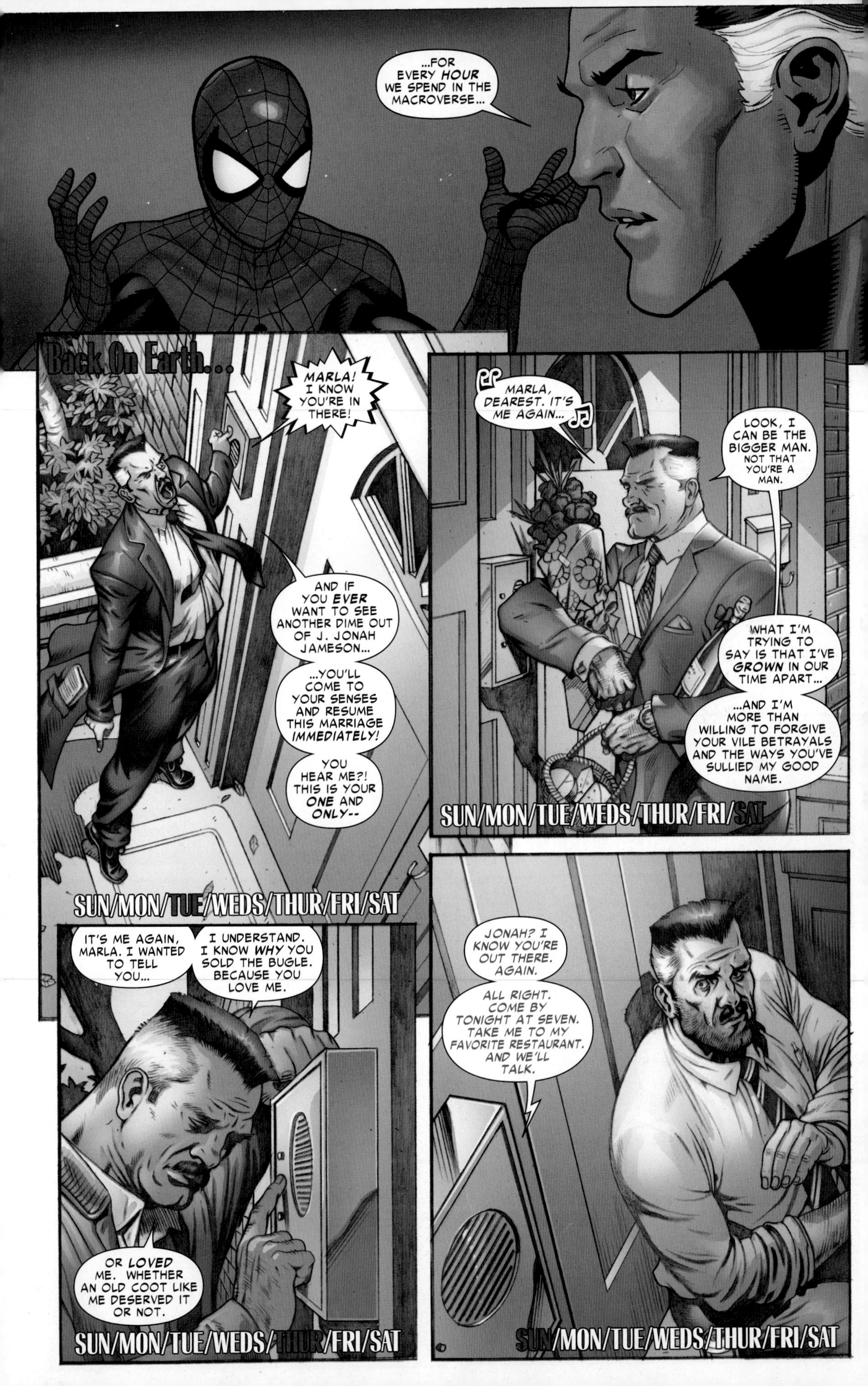
...FOR EVERY HOUR WE SPEND IN THE MACROVERSE...
Back On Earth...
MARLA! I KNOW YOU'RE IN THERE!
AND IF YOU EVER WANT TO SEE ANOTHER DIME OUT OF J. JONAH JAMESON...
...YOU'LL COME TO YOUR SENSES AND RESUME THIS MARRIAGE IMMEDIATELY!
YOU HEAR ME?! THIS IS YOUR ONE AND ONLY--
SUN/MON/TUE/WEDS/THUR/FRI/SAT
MARLA, DEAREST. IT'S ME AGAIN...
LOOK, I CAN BE THE BIGGER MAN. NOT THAT YOU'RE A MAN.
WHAT I'M TRYING TO SAY IS THAT I'VE GROWN IN OUR TIME APART...
...AND I'M MORE THAN WILLING TO FORGIVE YOUR VILE BETRAYALS AND THE WAYS YOU'VE SULLIED MY GOOD NAME.
SUN/MON/TUE/WEDS/THUR/FRI/SAT
IT'S ME AGAIN, MARLA. I WANTED TO TELL YOU...
I UNDERSTAND. I KNOW WHY YOU SOLD THE BUGLE. BECAUSE YOU LOVE ME.
OR LOVED ME. WHETHER AN OLD COOT LIKE ME DESERVED IT OR NOT.
SUN/MON/TUE/WEDS/THUR/FRI/SAT
JONAH? I KNOW YOU'RE OUT THERE. AGAIN.
ALL RIGHT. COME BY TONIGHT AT SEVEN. TAKE ME TO MY FAVORITE RESTAURANT. AND WE'LL TALK.
SUN/MON/TUE/WEDS/THUR/FRI/SAT

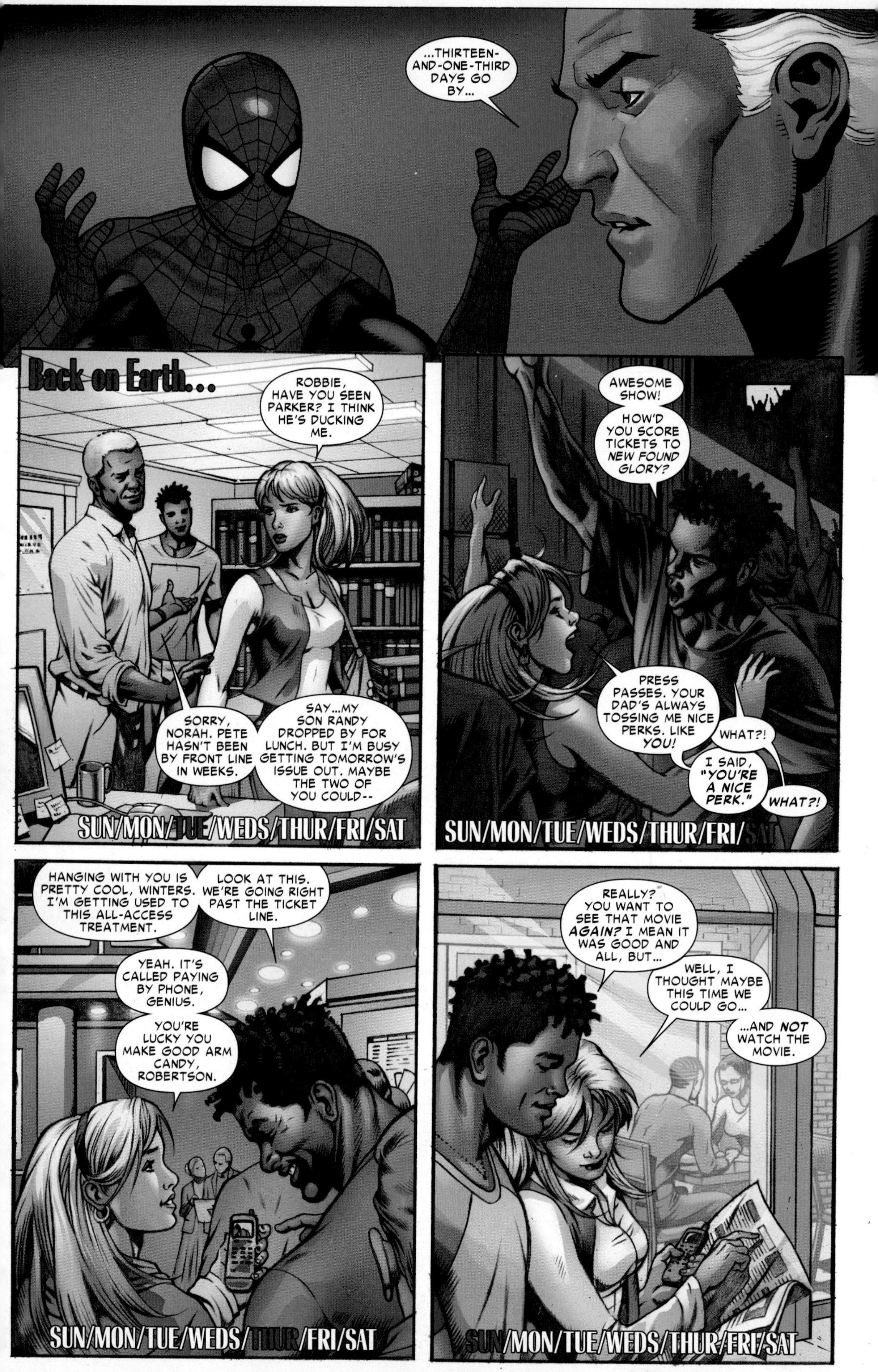
...THIRTEEN-AND-ONE-THIRD DAYS GO BY...
Back on Earth...
ROBBIE, HAVE YOU SEEN PARKER? I THINK HE'S DUCKING ME.
SORRY, NORAH. PETE HASN'T BEEN BY FRONT LINE IN WEEKS.
SAY...MY SON RANDY DROPPED BY FOR LUNCH. BUT I'M BUSY GETTING TOMORROW'S ISSUE OUT. MAYBE THE TWO OF YOU COULD--
SUN/MON/TUE/WEDS/THUR/FRI/SAT
AWESOME SHOW! HOW'D YOU SCORE TICKETS TO NEW FOUND GLORY?
PRESS PASSES. YOUR DAD'S ALWAYS TOSSING ME NICE PERKS. LIKE YOU!
WHAT?!
I SAID, "YOU'RE A NICE PERK."
WHAT?!
SUN/MON/TUE/WEDS/THUR/FRI/SAT
HANGING WITH YOU IS PRETTY COOL, WINTERS. I'M GETTING USED TO THIS ALL-ACCESS TREATMENT.
LOOK AT THIS. WE'RE GOING RIGHT PAST THE TICKET LINE.
YEAH. IT'S CALLED PAYING BY PHONE, GENIUS.
YOU'RE LUCKY YOU MAKE GOOD ARM CANDY, ROBERTSON.
SUN/MON/TUE/WEDS/THUR/FRI/SAT
REALLY? YOU WANT TO SEE THAT MOVIE AGAIN? I MEAN IT WAS GOOD AND ALL, BUT...
WELL, I THOUGHT MAYBE THIS TIME WE COULD GO...
...AND NOT WATCH THE MOVIE.
SUN/MON/TUE/WEDS/THUR/FRI/SAT

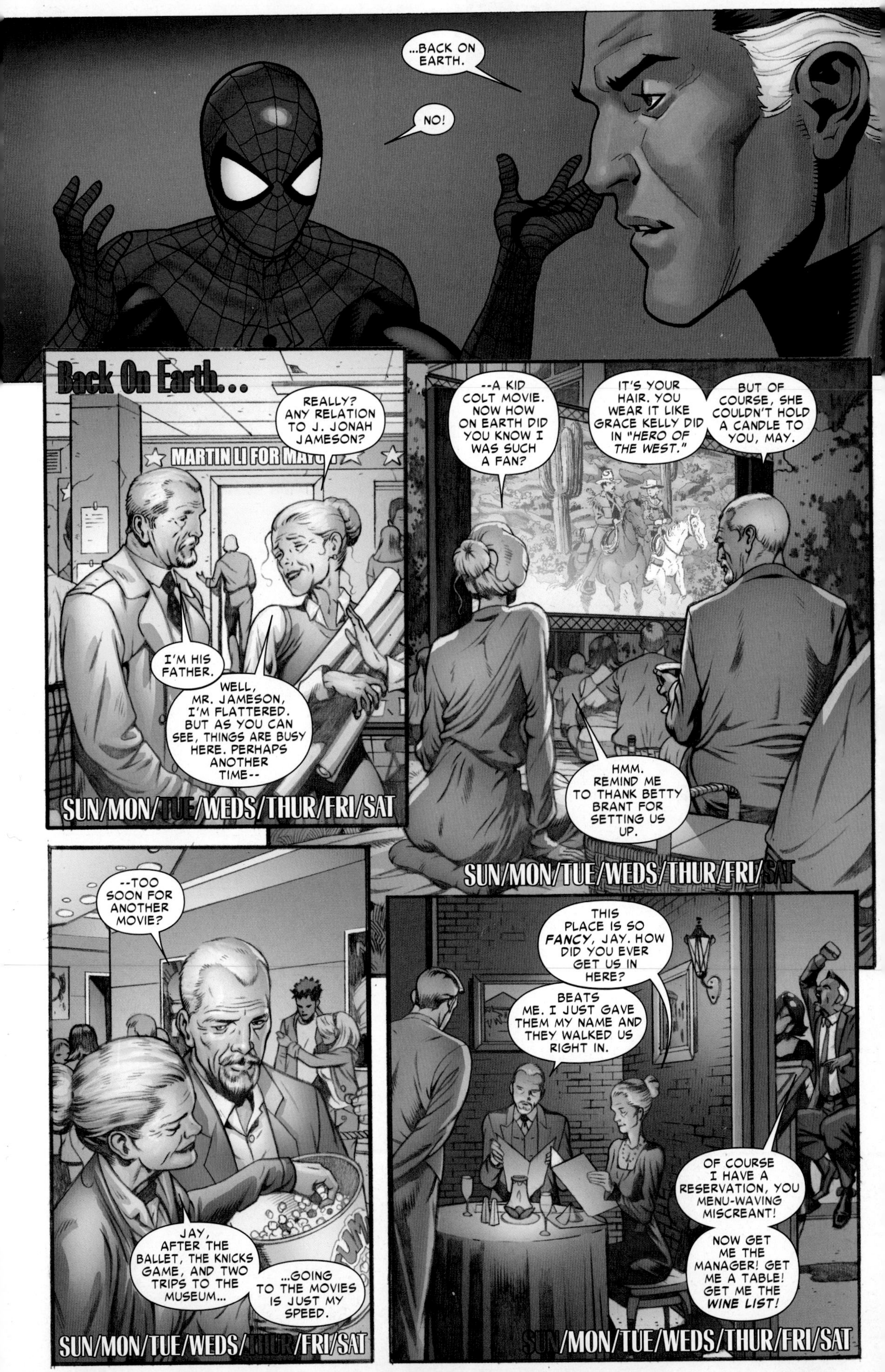
...BACK ON EARTH.
NO!
Back On Earth...
REALLY? ANY RELATION TO J. JONAH JAMESON?
MARTIN LI FOR MAY
I'M HIS FATHER.
WELL, MR. JAMESON, I'M FLATTERED. BUT AS YOU CAN SEE, THINGS ARE BUSY HERE. PERHAPS ANOTHER TIME--
SUN/MON/TUE/WEDS/THUR/FRI/SAT
--A KID COLT MOVIE. NOW HOW ON EARTH DID YOU KNOW I WAS SUCH A FAN?
IT'S YOUR HAIR. YOU WEAR IT LIKE GRACE KELLY DID IN "HERO OF THE WEST."
BUT OF COURSE, SHE COULDN'T HOLD A CANDLE TO YOU, MAY.
HMM. REMIND ME TO THANK BETTY BRANT FOR SETTING US UP.
SUN/MON/TUE/WEDS/THUR/FRI/SAT
--TOO SOON FOR ANOTHER MOVIE?
JAY, AFTER THE BALLET, THE KNICKS GAME, AND TWO TRIPS TO THE MUSEUM...
...GOING TO THE MOVIES IS JUST MY SPEED.
SUN/MON/TUE/WEDS/THUR/FRI/SAT
THIS PLACE IS SO FANCY, JAY. HOW DID YOU EVER GET US IN HERE?
BEATS ME. I JUST GAVE THEM MY NAME AND THEY WALKED US RIGHT IN.
OF COURSE I HAVE A RESERVATION, YOU MENU-WAVING MISCREANT!
NOW GET ME THE MANAGER! GET ME A TABLE! GET ME THE WINE LIST!
SUN/MON/TUE/WEDS/THUR/FRI/SAT

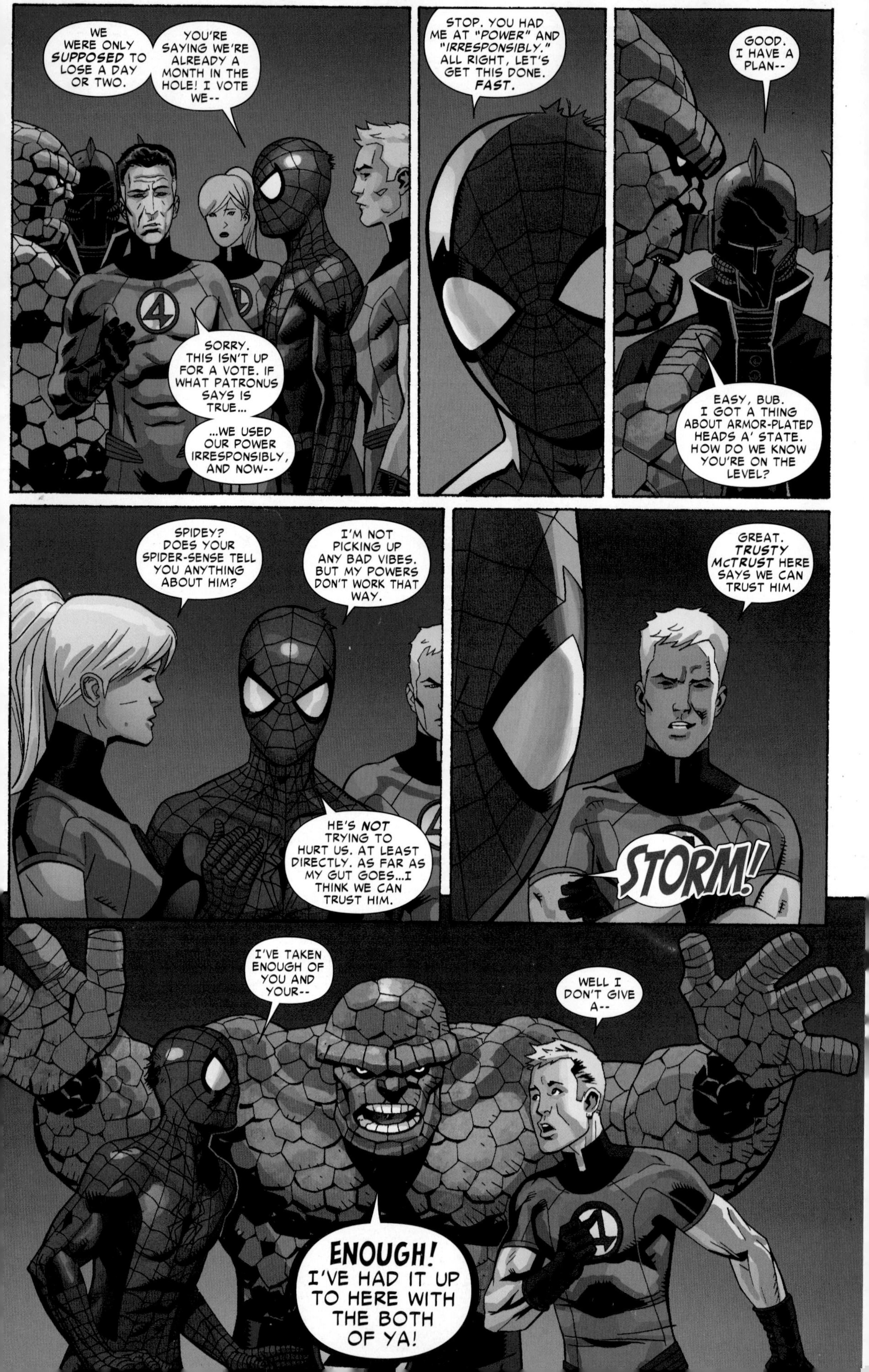
WE WERE ONLY SUPPOSED TO LOSE A DAY OR TWO.
YOU'RE SAYING WE'RE ALREADY A MONTH IN THE HOLE! I VOTE WE--
SORRY. THIS ISN'T UP FOR A VOTE. IF WHAT PATRONUS SAYS IS TRUE...
...WE USED OUR POWER IRRESPONSIBLY, AND NOW--
STOP. YOU HAD ME AT "POWER" AND "IRRESPONSIBLY." ALL RIGHT, LET'S GET THIS DONE. FAST.
GOOD. I HAVE A PLAN--
EASY, BUB. I GOT A THING ABOUT ARMOR-PLATED HEADS A' STATE. HOW DO WE KNOW YOU'RE ON THE LEVEL?
SPIDEY? DOES YOUR SPIDER-SENSE TELL YOU ANYTHING ABOUT HIM?
I'M NOT PICKING UP ANY BAD VIBES. BUT MY POWERS DON'T WORK THAT WAY.
HE'S NOT TRYING TO HURT US. AT LEAST DIRECTLY. AS FAR AS MY GUT GOES...I THINK WE CAN TRUST HIM.
GREAT. TRUSTY McTRUST HERE SAYS WE CAN TRUST HIM.
STORM!
I'VE TAKEN ENOUGH OF YOU AND YOUR--
WELL I DON'T GIVE A--
ENOUGH! I'VE HAD IT UP TO HERE WITH THE BOTH OF YA!

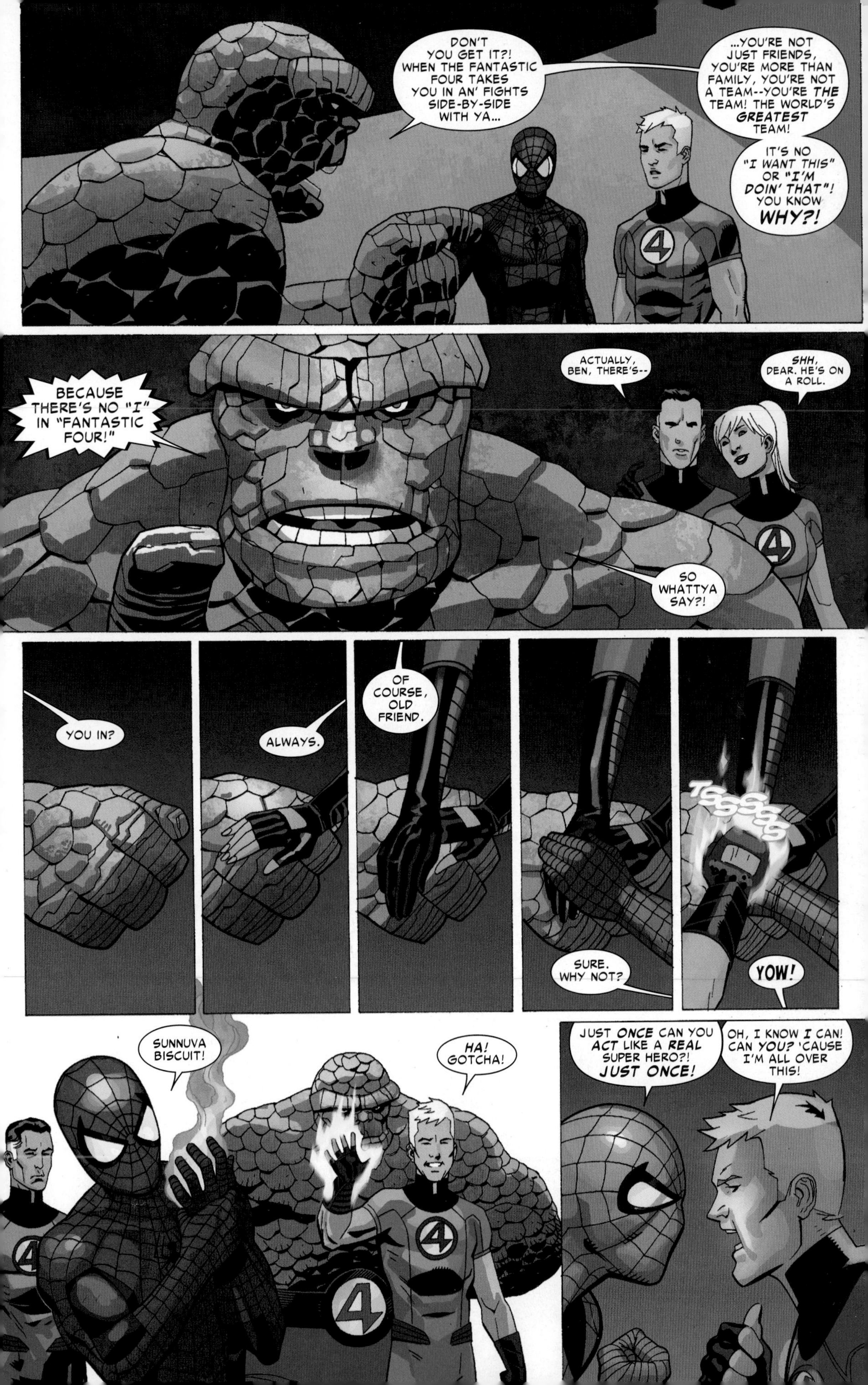
DON'T YOU GET IT?! WHEN THE FANTASTIC FOUR TAKES YOU IN AN' FIGHTS SIDE-BY-SIDE WITH YA...
...YOU'RE NOT JUST FRIENDS, YOU'RE MORE THAN FAMILY, YOU'RE NOT A TEAM--YOU'RE THE TEAM! THE WORLD'S GREATEST TEAM!
IT'S NO "I WANT THIS" OR "I'M DOIN' THAT"! YOU KNOW WHY?!
BECAUSE THERE'S NO "I" IN "FANTASTIC FOUR!"
ACTUALLY, BEN, THERE'S--
SHH, DEAR. HE'S ON A ROLL.
SO WHATTYA SAY?!
YOU IN?
ALWAYS.
OF COURSE, OLD FRIEND.
SURE. WHY NOT?
TSSSSS
YOW!
SUNNUVA BISCUIT!
HA! GOTCHA!
JUST ONCE CAN YOU ACT LIKE A REAL SUPER HERO?! JUST ONCE!
OH, I KNOW I CAN! CAN YOU? 'CAUSE I'M ALL OVER THIS!

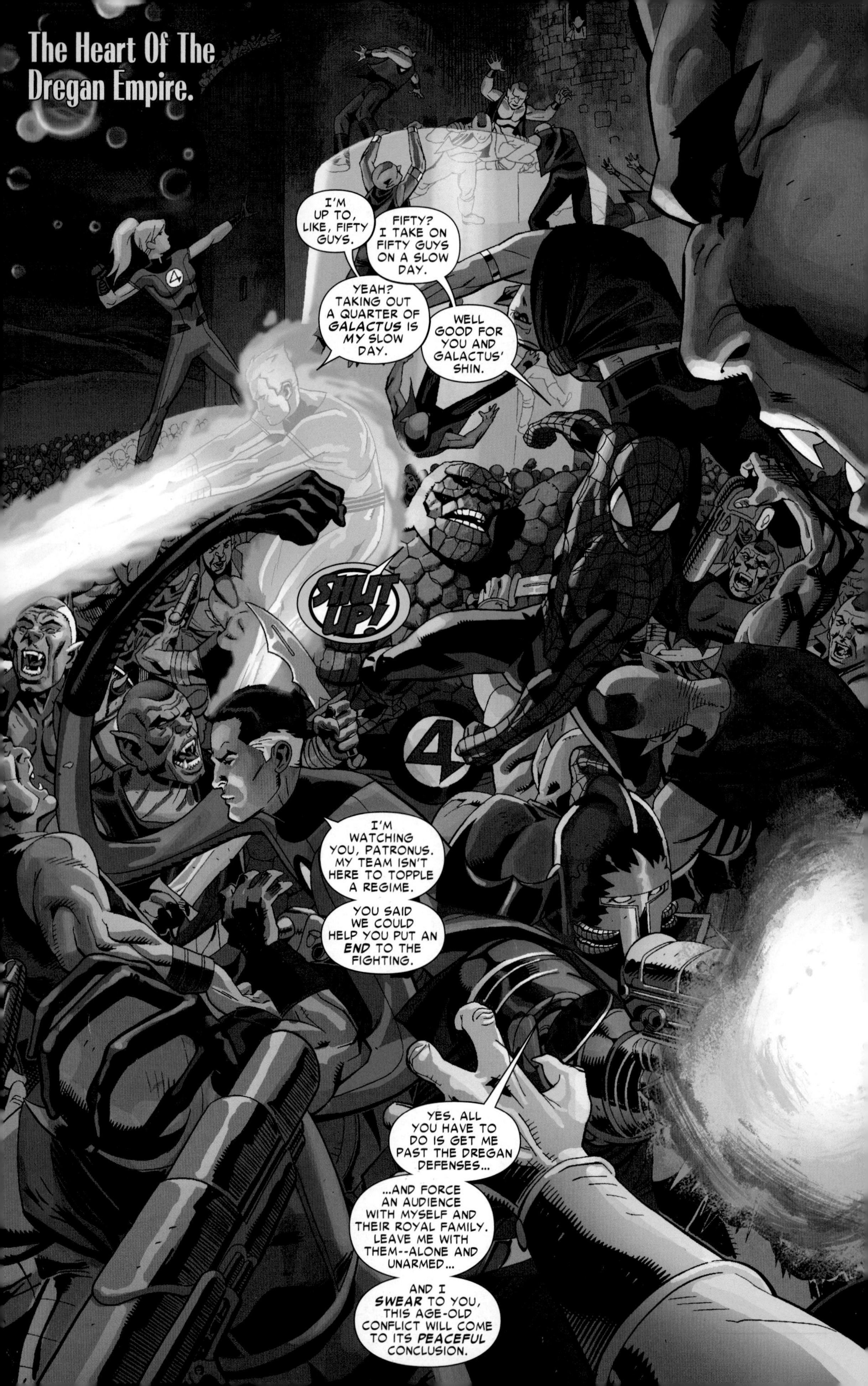
The Heart Of The Dregan Empire.
I'M UP TO, LIKE, FIFTY GUYS.
FIFTY? I TAKE ON FIFTY GUYS ON A SLOW DAY.
YEAH? TAKING OUT A QUARTER OF GALACTUS IS MY SLOW DAY.
WELL GOOD FOR YOU AND GALACTUS' SHIN.
SHUT UP!
I'M WATCHING YOU, PATRONUS. MY TEAM ISN'T HERE TO TOPPLE A REGIME.
YOU SAID WE COULD HELP YOU PUT AN END TO THE FIGHTING.
YES. ALL YOU HAVE TO DO IS GET ME PAST THE DREGAN DEFENSES...
...AND FORCE AN AUDIENCE WITH MYSELF AND THEIR ROYAL FAMILY. LEAVE ME WITH THEM--ALONE AND UNARMED...
AND I SWEAR TO YOU, THIS AGE-OLD CONFLICT WILL COME TO ITS PEACEFUL CONCLUSION.

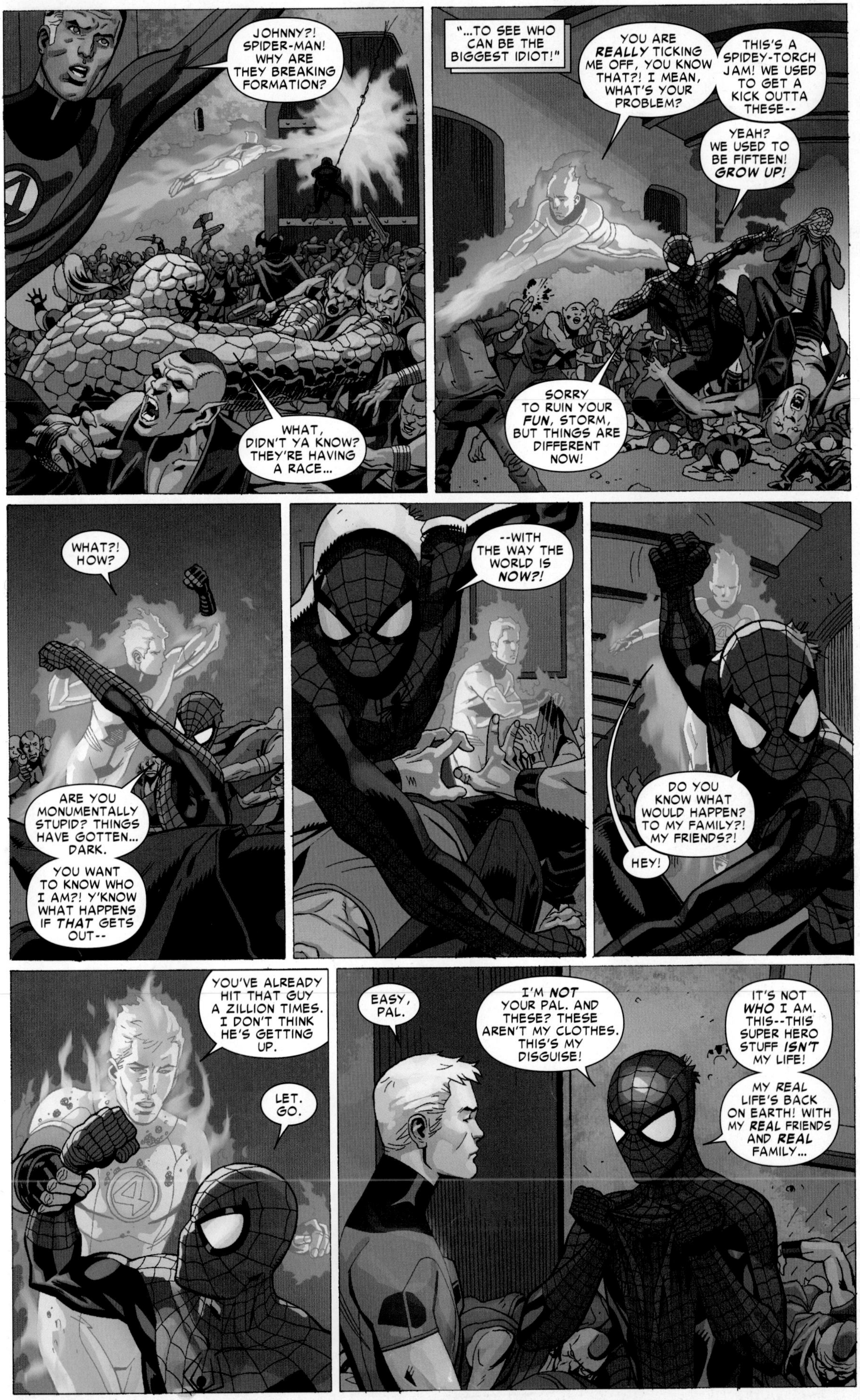
JOHNNY?! SPIDER-MAN! WHY ARE THEY BREAKING FORMATION?
WHAT, DIDN'T YA KNOW? THEY'RE HAVING A RACE...
"...TO SEE WHO CAN BE THE BIGGEST IDIOT!"
YOU ARE REALLY TICKING ME OFF, YOU KNOW THAT?! I MEAN, WHAT'S YOUR PROBLEM?
THIS'S A SPIDEY-TORCH JAM! WE USED TO GET A KICK OUTTA THESE--
YEAH? WE USED TO BE FIFTEEN! GROW UP!
SORRY TO RUIN YOUR FUN, STORM, BUT THINGS ARE DIFFERENT NOW!
WHAT?! HOW?
ARE YOU MONUMENTALLY STUPID? THINGS HAVE GOTTEN... DARK.
YOU WANT TO KNOW WHO I AM?! Y'KNOW WHAT HAPPENS IF THAT GETS OUT--
--WITH THE WAY THE WORLD IS NOW?!
DO YOU KNOW WHAT WOULD HAPPEN? TO MY FAMILY?! MY FRIENDS?!
HEY!
YOU'VE ALREADY HIT THAT GUY A ZILLION TIMES. I DON'T THINK HE'S GETTING UP.
LET. GO.
EASY, PAL.
I'M NOT YOUR PAL. AND THESE? THESE AREN'T MY CLOTHES. THIS'S MY DISGUISE!
IT'S NOT WHO I AM. THIS--THIS SUPER HERO STUFF ISN'T MY LIFE!
MY REAL LIFE'S BACK ON EARTH! WITH MY REAL FRIENDS AND REAL FAMILY...

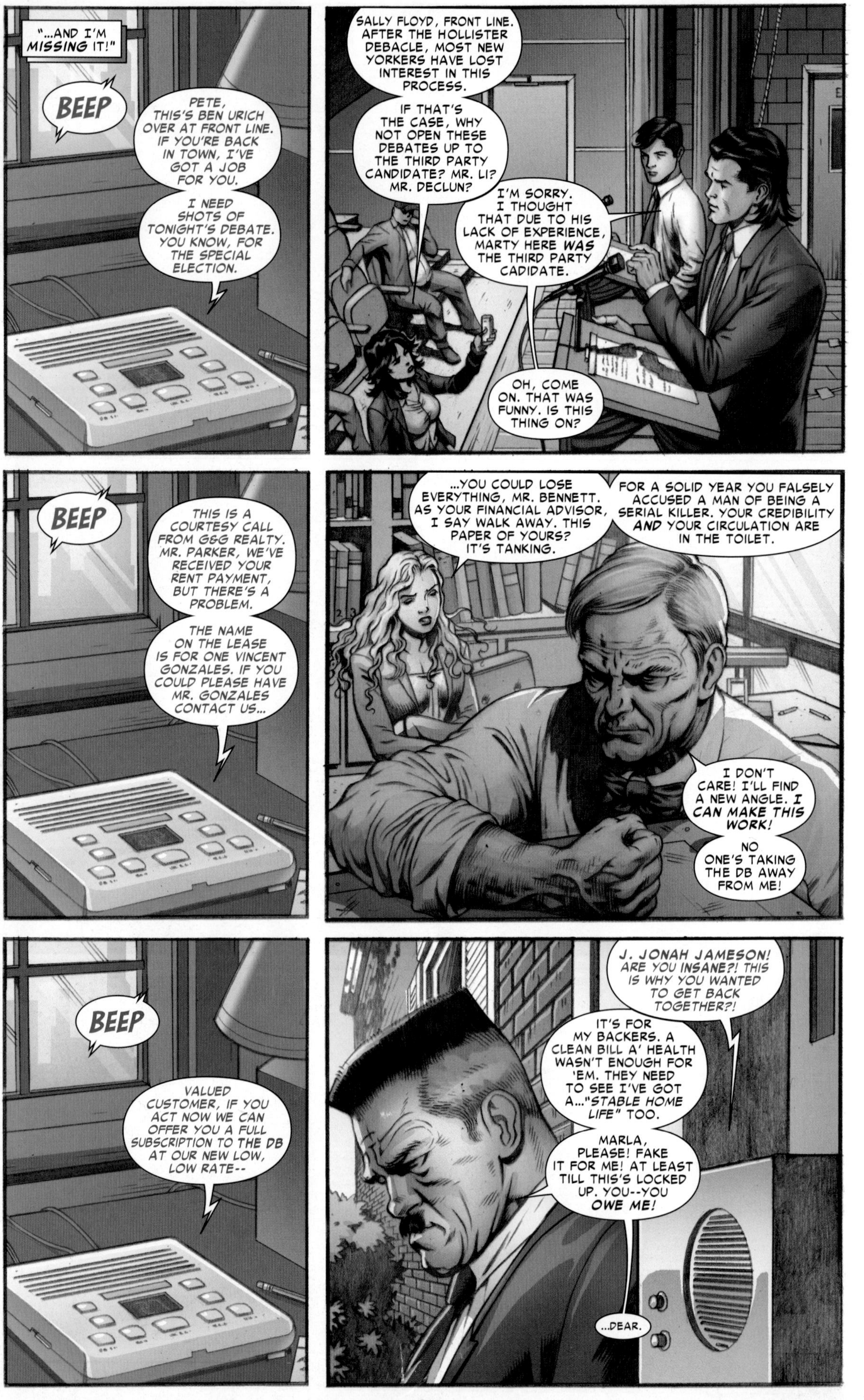
"...AND I'M *MISSING* IT!"
BEEP
PETE, THIS'S BEN URICH OVER AT FRONT LINE. IF YOU'RE BACK IN TOWN, I'VE GOT A JOB FOR YOU.
I NEED SHOTS OF TONIGHT'S DEBATE. YOU KNOW, FOR THE SPECIAL ELECTION.
SALLY FLOYD, FRONT LINE. AFTER THE HOLLISTER DEBACLE, MOST NEW YORKERS HAVE LOST INTEREST IN THIS PROCESS.
IF THAT'S THE CASE, WHY NOT OPEN THESE DEBATES UP TO THE THIRD PARTY CANDIDATE? MR. LI? MR. DECLUN?
I'M SORRY. I THOUGHT THAT DUE TO HIS LACK OF EXPERIENCE, MARTY HERE **WAS** THE THIRD PARTY CADIDATE.
OH, COME ON. THAT WAS FUNNY. IS THIS THING ON?
BEEP
THIS IS A COURTESY CALL FROM G&G REALTY. MR. PARKER, WE'VE RECEIVED YOUR RENT PAYMENT, BUT THERE'S A PROBLEM.
THE NAME ON THE LEASE IS FOR ONE VINCENT GONZALES. IF YOU COULD PLEASE HAVE MR. GONZALES CONTACT US...
...YOU COULD LOSE EVERYTHING, MR. BENNETT. AS YOUR FINANCIAL ADVISOR, I SAY WALK AWAY. THIS PAPER OF YOURS? IT'S TANKING.
FOR A SOLID YEAR YOU FALSELY ACCUSED A MAN OF BEING A SERIAL KILLER. YOUR CREDIBILITY **AND** YOUR CIRCULATION ARE IN THE TOILET.
I DON'T CARE! I'LL FIND A NEW ANGLE. ***I CAN MAKE THIS WORK!***
NO ONE'S TAKING THE DB AWAY FROM ME!
BEEP
VALUED CUSTOMER, IF YOU ACT NOW WE CAN OFFER YOU A FULL SUBSCRIPTION TO **THE DB** AT OUR NEW LOW, LOW RATE--
J. JONAH JAMESON! ARE YOU **INSANE?!** THIS IS WHY YOU WANTED TO GET BACK TOGETHER?!
IT'S FOR MY BACKERS. A CLEAN BILL A' HEALTH WASN'T ENOUGH FOR 'EM. THEY NEED TO SEE I'VE GOT A..."*STABLE HOME LIFE*" TOO.
MARLA, PLEASE! FAKE IT FOR ME! AT LEAST TILL THIS'S LOCKED UP. YOU--YOU **OWE ME!**
...DEAR.

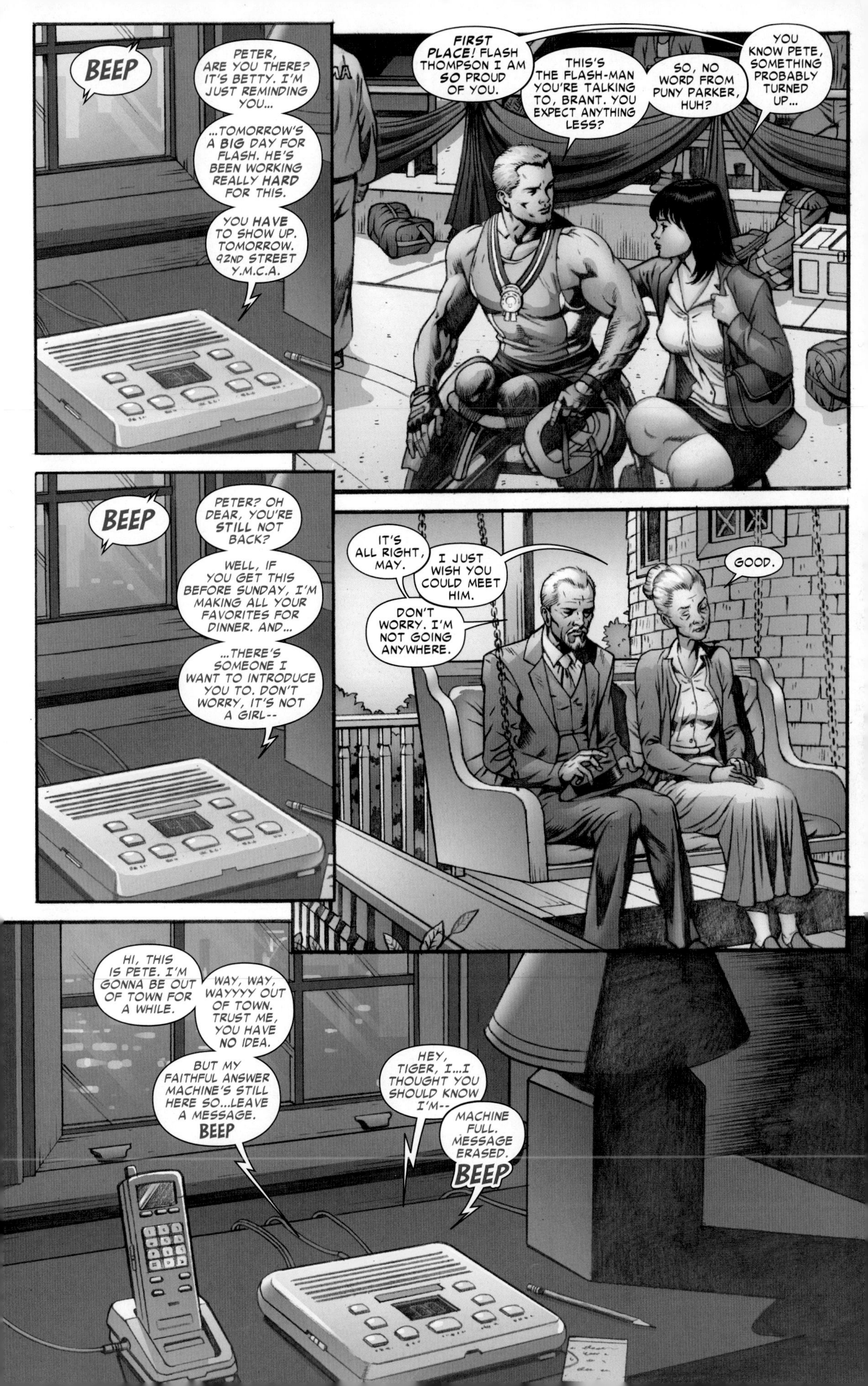
BEEP
PETER, ARE YOU THERE? IT'S BETTY. I'M JUST REMINDING YOU...
...TOMORROW'S A BIG DAY FOR FLASH. HE'S BEEN WORKING REALLY HARD FOR THIS.
YOU HAVE TO SHOW UP. TOMORROW. 92ND STREET Y.M.C.A.
FIRST PLACE! FLASH THOMPSON I AM SO PROUD OF YOU.
THIS'S THE FLASH-MAN YOU'RE TALKING TO, BRANT. YOU EXPECT ANYTHING LESS?
SO, NO WORD FROM PUNY PARKER, HUH?
YOU KNOW PETE, SOMETHING PROBABLY TURNED UP...
BEEP
PETER? OH DEAR, YOU'RE STILL NOT BACK?
WELL, IF YOU GET THIS BEFORE SUNDAY, I'M MAKING ALL YOUR FAVORITES FOR DINNER. AND...
...THERE'S SOMEONE I WANT TO INTRODUCE YOU TO. DON'T WORRY, IT'S NOT A GIRL--
IT'S ALL RIGHT, MAY.
I JUST WISH YOU COULD MEET HIM.
GOOD.
DON'T WORRY. I'M NOT GOING ANYWHERE.
HI, THIS IS PETE. I'M GONNA BE OUT OF TOWN FOR A WHILE.
WAY, WAY, WAYYYY OUT OF TOWN. TRUST ME, YOU HAVE NO IDEA.
BUT MY FAITHFUL ANSWER MACHINE'S STILL HERE SO...LEAVE A MESSAGE. BEEP
HEY, TIGER, I...I THOUGHT YOU SHOULD KNOW I'M--
MACHINE FULL. MESSAGE ERASED. BEEP

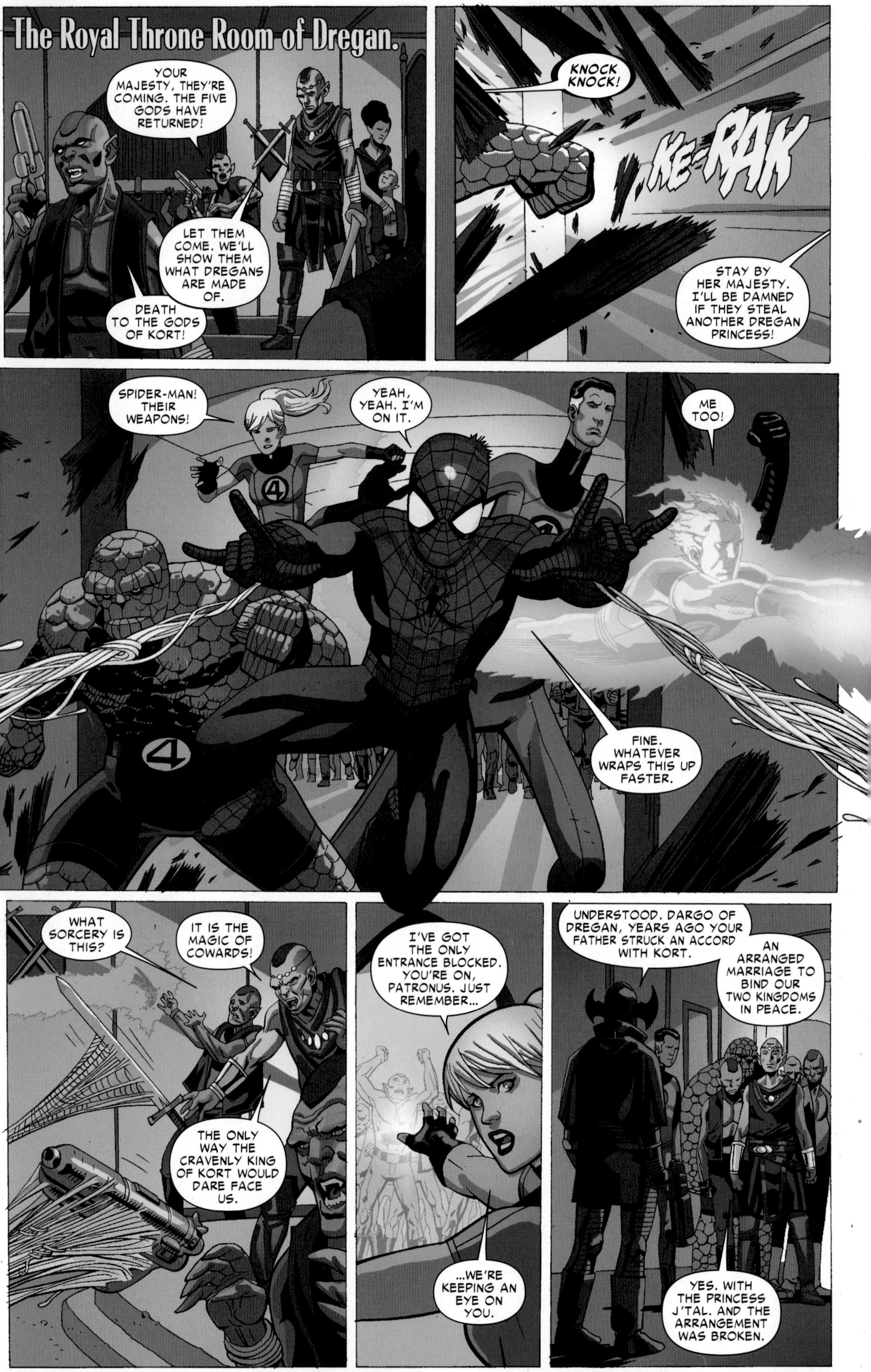
The Royal Throne Room of Dregan.
YOUR MAJESTY, THEY'RE COMING. THE FIVE GODS HAVE RETURNED!
LET THEM COME. WE'LL SHOW THEM WHAT DREGANS ARE MADE OF.
DEATH TO THE GODS OF KORT!
KNOCK KNOCK!
KE-RAK
STAY BY HER MAJESTY. I'LL BE DAMNED IF THEY STEAL ANOTHER DREGAN PRINCESS!
SPIDER-MAN! THEIR WEAPONS!
YEAH, YEAH. I'M ON IT.
ME TOO!
FINE. WHATEVER WRAPS THIS UP FASTER.
WHAT SORCERY IS THIS?
IT IS THE MAGIC OF COWARDS!
THE ONLY WAY THE CRAVENLY KING OF KORT WOULD DARE FACE US.
I'VE GOT THE ONLY ENTRANCE BLOCKED. YOU'RE ON, PATRONUS. JUST REMEMBER...
...WE'RE KEEPING AN EYE ON YOU.
UNDERSTOOD. DARGO OF DREGAN, YEARS AGO YOUR FATHER STRUCK AN ACCORD WITH KORT.
AN ARRANGED MARRIAGE TO BIND OUR TWO KINGDOMS IN PEACE.
YES. WITH THE PRINCESS J'TAL. AND THE ARRANGEMENT WAS BROKEN.

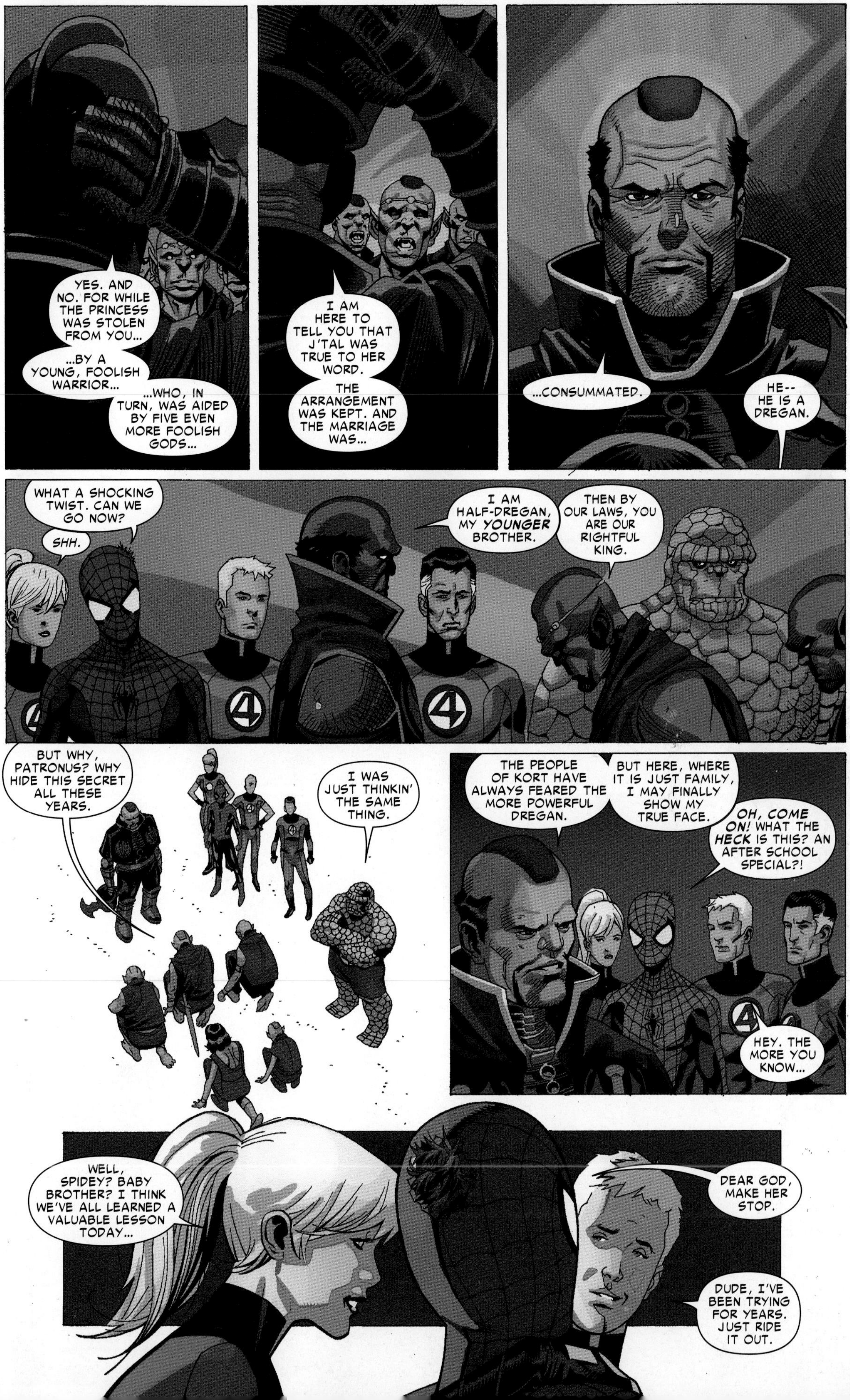
YES. AND NO. FOR WHILE THE PRINCESS WAS STOLEN FROM YOU...
...BY A YOUNG, FOOLISH WARRIOR...
...WHO, IN TURN, WAS AIDED BY FIVE EVEN MORE FOOLISH GODS...
I AM HERE TO TELL YOU THAT J'TAL WAS TRUE TO HER WORD.
THE ARRANGEMENT WAS KEPT. AND THE MARRIAGE WAS...
...CONSUMMATED.
HE--HE IS A DREGAN.
WHAT A SHOCKING TWIST. CAN WE GO NOW?
SHH.
I AM HALF-DREGAN, MY *YOUNGER* BROTHER.
THEN BY OUR LAWS, YOU ARE OUR RIGHTFUL KING.
BUT WHY, PATRONUS? WHY HIDE THIS SECRET ALL THESE YEARS.
I WAS JUST THINKIN' THE SAME THING.
THE PEOPLE OF KORT HAVE ALWAYS FEARED THE MORE POWERFUL DREGAN.
BUT HERE, WHERE IT IS JUST FAMILY, I MAY FINALLY SHOW MY TRUE FACE.
OH, COME ON! WHAT THE *HECK* IS THIS? AN AFTER SCHOOL SPECIAL?!
HEY. THE MORE YOU KNOW...
WELL, SPIDEY? BABY BROTHER? I THINK WE'VE ALL LEARNED A VALUABLE LESSON TODAY...
DEAR GOD, MAKE HER STOP.
DUDE, I'VE BEEN TRYING FOR YEARS. JUST RIDE IT OUT.

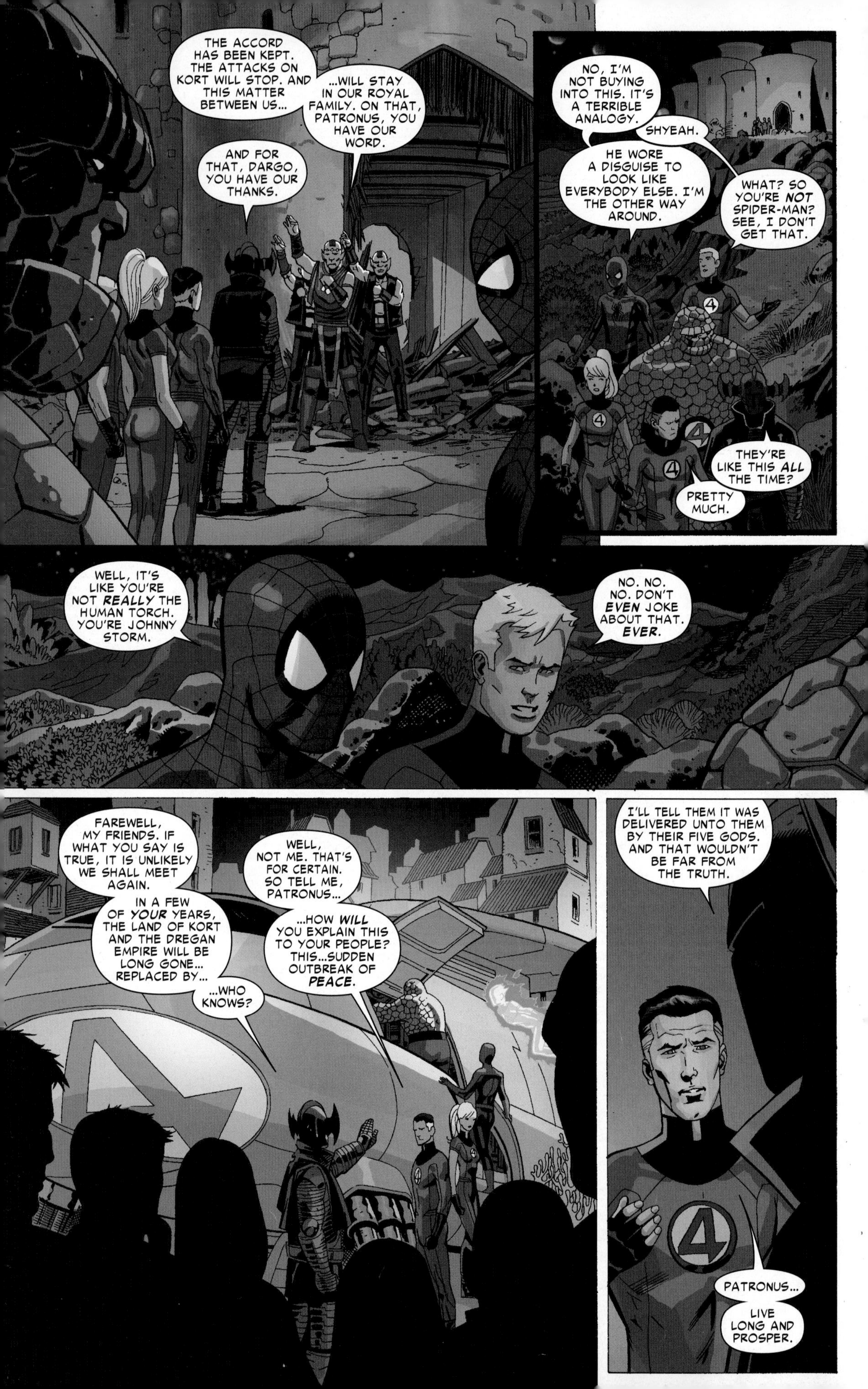
THE ACCORD HAS BEEN KEPT. THE ATTACKS ON KORT WILL STOP. AND THIS MATTER BETWEEN US...
...WILL STAY IN OUR ROYAL FAMILY. ON THAT, PATRONUS, YOU HAVE OUR WORD.
AND FOR THAT, DARGO, YOU HAVE OUR THANKS.
NO, I'M NOT BUYING INTO THIS. IT'S A TERRIBLE ANALOGY.
SHYEAH.
HE WORE A DISGUISE TO LOOK LIKE EVERYBODY ELSE. I'M THE OTHER WAY AROUND.
WHAT? SO YOU'RE **NOT** SPIDER-MAN? SEE, I DON'T GET THAT.
THEY'RE LIKE THIS **ALL** THE TIME?
PRETTY MUCH.
WELL, IT'S LIKE YOU'RE NOT **REALLY** THE HUMAN TORCH. YOU'RE JOHNNY STORM.
NO. NO. NO. DON'T **EVEN** JOKE ABOUT THAT. **EVER.**
FAREWELL, MY FRIENDS. IF WHAT YOU SAY IS TRUE, IT IS UNLIKELY WE SHALL MEET AGAIN.
IN A FEW OF **YOUR** YEARS, THE LAND OF KORT AND THE DREGAN EMPIRE WILL BE LONG GONE... REPLACED BY...
...WHO KNOWS?
WELL, NOT ME. THAT'S FOR CERTAIN. SO TELL ME, PATRONUS...
...HOW **WILL** YOU EXPLAIN THIS TO YOUR PEOPLE? THIS...SUDDEN OUTBREAK OF **PEACE**.
I'LL TELL THEM IT WAS DELIVERED UNTO THEM BY THEIR FIVE GODS. AND THAT WOULDN'T BE FAR FROM THE TRUTH.
PATRONUS...
LIVE LONG AND PROSPER.

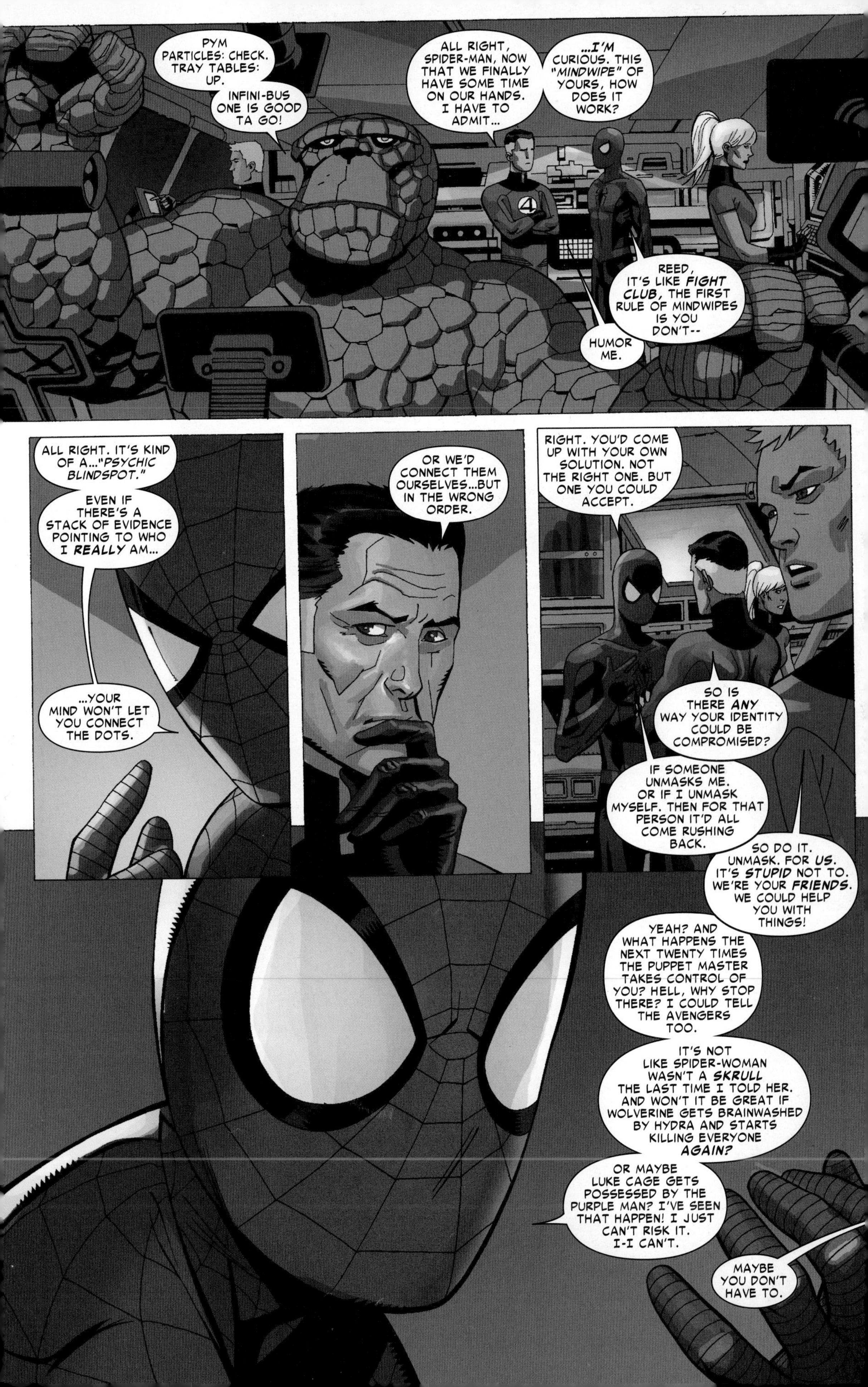
PYM PARTICLES: CHECK. TRAY TABLES: UP.
INFINI-BUS ONE IS GOOD TA GO!
ALL RIGHT, SPIDER-MAN, NOW THAT WE FINALLY HAVE SOME TIME ON OUR HANDS. I HAVE TO ADMIT...
...I'M CURIOUS. THIS "MINDWIPE" OF YOURS, HOW DOES IT WORK?
REED, IT'S LIKE FIGHT CLUB, THE FIRST RULE OF MINDWIPES IS YOU DON'T--
HUMOR ME.
ALL RIGHT. IT'S KIND OF A..."PSYCHIC BLINDSPOT."
EVEN IF THERE'S A STACK OF EVIDENCE POINTING TO WHO I REALLY AM...
...YOUR MIND WON'T LET YOU CONNECT THE DOTS.
OR WE'D CONNECT THEM OURSELVES...BUT IN THE WRONG ORDER.
RIGHT. YOU'D COME UP WITH YOUR OWN SOLUTION. NOT THE RIGHT ONE. BUT ONE YOU COULD ACCEPT.
SO IS THERE ANY WAY YOUR IDENTITY COULD BE COMPROMISED?
IF SOMEONE UNMASKS ME. OR IF I UNMASK MYSELF. THEN FOR THAT PERSON IT'D ALL COME RUSHING BACK.
SO DO IT. UNMASK. FOR US. IT'S STUPID NOT TO. WE'RE YOUR FRIENDS. WE COULD HELP YOU WITH THINGS!
YEAH? AND WHAT HAPPENS THE NEXT TWENTY TIMES THE PUPPET MASTER TAKES CONTROL OF YOU? HELL, WHY STOP THERE? I COULD TELL THE AVENGERS TOO.
IT'S NOT LIKE SPIDER-WOMAN WASN'T A SKRULL THE LAST TIME I TOLD HER. AND WON'T IT BE GREAT IF WOLVERINE GETS BRAINWASHED BY HYDRA AND STARTS KILLING EVERYONE AGAIN?
OR MAYBE LUKE CAGE GETS POSSESSED BY THE PURPLE MAN? I'VE SEEN THAT HAPPEN! I JUST CAN'T RISK IT. I-I CAN'T.
MAYBE YOU DON'T HAVE TO.

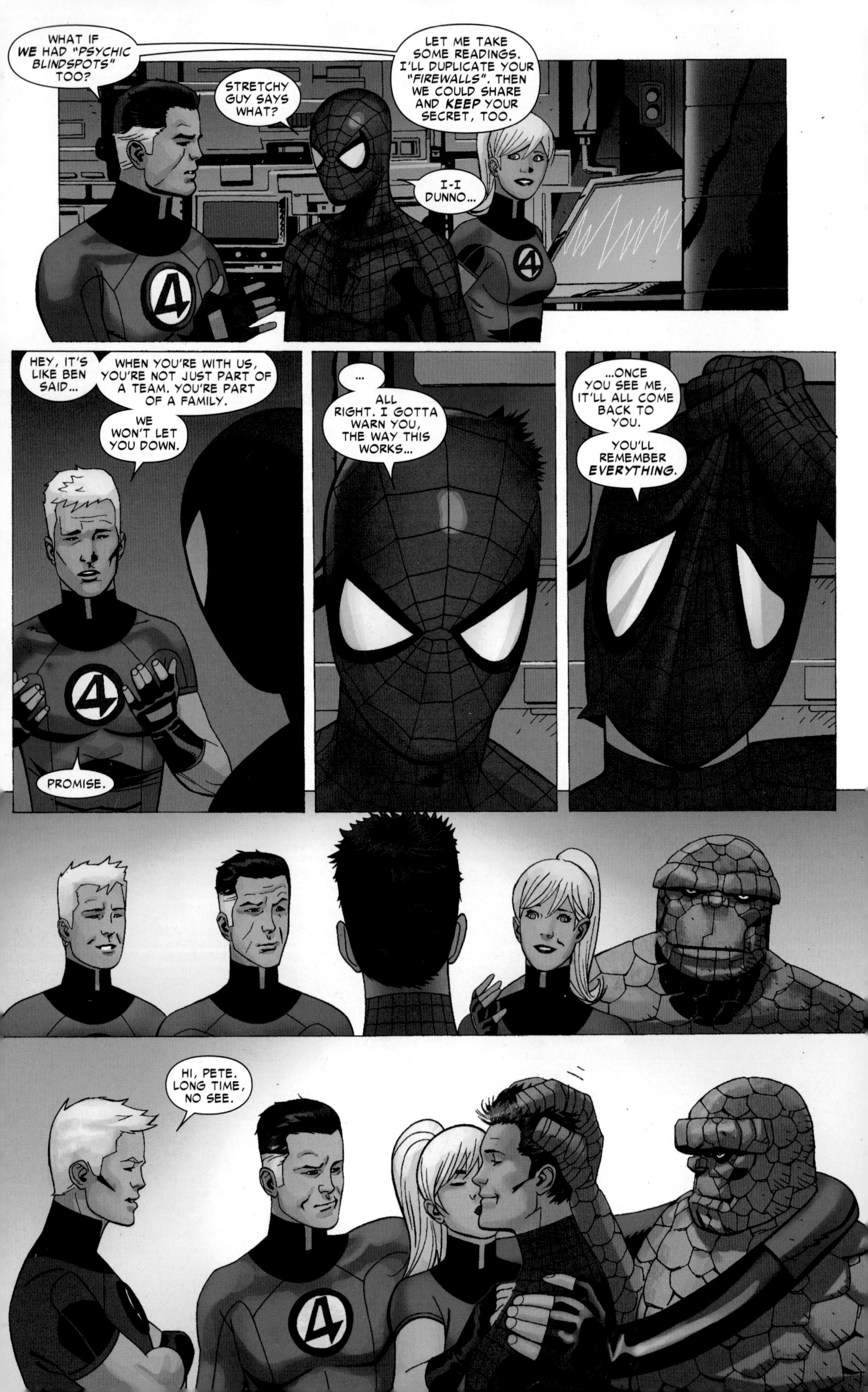
WHAT IF WE HAD "PSYCHIC BLINDSPOTS" TOO?
STRETCHY GUY SAYS WHAT?
LET ME TAKE SOME READINGS. I'LL DUPLICATE YOUR "FIREWALLS". THEN WE COULD SHARE AND KEEP YOUR SECRET, TOO.
I-I DUNNO...
HEY, IT'S LIKE BEN SAID...
WHEN YOU'RE WITH US, YOU'RE NOT JUST PART OF A TEAM. YOU'RE PART OF A FAMILY.
WE WON'T LET YOU DOWN.
PROMISE.
...
ALL RIGHT. I GOTTA WARN YOU, THE WAY THIS WORKS...
...ONCE YOU SEE ME, IT'LL ALL COME BACK TO YOU.
YOU'LL REMEMBER EVERYTHING.
HI, PETE. LONG TIME, NO SEE.

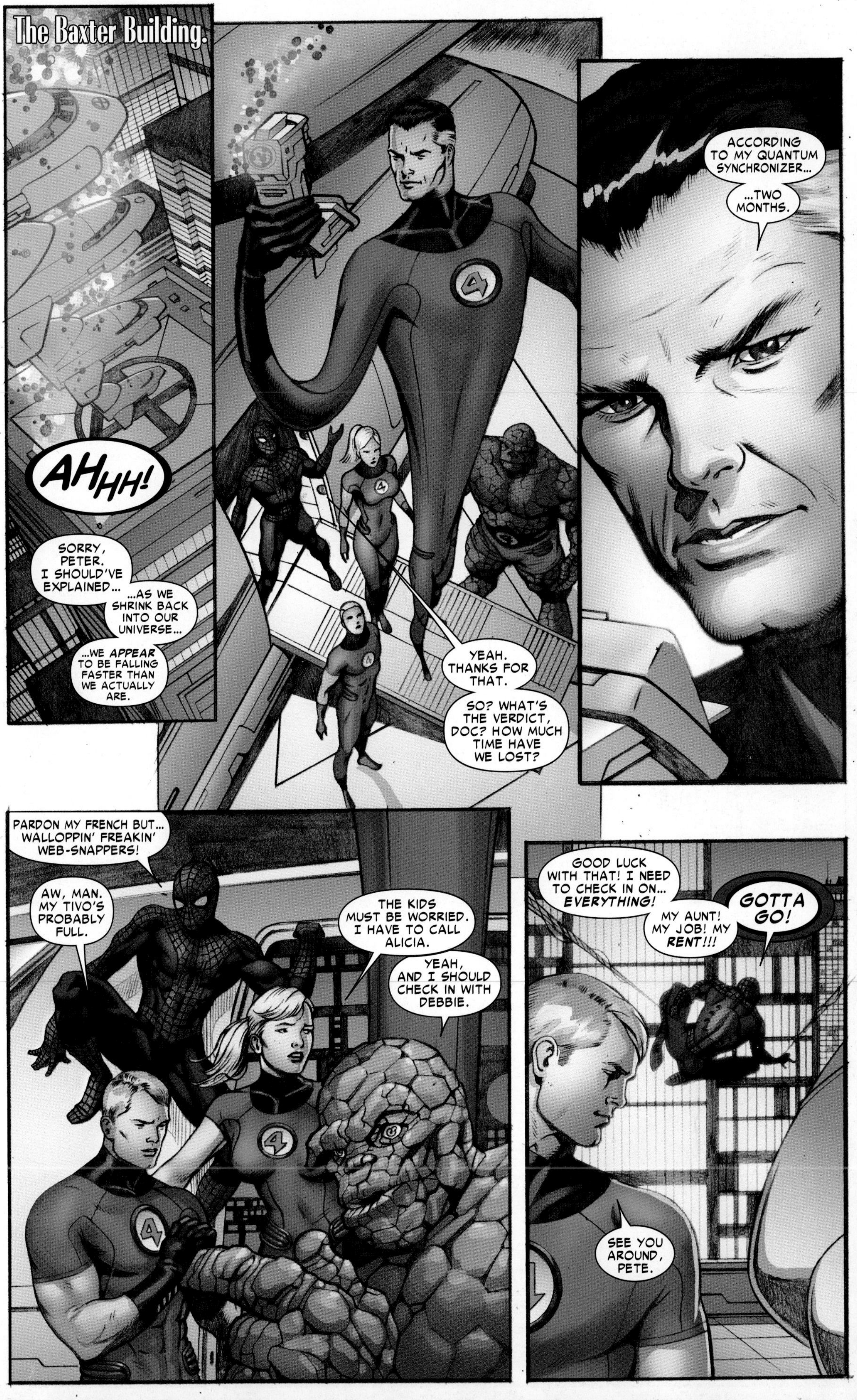
The Baxter Building.
AHHH!
SORRY, PETER. I SHOULD'VE EXPLAINED...
...AS WE SHRINK BACK INTO OUR UNIVERSE...
...WE *APPEAR* TO BE FALLING FASTER THAN WE ACTUALLY ARE.
YEAH. THANKS FOR THAT.
SO? WHAT'S THE VERDICT, DOC? HOW MUCH TIME HAVE WE LOST?
ACCORDING TO MY QUANTUM SYNCHRONIZER...
...TWO MONTHS.
PARDON MY FRENCH BUT... WALLOPPIN' FREAKIN' WEB-SNAPPERS!
AW, MAN. MY TIVO'S PROBABLY FULL.
THE KIDS MUST BE WORRIED. I HAVE TO CALL ALICIA.
YEAH, AND I SHOULD CHECK IN WITH DEBBIE.
GOOD LUCK WITH THAT! I NEED TO CHECK IN ON... *EVERYTHING!*
MY AUNT! MY JOB! MY *RENT!!!*
GOTTA GO!
SEE YOU AROUND, PETE.

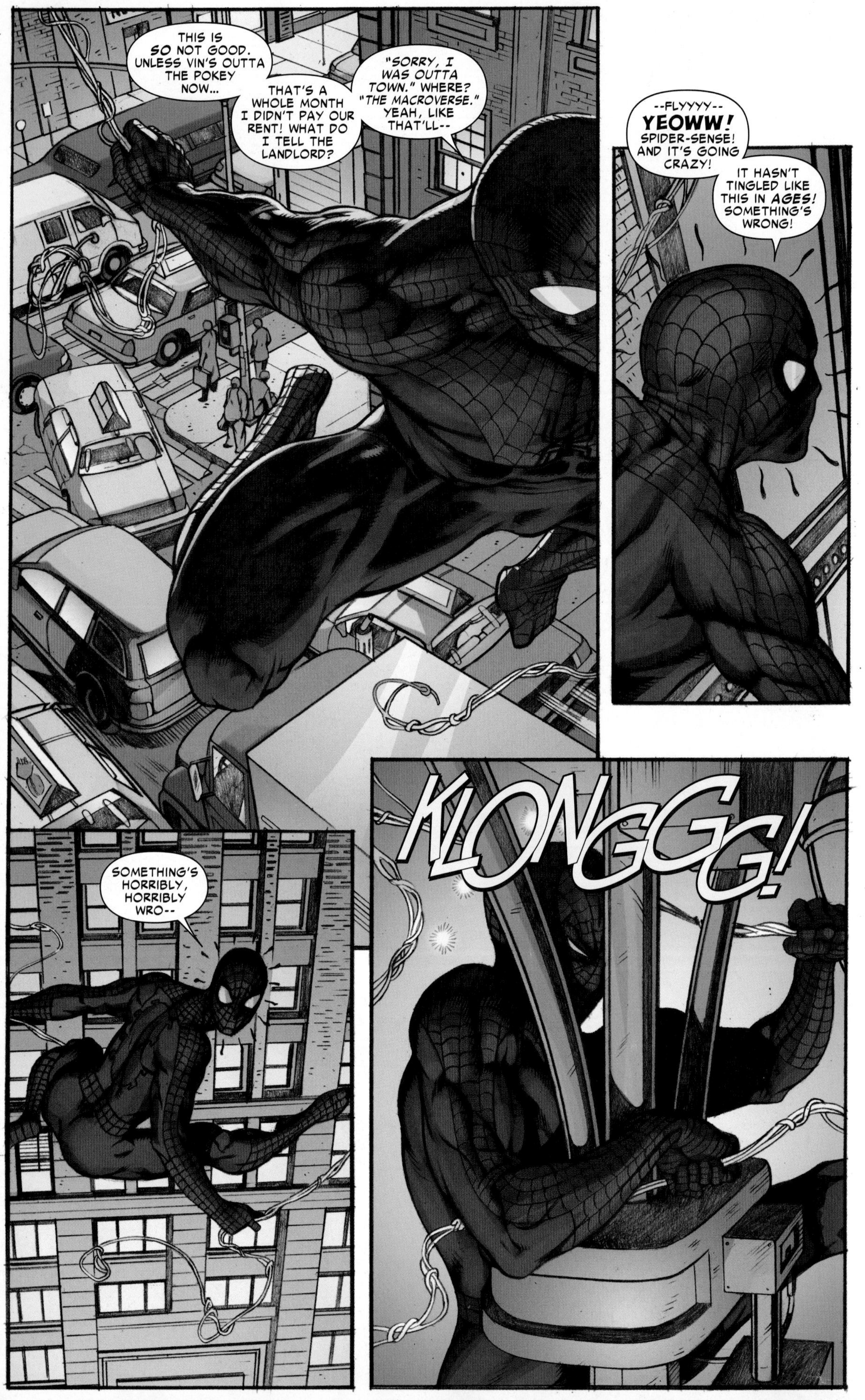
THIS IS SO NOT GOOD. UNLESS VIN'S OUTTA THE POKEY NOW...
THAT'S A WHOLE MONTH I DIDN'T PAY OUR RENT! WHAT DO I TELL THE LANDLORD?
"SORRY, I WAS OUTTA TOWN." WHERE? "THE MACROVERSE." YEAH, LIKE THAT'LL--
--FLYYYY--
YEOWW! SPIDER-SENSE! AND IT'S GOING CRAZY!
IT HASN'T TINGLED LIKE THIS IN AGES! SOMETHING'S WRONG!
SOMETHING'S HORRIBLY, HORRIBLY WRO--
KLONGGG!

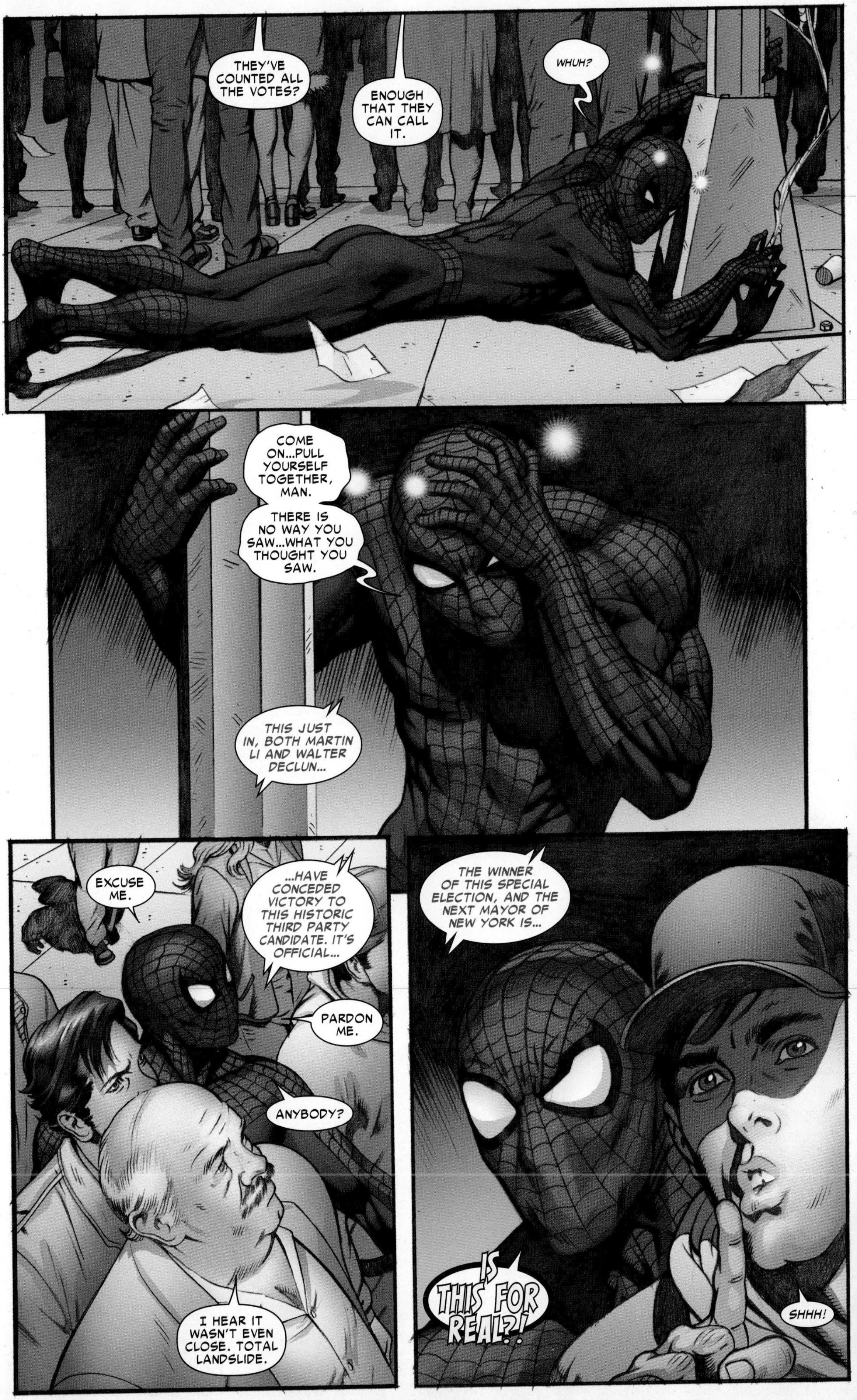
THEY'VE COUNTED ALL THE VOTES?
ENOUGH THAT THEY CAN CALL IT.
WHUH?
COME ON...PULL YOURSELF TOGETHER, MAN.
THERE IS NO WAY YOU SAW...WHAT YOU THOUGHT YOU SAW.
THIS JUST IN, BOTH MARTIN LI AND WALTER DECLUN...
EXCUSE ME.
...HAVE CONCEDED VICTORY TO THIS HISTORIC THIRD PARTY CANDIDATE. IT'S OFFICIAL...
PARDON ME.
ANYBODY?
I HEAR IT WASN'T EVEN CLOSE. TOTAL LANDSLIDE.
THE WINNER OF THIS SPECIAL ELECTION, AND THE NEXT MAYOR OF NEW YORK IS...
IS THIS FOR REAL?!
SHHH!

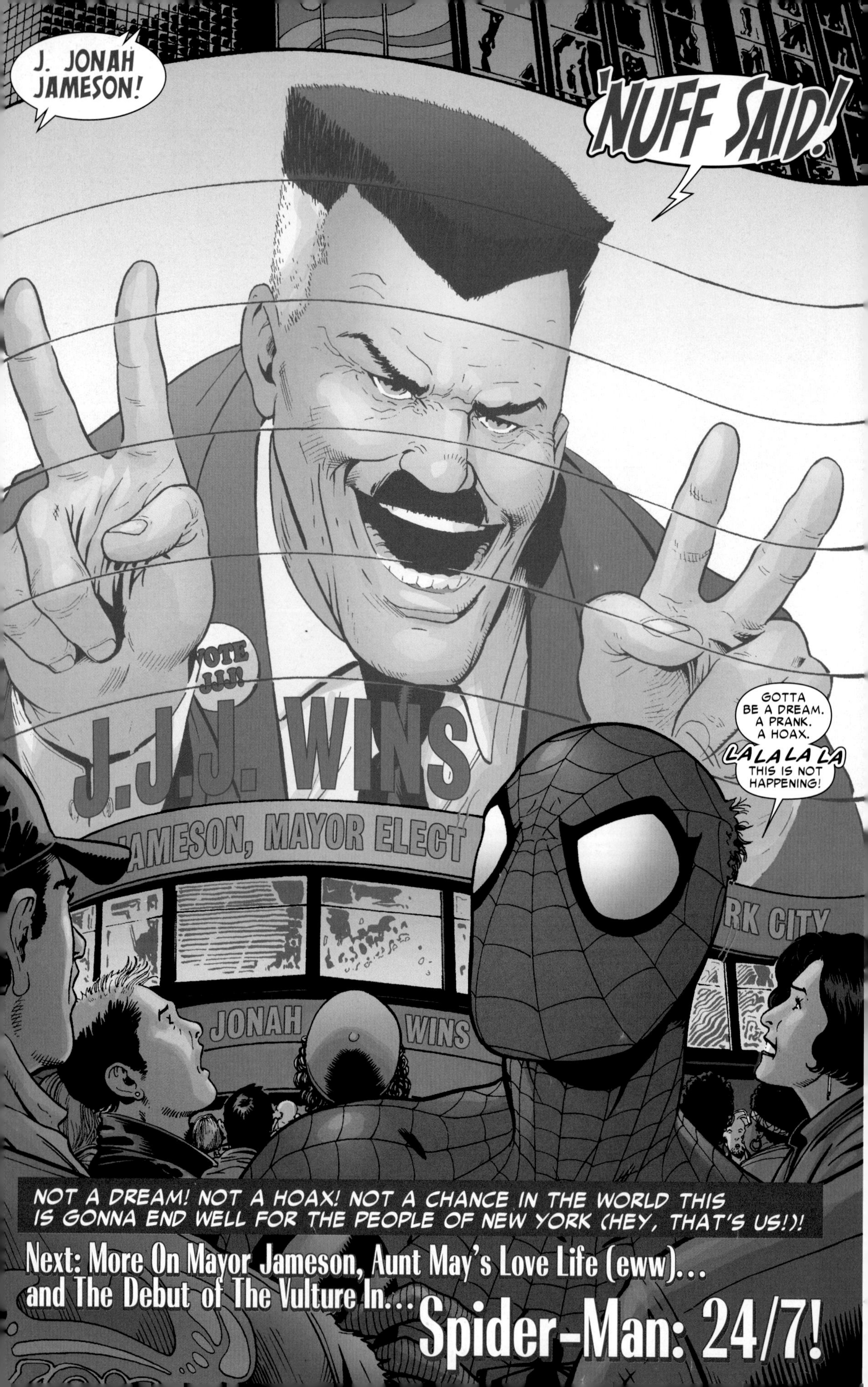
J. JONAH JAMESON!
'NUFF SAID!
VOTE J.J.J.!
J.J.J. WINS
JAMESON, MAYOR ELECT
RK CITY
JONAH WINS
GOTTA BE A DREAM. A PRANK. A HOAX. LA LA LA LA THIS IS NOT HAPPENING!
NOT A DREAM! NOT A HOAX! NOT A CHANCE IN THE WORLD THIS IS GONNA END WELL FOR THE PEOPLE OF NEW YORK (HEY, THAT'S US!)!
Next: More On Mayor Jameson, Aunt May's Love Life (eww)... and The Debut of The Vulture In... Spider-Man: 24/7!

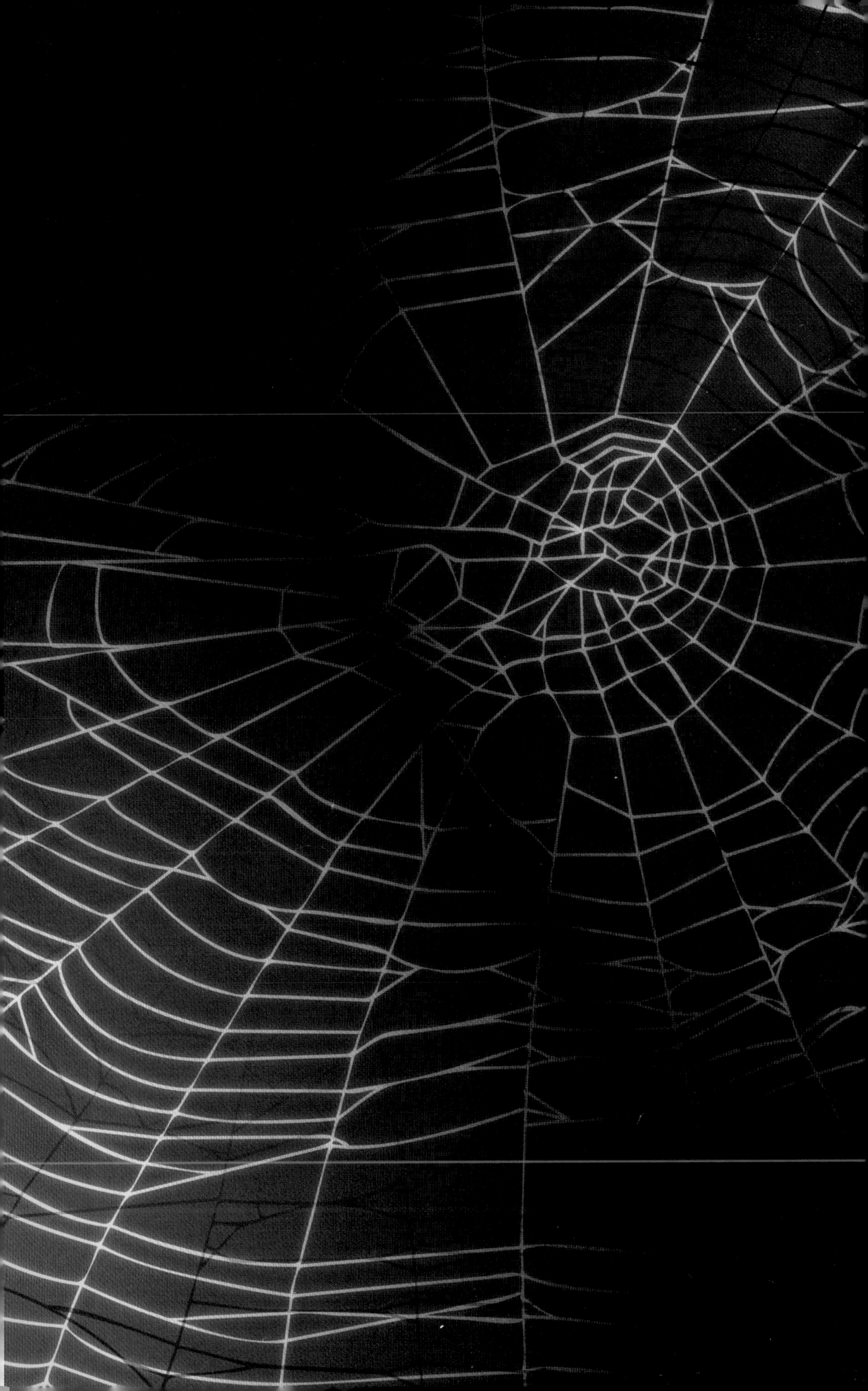

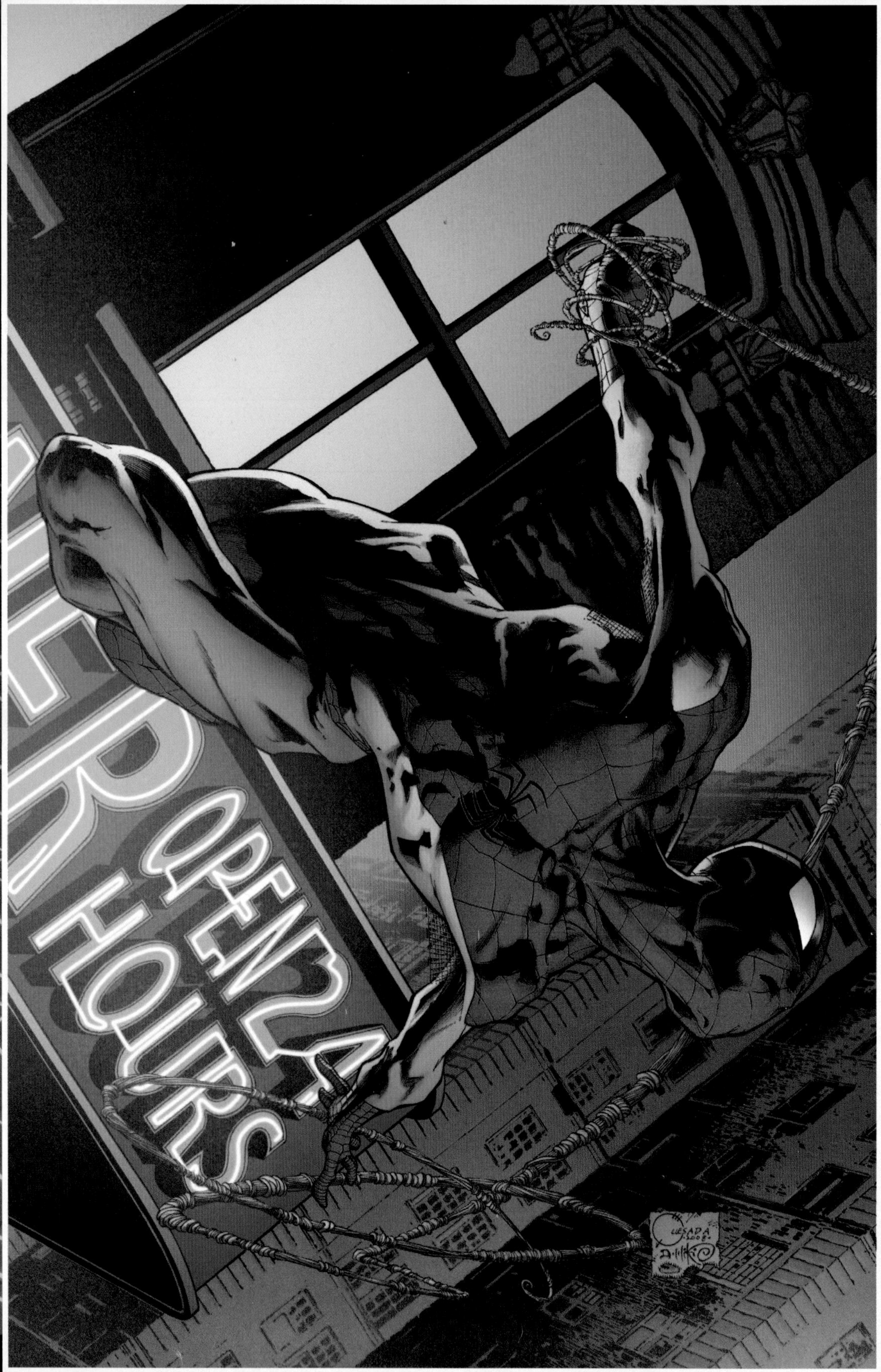
OPEN 24 HOURS

AMAZING SPIDER-MAN #592

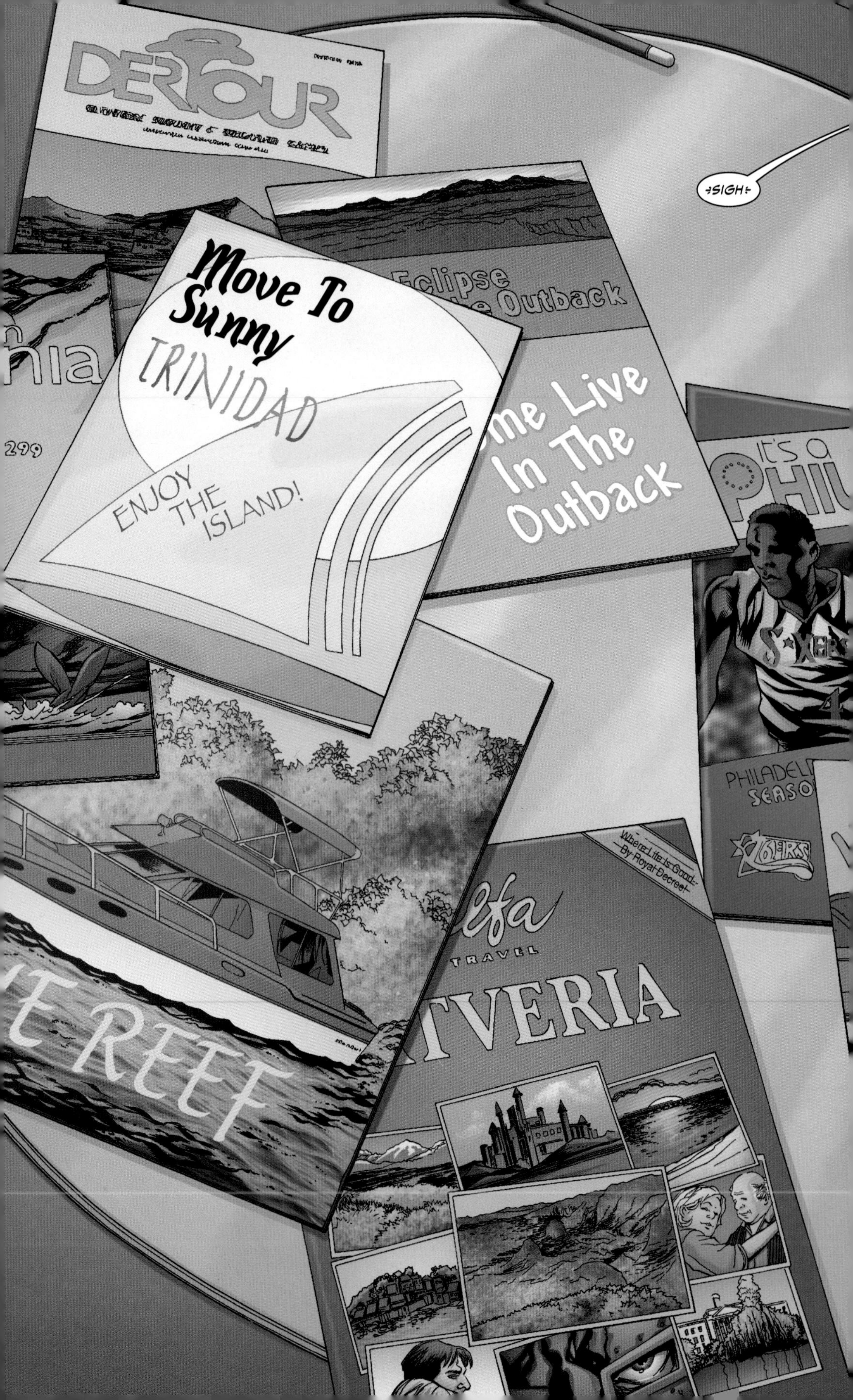

DETOUR
Move To Sunny
TRINIDAD
ENJOY THE ISLAND!
Eclipse
e Outback
me Live In The Outback
It's a
PHI
299
PHILADEL
SEASO
76ERS
Where Life Is Good-
By Royal Decree!
TRAVEL
TVERIA
E REEF
SIGH

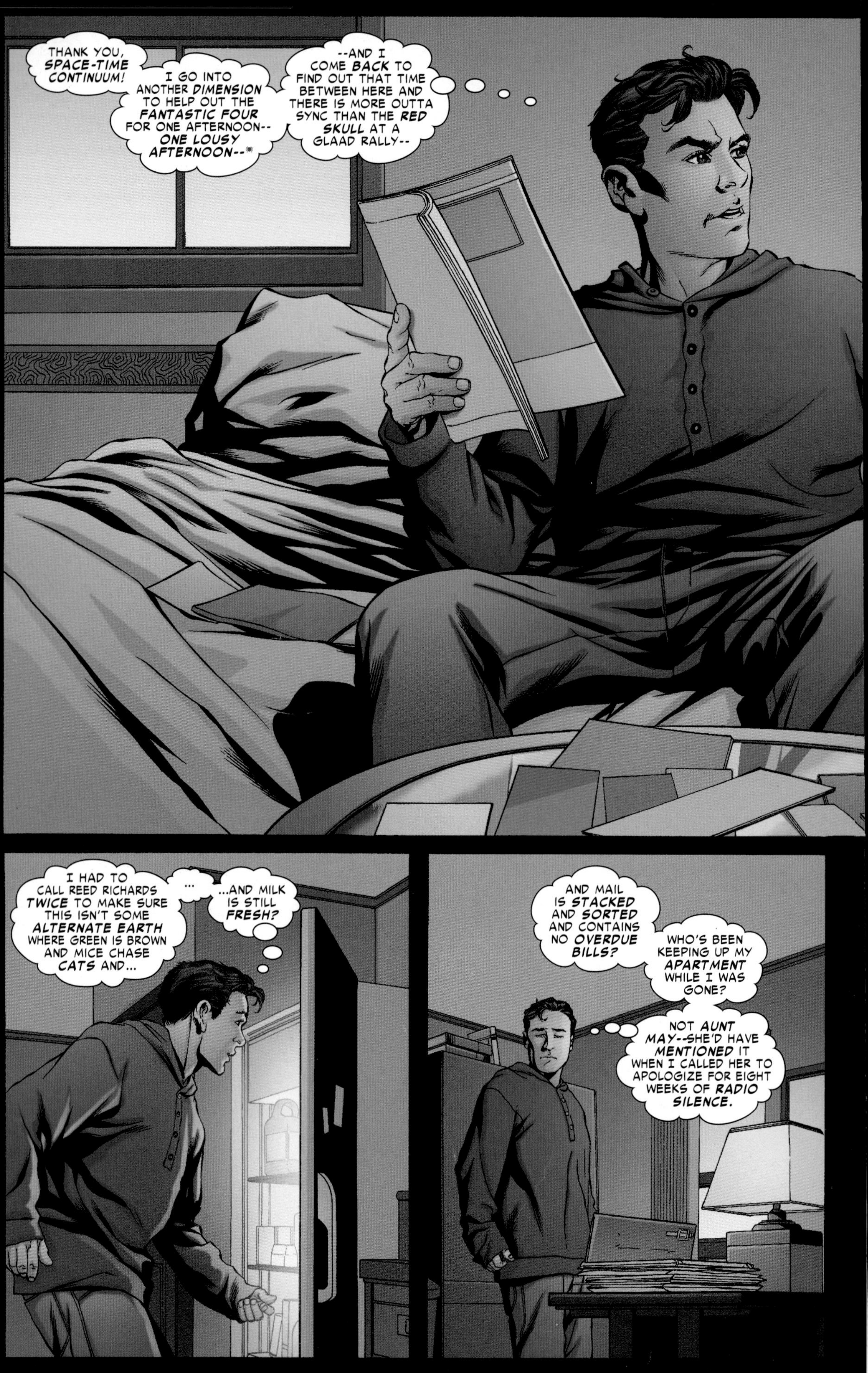
THANK YOU, SPACE-TIME CONTINUUM!
I GO INTO ANOTHER DIMENSION TO HELP OUT THE FANTASTIC FOUR FOR ONE AFTERNOON-- ONE LOUSY AFTERNOON--
--AND I COME BACK TO FIND OUT THAT TIME BETWEEN HERE AND THERE IS MORE OUTTA SYNC THAN THE RED SKULL AT A GLAAD RALLY--
I HAD TO CALL REED RICHARDS TWICE TO MAKE SURE THIS ISN'T SOME ALTERNATE EARTH WHERE GREEN IS BROWN AND MICE CHASE CATS AND...
...
...AND MILK IS STILL FRESH?
AND MAIL IS STACKED AND SORTED AND CONTAINS NO OVERDUE BILLS?
WHO'S BEEN KEEPING UP MY APARTMENT WHILE I WAS GONE?
NOT AUNT MAY--SHE'D HAVE MENTIONED IT WHEN I CALLED HER TO APOLOGIZE FOR EIGHT WEEKS OF RADIO SILENCE.

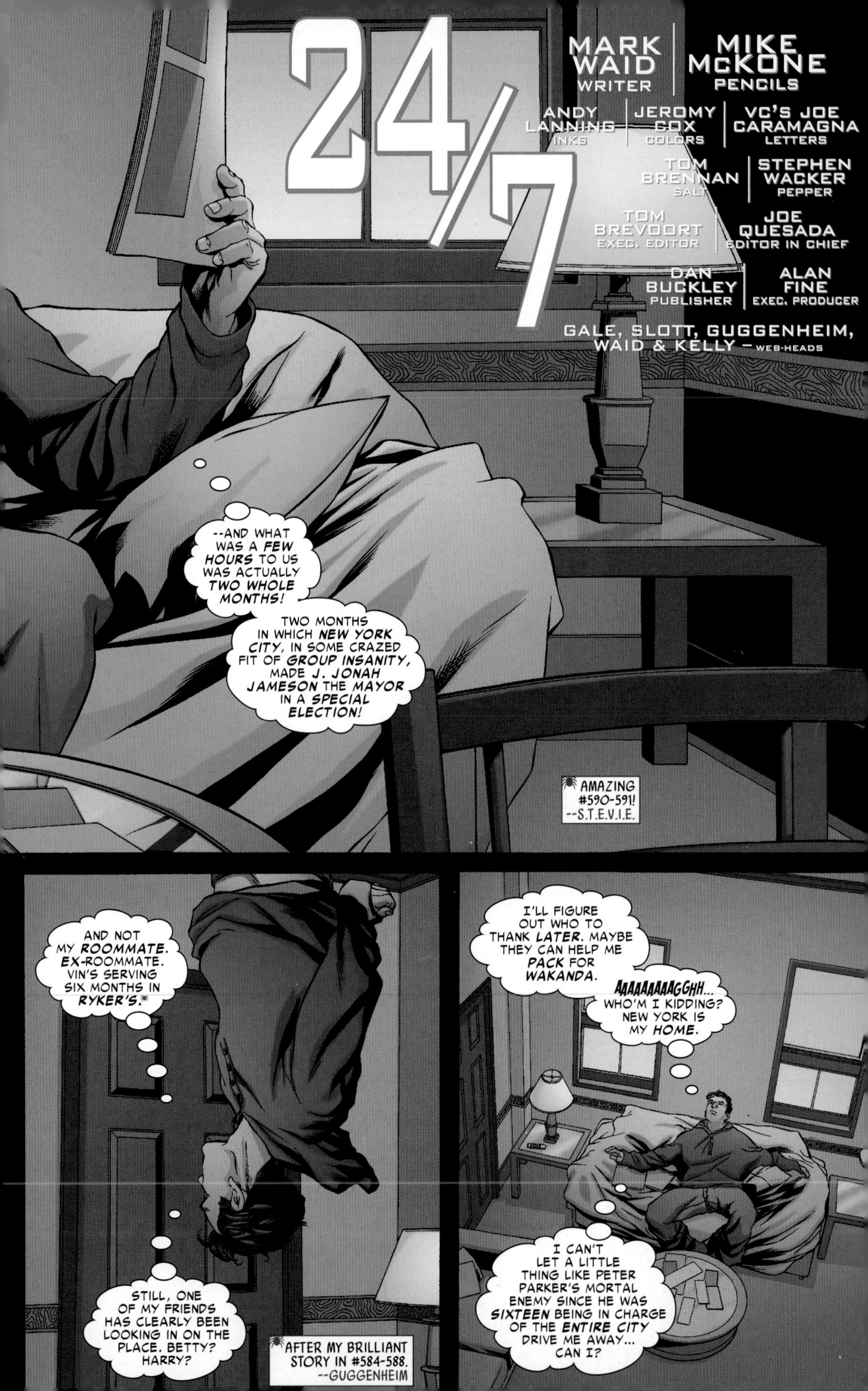
24/7
MARK WAID WRITER
MIKE McKONE PENCILS
ANDY LANNING INKS
JEROMY COX COLORS
VC'S JOE CARAMAGNA LETTERS
TOM BRENNAN SALT
STEPHEN WACKER PEPPER
TOM BREVOORT EXEC. EDITOR
JOE QUESADA EDITOR IN CHIEF
DAN BUCKLEY PUBLISHER
ALAN FINE EXEC. PRODUCER
GALE, SLOTT, GUGGENHEIM, WAID & KELLY – WEB-HEADS
--AND WHAT WAS A FEW HOURS TO US WAS ACTUALLY TWO WHOLE MONTHS!
TWO MONTHS IN WHICH NEW YORK CITY, IN SOME CRAZED FIT OF GROUP INSANITY, MADE J. JONAH JAMESON THE MAYOR IN A SPECIAL ELECTION!
AMAZING #590-591! --S.T.E.V.I.E.
AND NOT MY ROOMMATE. EX-ROOMMATE. VIN'S SERVING SIX MONTHS IN RYKER'S.*
STILL, ONE OF MY FRIENDS HAS CLEARLY BEEN LOOKING IN ON THE PLACE. BETTY? HARRY?
*AFTER MY BRILLIANT STORY IN #584-588. --GUGGENHEIM
I'LL FIGURE OUT WHO TO THANK LATER. MAYBE THEY CAN HELP ME PACK FOR WAKANDA.
AAAAAAAAAGGHH... WHO'M I KIDDING? NEW YORK IS MY HOME.
I CAN'T LET A LITTLE THING LIKE PETER PARKER'S MORTAL ENEMY SINCE HE WAS SIXTEEN BEING IN CHARGE OF THE ENTIRE CITY DRIVE ME AWAY... CAN I?

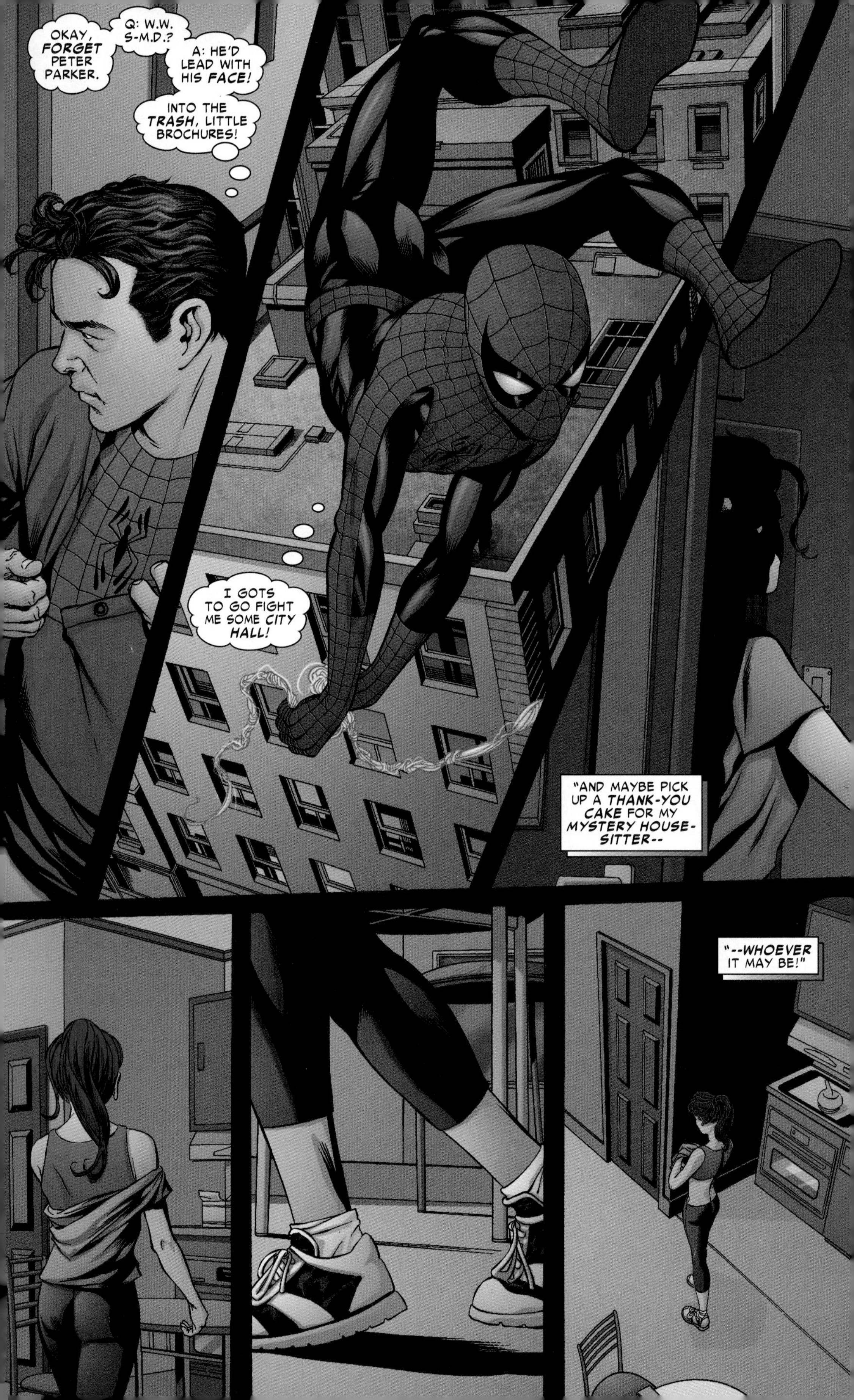
OKAY, FORGET PETER PARKER.
Q: W.W. S-M.D.?
A: HE'D LEAD WITH HIS FACE!
INTO THE TRASH, LITTLE BROCHURES!
I GOTS TO GO FIGHT ME SOME CITY HALL!
"AND MAYBE PICK UP A THANK-YOU CAKE FOR MY MYSTERY HOUSE-SITTER--
"--WHOEVER IT MAY BE!"

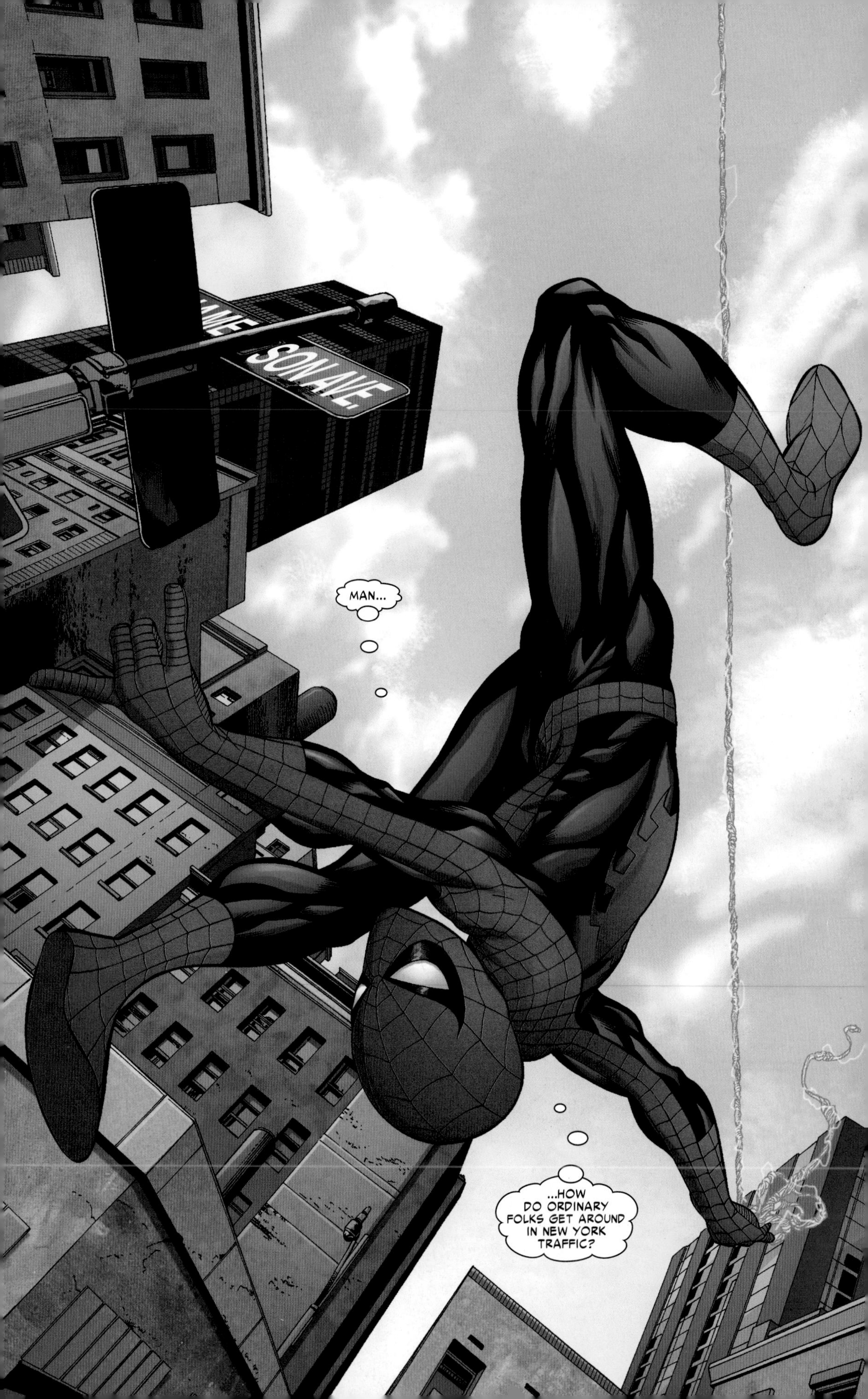
SON AVE.
MAN...
...HOW DO ORDINARY FOLKS GET AROUND IN NEW YORK TRAFFIC?

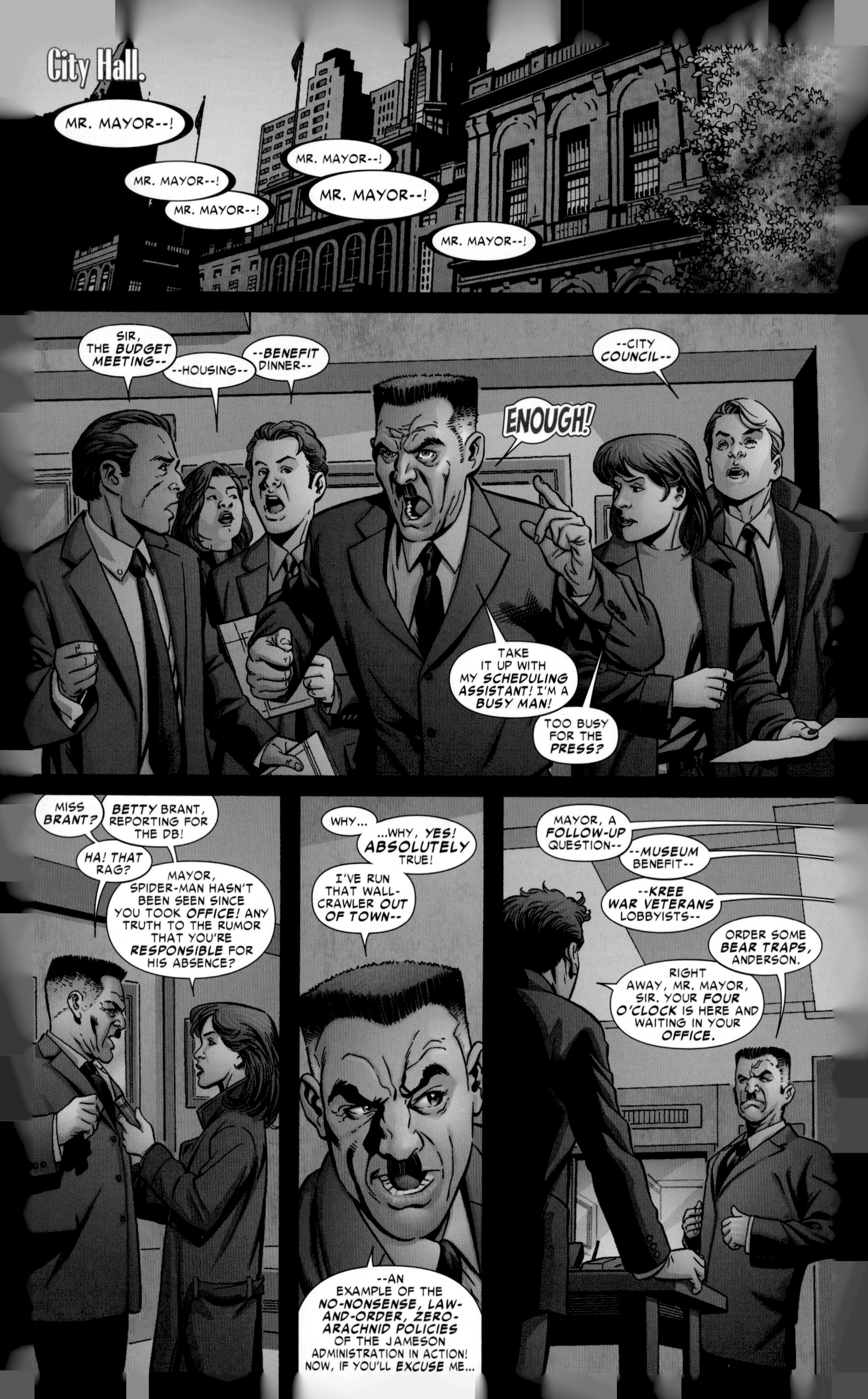
City Hall.
MR. MAYOR--!
MR. MAYOR--!
MR. MAYOR--!
MR. MAYOR--!
MR. MAYOR--!
MR. MAYOR--!
SIR, THE BUDGET MEETING--
--HOUSING--
--BENEFIT DINNER--
--CITY COUNCIL--
ENOUGH!
TAKE IT UP WITH MY SCHEDULING ASSISTANT! I'M A BUSY MAN!
TOO BUSY FOR THE PRESS?
MISS BRANT?
BETTY BRANT, REPORTING FOR THE DB!
HA! THAT RAG?
MAYOR, SPIDER-MAN HASN'T BEEN SEEN SINCE YOU TOOK OFFICE! ANY TRUTH TO THE RUMOR THAT YOU'RE RESPONSIBLE FOR HIS ABSENCE?
WHY...
...WHY, YES! ABSOLUTELY TRUE!
I'VE RUN THAT WALL-CRAWLER OUT OF TOWN--
--AN EXAMPLE OF THE NO-NONSENSE, LAW-AND-ORDER, ZERO-ARACHNID POLICIES OF THE JAMESON ADMINISTRATION IN ACTION! NOW, IF YOU'LL EXCUSE ME...
MAYOR, A FOLLOW-UP QUESTION--
--MUSEUM BENEFIT--
--KREE WAR VETERANS LOBBYISTS--
ORDER SOME BEAR TRAPS, ANDERSON.
RIGHT AWAY, MR. MAYOR, SIR. YOUR FOUR O'CLOCK IS HERE AND WAITING IN YOUR OFFICE.

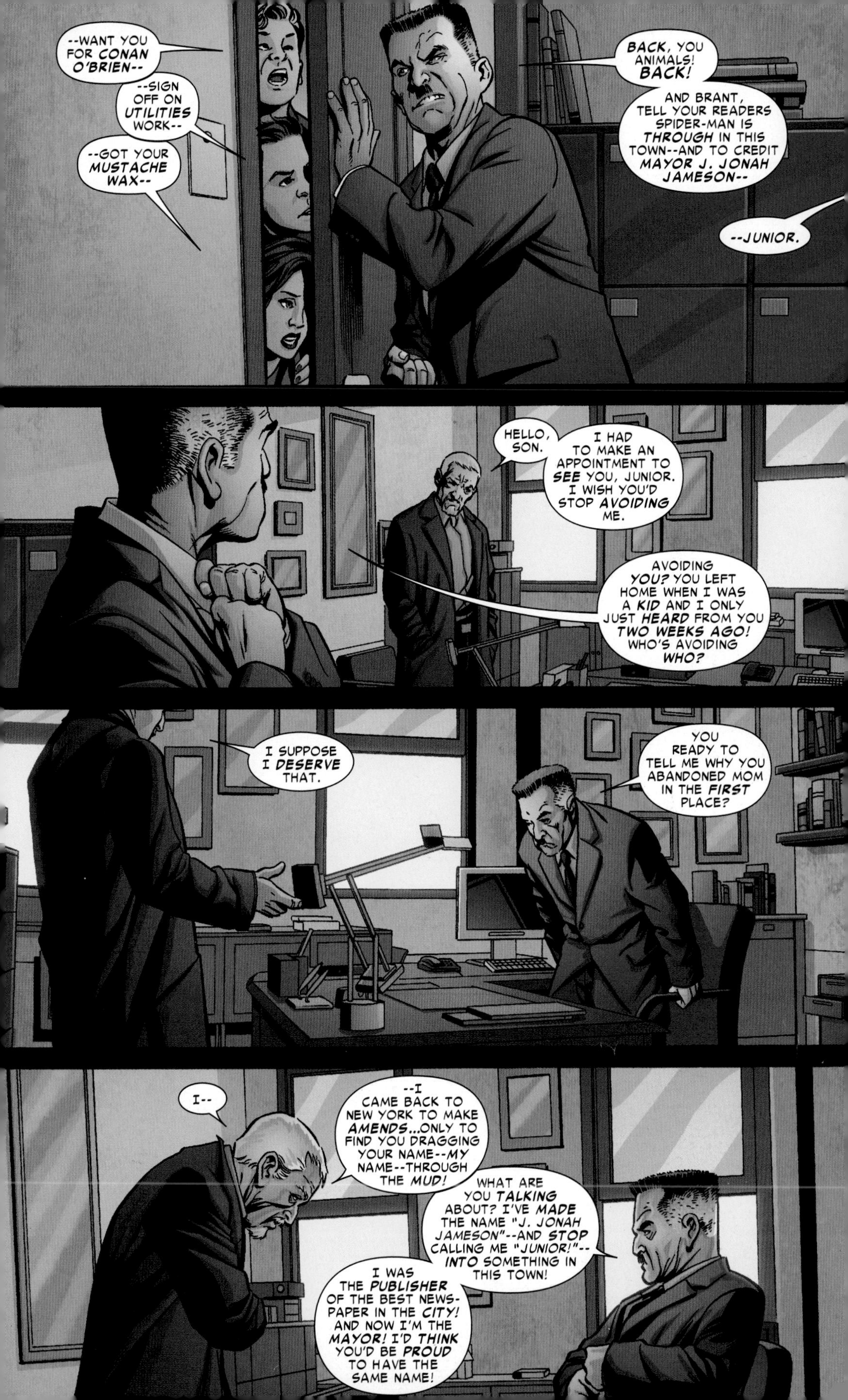
--WANT YOU FOR CONAN O'BRIEN--
--SIGN OFF ON UTILITIES WORK--
--GOT YOUR MUSTACHE WAX--
BACK, YOU ANIMALS! BACK!
AND BRANT, TELL YOUR READERS SPIDER-MAN IS THROUGH IN THIS TOWN--AND TO CREDIT MAYOR J. JONAH JAMESON--
--JUNIOR.
HELLO, SON.
I HAD TO MAKE AN APPOINTMENT TO SEE YOU, JUNIOR. I WISH YOU'D STOP AVOIDING ME.
AVOIDING YOU? YOU LEFT HOME WHEN I WAS A KID AND I ONLY JUST HEARD FROM YOU TWO WEEKS AGO! WHO'S AVOIDING WHO?
I SUPPOSE I DESERVE THAT.
YOU READY TO TELL ME WHY YOU ABANDONED MOM IN THE FIRST PLACE?
I--
--I CAME BACK TO NEW YORK TO MAKE AMENDS...ONLY TO FIND YOU DRAGGING YOUR NAME--MY NAME--THROUGH THE MUD!
WHAT ARE YOU TALKING ABOUT? I'VE MADE THE NAME "J. JONAH JAMESON"--AND STOP CALLING ME "JUNIOR!"--INTO SOMETHING IN THIS TOWN!
I WAS THE PUBLISHER OF THE BEST NEWS-PAPER IN THE CITY! AND NOW I'M THE MAYOR! I'D THINK YOU'D BE PROUD TO HAVE THE SAME NAME!

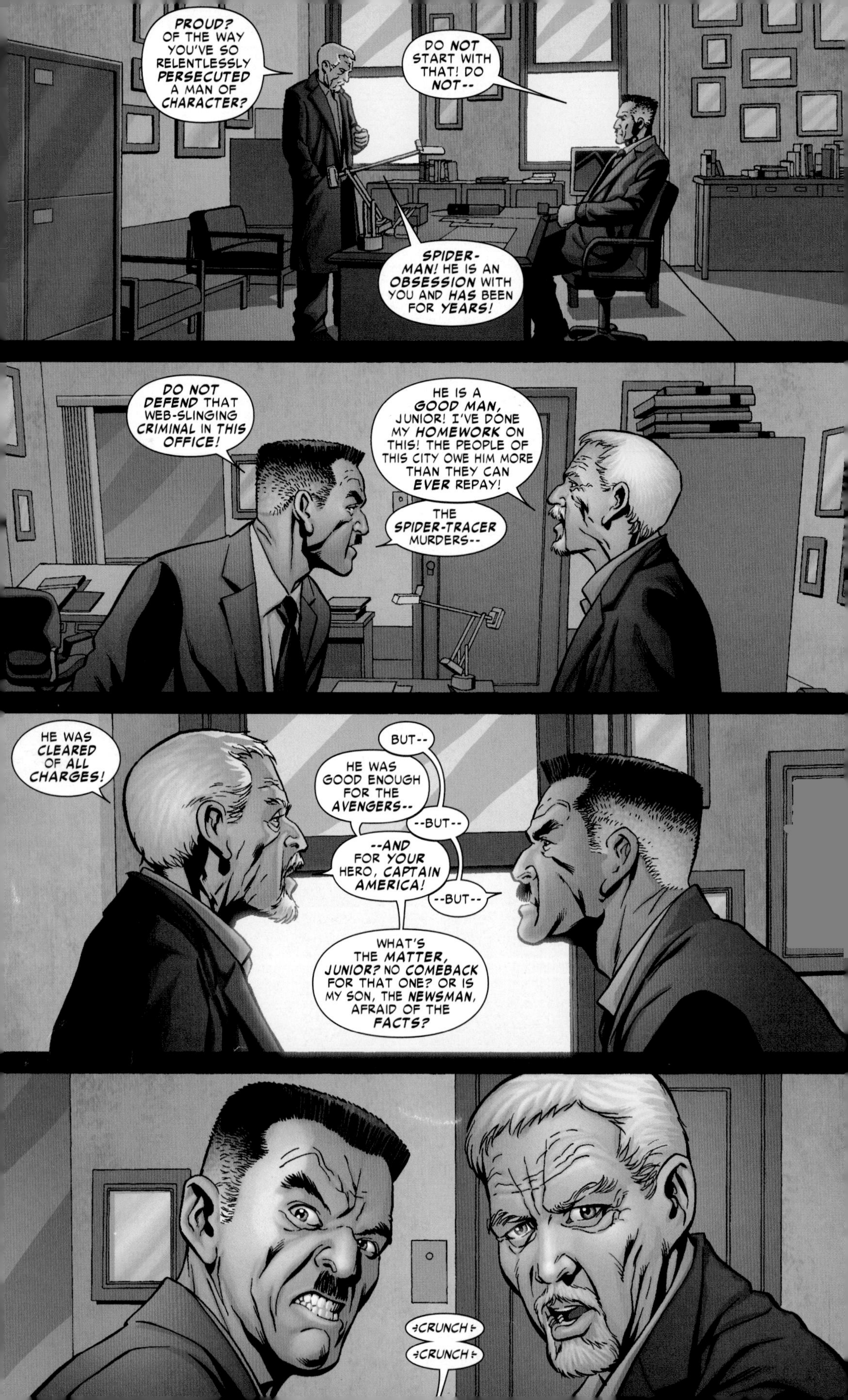
PROUD? OF THE WAY YOU'VE SO RELENTLESSLY PERSECUTED A MAN OF CHARACTER?
DO NOT START WITH THAT! DO NOT--
SPIDER-MAN! HE IS AN OBSESSION WITH YOU AND HAS BEEN FOR YEARS!
DO NOT DEFEND THAT WEB-SLINGING CRIMINAL IN THIS OFFICE!
HE IS A GOOD MAN, JUNIOR! I'VE DONE MY HOMEWORK ON THIS! THE PEOPLE OF THIS CITY OWE HIM MORE THAN THEY CAN EVER REPAY!
THE SPIDER-TRACER MURDERS--
HE WAS CLEARED OF ALL CHARGES!
BUT--
HE WAS GOOD ENOUGH FOR THE AVENGERS--
--BUT--
--AND FOR YOUR HERO, CAPTAIN AMERICA!
--BUT--
WHAT'S THE MATTER, JUNIOR? NO COMEBACK FOR THAT ONE? OR IS MY SON, THE NEWSMAN, AFRAID OF THE FACTS?
CRUNCH
CRUNCH

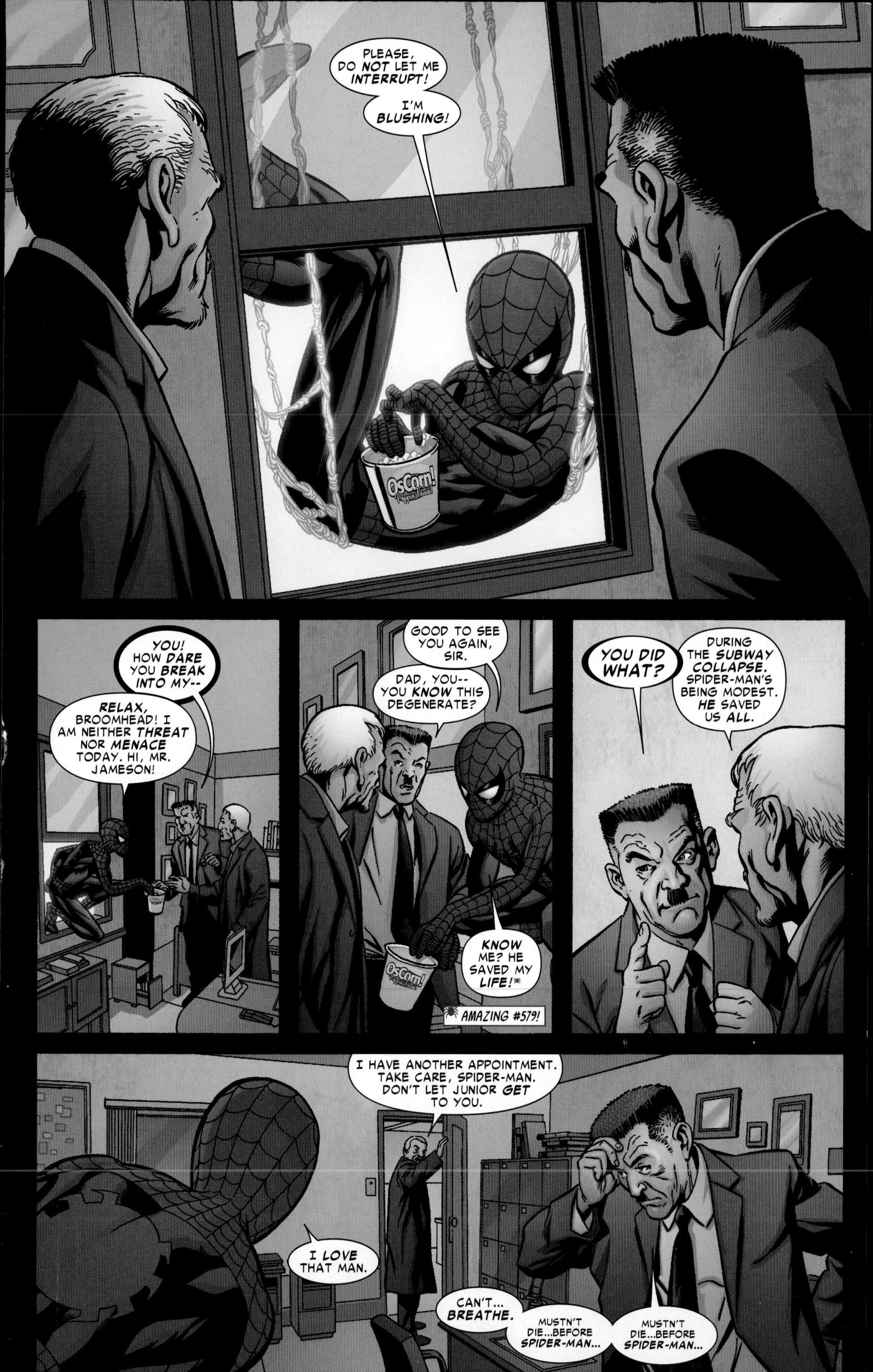
PLEASE, DO NOT LET ME INTERRUPT!
I'M BLUSHING!
YOU! HOW DARE YOU BREAK INTO MY--
RELAX, BROOMHEAD! I AM NEITHER THREAT NOR MENACE TODAY. HI, MR. JAMESON!
GOOD TO SEE YOU AGAIN, SIR.
DAD, YOU-- YOU KNOW THIS DEGENERATE?
KNOW ME? HE SAVED MY LIFE!
AMAZING #579!
YOU DID WHAT?
DURING THE SUBWAY COLLAPSE. SPIDER-MAN'S BEING MODEST. HE SAVED US ALL.
I HAVE ANOTHER APPOINTMENT. TAKE CARE, SPIDER-MAN. DON'T LET JUNIOR GET TO YOU.
I LOVE THAT MAN.
CAN'T... BREATHE.
MUSTN'T DIE...BEFORE SPIDER-MAN...
MUSTN'T DIE...BEFORE SPIDER-MAN...

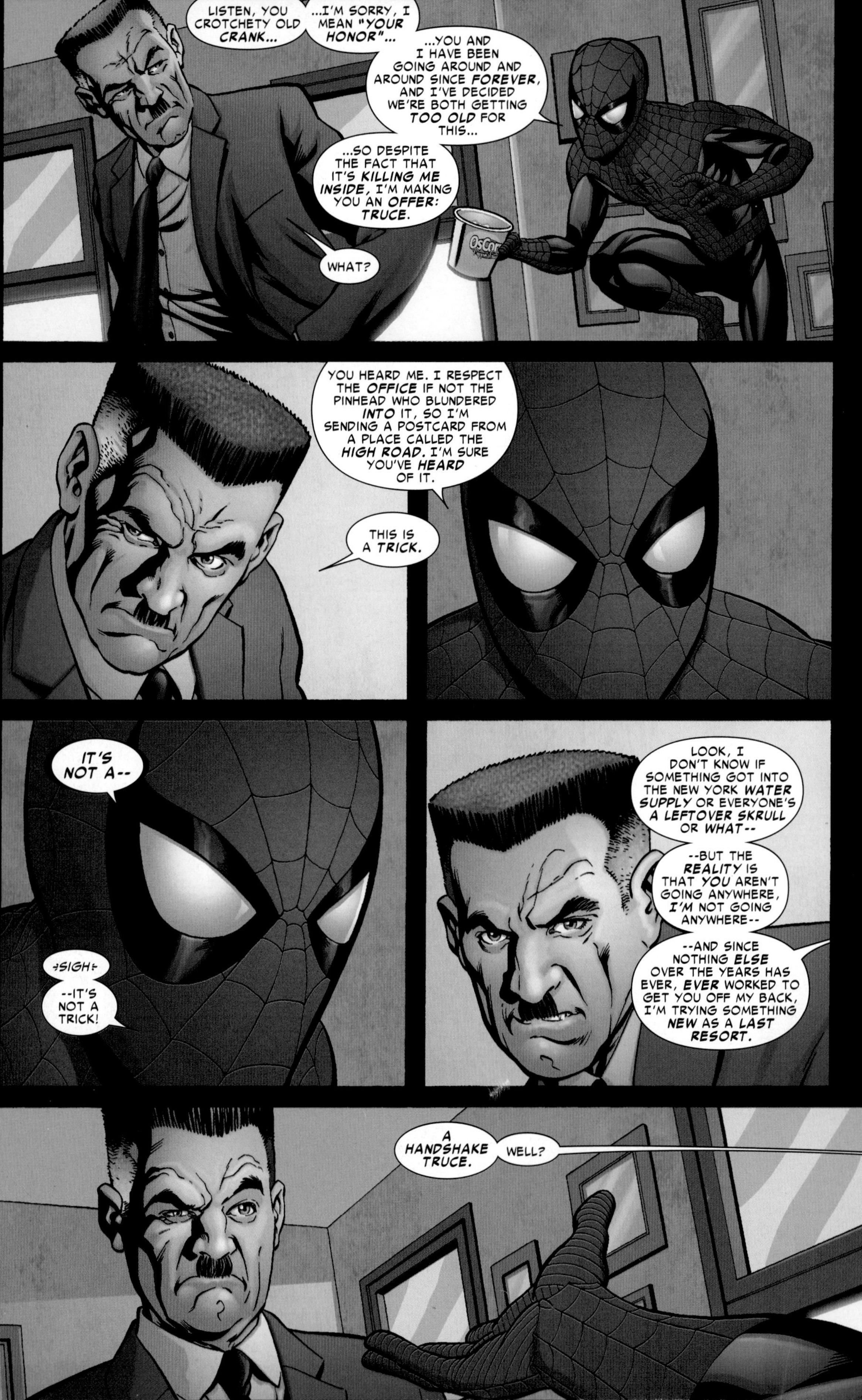
LISTEN, YOU CROTCHETY OLD CRANK...
...I'M SORRY, I MEAN "YOUR HONOR"...
...YOU AND I HAVE BEEN GOING AROUND AND AROUND SINCE FOREVER, AND I'VE DECIDED WE'RE BOTH GETTING TOO OLD FOR THIS...
...SO DESPITE THE FACT THAT IT'S KILLING ME INSIDE, I'M MAKING YOU AN OFFER: TRUCE.
WHAT?
YOU HEARD ME. I RESPECT THE OFFICE IF NOT THE PINHEAD WHO BLUNDERED INTO IT, SO I'M SENDING A POSTCARD FROM A PLACE CALLED THE HIGH ROAD. I'M SURE YOU'VE HEARD OF IT.
THIS IS A TRICK.
IT'S NOT A--
SIGH
--IT'S NOT A TRICK!
LOOK, I DON'T KNOW IF SOMETHING GOT INTO THE NEW YORK WATER SUPPLY OR EVERYONE'S A LEFTOVER SKRULL OR WHAT--
--BUT THE REALITY IS THAT YOU AREN'T GOING ANYWHERE, I'M NOT GOING ANYWHERE--
--AND SINCE NOTHING ELSE OVER THE YEARS HAS EVER, EVER WORKED TO GET YOU OFF MY BACK, I'M TRYING SOMETHING NEW AS A LAST RESORT.
A HANDSHAKE TRUCE.
WELL?

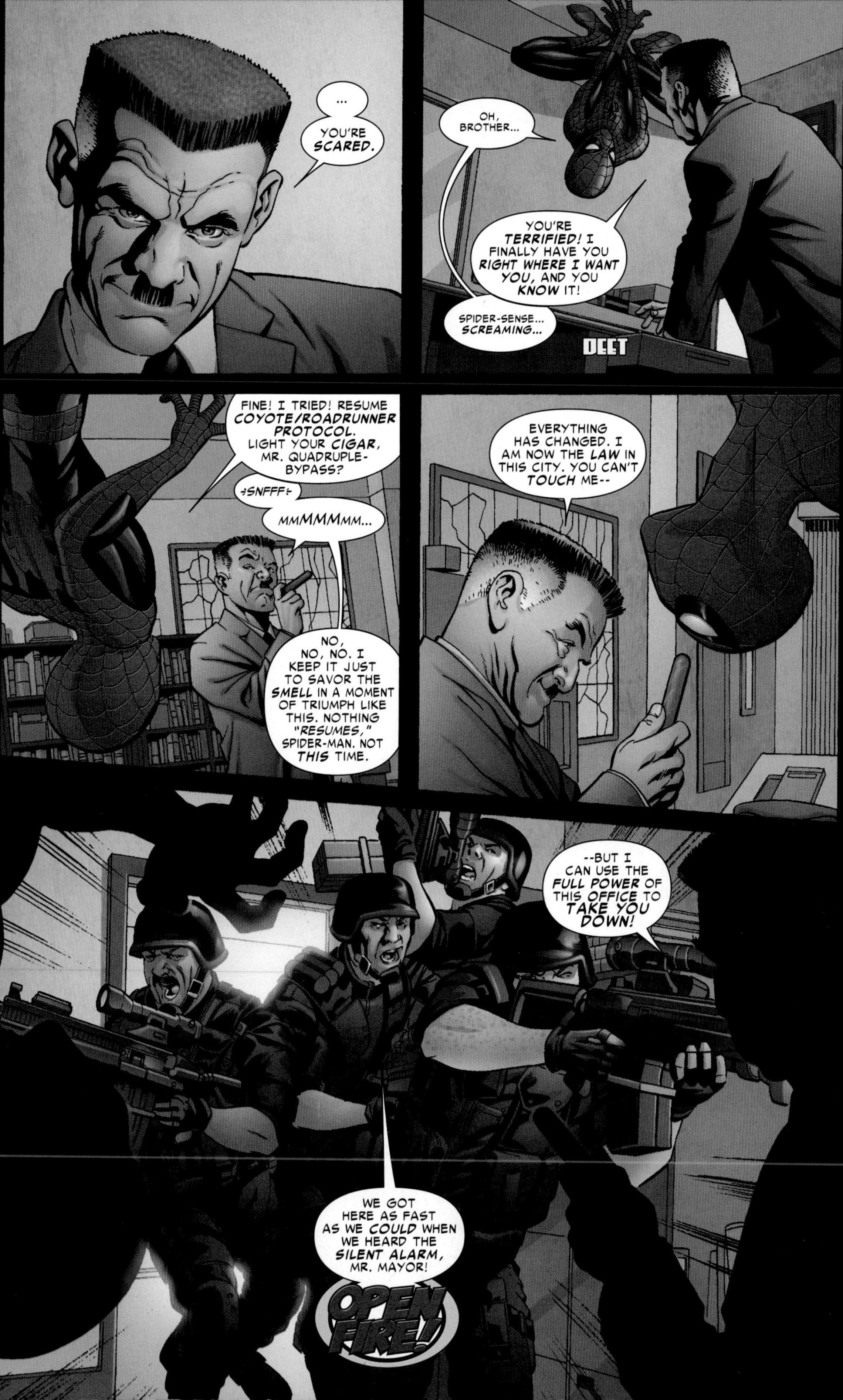
...
YOU'RE SCARED.
OH, BROTHER...
YOU'RE TERRIFIED! I FINALLY HAVE YOU RIGHT WHERE I WANT YOU, AND YOU KNOW IT!
SPIDER-SENSE... SCREAMING...
DEET
FINE! I TRIED! RESUME COYOTE/ROADRUNNER PROTOCOL. LIGHT YOUR CIGAR, MR. QUADRUPLE-BYPASS?
SNFFF
MMMMMMM...
NO, NO, NO. I KEEP IT JUST TO SAVOR THE SMELL IN A MOMENT OF TRIUMPH LIKE THIS. NOTHING "RESUMES," SPIDER-MAN. NOT THIS TIME.
EVERYTHING HAS CHANGED. I AM NOW THE LAW IN THIS CITY. YOU CAN'T TOUCH ME--
--BUT I CAN USE THE FULL POWER OF THIS OFFICE TO TAKE YOU DOWN!
WE GOT HERE AS FAST AS WE COULD WHEN WE HEARD THE SILENT ALARM, MR. MAYOR!
OPEN FIRE!

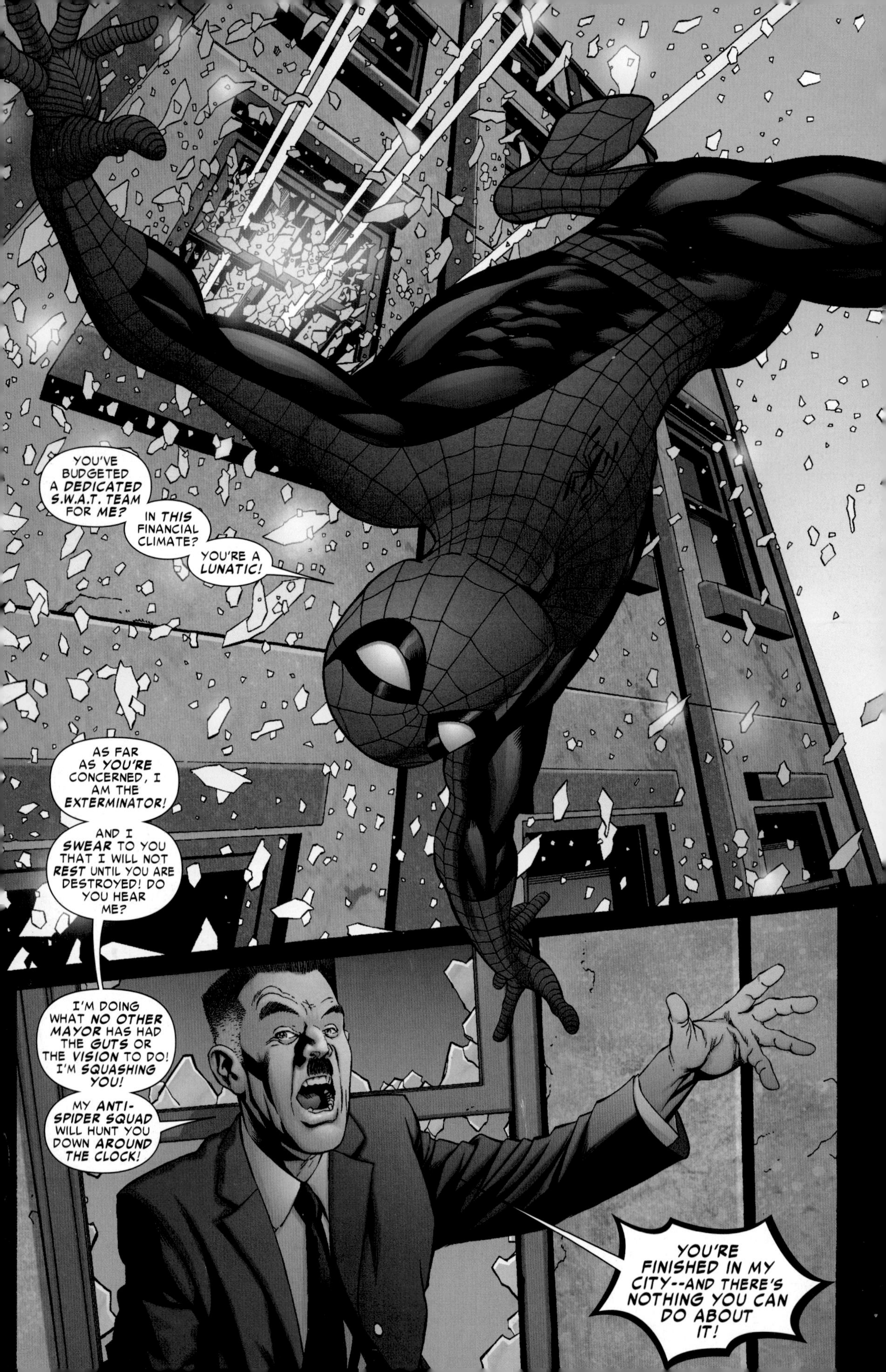
YOU'VE BUDGETED A DEDICATED S.W.A.T. TEAM FOR ME?
IN THIS FINANCIAL CLIMATE?
YOU'RE A LUNATIC!
AS FAR AS YOU'RE CONCERNED, I AM THE EXTERMINATOR!
AND I SWEAR TO YOU THAT I WILL NOT REST UNTIL YOU ARE DESTROYED! DO YOU HEAR ME?
I'M DOING WHAT NO OTHER MAYOR HAS HAD THE GUTS OR THE VISION TO DO! I'M SQUASHING YOU!
MY ANTI-SPIDER SQUAD WILL HUNT YOU DOWN AROUND THE CLOCK!
YOU'RE FINISHED IN MY CITY--AND THERE'S NOTHING YOU CAN DO ABOUT IT!

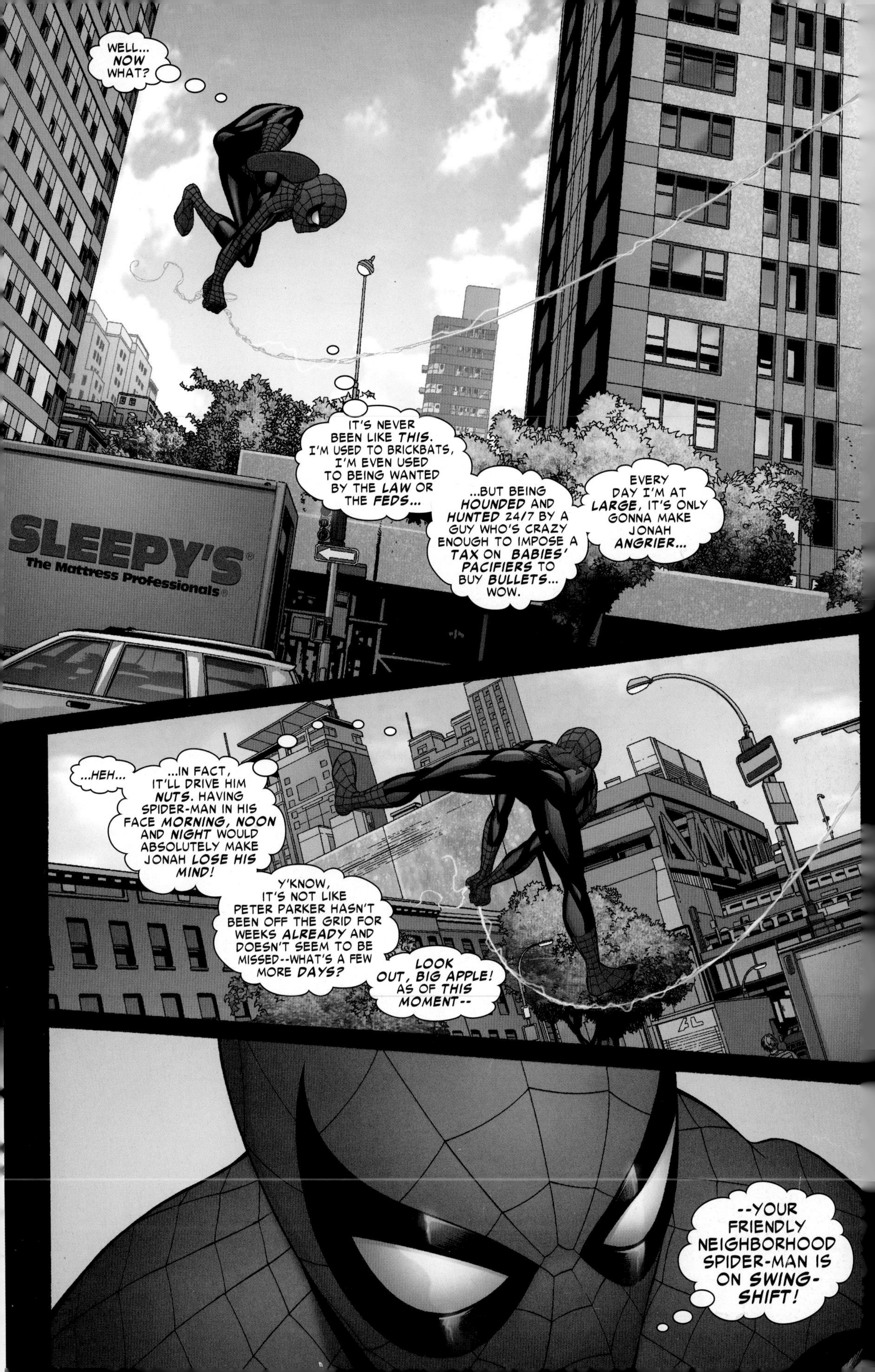
WELL... NOW WHAT?
IT'S NEVER BEEN LIKE THIS. I'M USED TO BRICKBATS, I'M EVEN USED TO BEING WANTED BY THE LAW OR THE FEDS...
...BUT BEING HOUNDED AND HUNTED 24/7 BY A GUY WHO'S CRAZY ENOUGH TO IMPOSE A TAX ON BABIES' PACIFIERS TO BUY BULLETS... WOW.
EVERY DAY I'M AT LARGE, IT'S ONLY GONNA MAKE JONAH ANGRIER...
SLEEPY'S
The Mattress Professionals
...HEH...
...IN FACT, IT'LL DRIVE HIM NUTS. HAVING SPIDER-MAN IN HIS FACE MORNING, NOON AND NIGHT WOULD ABSOLUTELY MAKE JONAH LOSE HIS MIND!
Y'KNOW, IT'S NOT LIKE PETER PARKER HASN'T BEEN OFF THE GRID FOR WEEKS ALREADY AND DOESN'T SEEM TO BE MISSED--WHAT'S A FEW MORE DAYS?
LOOK OUT, BIG APPLE! AS OF THIS MOMENT--
--YOUR FRIENDLY NEIGHBORHOOD SPIDER-MAN IS ON SWING-SHIFT!

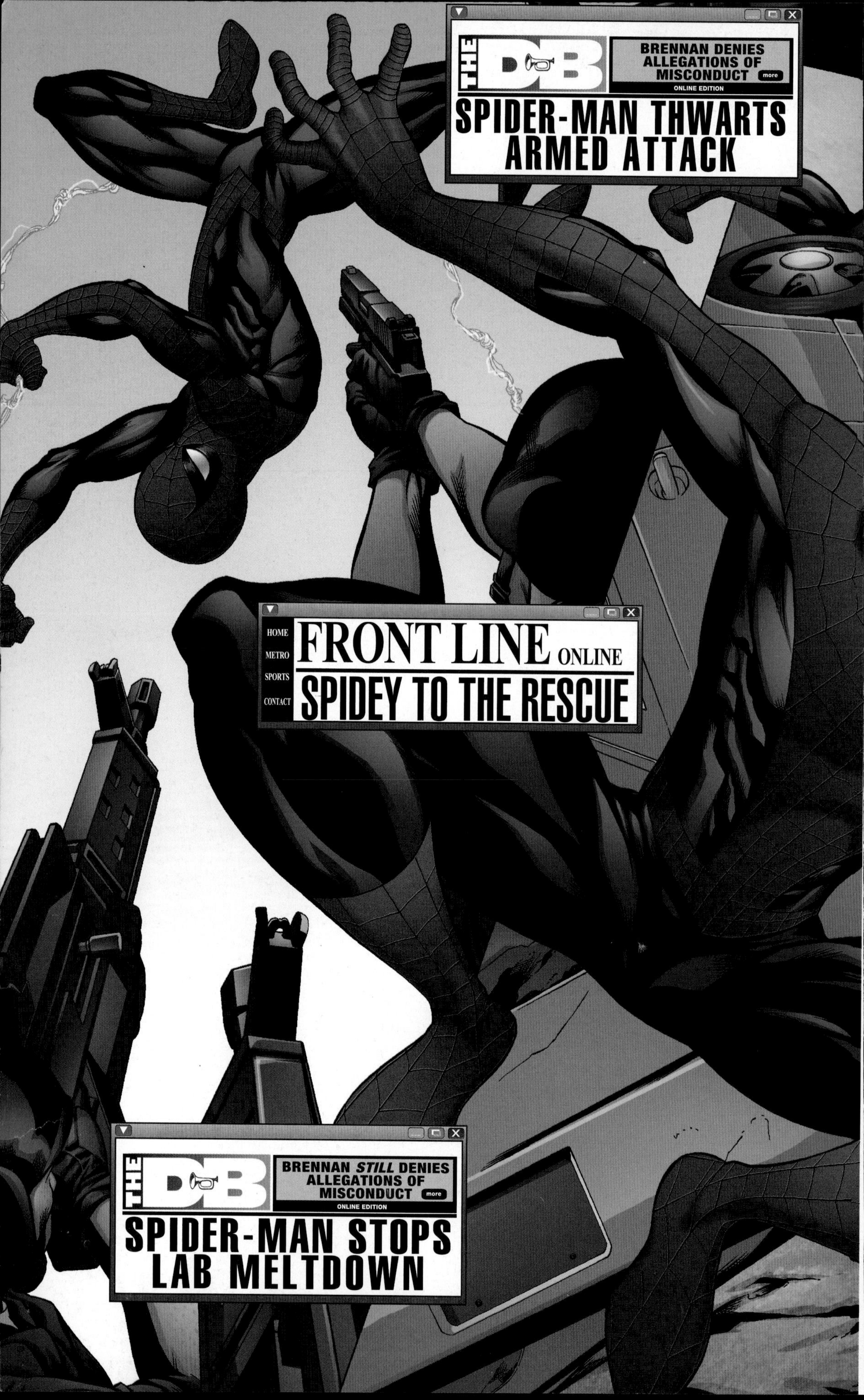
THE DB
BRENNAN DENIES ALLEGATIONS OF MISCONDUCT
more
ONLINE EDITION
SPIDER-MAN THWARTS ARMED ATTACK
HOME
METRO
SPORTS
CONTACT
FRONT LINE ONLINE
SPIDEY TO THE RESCUE
THE DB
BRENNAN STILL DENIES ALLEGATIONS OF MISCONDUCT
more
ONLINE EDITION
SPIDER-MAN STOPS LAB MELTDOWN

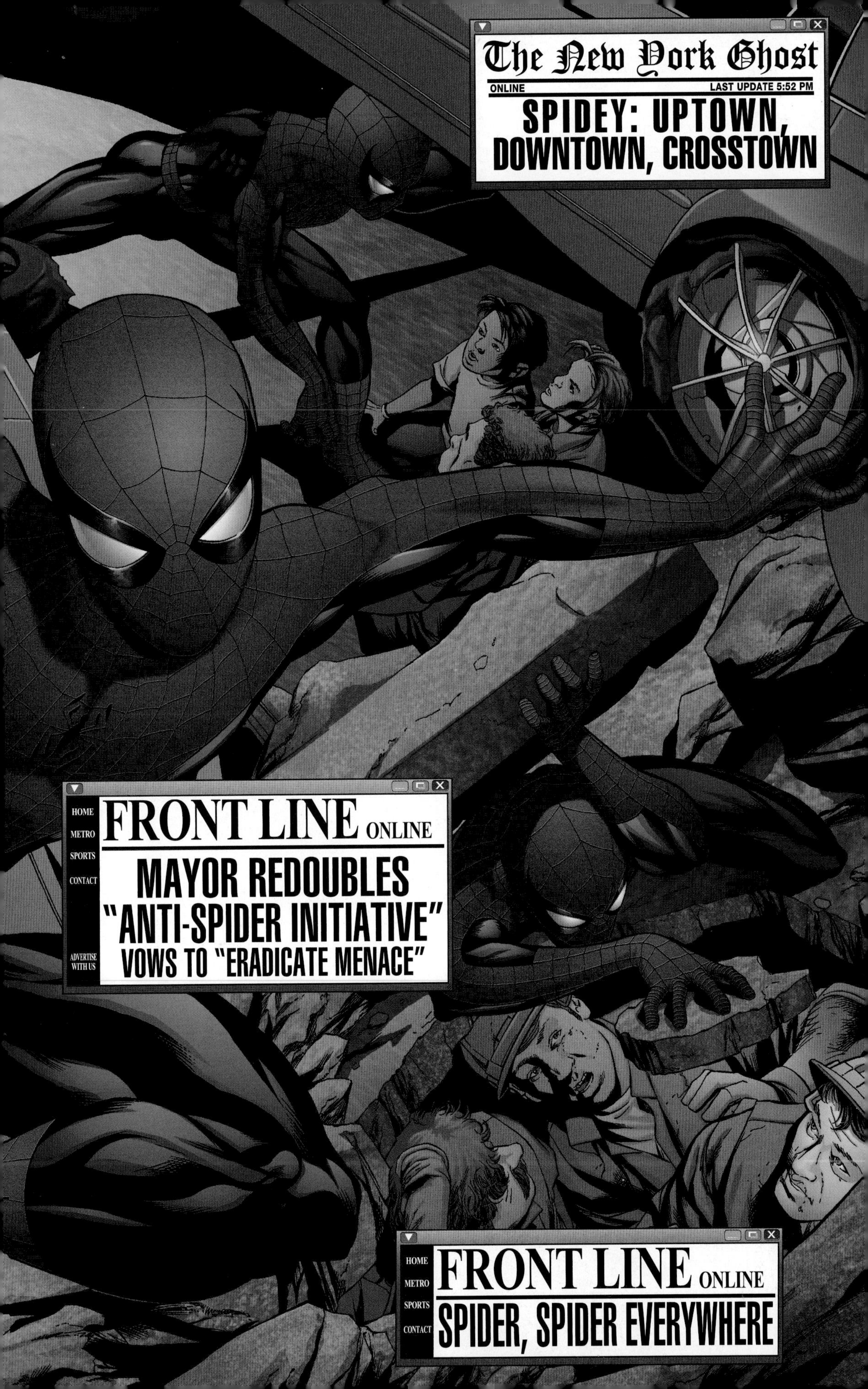
The New York Ghost
ONLINE
LAST UPDATE 5:52 PM
SPIDEY: UPTOWN, DOWNTOWN, CROSSTOWN
HOME
METRO
SPORTS
CONTACT
ADVERTISE WITH US
FRONT LINE ONLINE
MAYOR REDOUBLES "ANTI-SPIDER INITIATIVE" VOWS TO "ERADICATE MENACE"
HOME
METRO
SPORTS
CONTACT
FRONT LINE ONLINE
SPIDER, SPIDER EVERYWHERE

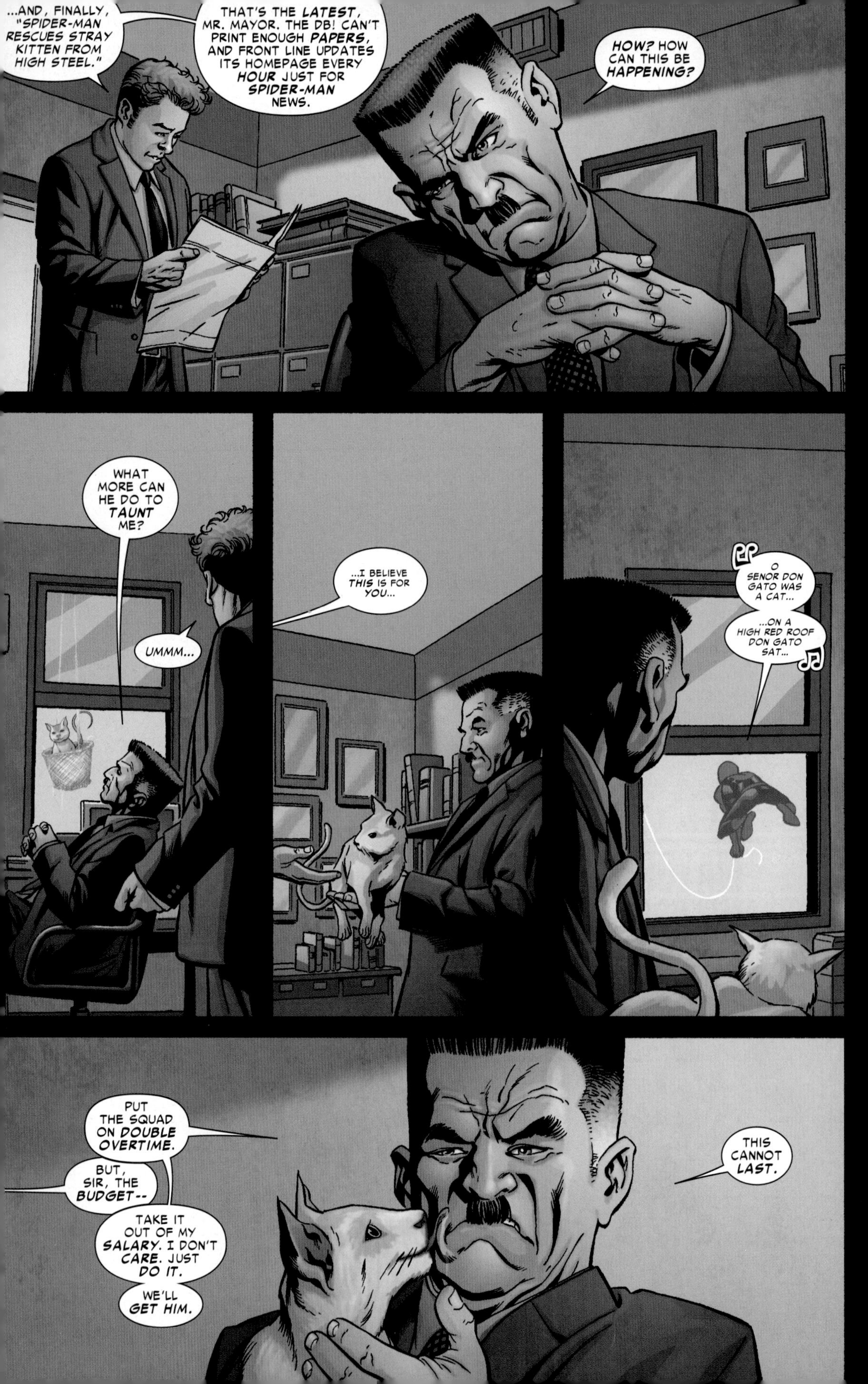
...AND, FINALLY, "SPIDER-MAN RESCUES STRAY KITTEN FROM HIGH STEEL."
THAT'S THE LATEST, MR. MAYOR. THE DB! CAN'T PRINT ENOUGH PAPERS, AND FRONT LINE UPDATES ITS HOMEPAGE EVERY HOUR JUST FOR SPIDER-MAN NEWS.
HOW? HOW CAN THIS BE HAPPENING?
WHAT MORE CAN HE DO TO TAUNT ME?
UMMM...
...I BELIEVE THIS IS FOR YOU...
O SENOR DON GATO WAS A CAT...
...ON A HIGH RED ROOF DON GATO SAT...
PUT THE SQUAD ON DOUBLE OVERTIME.
BUT, SIR, THE BUDGET--
TAKE IT OUT OF MY SALARY. I DON'T CARE. JUST DO IT.
WE'LL GET HIM.
THIS CANNOT LAST.

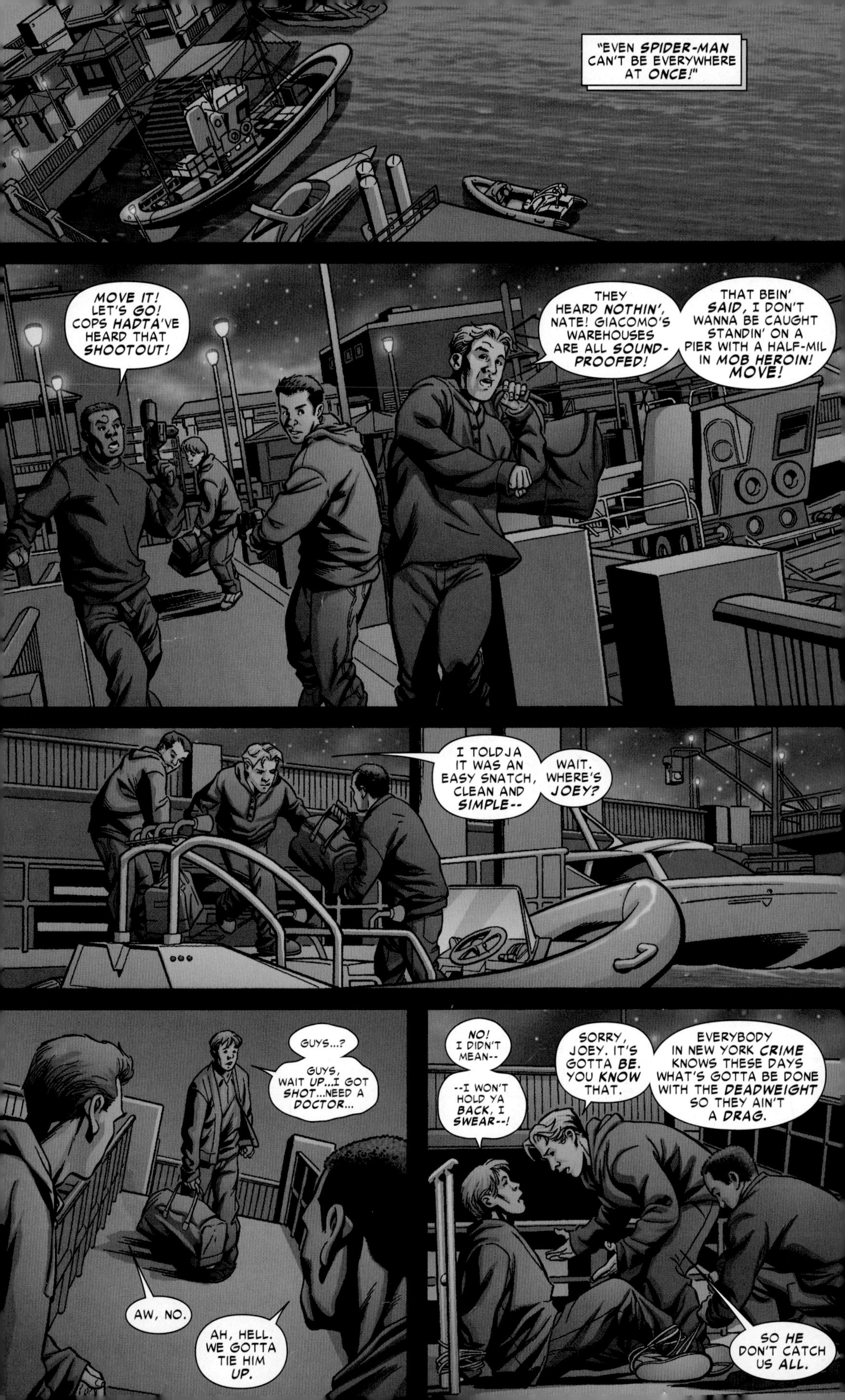
"EVEN SPIDER-MAN CAN'T BE EVERYWHERE AT ONCE!"
MOVE IT! LET'S GO! COPS HADTA'VE HEARD THAT SHOOTOUT!
THEY HEARD NOTHIN', NATE! GIACOMO'S WAREHOUSES ARE ALL SOUND-PROOFED!
THAT BEIN' SAID, I DON'T WANNA BE CAUGHT STANDIN' ON A PIER WITH A HALF-MIL IN MOB HEROIN! MOVE!
I TOLDJA IT WAS AN EASY SNATCH, CLEAN AND SIMPLE--
WAIT. WHERE'S JOEY?
GUYS...?
GUYS, WAIT UP...I GOT SHOT...NEED A DOCTOR...
AW, NO.
AH, HELL. WE GOTTA TIE HIM UP.
NO! I DIDN'T MEAN--
--I WON'T HOLD YA BACK, I SWEAR--!
SORRY, JOEY. IT'S GOTTA BE. YOU KNOW THAT.
EVERYBODY IN NEW YORK CRIME KNOWS THESE DAYS WHAT'S GOTTA BE DONE WITH THE DEADWEIGHT SO THEY AIN'T A DRAG.
SO HE DON'T CATCH US ALL.

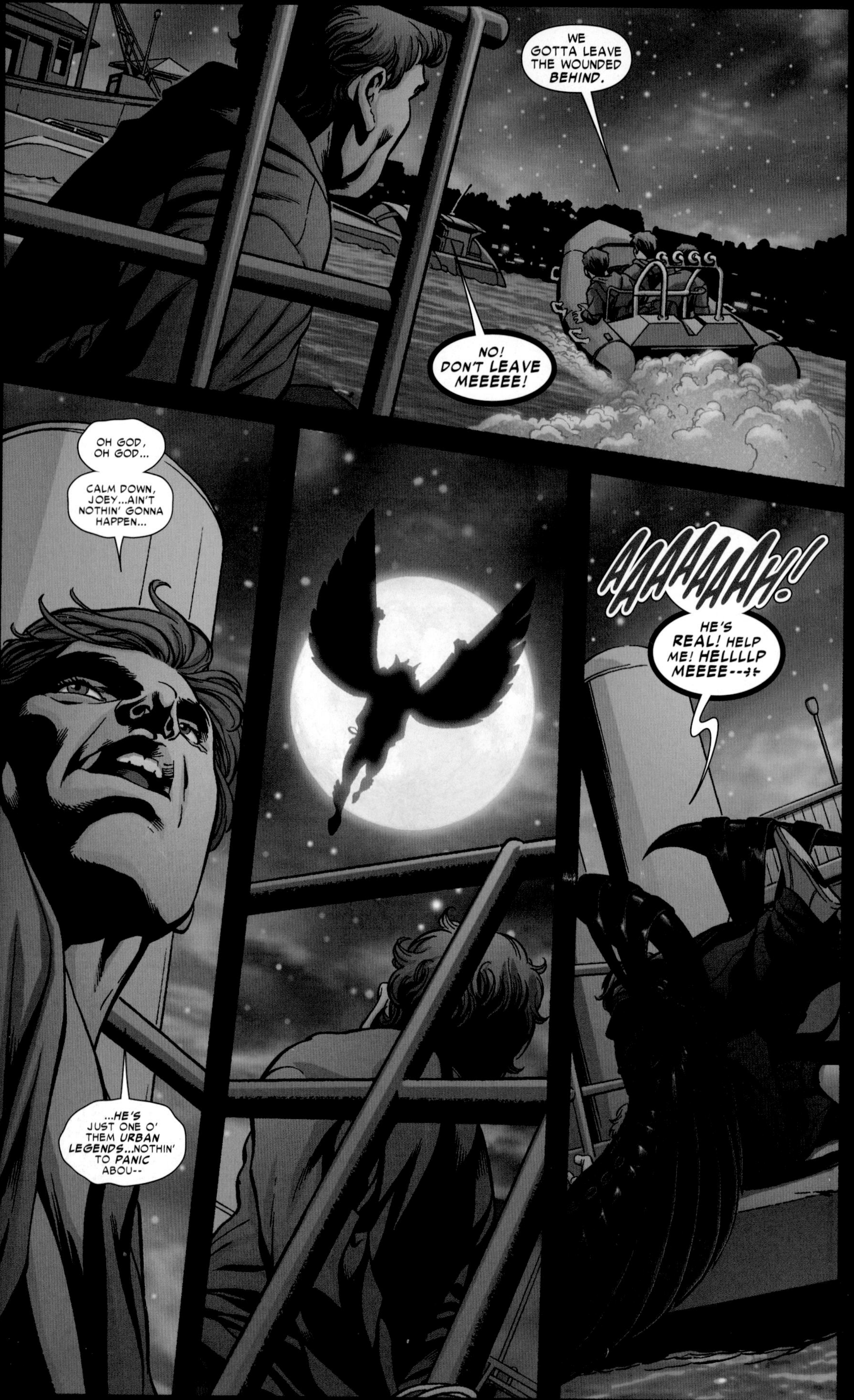
WE GOTTA LEAVE THE WOUNDED BEHIND.
NO! DON'T LEAVE MEEEEE!
OH GOD, OH GOD...
CALM DOWN, JOEY...AIN'T NOTHIN' GONNA HAPPEN...
...HE'S JUST ONE O' THEM URBAN LEGENDS...NOTHIN' TO PANIC ABOU--
AAAAAAAAH!
HE'S REAL! HELP ME! HELLLLP MEEEE--

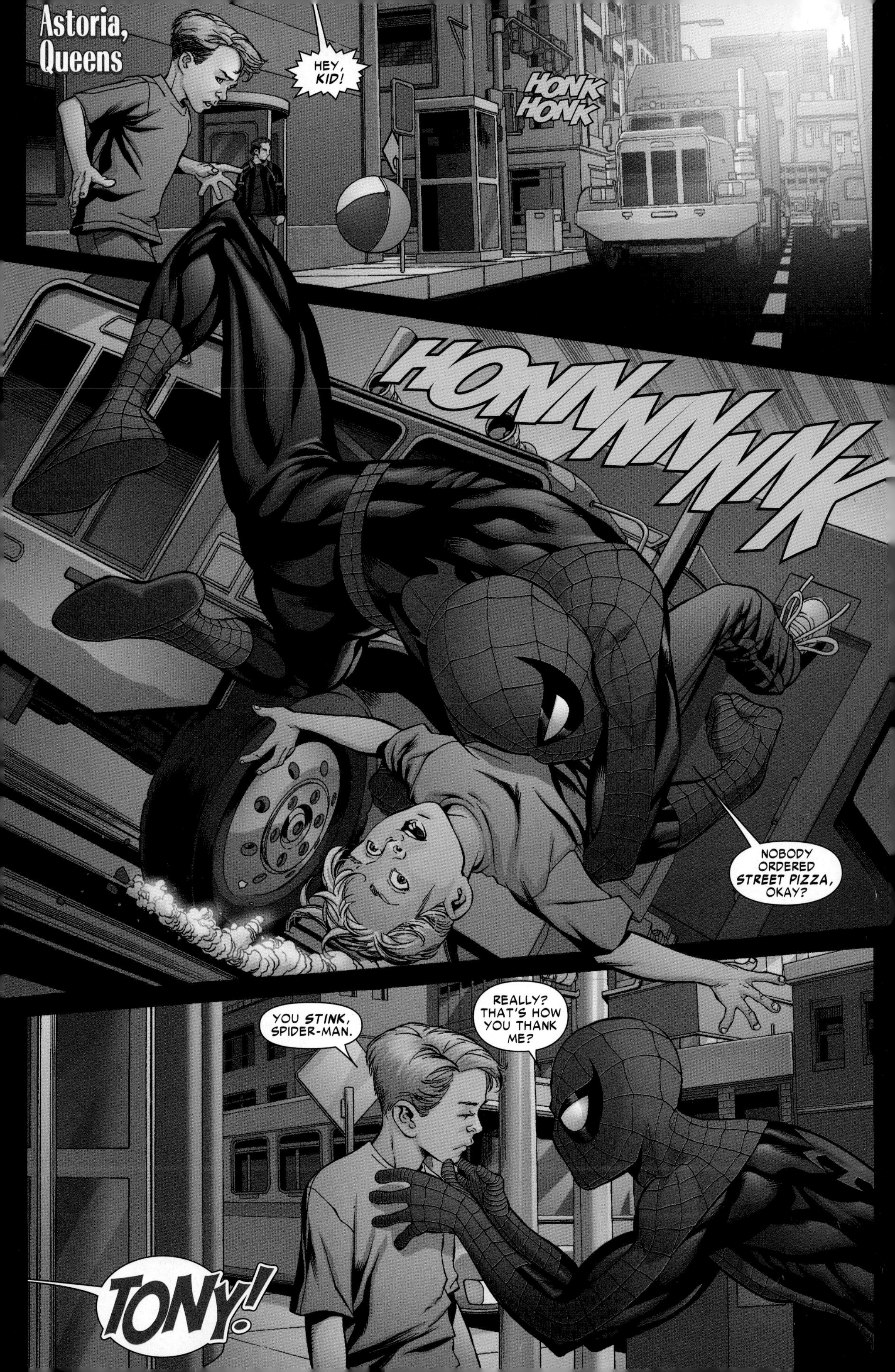
Astoria, Queens
HEY, KID!
HONK HONK
HONNNNNK
NOBODY ORDERED STREET PIZZA, OKAY?
YOU STINK, SPIDER-MAN.
REALLY? THAT'S HOW YOU THANK ME?
TONY!

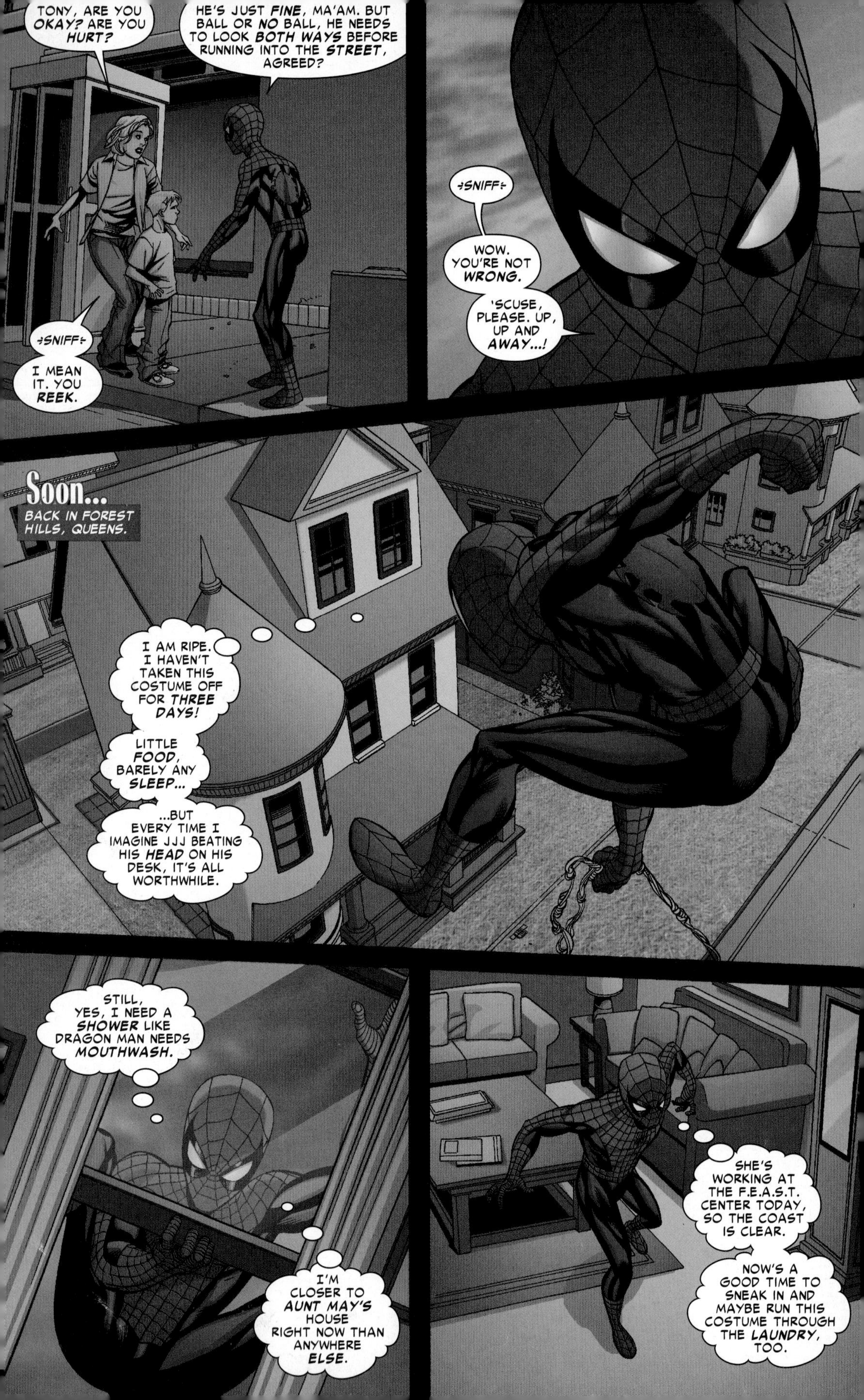
TONY, ARE YOU OKAY? ARE YOU HURT?
HE'S JUST FINE, MA'AM. BUT BALL OR NO BALL, HE NEEDS TO LOOK BOTH WAYS BEFORE RUNNING INTO THE STREET, AGREED?
≠SNIFF≠
I MEAN IT. YOU REEK.
≠SNIFF≠
WOW. YOU'RE NOT WRONG.
'SCUSE, PLEASE. UP, UP AND AWAY...!
Soon...
BACK IN FOREST HILLS, QUEENS.
I AM RIPE. I HAVEN'T TAKEN THIS COSTUME OFF FOR THREE DAYS!
LITTLE FOOD, BARELY ANY SLEEP...
...BUT EVERY TIME I IMAGINE JJJ BEATING HIS HEAD ON HIS DESK, IT'S ALL WORTHWHILE.
STILL, YES, I NEED A SHOWER LIKE DRAGON MAN NEEDS MOUTHWASH.
I'M CLOSER TO AUNT MAY'S HOUSE RIGHT NOW THAN ANYWHERE ELSE.
SHE'S WORKING AT THE F.E.A.S.T. CENTER TODAY, SO THE COAST IS CLEAR.
NOW'S A GOOD TIME TO SNEAK IN AND MAYBE RUN THIS COSTUME THROUGH THE LAUNDRY, TOO.

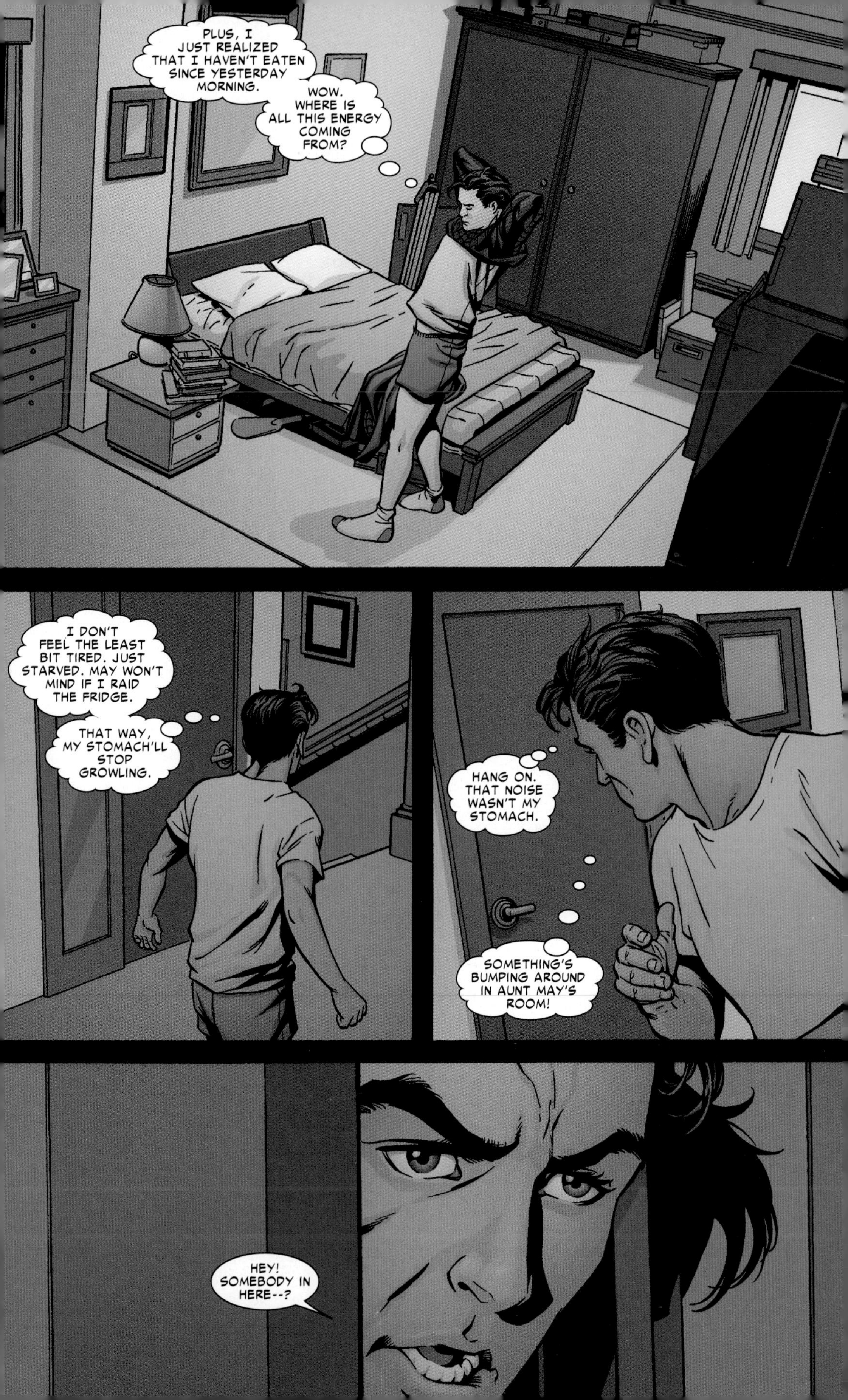
PLUS, I JUST REALIZED THAT I HAVEN'T EATEN SINCE YESTERDAY MORNING.
WOW. WHERE IS ALL THIS ENERGY COMING FROM?
I DON'T FEEL THE LEAST BIT TIRED. JUST STARVED. MAY WON'T MIND IF I RAID THE FRIDGE.
THAT WAY, MY STOMACH'LL STOP GROWLING.
HANG ON. THAT NOISE WASN'T MY STOMACH.
SOMETHING'S BUMPING AROUND IN AUNT MAY'S ROOM!
HEY! SOMEBODY IN HERE--?

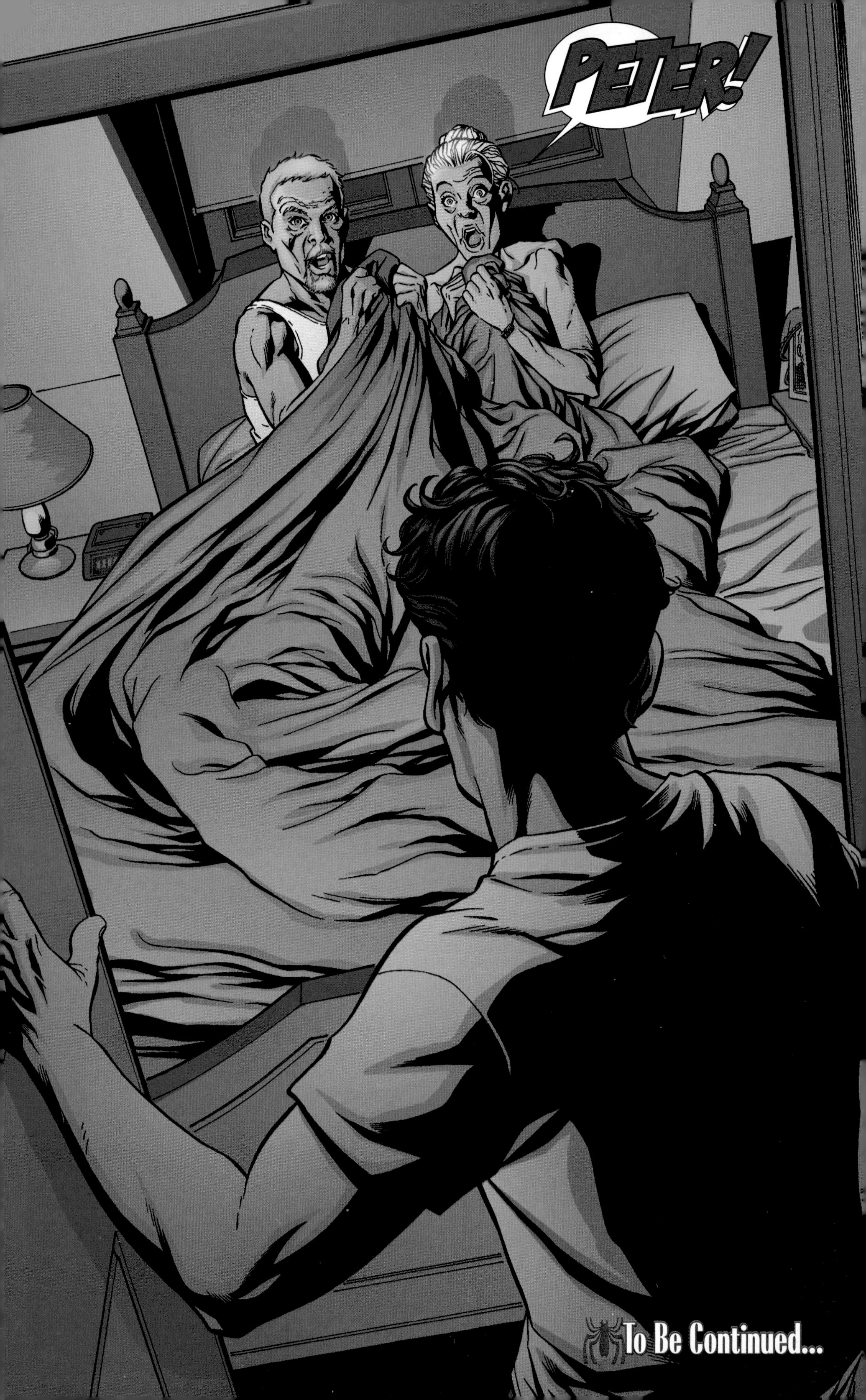
PETER!
To Be Continued...

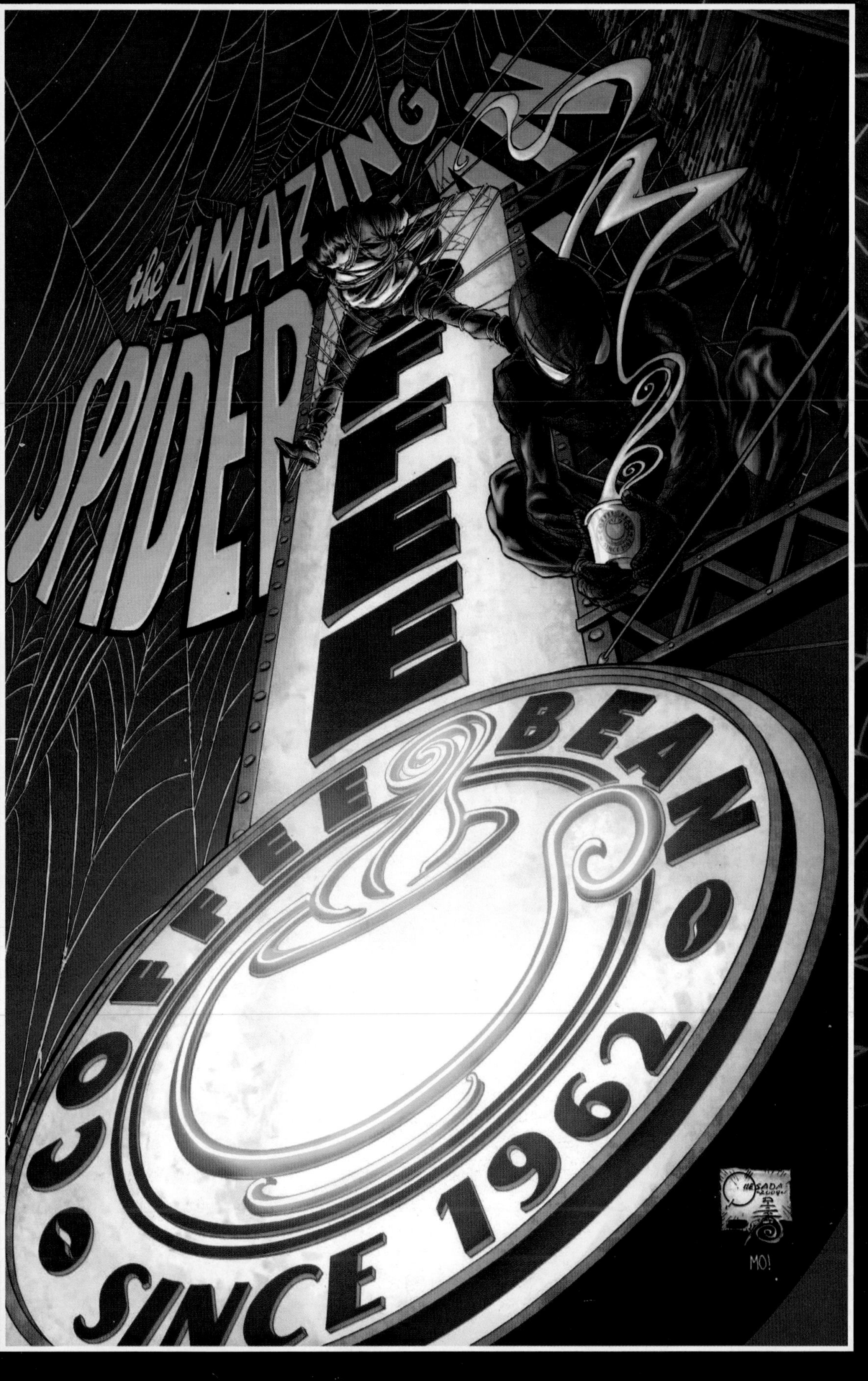
the AMAZING
SPIDER
BEAN
SINCE 1962
MO!

AMAZING SPIDER-MAN #593

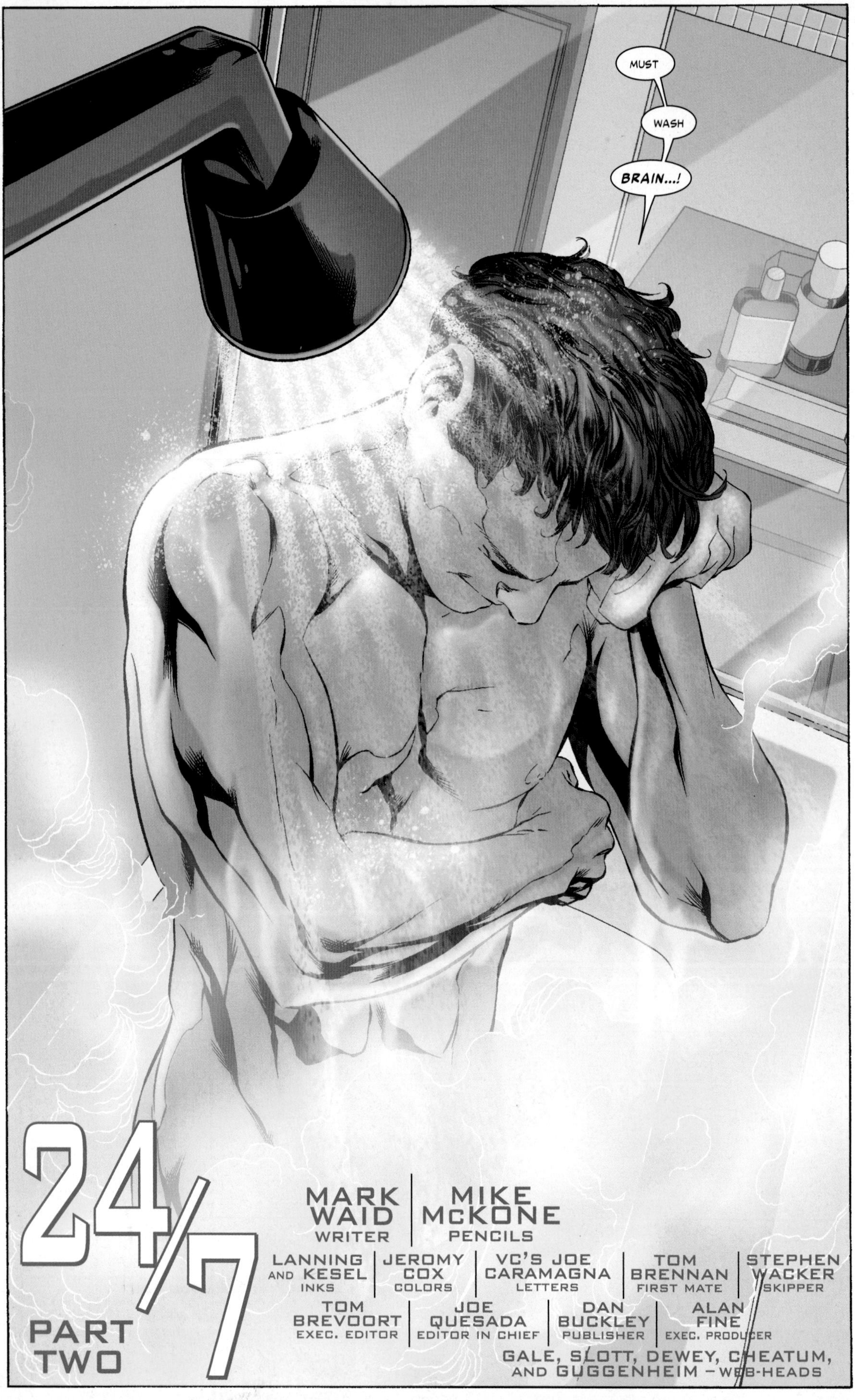
MUST
WASH
BRAIN...!
24/7
PART TWO
MARK WAID WRITER
MIKE McKONE PENCILS
LANNING AND KESEL INKS
JEROMY COX COLORS
VC'S JOE CARAMAGNA LETTERS
TOM BRENNAN FIRST MATE
STEPHEN WACKER SKIPPER
TOM BREVOORT EXEC. EDITOR
JOE QUESADA EDITOR IN CHIEF
DAN BUCKLEY PUBLISHER
ALAN FINE EXEC. PRODUCER
GALE, SLOTT, DEWEY, CHEATUM, AND GUGGENHEIM –WEB-HEADS

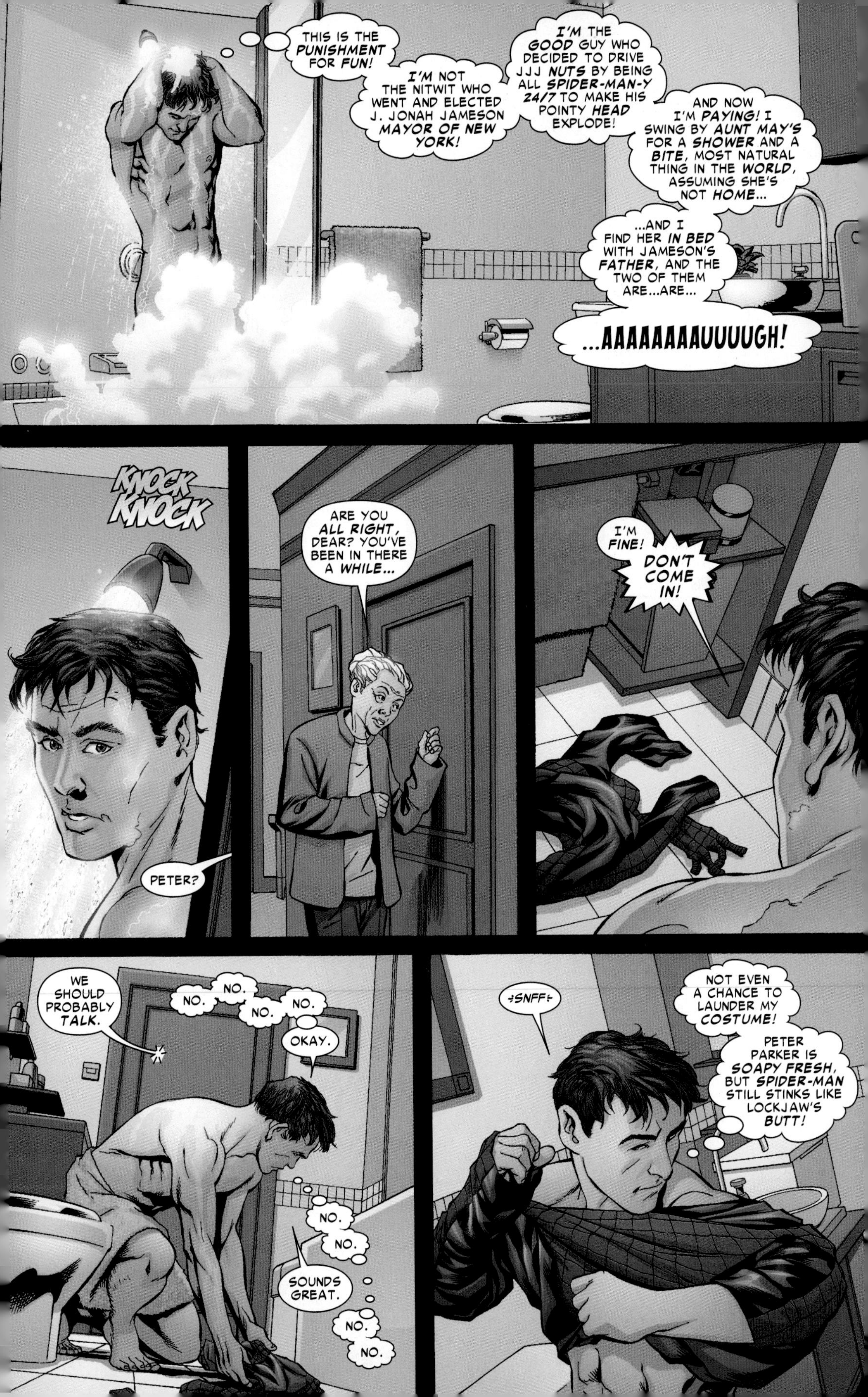
THIS IS THE PUNISHMENT FOR FUN!
I'M NOT THE NITWIT WHO WENT AND ELECTED J. JONAH JAMESON MAYOR OF NEW YORK!
I'M THE GOOD GUY WHO DECIDED TO DRIVE JJJ NUTS BY BEING ALL SPIDER-MAN-Y 24/7 TO MAKE HIS POINTY HEAD EXPLODE!
AND NOW I'M PAYING! I SWING BY AUNT MAY'S FOR A SHOWER AND A BITE, MOST NATURAL THING IN THE WORLD, ASSUMING SHE'S NOT HOME...
...AND I FIND HER IN BED WITH JAMESON'S FATHER, AND THE TWO OF THEM ARE...ARE...
...AAAAAAAAUUUUGH!
KNOCK KNOCK
PETER?
ARE YOU ALL RIGHT, DEAR? YOU'VE BEEN IN THERE A WHILE...
I'M FINE!
DON'T COME IN!
WE SHOULD PROBABLY TALK.
NO.
NO.
NO.
NO.
OKAY.
NO.
NO.
SOUNDS GREAT.
NO.
NO.
-SNFF-
NOT EVEN A CHANCE TO LAUNDER MY COSTUME!
PETER PARKER IS SOAPY FRESH, BUT SPIDER-MAN STILL STINKS LIKE LOCKJAW'S BUTT!

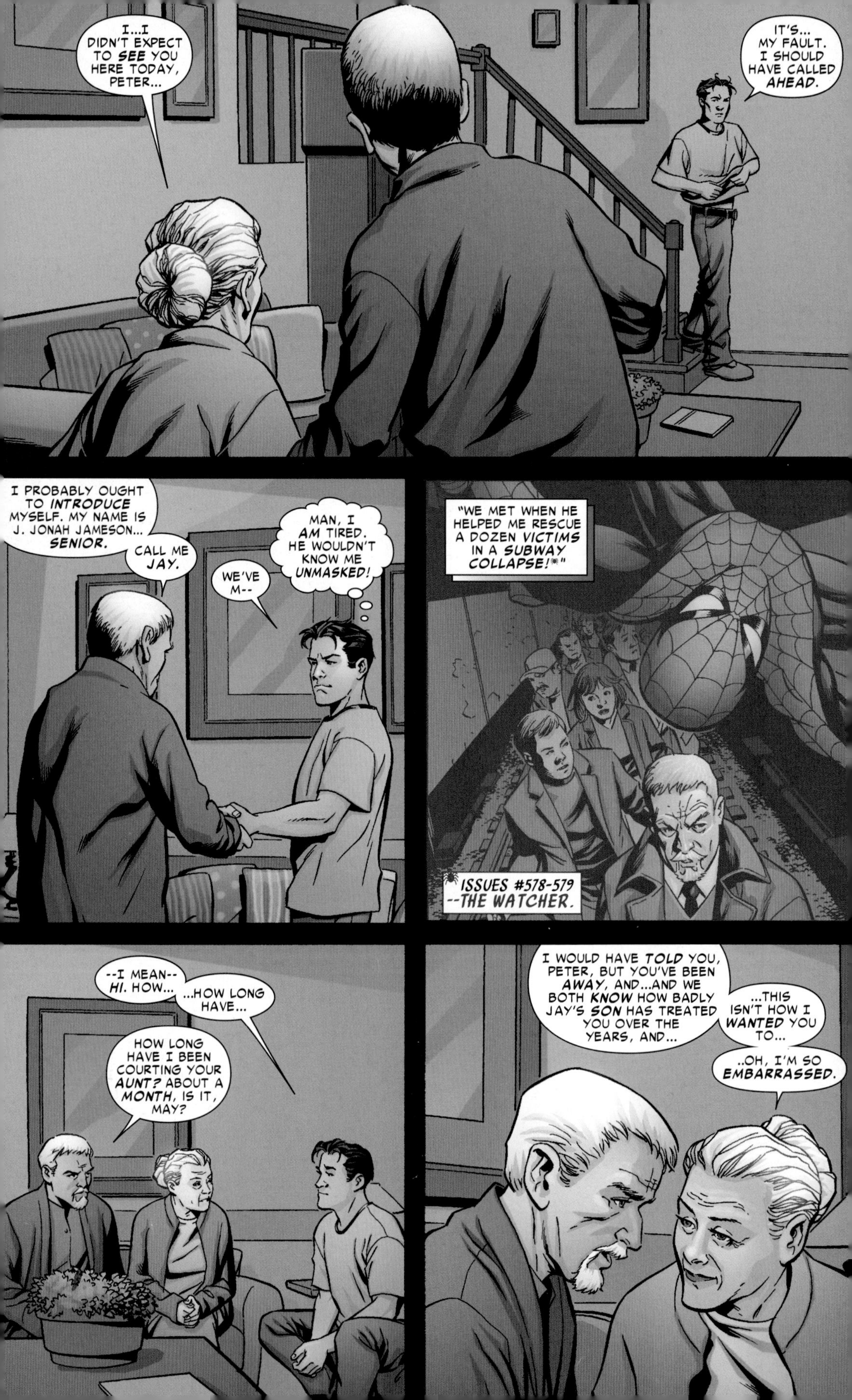
I...I DIDN'T EXPECT TO SEE YOU HERE TODAY, PETER...
IT'S... MY FAULT. I SHOULD HAVE CALLED AHEAD.
I PROBABLY OUGHT TO INTRODUCE MYSELF. MY NAME IS J. JONAH JAMESON... SENIOR.
CALL ME JAY.
WE'VE M--
MAN, I AM TIRED. HE WOULDN'T KNOW ME UNMASKED!
"WE MET WHEN HE HELPED ME RESCUE A DOZEN VICTIMS IN A SUBWAY COLLAPSE!*"
*ISSUES #578-579 --THE WATCHER.
--I MEAN-- HI. HOW...
...HOW LONG HAVE...
HOW LONG HAVE I BEEN COURTING YOUR AUNT? ABOUT A MONTH, IS IT, MAY?
I WOULD HAVE TOLD YOU, PETER, BUT YOU'VE BEEN AWAY, AND...AND WE BOTH KNOW HOW BADLY JAY'S SON HAS TREATED YOU OVER THE YEARS, AND...
...THIS ISN'T HOW I WANTED YOU TO...
..OH, I'M SO EMBARRASSED.

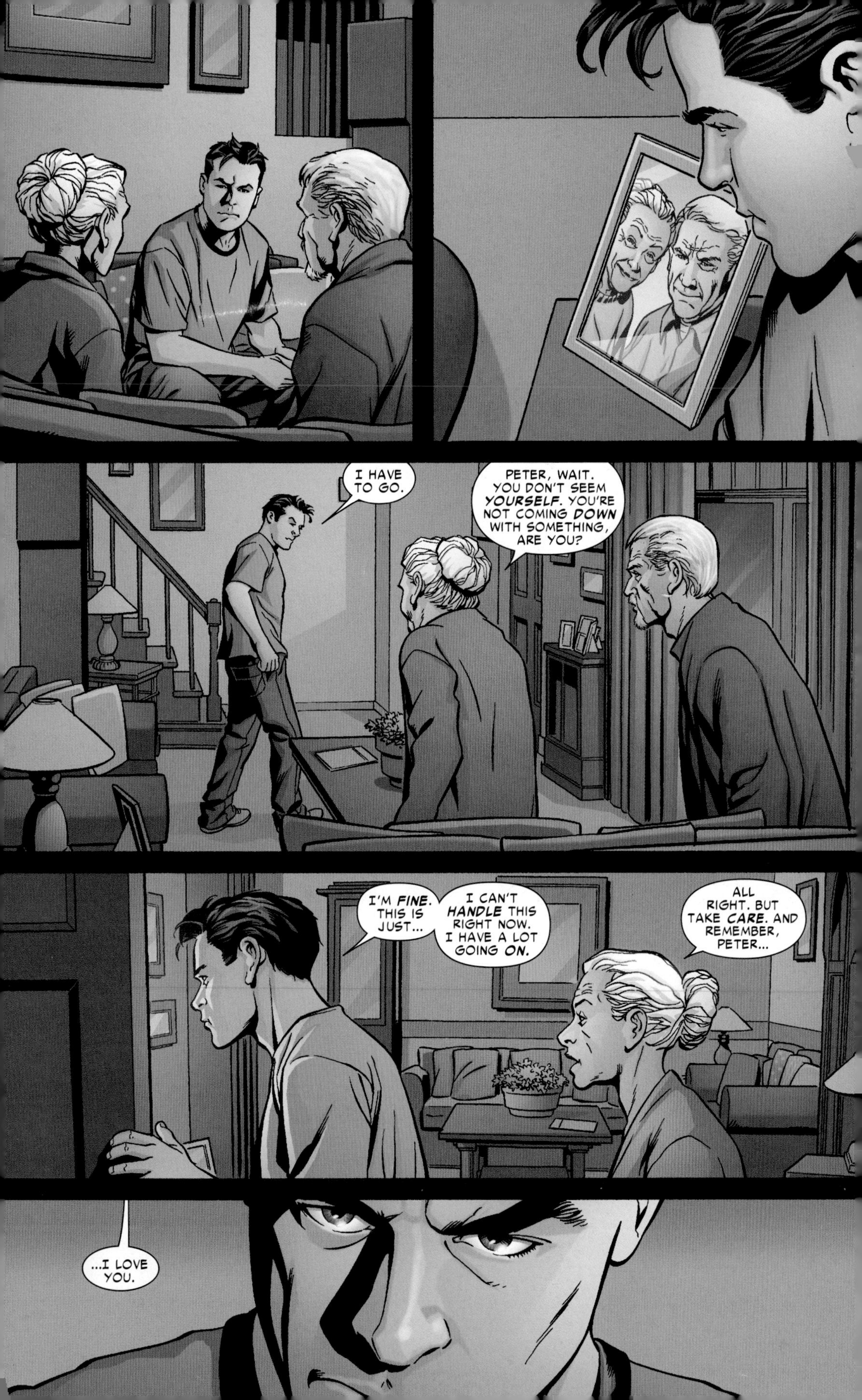
I HAVE TO GO.
PETER, WAIT. YOU DON'T SEEM *YOURSELF*. YOU'RE NOT COMING *DOWN* WITH SOMETHING, ARE YOU?
I'M *FINE*. THIS IS JUST...
I CAN'T *HANDLE* THIS RIGHT NOW. I HAVE A LOT GOING *ON*.
ALL RIGHT. BUT TAKE *CARE*. AND REMEMBER, PETER...
...I LOVE YOU.

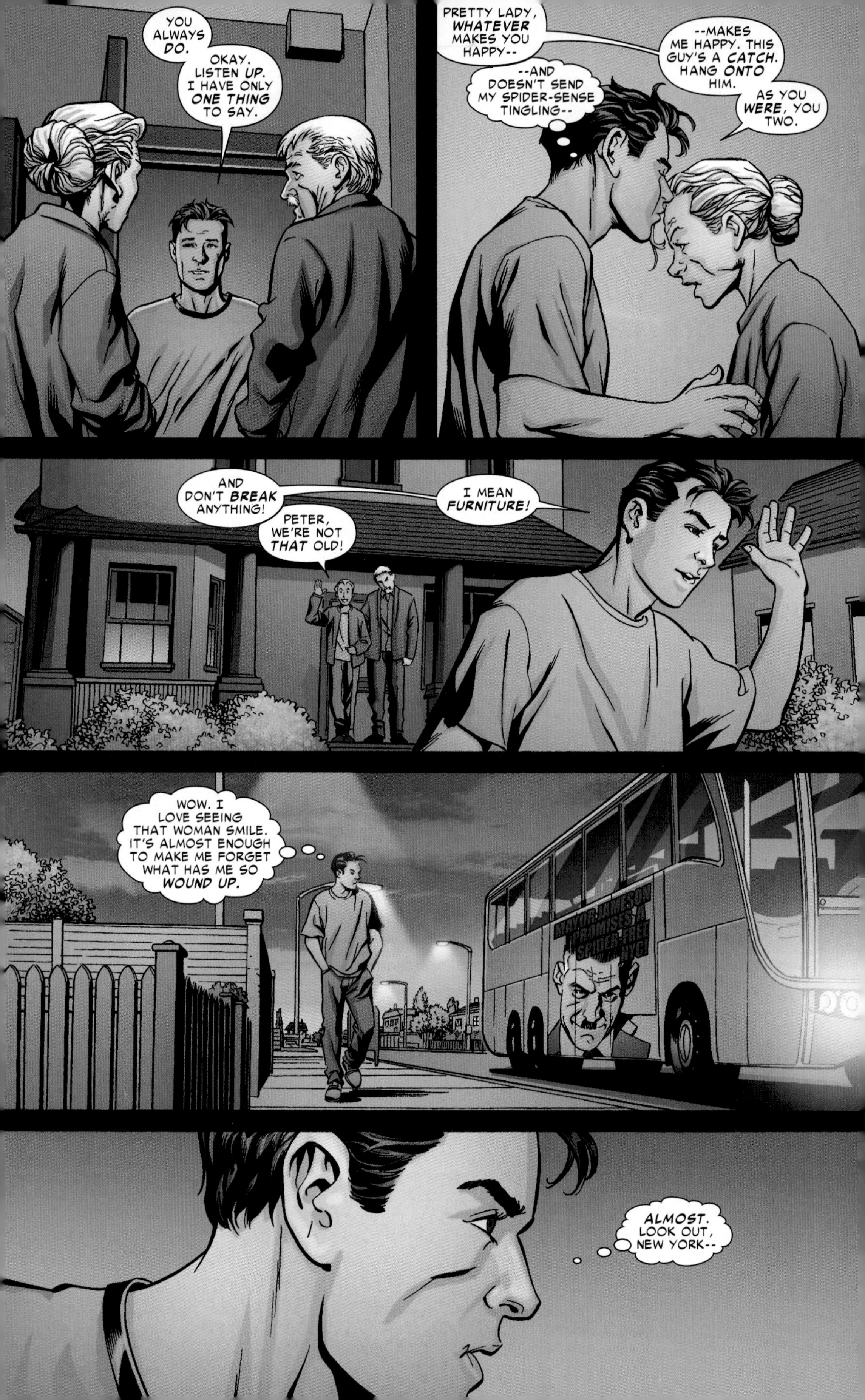

YOU ALWAYS DO.
OKAY. LISTEN UP. I HAVE ONLY ONE THING TO SAY.
PRETTY LADY, WHATEVER MAKES YOU HAPPY--
--AND DOESN'T SEND MY SPIDER-SENSE TINGLING--
--MAKES ME HAPPY. THIS GUY'S A CATCH. HANG ONTO HIM.
AS YOU WERE, YOU TWO.
AND DON'T BREAK ANYTHING!
I MEAN FURNITURE!
PETER, WE'RE NOT THAT OLD!
WOW. I LOVE SEEING THAT WOMAN SMILE. IT'S ALMOST ENOUGH TO MAKE ME FORGET WHAT HAS ME SO WOUND UP.
MAYOR JAMESON PROMISES A SPIDER-FREE NYC!
ALMOST. LOOK OUT, NEW YORK--

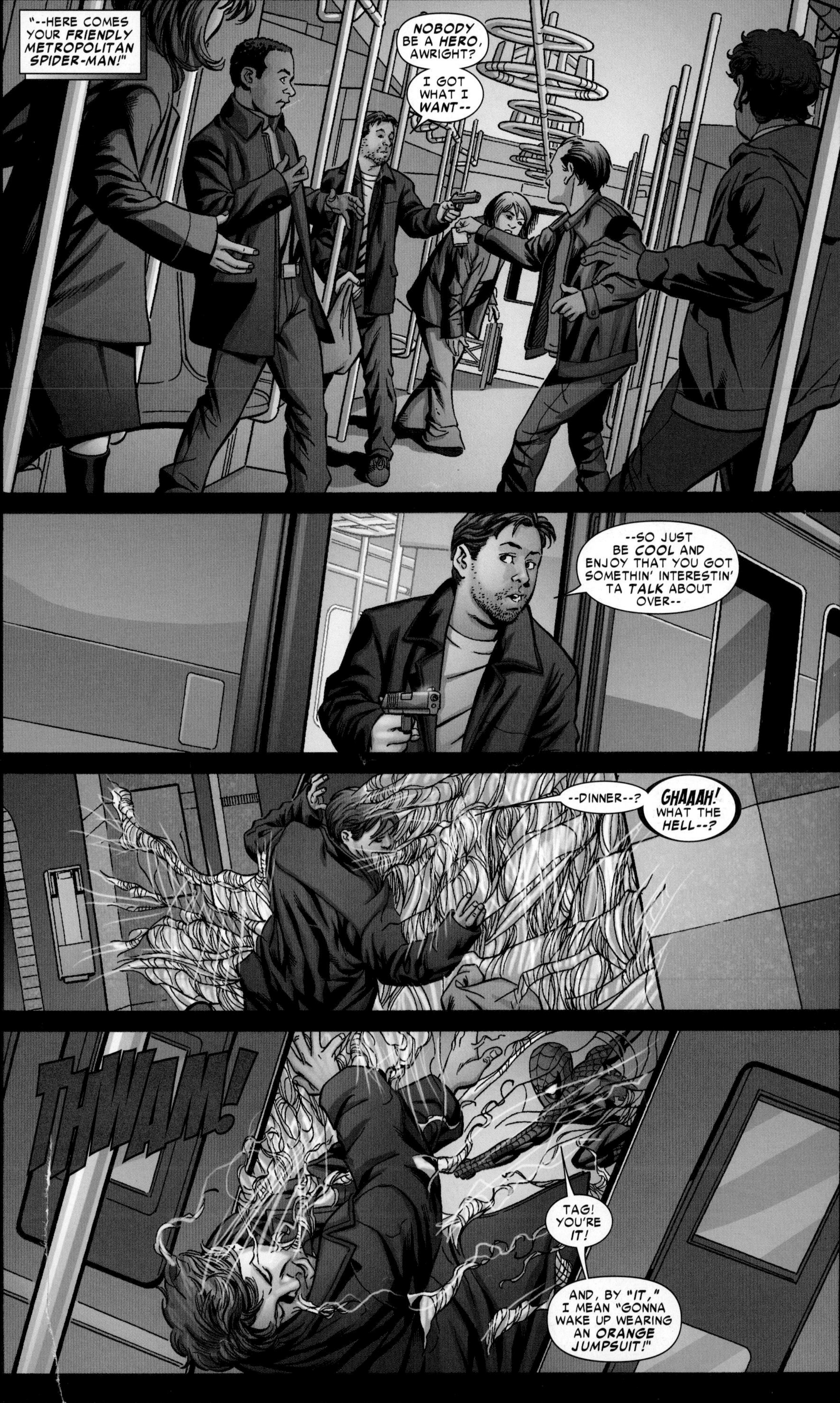
"--HERE COMES YOUR FRIENDLY METROPOLITAN SPIDER-MAN!"
NOBODY BE A HERO, AWRIGHT?
I GOT WHAT I WANT--
--SO JUST BE COOL AND ENJOY THAT YOU GOT SOMETHIN' INTERESTIN' TA TALK ABOUT OVER--
--DINNER--?
GHAAAH! WHAT THE HELL--?
THWAK!
TAG! YOU'RE IT!
AND, BY "IT," I MEAN "GONNA WAKE UP WEARING AN ORANGE JUMPSUIT!"

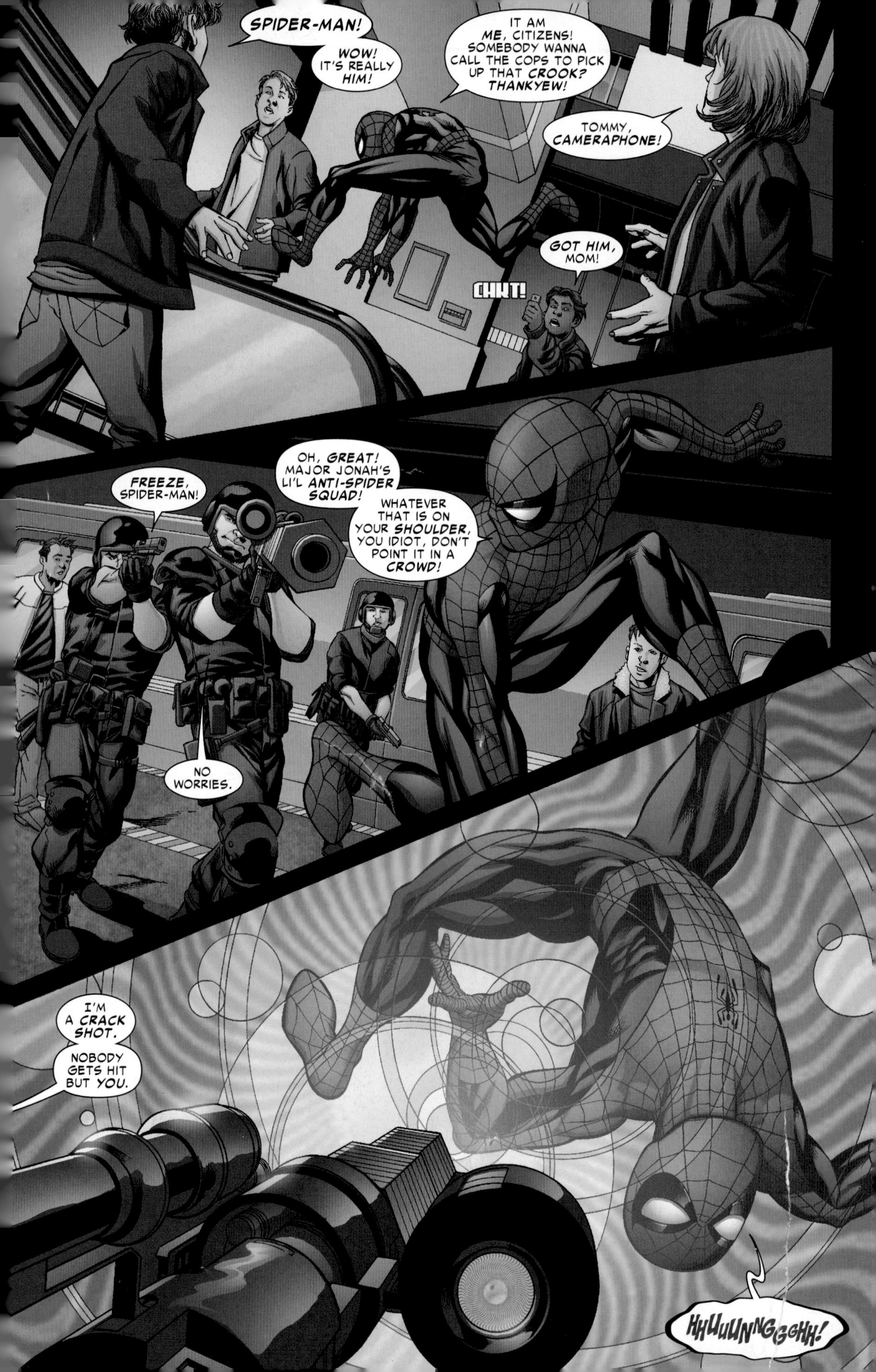
SPIDER-MAN!
WOW! IT'S REALLY HIM!
IT AM ME, CITIZENS! SOMEBODY WANNA CALL THE COPS TO PICK UP THAT CROOK? THANKYEW!
TOMMY, CAMERAPHONE!
GOT HIM, MOM!
CHKT!
FREEZE, SPIDER-MAN!
OH, GREAT! MAJOR JONAH'S LI'L ANTI-SPIDER SQUAD!
WHATEVER THAT IS ON YOUR SHOULDER, YOU IDIOT, DON'T POINT IT IN A CROWD!
NO WORRIES.
I'M A CRACK SHOT.
NOBODY GETS HIT BUT YOU.
HHUUUNNGGGHH!

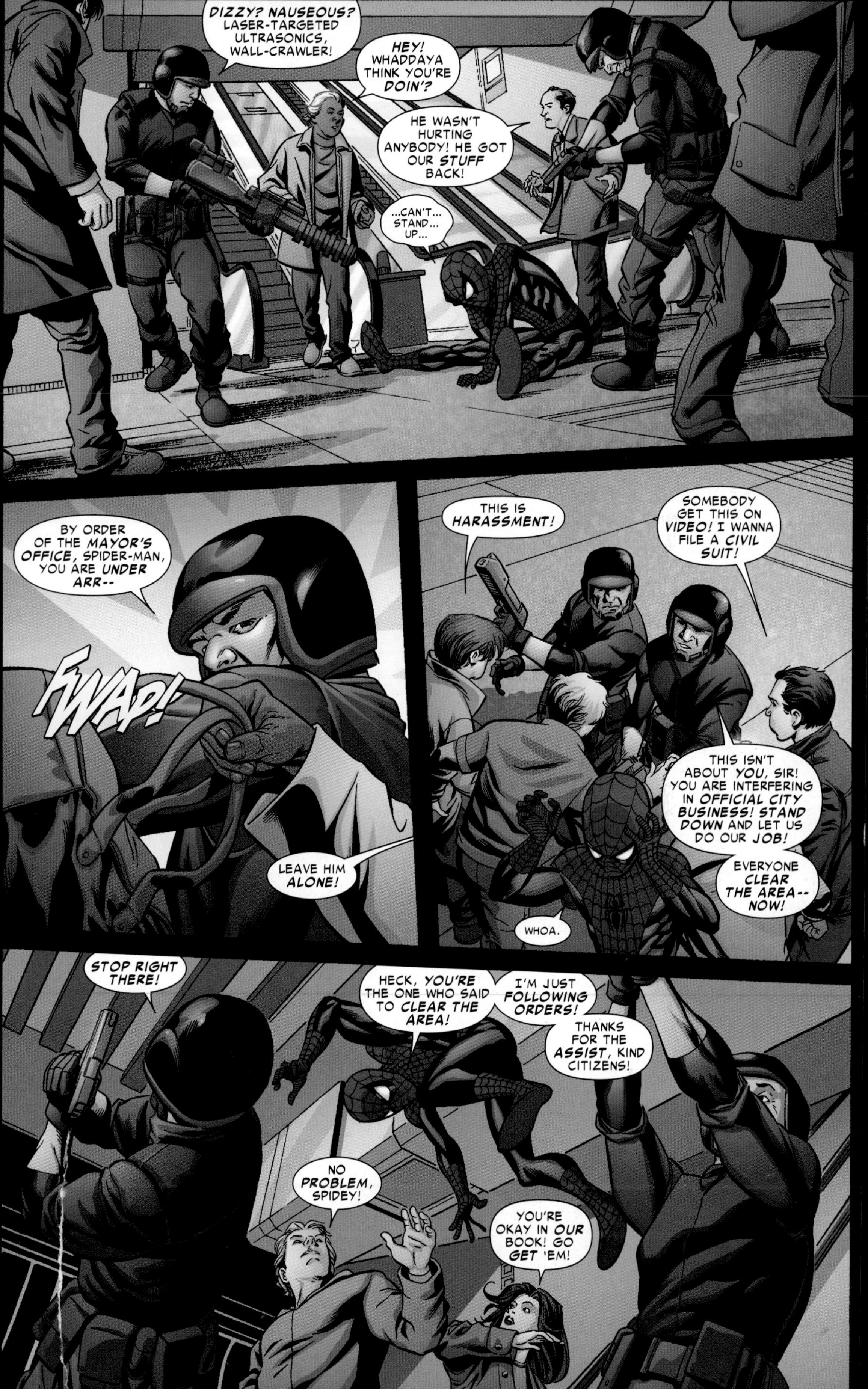
DIZZY? NAUSEOUS? LASER-TARGETED ULTRASONICS, WALL-CRAWLER!
HEY! WHADDAYA THINK YOU'RE DOIN'?
HE WASN'T HURTING ANYBODY! HE GOT OUR STUFF BACK!
...CAN'T... STAND... UP...
BY ORDER OF THE MAYOR'S OFFICE, SPIDER-MAN, YOU ARE UNDER ARR--
FWAP!
LEAVE HIM ALONE!
THIS IS HARASSMENT!
SOMEBODY GET THIS ON VIDEO! I WANNA FILE A CIVIL SUIT!
THIS ISN'T ABOUT YOU, SIR! YOU ARE INTERFERING IN OFFICIAL CITY BUSINESS! STAND DOWN AND LET US DO OUR JOB!
EVERYONE CLEAR THE AREA-- NOW!
WHOA.
STOP RIGHT THERE!
HECK, YOU'RE THE ONE WHO SAID TO CLEAR THE AREA!
I'M JUST FOLLOWING ORDERS!
THANKS FOR THE ASSIST, KIND CITIZENS!
NO PROBLEM, SPIDEY!
YOU'RE OKAY IN OUR BOOK! GO GET 'EM!

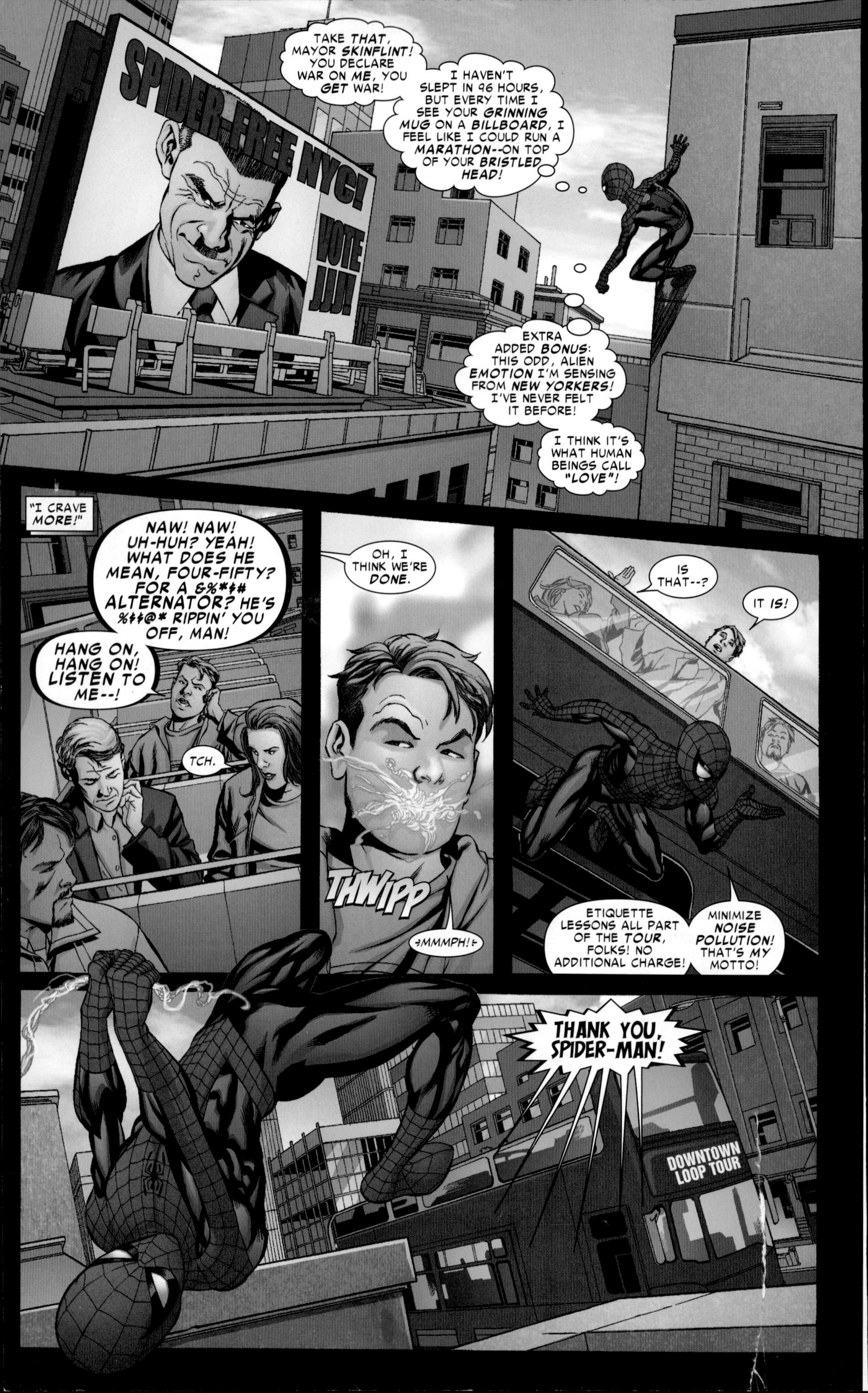

SPIDER-FREE NYC!
VOTE JJJ!
TAKE THAT, MAYOR SKINFLINT! YOU DECLARE WAR ON ME, YOU GET WAR!
I HAVEN'T SLEPT IN 96 HOURS, BUT EVERY TIME I SEE YOUR GRINNING MUG ON A BILLBOARD, I FEEL LIKE I COULD RUN A MARATHON--ON TOP OF YOUR BRISTLED HEAD!
EXTRA ADDED BONUS: THIS ODD, ALIEN EMOTION I'M SENSING FROM NEW YORKERS! I'VE NEVER FELT IT BEFORE!
I THINK IT'S WHAT HUMAN BEINGS CALL "LOVE"!
"I CRAVE MORE!"
NAW! NAW! UH-HUH? YEAH! WHAT DOES HE MEAN, FOUR-FIFTY? FOR A &%*$# ALTERNATOR? HE'S %$$@* RIPPIN' YOU OFF, MAN!
HANG ON, HANG ON! LISTEN TO ME--!
TCH.
OH, I THINK WE'RE DONE.
THWIPP
MMMPH!
IS THAT--?
IT IS!
ETIQUETTE LESSONS ALL PART OF THE TOUR, FOLKS! NO ADDITIONAL CHARGE!
MINIMIZE NOISE POLLUTION! THAT'S MY MOTTO!
THANK YOU, SPIDER-MAN!
DOWNTOWN LOOP TOUR

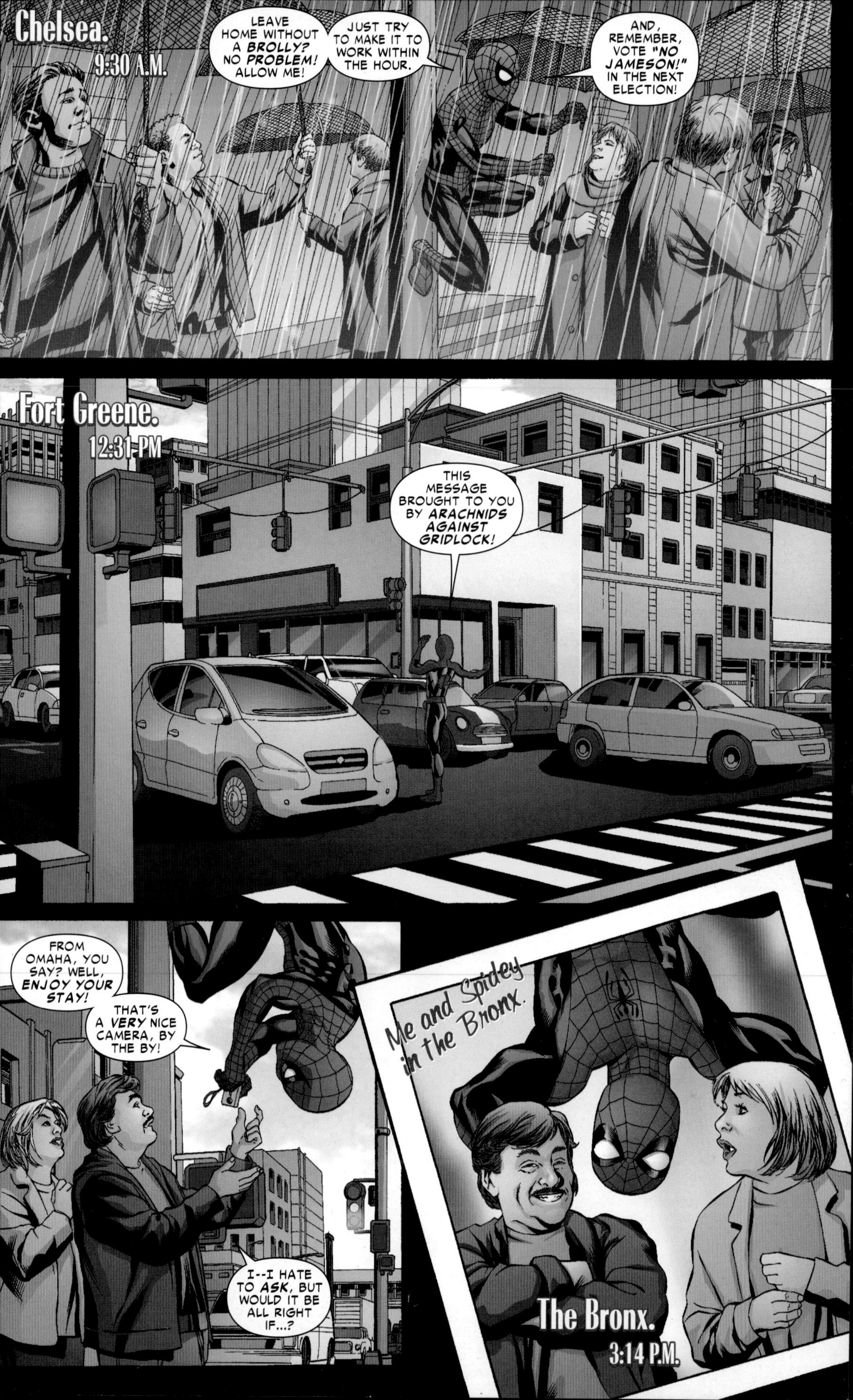
Chelsea.
9:30 A.M.
LEAVE HOME WITHOUT A BROLLY? NO PROBLEM! ALLOW ME!
JUST TRY TO MAKE IT TO WORK WITHIN THE HOUR.
AND, REMEMBER, VOTE "NO JAMESON!" IN THE NEXT ELECTION!
Fort Greene.
12:31 PM
THIS MESSAGE BROUGHT TO YOU BY ARACHNIDS AGAINST GRIDLOCK!
FROM OMAHA, YOU SAY? WELL, ENJOY YOUR STAY!
THAT'S A VERY NICE CAMERA, BY THE BY!
I--I HATE TO ASK, BUT WOULD IT BE ALL RIGHT IF...?
Me and Spidey in the Bronx.
The Bronx.
3:14 P.M.

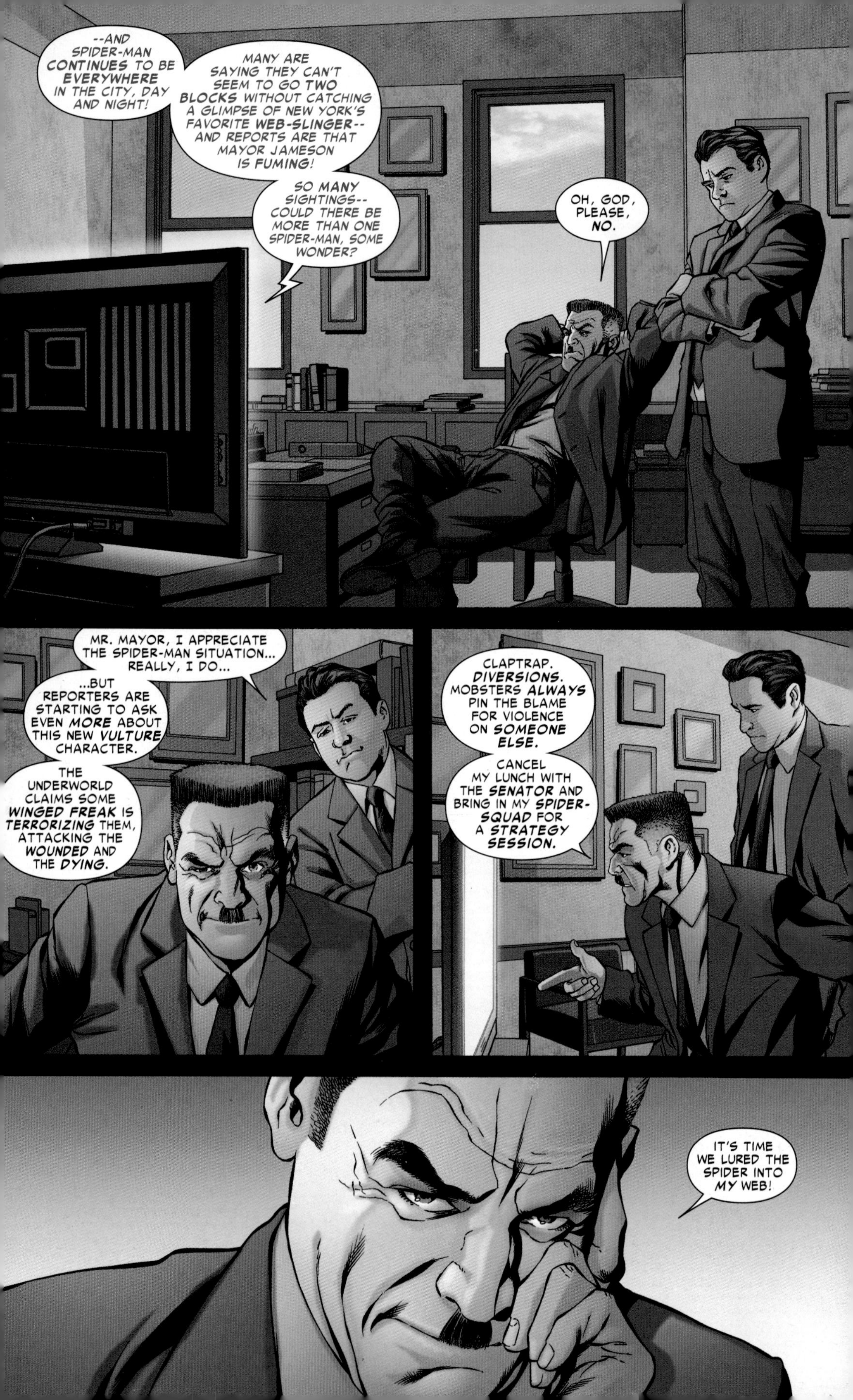
--AND SPIDER-MAN CONTINUES TO BE EVERYWHERE IN THE CITY, DAY AND NIGHT!
MANY ARE SAYING THEY CAN'T SEEM TO GO TWO BLOCKS WITHOUT CATCHING A GLIMPSE OF NEW YORK'S FAVORITE WEB-SLINGER-- AND REPORTS ARE THAT MAYOR JAMESON IS FUMING!
SO MANY SIGHTINGS-- COULD THERE BE MORE THAN ONE SPIDER-MAN, SOME WONDER?
OH, GOD, PLEASE, NO.
MR. MAYOR, I APPRECIATE THE SPIDER-MAN SITUATION... REALLY, I DO...
...BUT REPORTERS ARE STARTING TO ASK EVEN MORE ABOUT THIS NEW VULTURE CHARACTER.
THE UNDERWORLD CLAIMS SOME WINGED FREAK IS TERRORIZING THEM, ATTACKING THE WOUNDED AND THE DYING.
CLAPTRAP. DIVERSIONS. MOBSTERS ALWAYS PIN THE BLAME FOR VIOLENCE ON SOMEONE ELSE.
CANCEL MY LUNCH WITH THE SENATOR AND BRING IN MY SPIDER-SQUAD FOR A STRATEGY SESSION.
IT'S TIME WE LURED THE SPIDER INTO MY WEB!

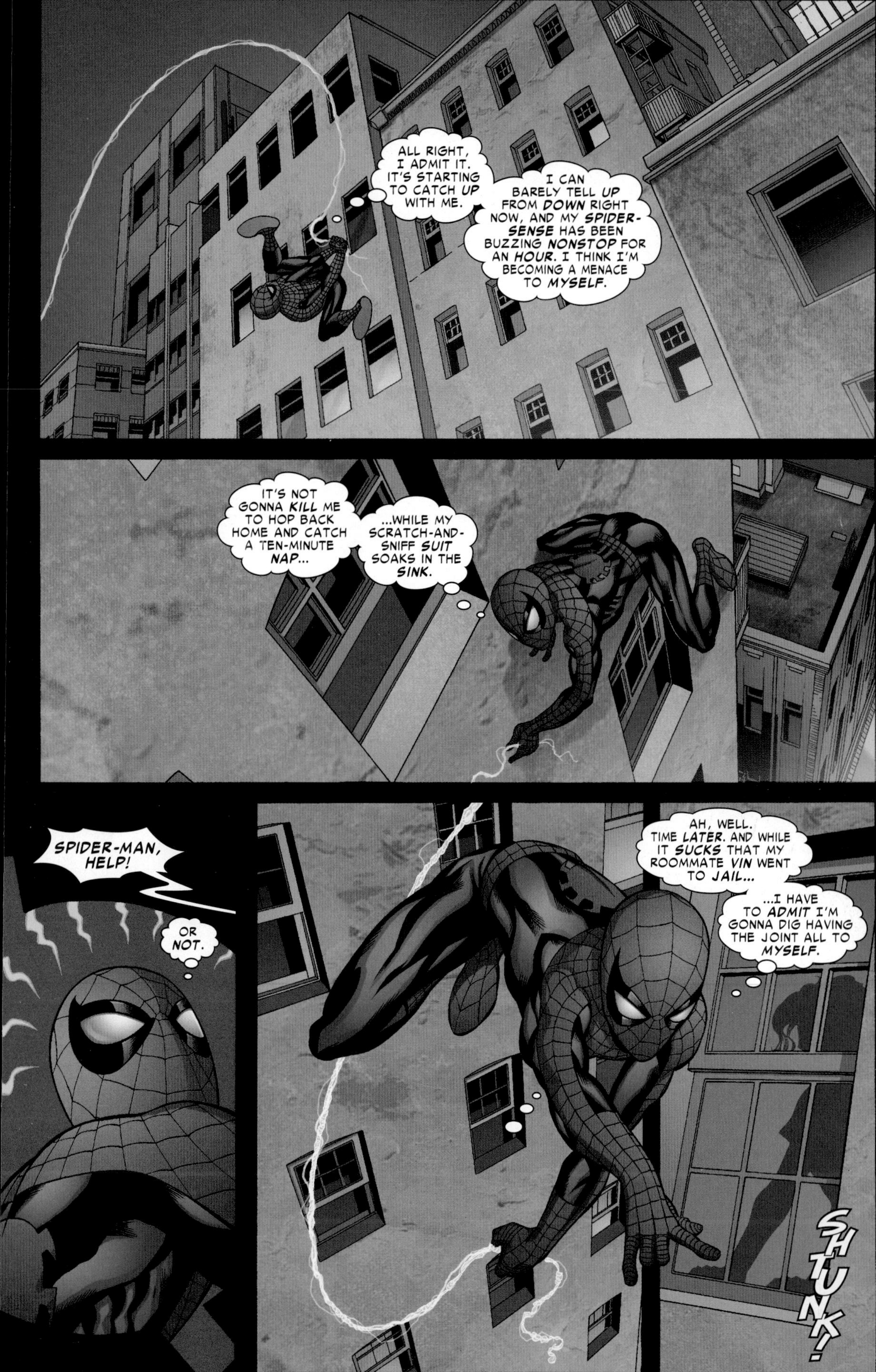
ALL RIGHT, I ADMIT IT. IT'S STARTING TO CATCH UP WITH ME.
I CAN BARELY TELL UP FROM DOWN RIGHT NOW, AND MY SPIDER-SENSE HAS BEEN BUZZING NONSTOP FOR AN HOUR. I THINK I'M BECOMING A MENACE TO MYSELF.
IT'S NOT GONNA KILL ME TO HOP BACK HOME AND CATCH A TEN-MINUTE NAP...
...WHILE MY SCRATCH-AND-SNIFF SUIT SOAKS IN THE SINK.
AH, WELL. TIME LATER. AND WHILE IT SUCKS THAT MY ROOMMATE VIN WENT TO JAIL...
...I HAVE TO ADMIT I'M GONNA DIG HAVING THE JOINT ALL TO MYSELF.
SHTUNK!
SPIDER-MAN, HELP!
OR NOT.

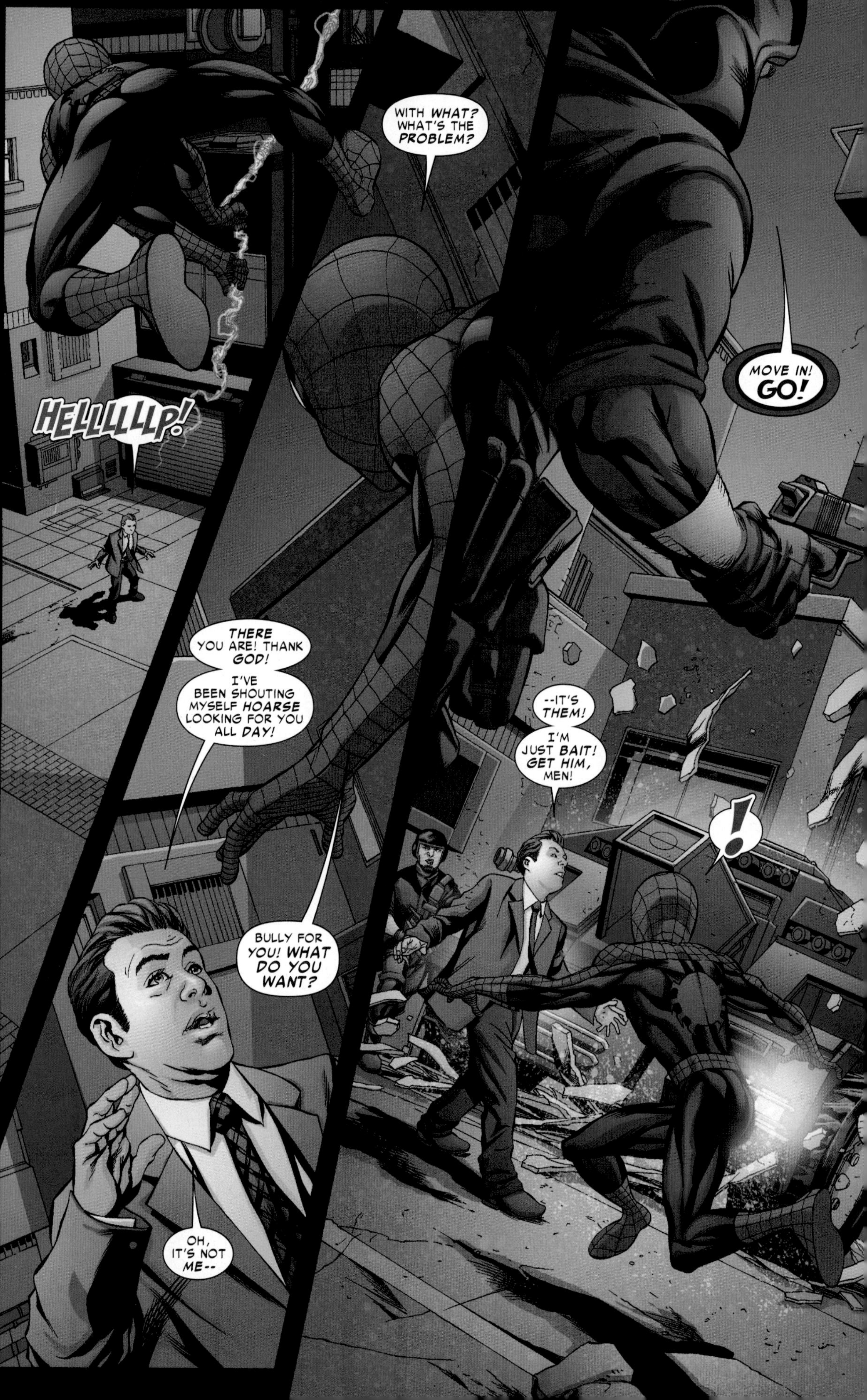
HELLLLLLP!
WITH WHAT? WHAT'S THE PROBLEM?
THERE YOU ARE! THANK GOD!
I'VE BEEN SHOUTING MYSELF HOARSE LOOKING FOR YOU ALL DAY!
BULLY FOR YOU! WHAT DO YOU WANT?
OH, IT'S NOT ME--
--IT'S THEM!
I'M JUST BAIT! GET HIM, MEN!
MOVE IN! GO!
!

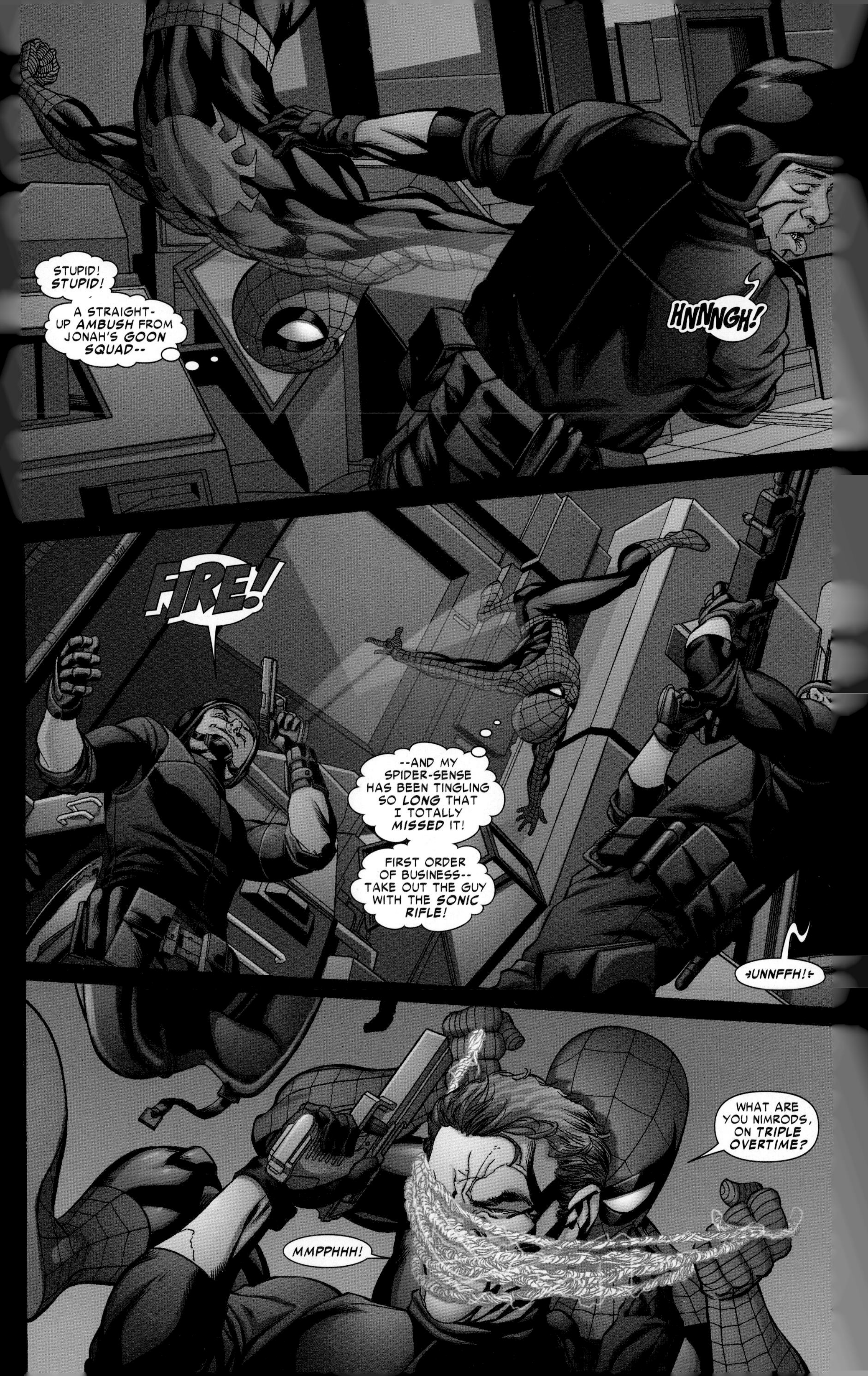

STUPID! STUPID!
A STRAIGHT-UP AMBUSH FROM JONAH'S GOON SQUAD--
HNNNGH!
FIRE!
--AND MY SPIDER-SENSE HAS BEEN TINGLING SO LONG THAT I TOTALLY MISSED IT!
FIRST ORDER OF BUSINESS--TAKE OUT THE GUY WITH THE SONIC RIFLE!
UNNFFH!
WHAT ARE YOU NIMRODS, ON TRIPLE OVERTIME?
MMPPHHH!

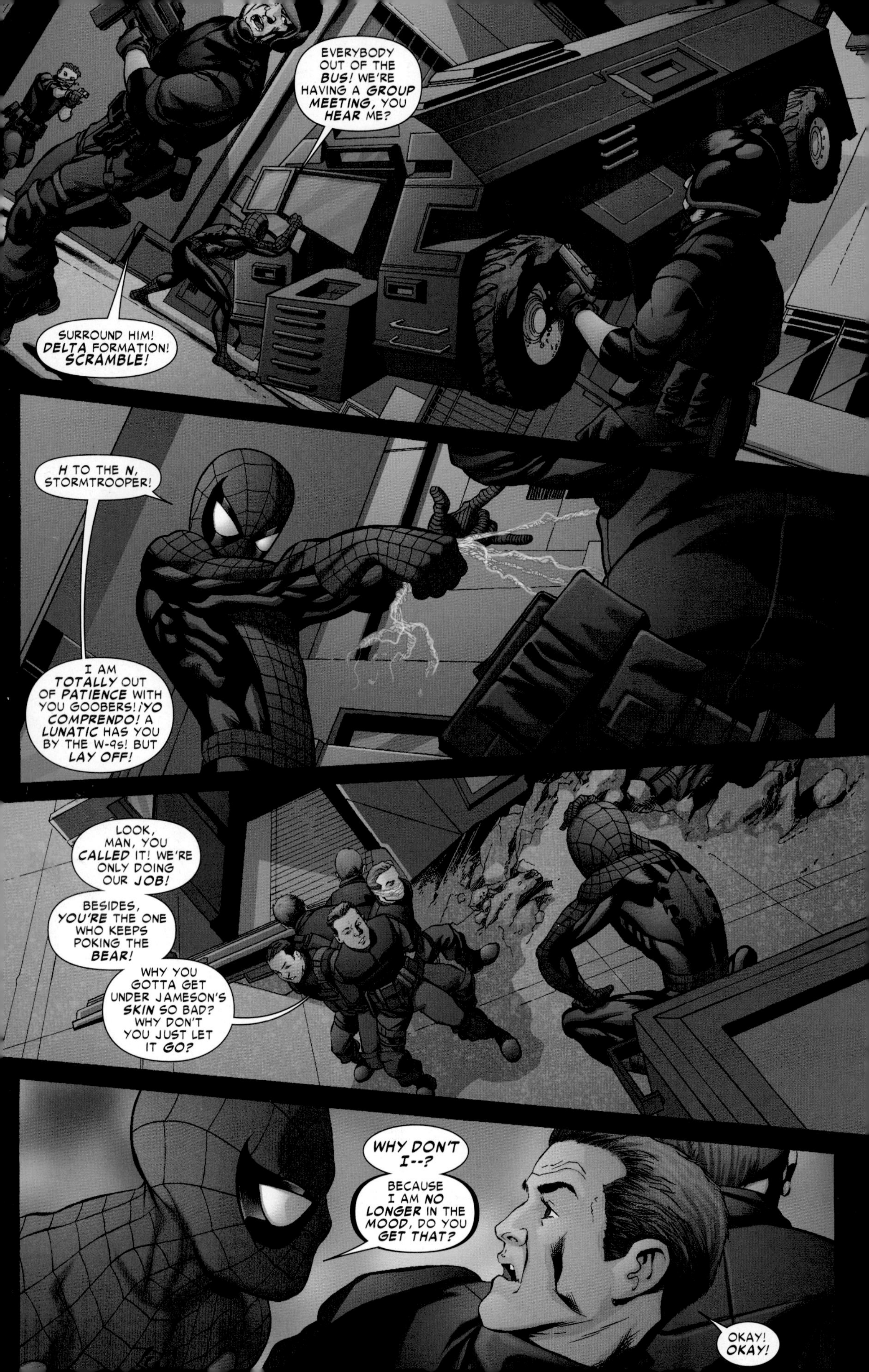

EVERYBODY OUT OF THE BUS! WE'RE HAVING A GROUP MEETING, YOU HEAR ME?
SURROUND HIM! DELTA FORMATION! SCRAMBLE!
H TO THE N, STORMTROOPER!
I AM TOTALLY OUT OF PATIENCE WITH YOU GOOBERS! ¡YO COMPRENDO! A LUNATIC HAS YOU BY THE W-9s! BUT LAY OFF!
LOOK, MAN, YOU CALLED IT! WE'RE ONLY DOING OUR JOB!
BESIDES, YOU'RE THE ONE WHO KEEPS POKING THE BEAR!
WHY YOU GOTTA GET UNDER JAMESON'S SKIN SO BAD? WHY DON'T YOU JUST LET IT GO?
WHY DON'T I--?
BECAUSE I AM NO LONGER IN THE MOOD, DO YOU GET THAT?
OKAY! OKAY!

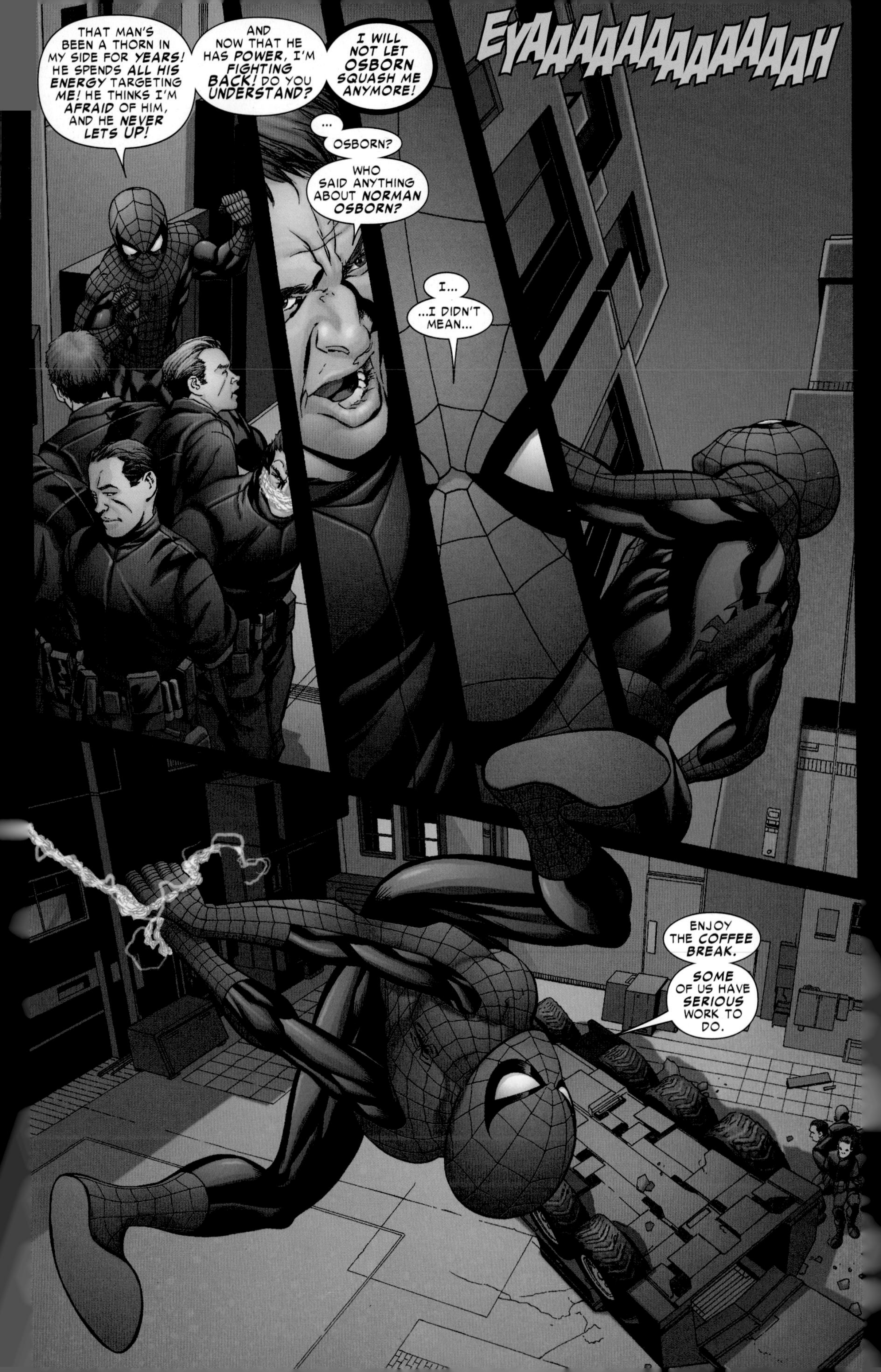
EYAAAAAAAAAAAAH
THAT MAN'S BEEN A THORN IN MY SIDE FOR YEARS! HE SPENDS ALL HIS ENERGY TARGETING ME! HE THINKS I'M AFRAID OF HIM, AND HE NEVER LETS UP!
AND NOW THAT HE HAS POWER, I'M FIGHTING BACK! DO YOU UNDERSTAND?
I WILL NOT LET OSBORN SQUASH ME ANYMORE!
...
OSBORN?
WHO SAID ANYTHING ABOUT NORMAN OSBORN?
I...
...I DIDN'T MEAN...
ENJOY THE COFFEE BREAK.
SOME OF US HAVE SERIOUS WORK TO DO.

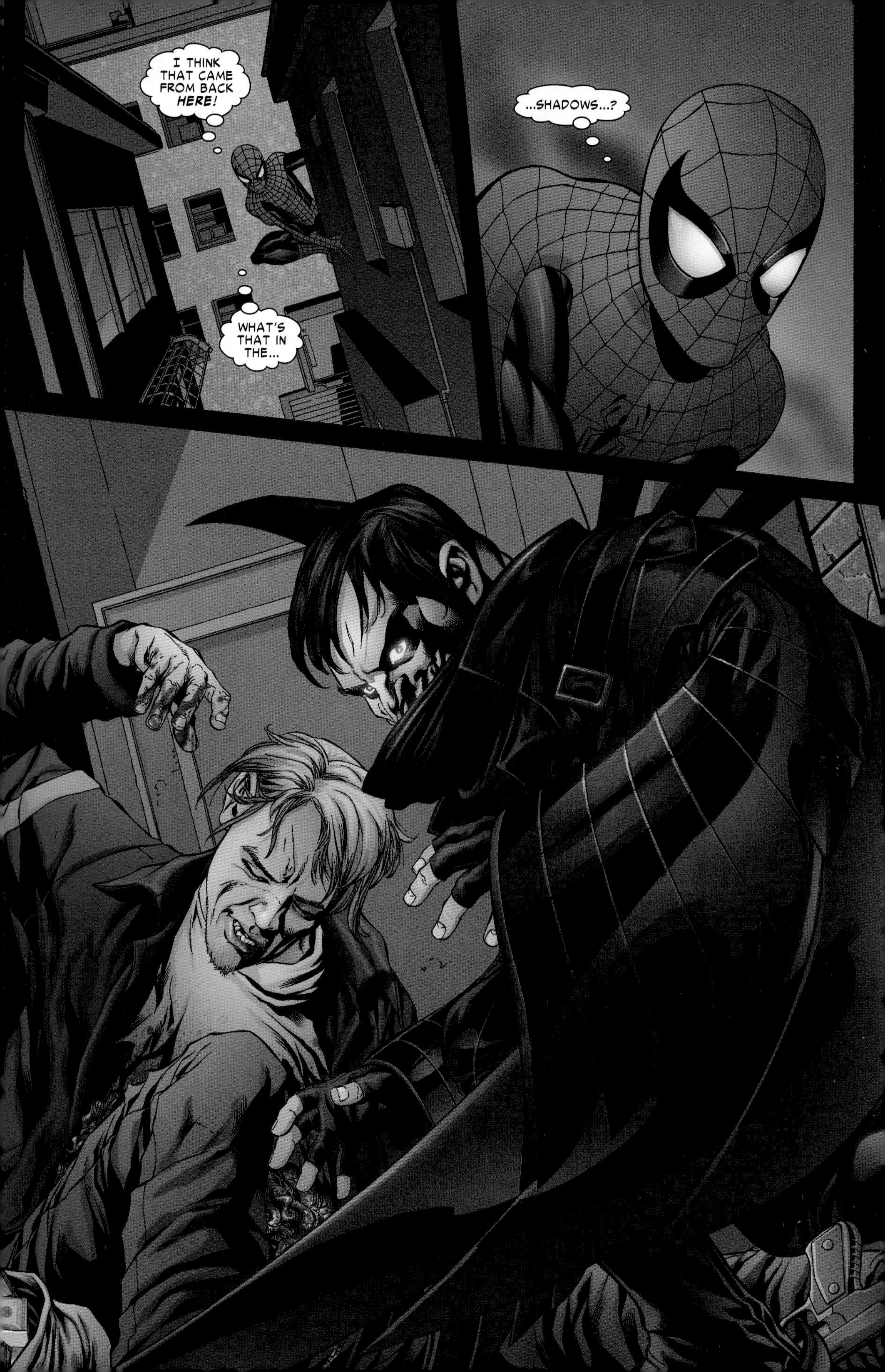
I THINK THAT CAME FROM BACK *HERE!*
WHAT'S THAT IN THE...
...SHADOWS...?

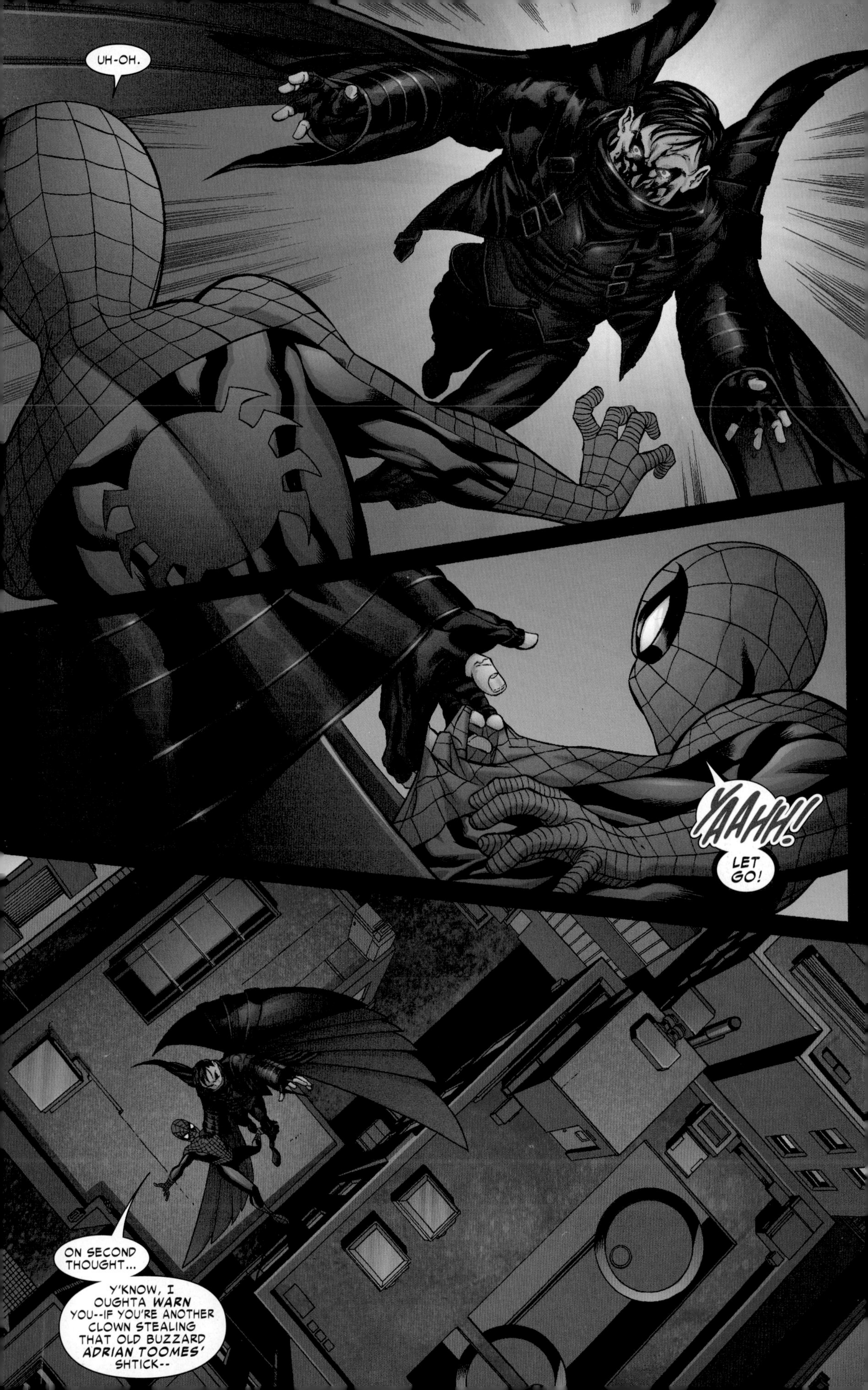
UH-OH.
YAAHH!
LET GO!
ON SECOND THOUGHT...
Y'KNOW, I OUGHTA *WARN* YOU--IF YOU'RE ANOTHER CLOWN STEALING THAT OLD BUZZARD *ADRIAN TOOMES'* SHTICK--

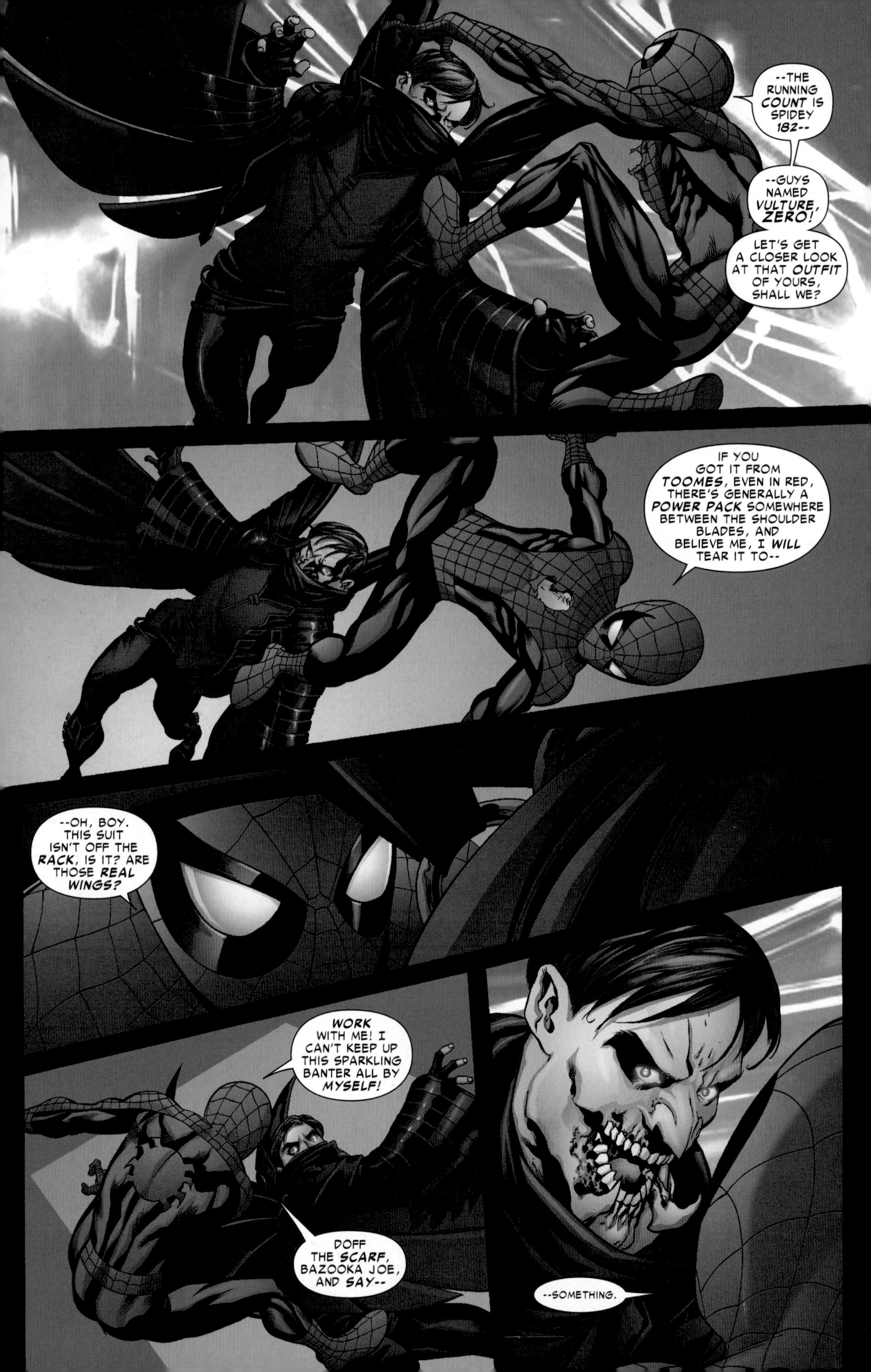
--THE RUNNING COUNT IS SPIDEY 182--
--GUYS NAMED VULTURE, ZERO!
LET'S GET A CLOSER LOOK AT THAT OUTFIT OF YOURS, SHALL WE?
IF YOU GOT IT FROM TOOMES, EVEN IN RED, THERE'S GENERALLY A POWER PACK SOMEWHERE BETWEEN THE SHOULDER BLADES, AND BELIEVE ME, I WILL TEAR IT TO--
--OH, BOY. THIS SUIT ISN'T OFF THE RACK, IS IT? ARE THOSE REAL WINGS?
WORK WITH ME! I CAN'T KEEP UP THIS SPARKLING BANTER ALL BY MYSELF!
DOFF THE SCARF, BAZOOKA JOE, AND SAY--
--SOMETHING.

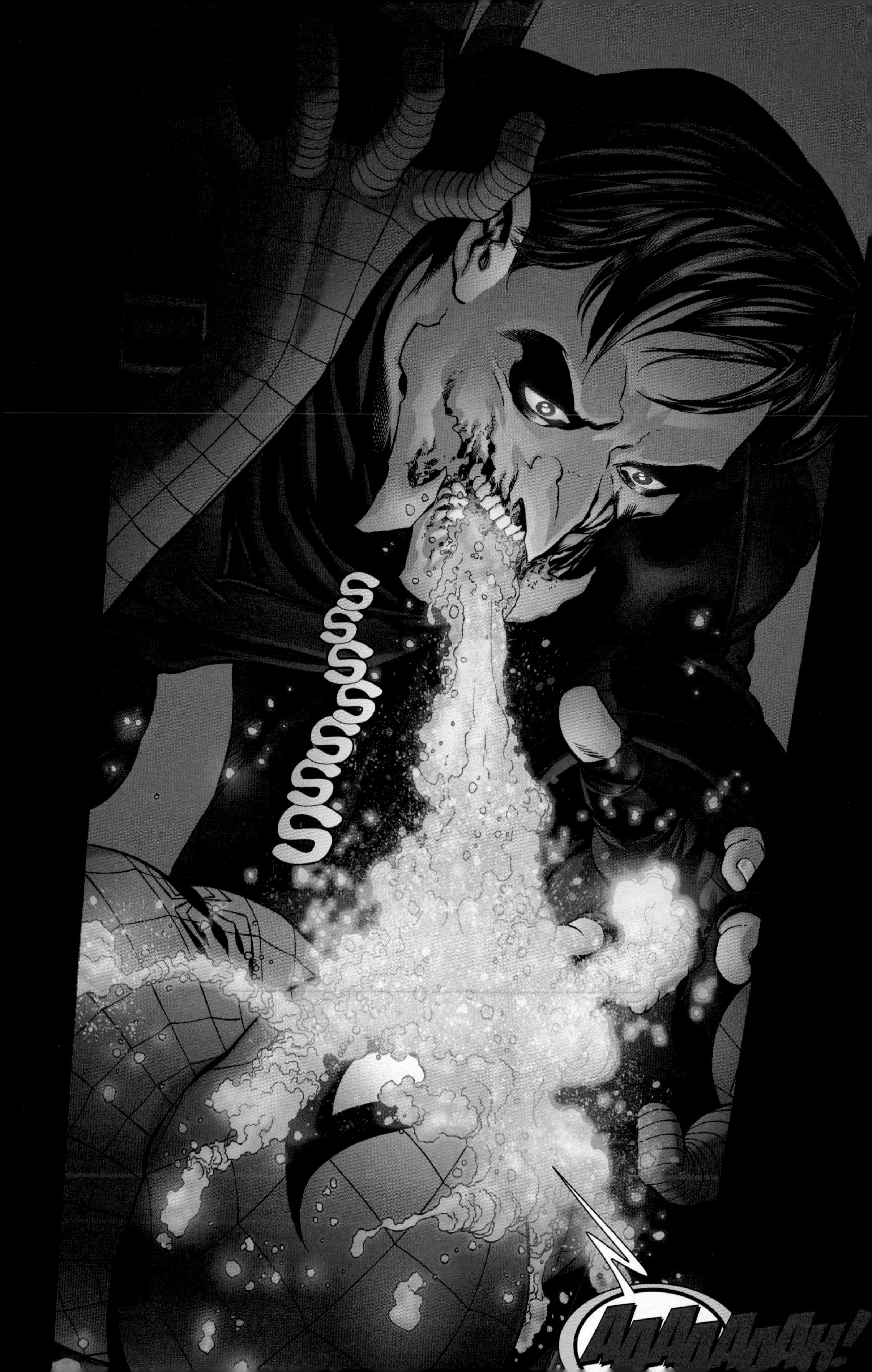
SSSSSSSSS

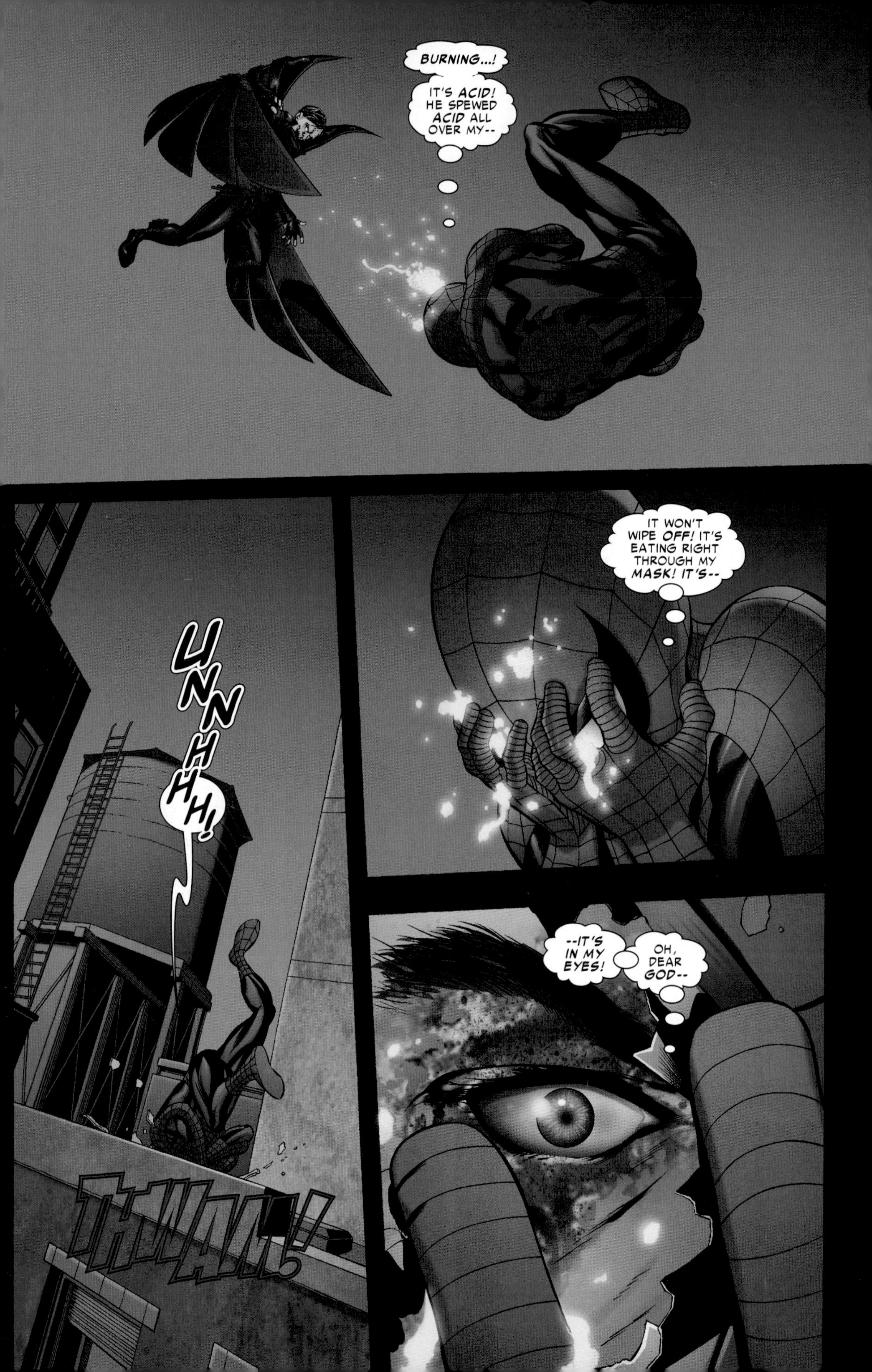
BURNING...!
IT'S ACID! HE SPEWED ACID ALL OVER MY--
UNNHHH!
THWAM!
IT WON'T WIPE OFF! IT'S EATING RIGHT THROUGH MY MASK! IT'S--
--IT'S IN MY EYES!
OH, DEAR GOD--

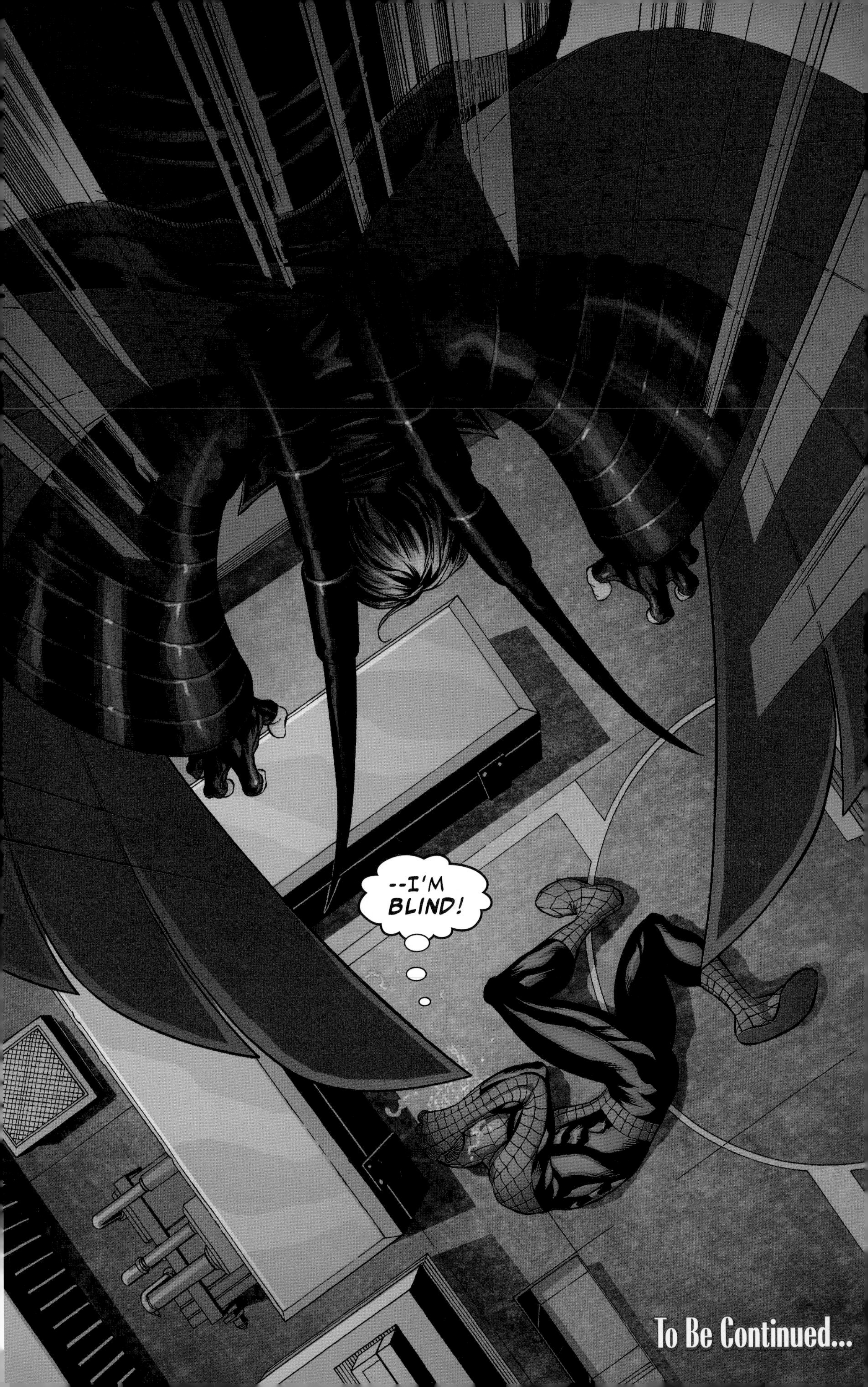
--I'M BLIND!
To Be Continued...

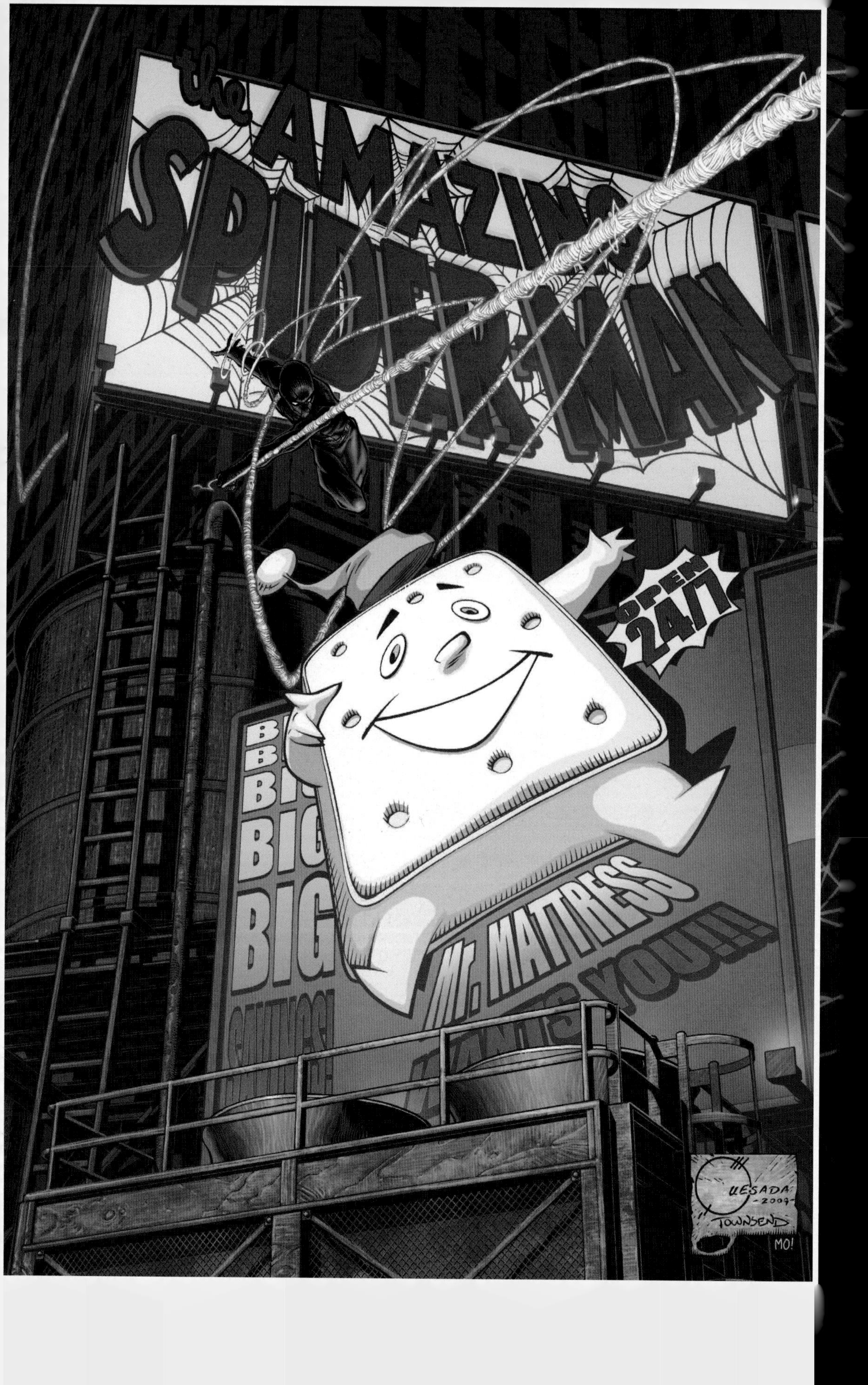
the AMAZING SPIDER-MAN
OPEN 24/7
BIG
BIG
Mr. MATRESS
YOU!!!
QUESADA 2007
TOWNSEND
MO!

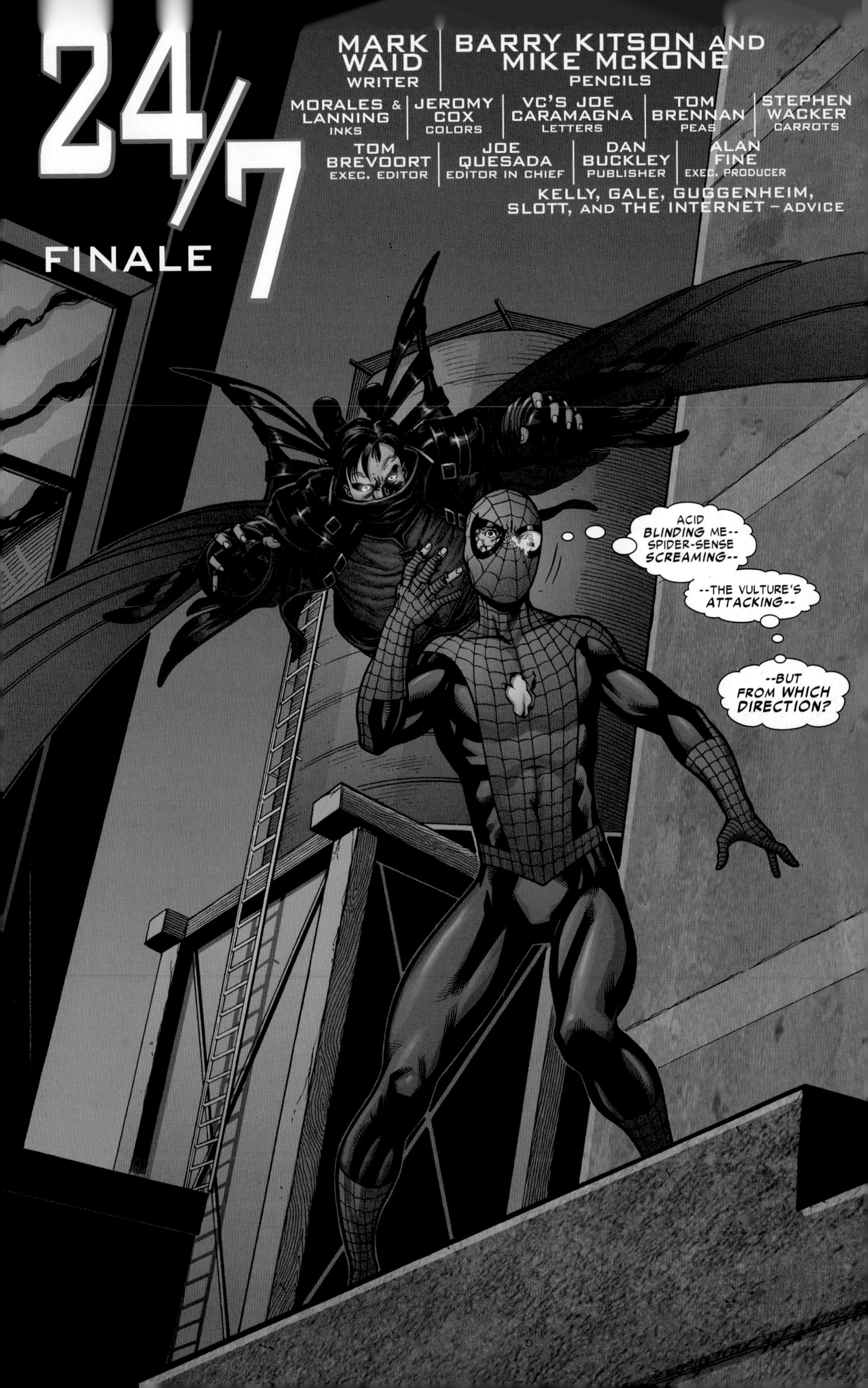
24/7
FINALE
MARK WAID WRITER
BARRY KITSON AND MIKE McKONE PENCILS
MORALES & LANNING INKS
JEROMY COX COLORS
VC'S JOE CARAMAGNA LETTERS
TOM BRENNAN PEAS
STEPHEN WACKER CARROTS
TOM BREVOORT EXEC. EDITOR
JOE QUESADA EDITOR IN CHIEF
DAN BUCKLEY PUBLISHER
ALAN FINE EXEC. PRODUCER
KELLY, GALE, GUGGENHEIM, SLOTT, AND THE INTERNET – ADVICE
ACID BLINDING ME--SPIDER-SENSE SCREAMING--
--THE VULTURE'S ATTACKING--
--BUT FROM WHICH DIRECTION?

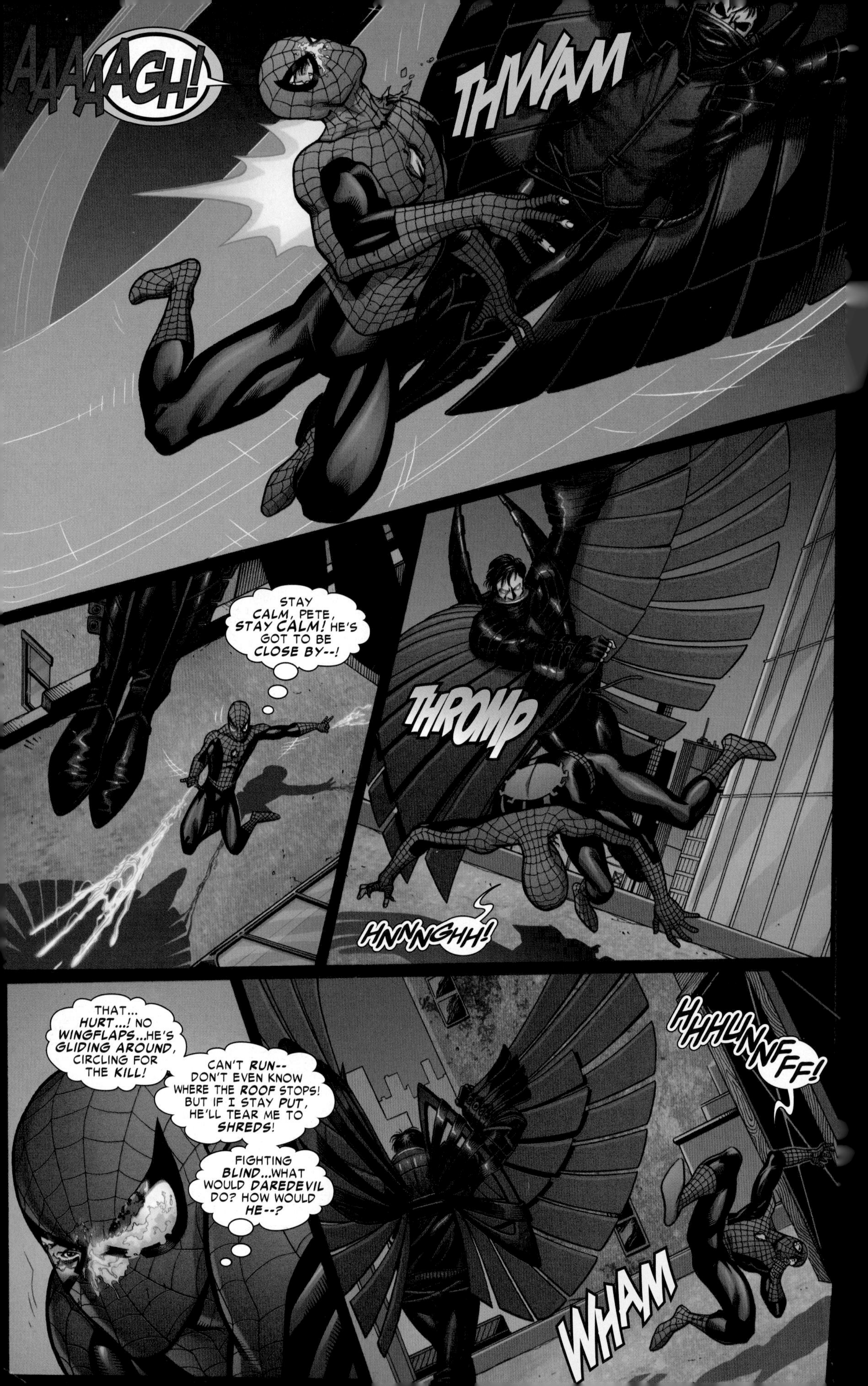
AAAAAGH!
THWAM
STAY CALM, PETE, STAY CALM! HE'S GOT TO BE CLOSE BY--!
THROMP
HNNNGHH!
THAT... HURT...! NO WINGFLAPS...HE'S GLIDING AROUND, CIRCLING FOR THE KILL!
CAN'T RUN-- DON'T EVEN KNOW WHERE THE ROOF STOPS! BUT IF I STAY PUT, HE'LL TEAR ME TO SHREDS!
FIGHTING BLIND...WHAT WOULD DAREDEVIL DO? HOW WOULD HE--?
HHHLUNNFFF!
WHAM

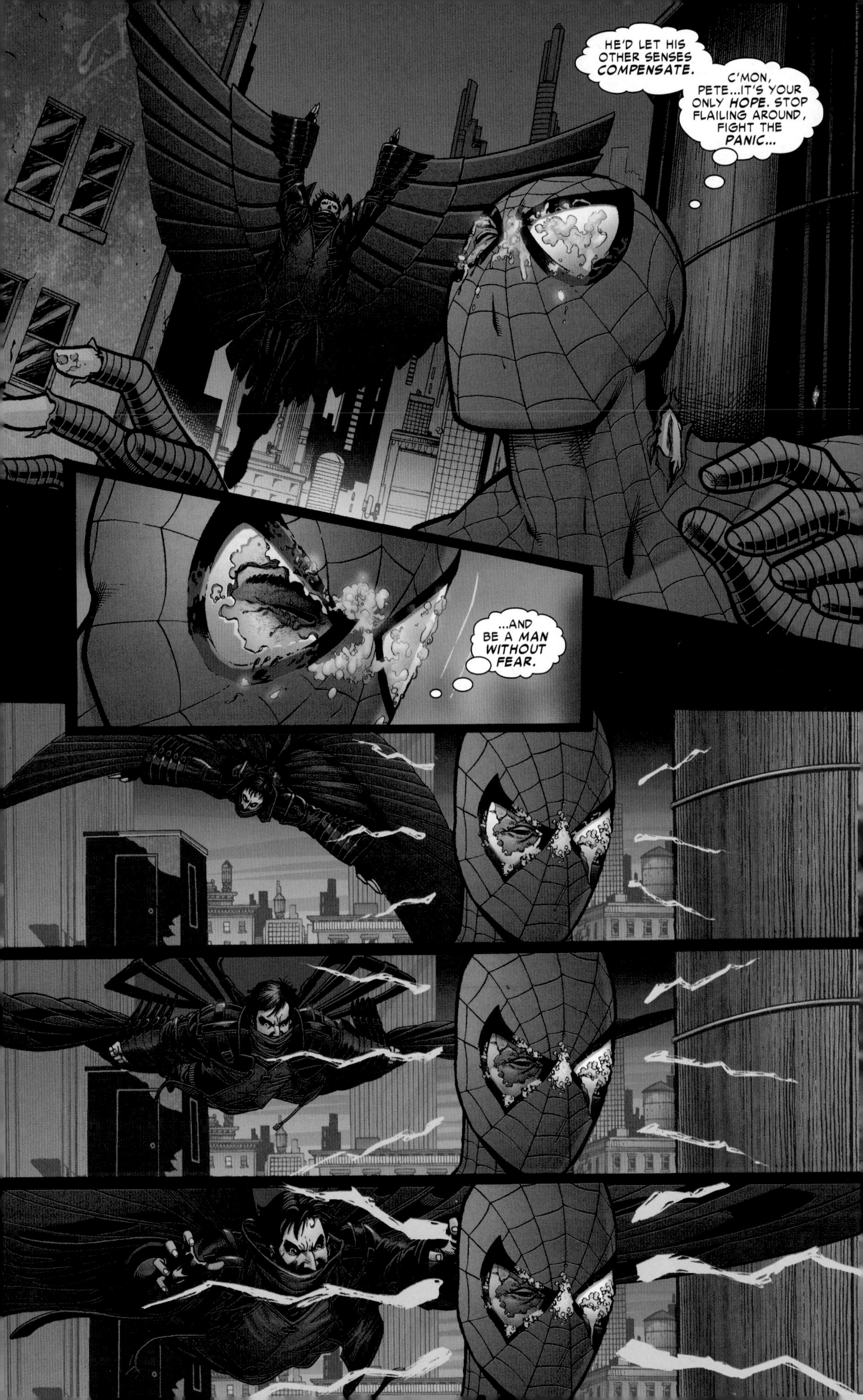
HE'D LET HIS OTHER SENSES COMPENSATE.
C'MON, PETE...IT'S YOUR ONLY HOPE. STOP FLAILING AROUND, FIGHT THE PANIC...
...AND BE A MAN WITHOUT FEAR.

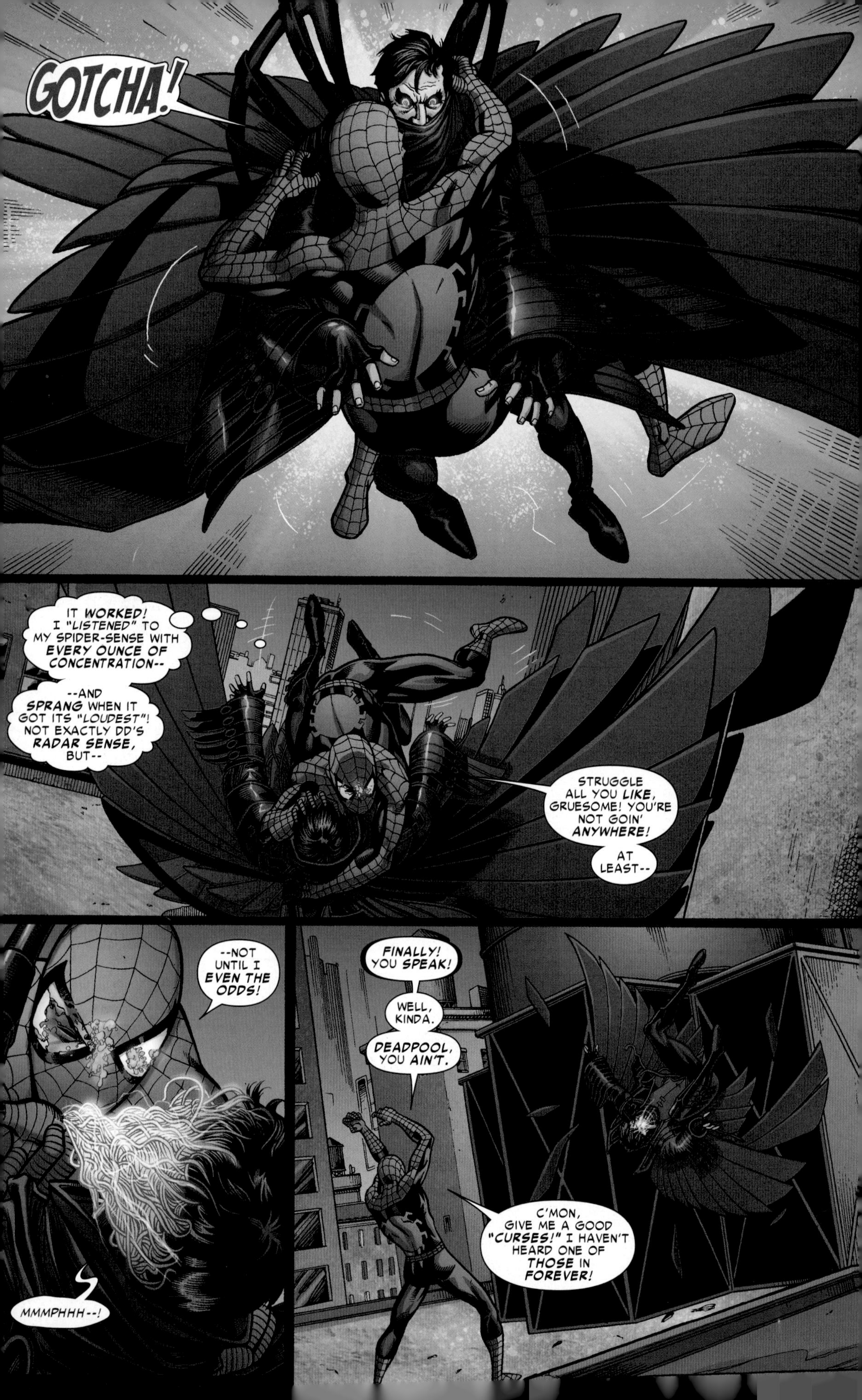
GOTCHA!
IT WORKED! I "LISTENED" TO MY SPIDER-SENSE WITH EVERY OUNCE OF CONCENTRATION--
--AND SPRANG WHEN IT GOT ITS "LOUDEST"! NOT EXACTLY DD'S RADAR SENSE, BUT--
STRUGGLE ALL YOU LIKE, GRUESOME! YOU'RE NOT GOIN' ANYWHERE!
AT LEAST--
--NOT UNTIL I EVEN THE ODDS!
MMMPHHH--!
FINALLY! YOU SPEAK!
WELL, KINDA.
DEADPOOL, YOU AIN'T.
C'MON, GIVE ME A GOOD "CURSES!" I HAVEN'T HEARD ONE OF THOSE IN FOREVER!

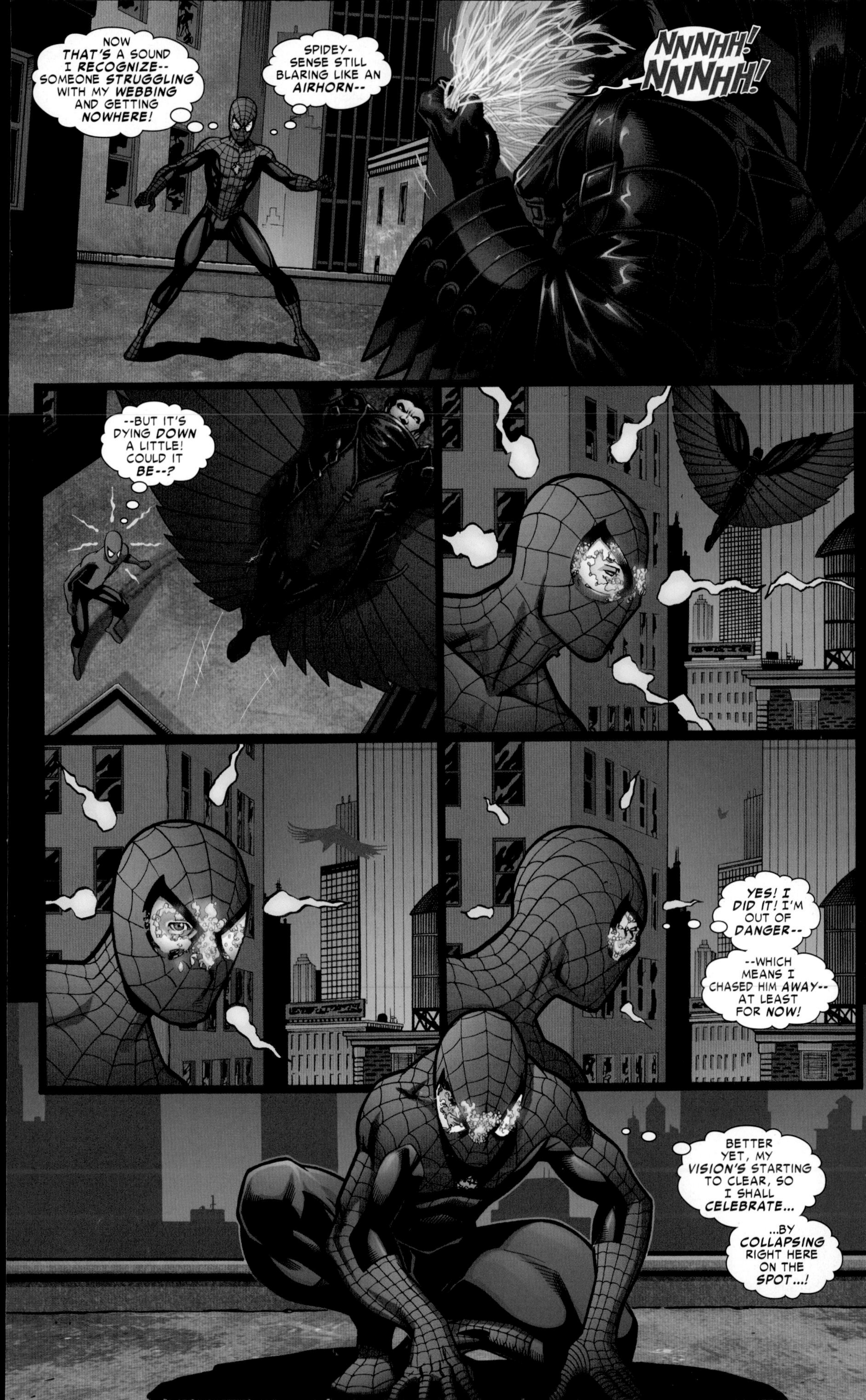
NOW THAT'S A SOUND I RECOGNIZE-- SOMEONE STRUGGLING WITH MY WEBBING AND GETTING NOWHERE!
SPIDEY-SENSE STILL BLARING LIKE AN AIRHORN--
NNNHH! NNNHH!
--BUT IT'S DYING DOWN A LITTLE! COULD IT BE--?
YES! I DID IT! I'M OUT OF DANGER--
--WHICH MEANS I CHASED HIM AWAY-- AT LEAST FOR NOW!
BETTER YET, MY VISION'S STARTING TO CLEAR, SO I SHALL CELEBRATE...
...BY COLLAPSING RIGHT HERE ON THE SPOT...!

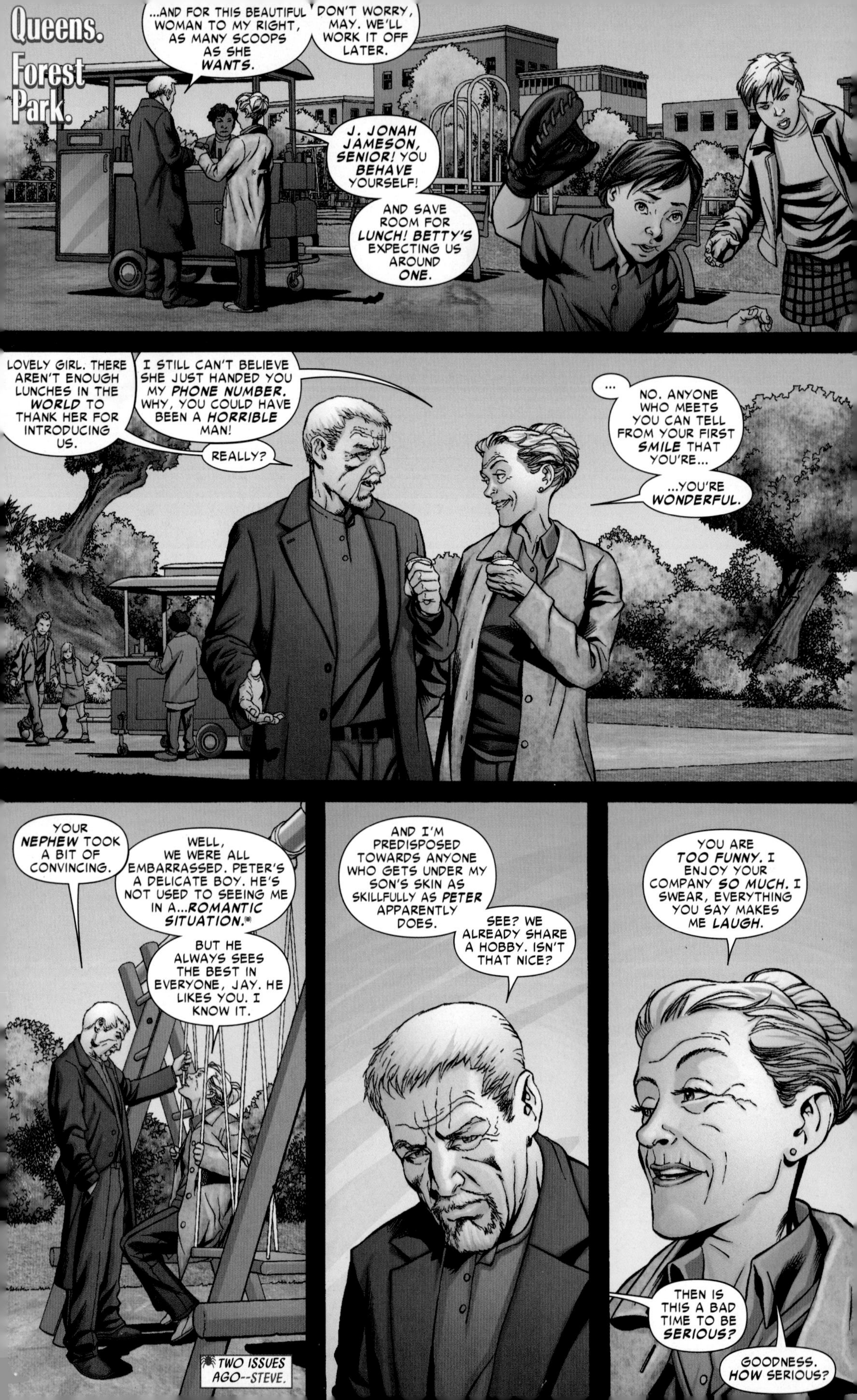
Queens. Forest Park.
...AND FOR THIS BEAUTIFUL WOMAN TO MY RIGHT, AS MANY SCOOPS AS SHE WANTS.
DON'T WORRY, MAY. WE'LL WORK IT OFF LATER.
J. JONAH JAMESON, SENIOR! YOU BEHAVE YOURSELF!
AND SAVE ROOM FOR LUNCH! BETTY'S EXPECTING US AROUND ONE.
LOVELY GIRL. THERE AREN'T ENOUGH LUNCHES IN THE WORLD TO THANK HER FOR INTRODUCING US.
I STILL CAN'T BELIEVE SHE JUST HANDED YOU MY PHONE NUMBER. WHY, YOU COULD HAVE BEEN A HORRIBLE MAN!
REALLY?
...
NO. ANYONE WHO MEETS YOU CAN TELL FROM YOUR FIRST SMILE THAT YOU'RE...
...YOU'RE WONDERFUL.
YOUR NEPHEW TOOK A BIT OF CONVINCING.
WELL, WE WERE ALL EMBARRASSED. PETER'S A DELICATE BOY. HE'S NOT USED TO SEEING ME IN A...ROMANTIC SITUATION.*
BUT HE ALWAYS SEES THE BEST IN EVERYONE, JAY. HE LIKES YOU. I KNOW IT.
*TWO ISSUES AGO--STEVE.
AND I'M PREDISPOSED TOWARDS ANYONE WHO GETS UNDER MY SON'S SKIN AS SKILLFULLY AS PETER APPARENTLY DOES.
SEE? WE ALREADY SHARE A HOBBY. ISN'T THAT NICE?
YOU ARE TOO FUNNY. I ENJOY YOUR COMPANY SO MUCH. I SWEAR, EVERYTHING YOU SAY MAKES ME LAUGH.
THEN IS THIS A BAD TIME TO BE SERIOUS?
GOODNESS. HOW SERIOUS?

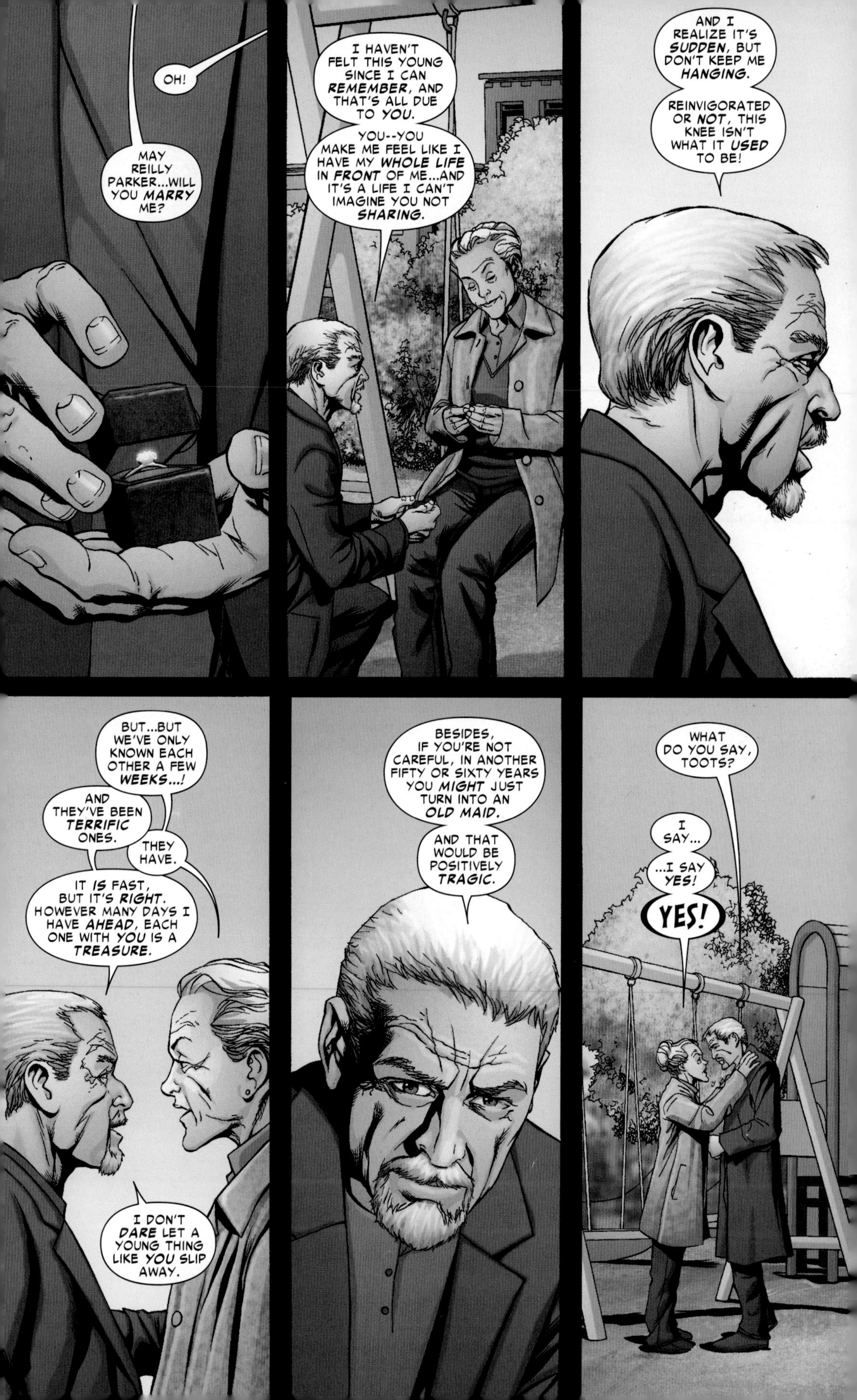
OH!
MAY REILLY PARKER...WILL YOU MARRY ME?
I HAVEN'T FELT THIS YOUNG SINCE I CAN REMEMBER, AND THAT'S ALL DUE TO YOU.
YOU--YOU MAKE ME FEEL LIKE I HAVE MY WHOLE LIFE IN FRONT OF ME...AND IT'S A LIFE I CAN'T IMAGINE YOU NOT SHARING.
AND I REALIZE IT'S SUDDEN, BUT DON'T KEEP ME HANGING.
REINVIGORATED OR NOT, THIS KNEE ISN'T WHAT IT USED TO BE!
BUT...BUT WE'VE ONLY KNOWN EACH OTHER A FEW WEEKS...!
AND THEY'VE BEEN TERRIFIC ONES.
THEY HAVE.
IT IS FAST, BUT IT'S RIGHT. HOWEVER MANY DAYS I HAVE AHEAD, EACH ONE WITH YOU IS A TREASURE.
I DON'T DARE LET A YOUNG THING LIKE YOU SLIP AWAY.
BESIDES, IF YOU'RE NOT CAREFUL, IN ANOTHER FIFTY OR SIXTY YEARS YOU MIGHT JUST TURN INTO AN OLD MAID.
AND THAT WOULD BE POSITIVELY TRAGIC.
WHAT DO YOU SAY, TOOTS?
I SAY...
...I SAY YES!
YES!

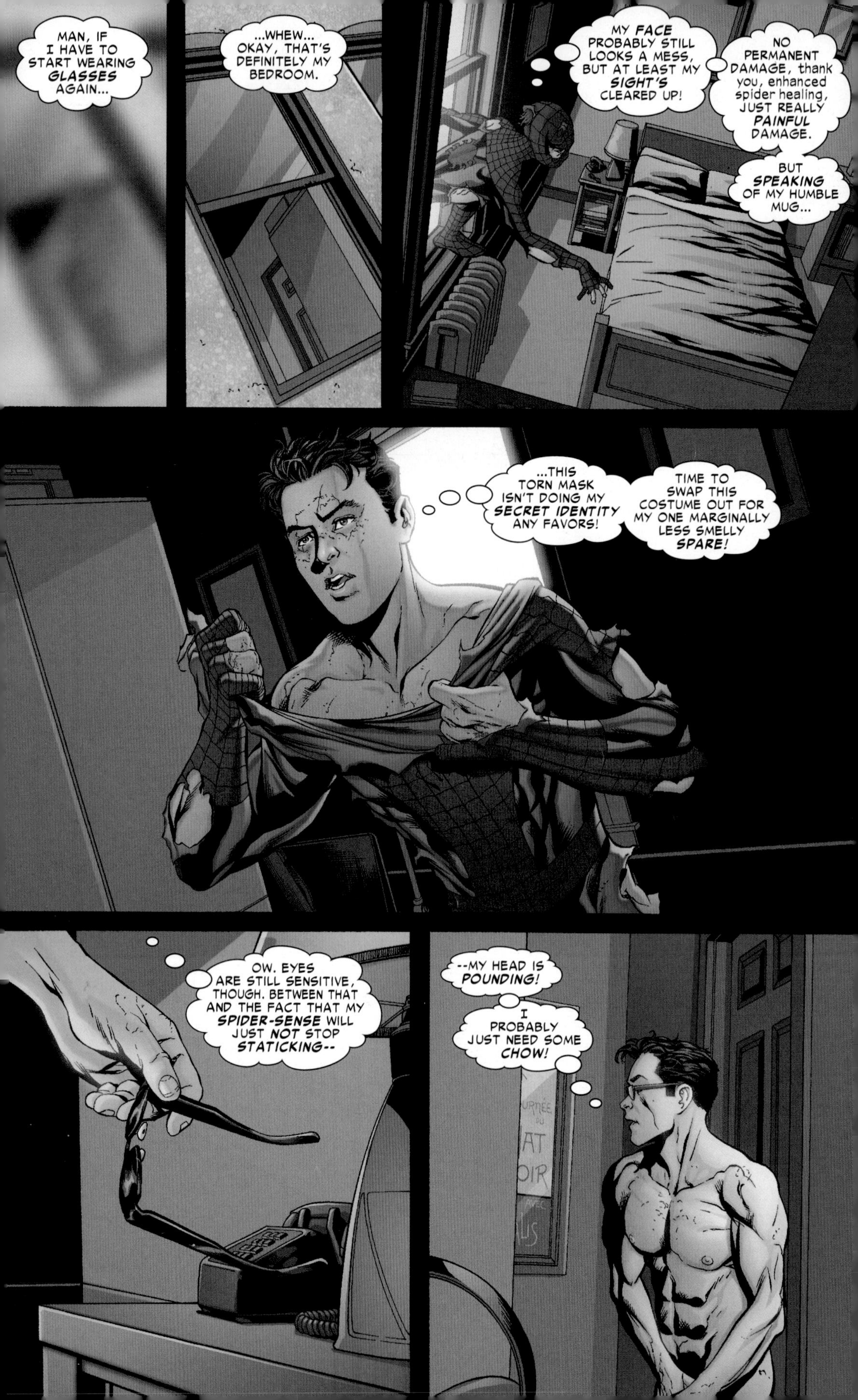
MAN, IF I HAVE TO START WEARING GLASSES AGAIN...
...WHEW... OKAY, THAT'S DEFINITELY MY BEDROOM.
MY FACE PROBABLY STILL LOOKS A MESS, BUT AT LEAST MY SIGHT'S CLEARED UP!
NO PERMANENT DAMAGE, thank you, enhanced spider healing, JUST REALLY PAINFUL DAMAGE.
BUT SPEAKING OF MY HUMBLE MUG...
...THIS TORN MASK ISN'T DOING MY SECRET IDENTITY ANY FAVORS!
TIME TO SWAP THIS COSTUME OUT FOR MY ONE MARGINALLY LESS SMELLY SPARE!
OW. EYES ARE STILL SENSITIVE, THOUGH. BETWEEN THAT AND THE FACT THAT MY SPIDER-SENSE WILL JUST NOT STOP STATICKING--
--MY HEAD IS POUNDING!
I PROBABLY JUST NEED SOME CHOW!

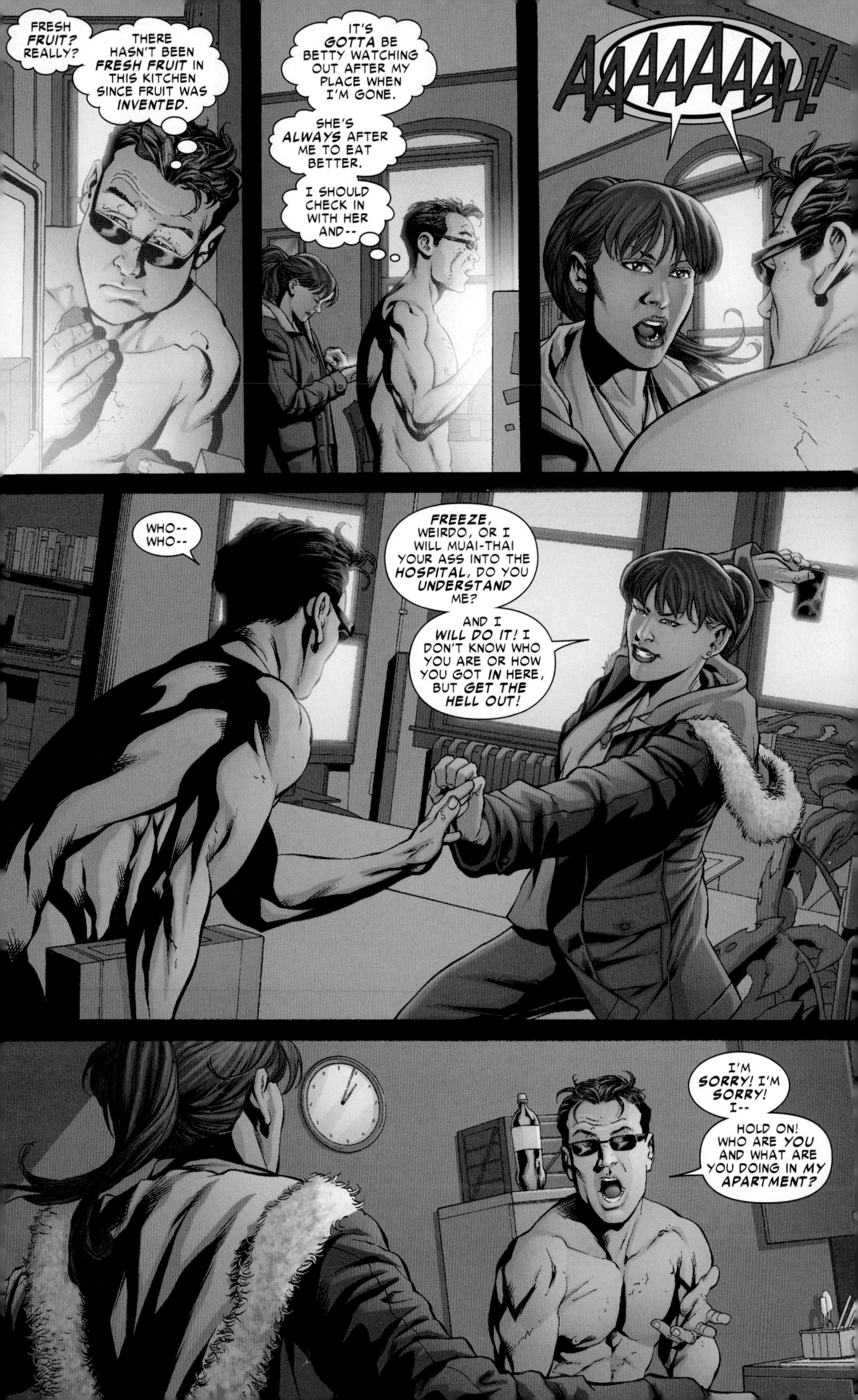
FRESH FRUIT? REALLY?
THERE HASN'T BEEN FRESH FRUIT IN THIS KITCHEN SINCE FRUIT WAS INVENTED.
IT'S GOTTA BE BETTY WATCHING OUT AFTER MY PLACE WHEN I'M GONE.
SHE'S ALWAYS AFTER ME TO EAT BETTER.
I SHOULD CHECK IN WITH HER AND--
AAAAAAAAH!
WHO-- WHO--
FREEZE, WEIRDO, OR I WILL MUAI-THAI YOUR ASS INTO THE HOSPITAL, DO YOU UNDERSTAND ME?
AND I WILL DO IT! I DON'T KNOW WHO YOU ARE OR HOW YOU GOT IN HERE, BUT GET THE HELL OUT!
I'M SORRY! I'M SORRY! I--
HOLD ON! WHO ARE YOU AND WHAT ARE YOU DOING IN MY APARTMENT?

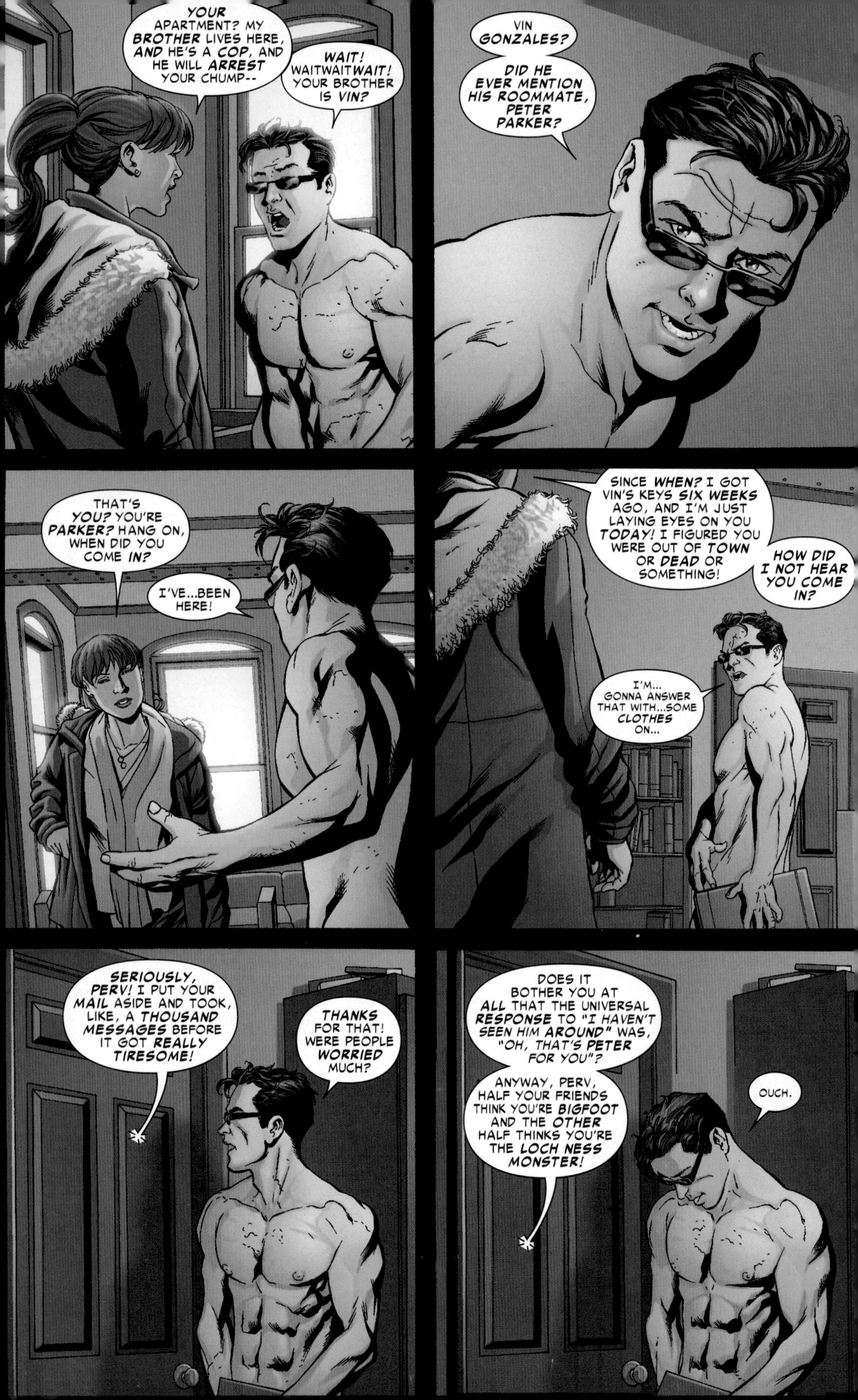
YOUR APARTMENT? MY BROTHER LIVES HERE, AND HE'S A COP, AND HE WILL ARREST YOUR CHUMP--
WAIT! WAITWAITWAIT! YOUR BROTHER IS VIN?
VIN GONZALES?
DID HE EVER MENTION HIS ROOMMATE, PETER PARKER?
THAT'S YOU? YOU'RE PARKER? HANG ON, WHEN DID YOU COME IN?
I'VE...BEEN HERE!
SINCE WHEN? I GOT VIN'S KEYS SIX WEEKS AGO, AND I'M JUST LAYING EYES ON YOU TODAY! I FIGURED YOU WERE OUT OF TOWN OR DEAD OR SOMETHING!
HOW DID I NOT HEAR YOU COME IN?
I'M... GONNA ANSWER THAT WITH...SOME CLOTHES ON...
SERIOUSLY, PERV! I PUT YOUR MAIL ASIDE AND TOOK, LIKE, A THOUSAND MESSAGES BEFORE IT GOT REALLY TIRESOME!
THANKS FOR THAT! WERE PEOPLE WORRIED MUCH?
DOES IT BOTHER YOU AT ALL THAT THE UNIVERSAL RESPONSE TO "I HAVEN'T SEEN HIM AROUND" WAS, "OH, THAT'S PETER FOR YOU"?
ANYWAY, PERV, HALF YOUR FRIENDS THINK YOU'RE BIGFOOT AND THE OTHER HALF THINKS YOU'RE THE LOCH NESS MONSTER!
OUCH.

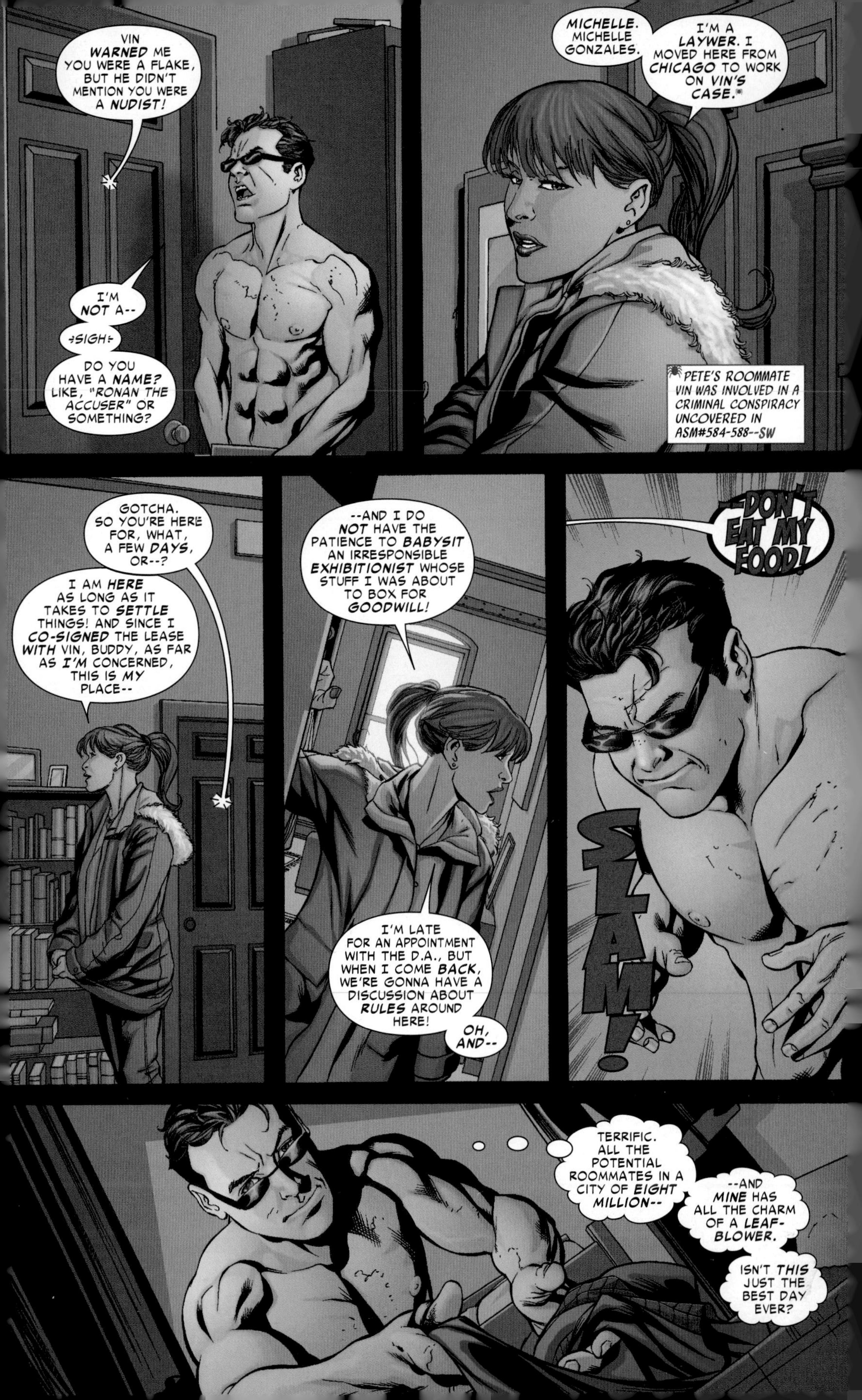

VIN WARNED ME YOU WERE A FLAKE, BUT HE DIDN'T MENTION YOU WERE A NUDIST!
I'M NOT A--
-SIGH-
DO YOU HAVE A NAME? LIKE, "RONAN THE ACCUSER" OR SOMETHING?
MICHELLE. MICHELLE GONZALES.
I'M A LAYWER. I MOVED HERE FROM CHICAGO TO WORK ON VIN'S CASE.*
*PETE'S ROOMMATE VIN WAS INVOLVED IN A CRIMINAL CONSPIRACY UNCOVERED IN ASM#584-588--SW
GOTCHA. SO YOU'RE HERE FOR, WHAT, A FEW DAYS, OR--?
I AM HERE AS LONG AS IT TAKES TO SETTLE THINGS! AND SINCE I CO-SIGNED THE LEASE WITH VIN, BUDDY, AS FAR AS I'M CONCERNED, THIS IS MY PLACE--
--AND I DO NOT HAVE THE PATIENCE TO BABYSIT AN IRRESPONSIBLE EXHIBITIONIST WHOSE STUFF I WAS ABOUT TO BOX FOR GOODWILL!
I'M LATE FOR AN APPOINTMENT WITH THE D.A., BUT WHEN I COME BACK, WE'RE GONNA HAVE A DISCUSSION ABOUT RULES AROUND HERE!
OH, AND--
--DON'T EAT MY FOOD!
SLAM!
TERRIFIC. ALL THE POTENTIAL ROOMMATES IN A CITY OF EIGHT MILLION--
--AND MINE HAS ALL THE CHARM OF A LEAF-BLOWER.
ISN'T THIS JUST THE BEST DAY EVER?

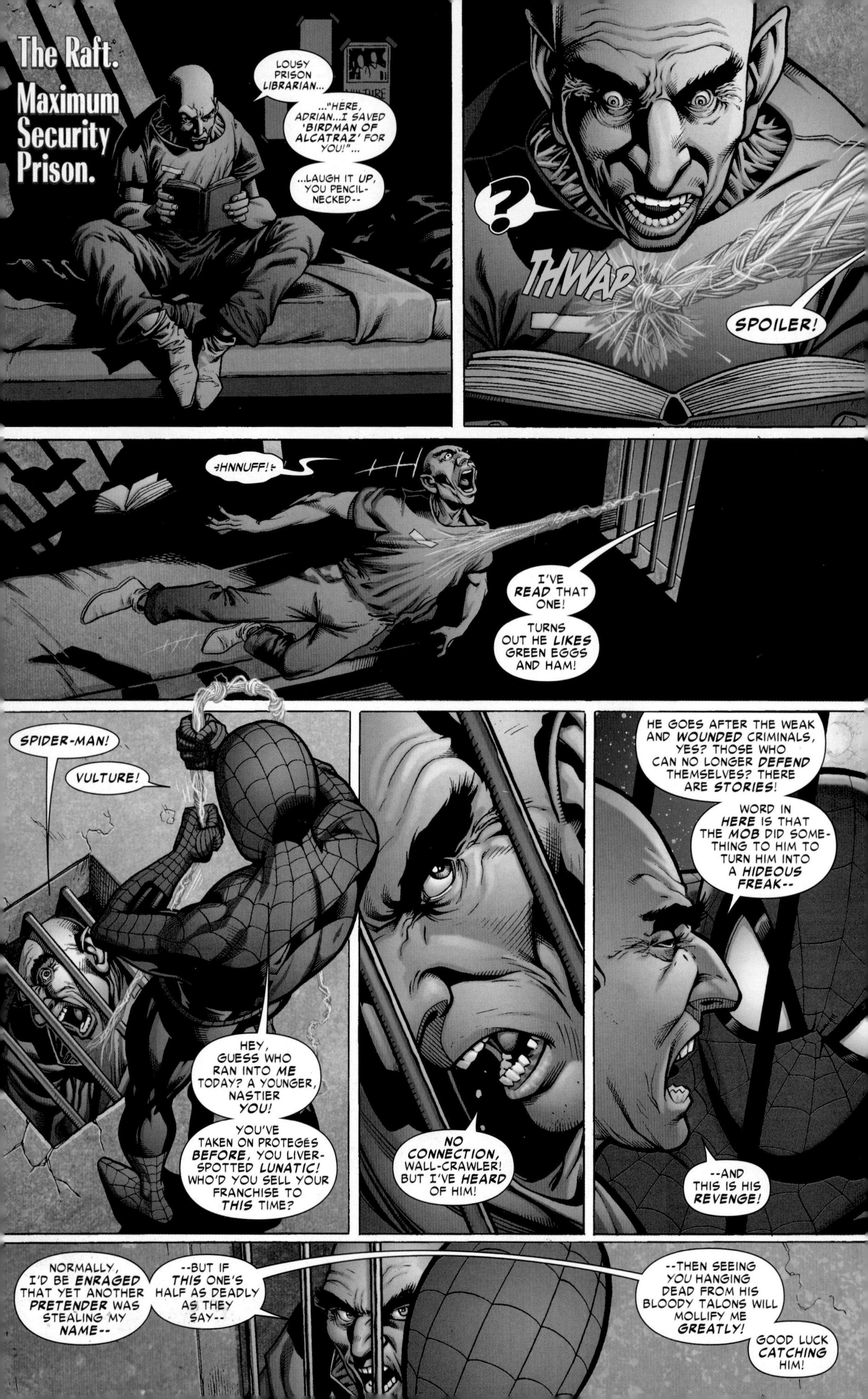
The Raft.
Maximum Security Prison.
LOUSY PRISON LIBRARIAN...
..."HERE, ADRIAN...I SAVED 'BIRDMAN OF ALCATRAZ' FOR YOU!"...
...LAUGH IT UP, YOU PENCIL-NECKED--
?
THWAP
SPOILER!
HNNUFF!
I'VE READ THAT ONE!
TURNS OUT HE LIKES GREEN EGGS AND HAM!
SPIDER-MAN!
VULTURE!
HEY, GUESS WHO RAN INTO ME TODAY? A YOUNGER, NASTIER YOU!
YOU'VE TAKEN ON PROTEGES BEFORE, YOU LIVER-SPOTTED LUNATIC! WHO'D YOU SELL YOUR FRANCHISE TO THIS TIME?
NO CONNECTION, WALL-CRAWLER! BUT I'VE HEARD OF HIM!
HE GOES AFTER THE WEAK AND WOUNDED CRIMINALS, YES? THOSE WHO CAN NO LONGER DEFEND THEMSELVES? THERE ARE STORIES!
WORD IN HERE IS THAT THE MOB DID SOME-THING TO HIM TO TURN HIM INTO A HIDEOUS FREAK--
--AND THIS IS HIS REVENGE!
NORMALLY, I'D BE ENRAGED THAT YET ANOTHER PRETENDER WAS STEALING MY NAME--
--BUT IF THIS ONE'S HALF AS DEADLY AS THEY SAY--
--THEN SEEING YOU HANGING DEAD FROM HIS BLOODY TALONS WILL MOLLIFY ME GREATLY!
GOOD LUCK CATCHING HIM!

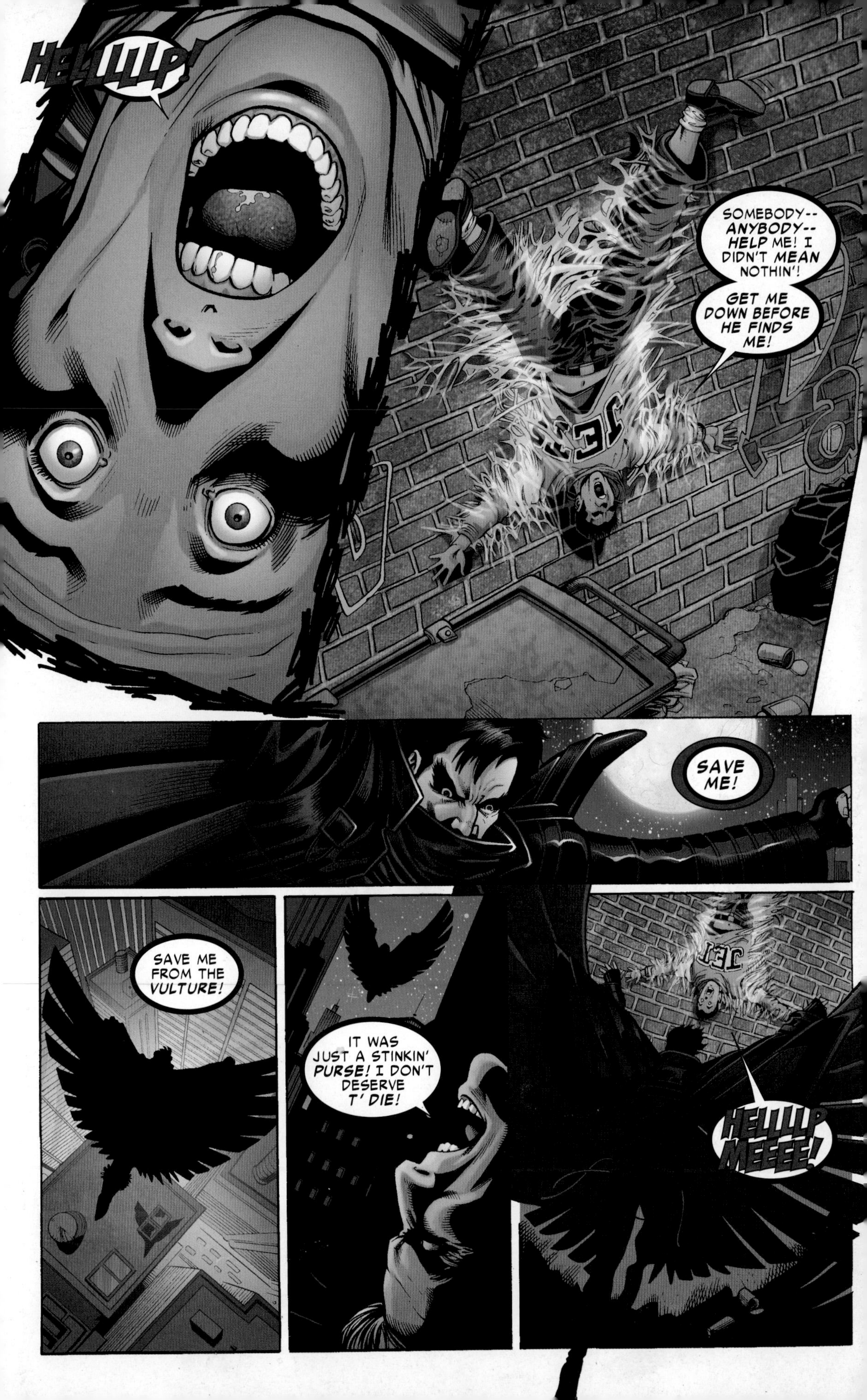
HELLLLP!
SOMEBODY-- ANYBODY-- HELP ME! I DIDN'T MEAN NOTHIN'!
GET ME DOWN BEFORE HE FINDS ME!
SAVE ME!
SAVE ME FROM THE VULTURE!
IT WAS JUST A STINKIN' PURSE! I DON'T DESERVE T' DIE!
HELLLLP MEEEE!

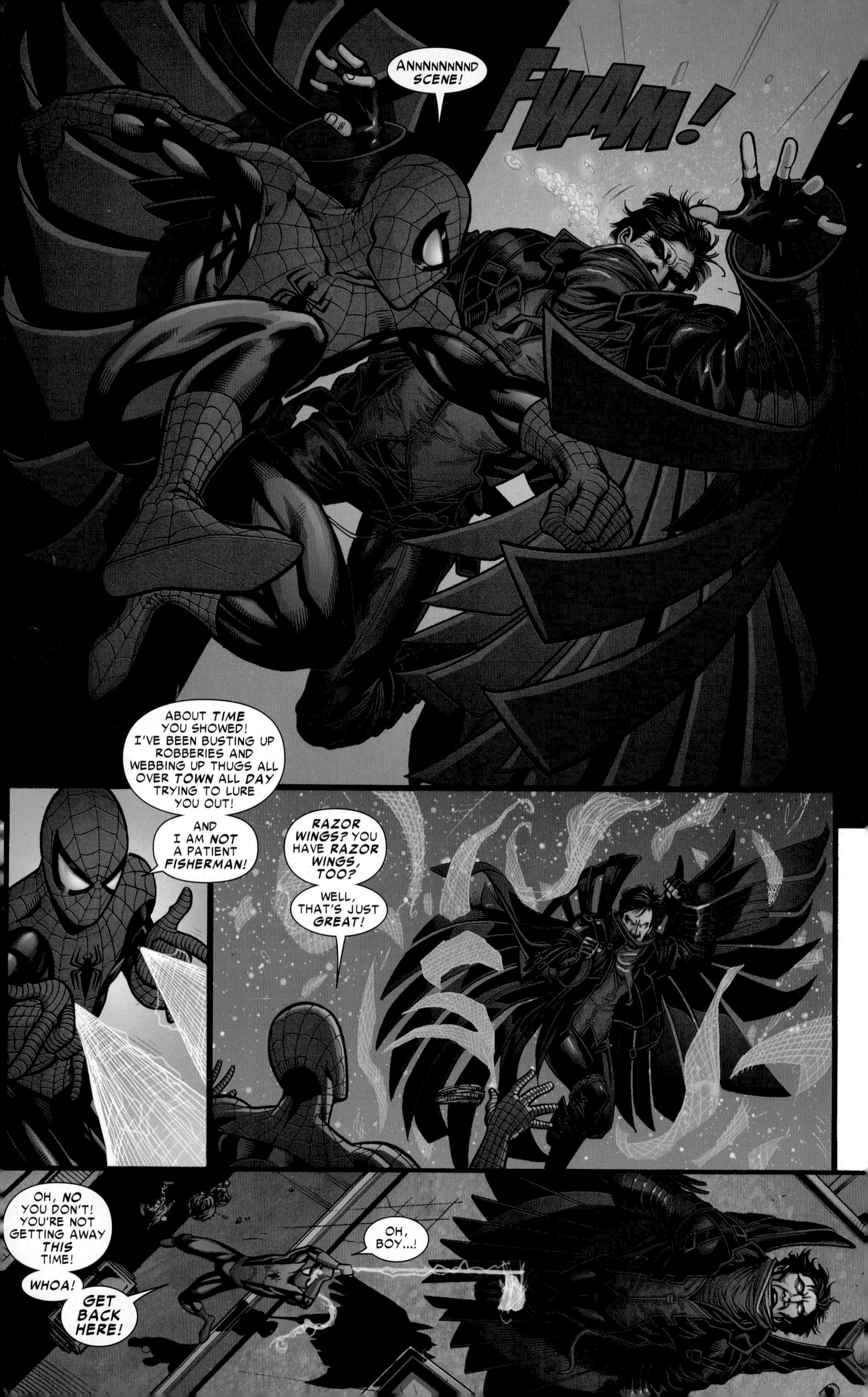
ANNNNNNNND SCENE!
FWAM!
ABOUT TIME YOU SHOWED! I'VE BEEN BUSTING UP ROBBERIES AND WEBBING UP THUGS ALL OVER TOWN ALL DAY TRYING TO LURE YOU OUT!
AND I AM NOT A PATIENT FISHERMAN!
RAZOR WINGS? YOU HAVE RAZOR WINGS, TOO?
WELL, THAT'S JUST GREAT!
OH, NO YOU DON'T! YOU'RE NOT GETTING AWAY THIS TIME!
OH, BOY...!
WHOA!
GET BACK HERE!

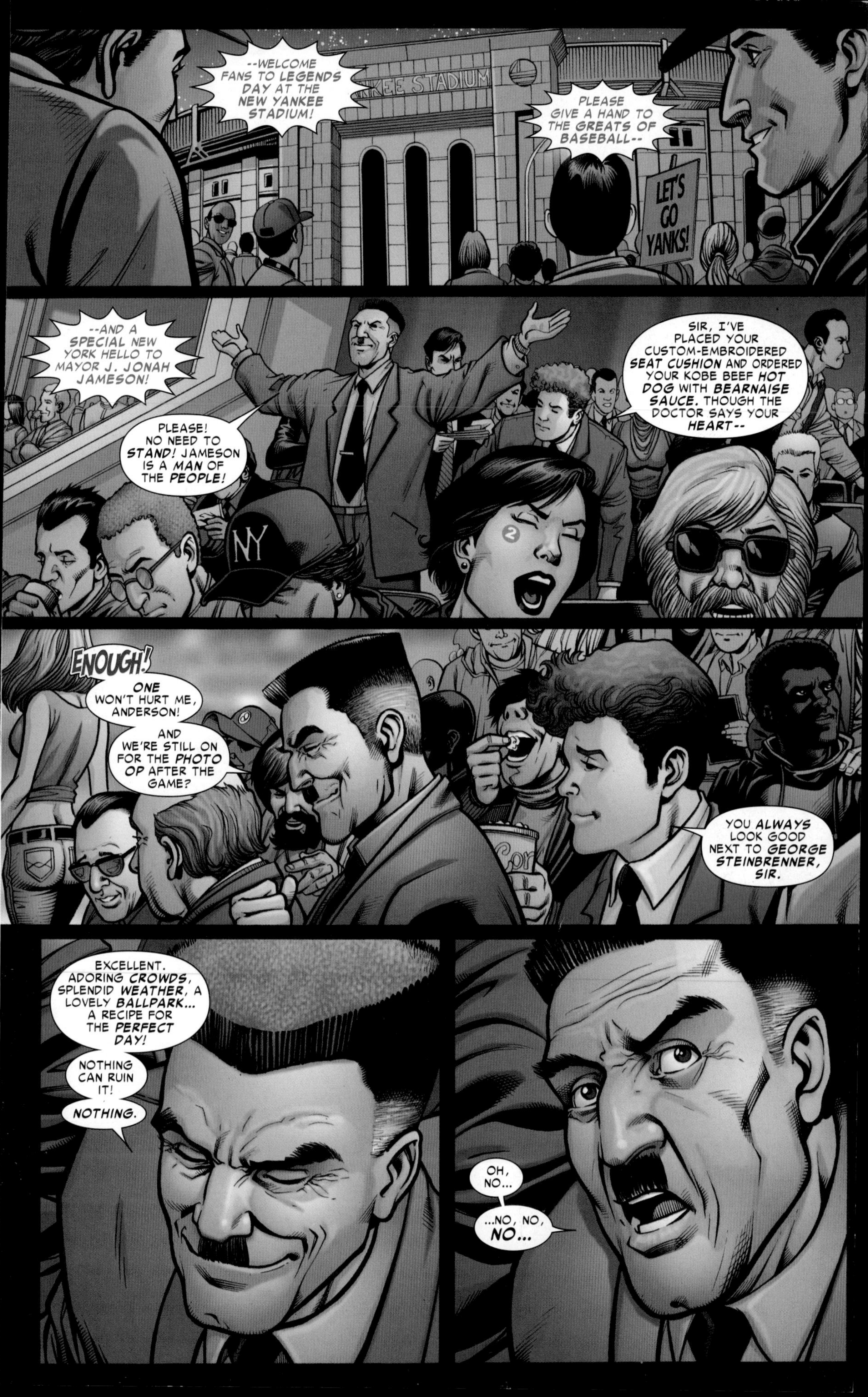
--WELCOME FANS TO LEGENDS DAY AT THE NEW YANKEE STADIUM!
PLEASE GIVE A HAND TO THE GREATS OF BASEBALL--
KEE STADIUM
LET'S GO YANKS!
--AND A SPECIAL NEW YORK HELLO TO MAYOR J. JONAH JAMESON!
PLEASE! NO NEED TO STAND! JAMESON IS A MAN OF THE PEOPLE!
SIR, I'VE PLACED YOUR CUSTOM-EMBROIDERED SEAT CUSHION AND ORDERED YOUR KOBE BEEF HOT DOG WITH BEARNAISE SAUCE. THOUGH THE DOCTOR SAYS YOUR HEART--
NY
ENOUGH!
ONE WON'T HURT ME, ANDERSON!
AND WE'RE STILL ON FOR THE PHOTO OP AFTER THE GAME?
YOU ALWAYS LOOK GOOD NEXT TO GEORGE STEINBRENNER, SIR.
EXCELLENT. ADORING CROWDS, SPLENDID WEATHER, A LOVELY BALLPARK... A RECIPE FOR THE PERFECT DAY!
NOTHING CAN RUIN IT!
NOTHING.
OH, NO...
...NO, NO, NO...

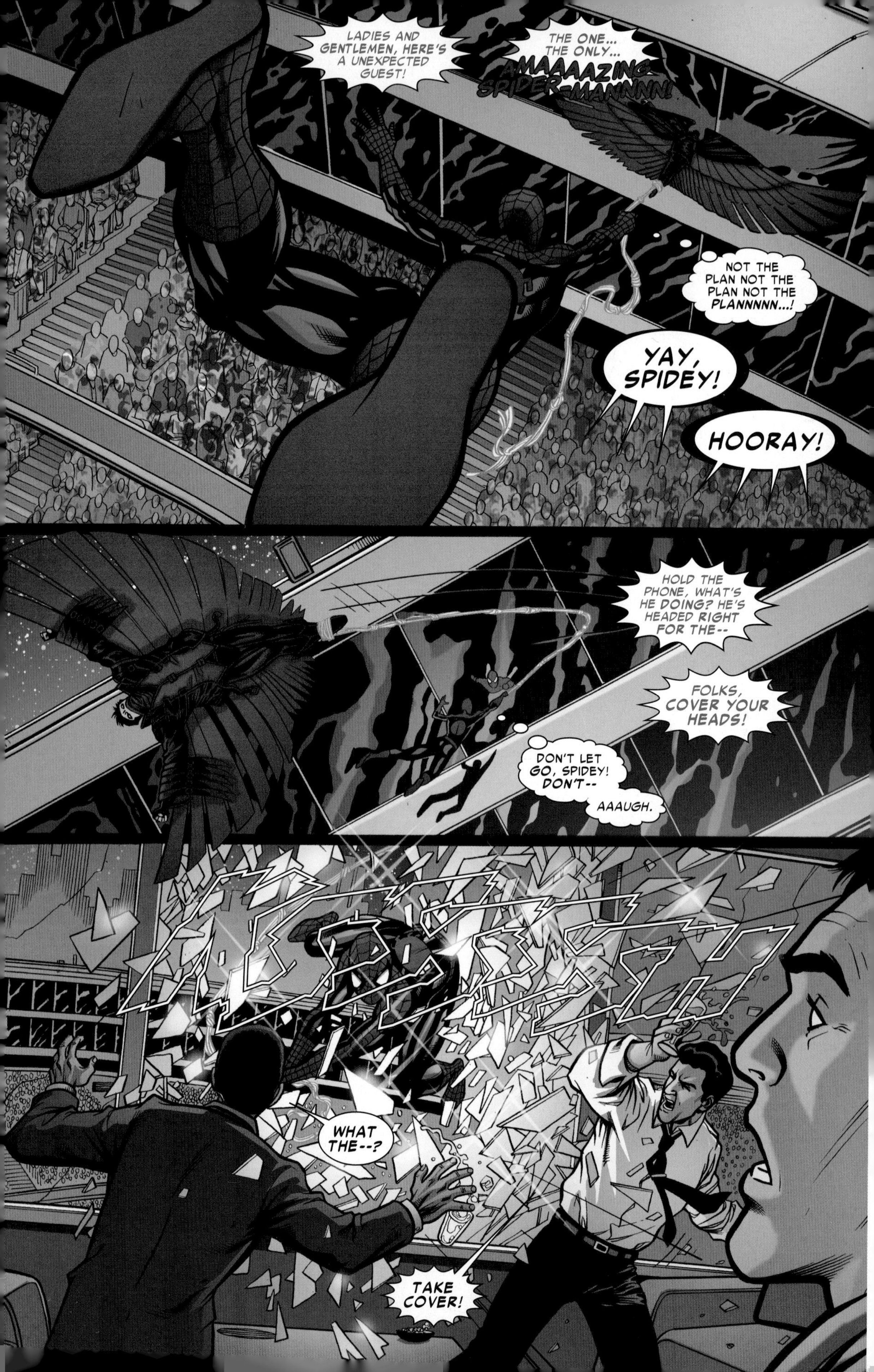
LADIES AND GENTLEMEN, HERE'S A UNEXPECTED GUEST!
THE ONE... THE ONLY...
AMAAAAAZING SPIDER-MANNNNN!
NOT THE PLAN NOT THE PLAN NOT THE PLANNNNN...!
YAY, SPIDEY!
HOORAY!
HOLD THE PHONE, WHAT'S HE DOING? HE'S HEADED RIGHT FOR THE--
FOLKS, COVER YOUR HEADS!
DON'T LET GO, SPIDEY! DON'T--
AAAUGH.
WHAT THE--?
TAKE COVER!

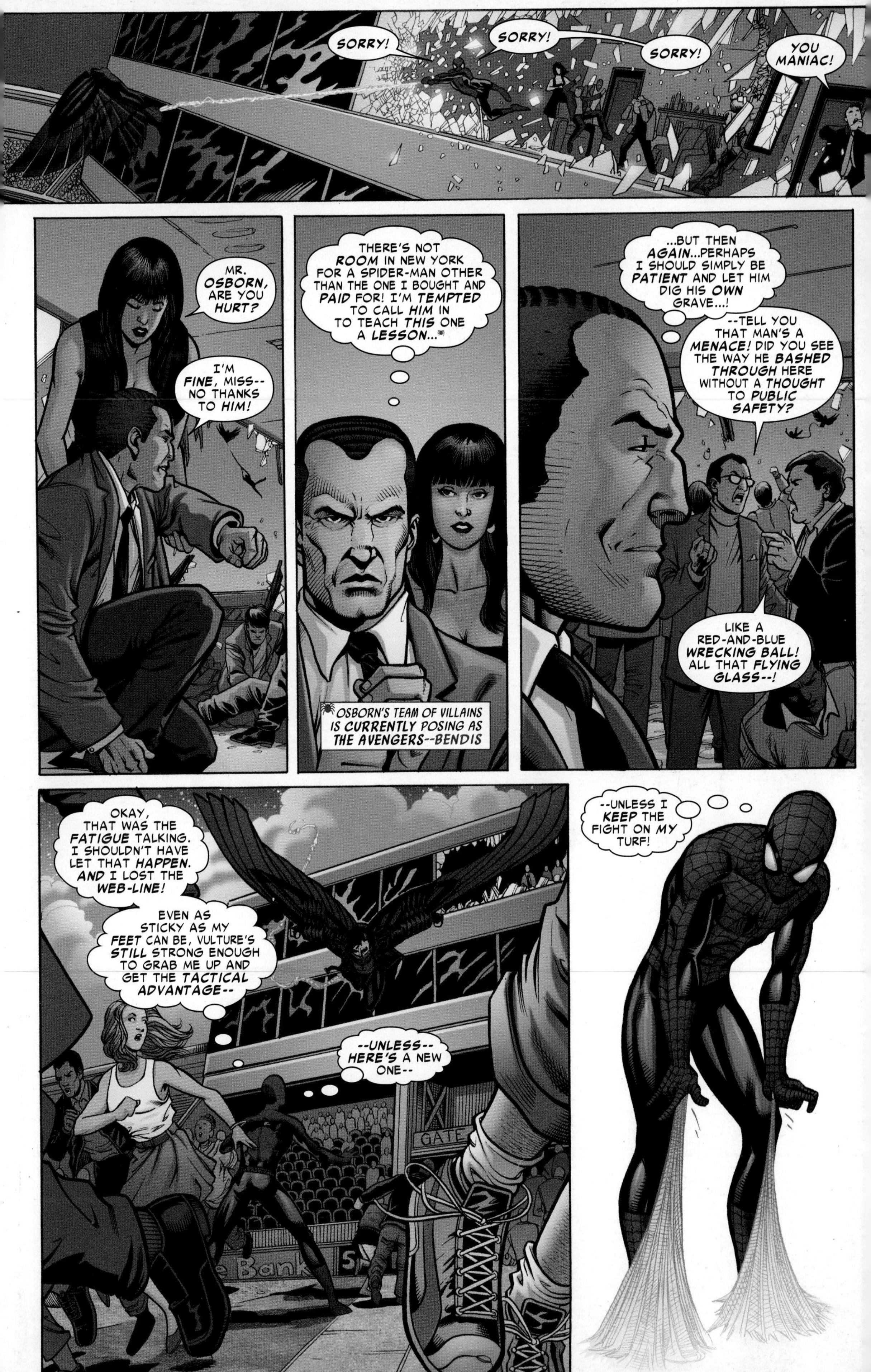
SORRY!
SORRY!
SORRY!
YOU MANIAC!
MR. OSBORN, ARE YOU HURT?
I'M FINE, MISS-- NO THANKS TO HIM!
THERE'S NOT ROOM IN NEW YORK FOR A SPIDER-MAN OTHER THAN THE ONE I BOUGHT AND PAID FOR! I'M TEMPTED TO CALL HIM IN TO TEACH THIS ONE A LESSON...
OSBORN'S TEAM OF VILLAINS IS CURRENTLY POSING AS THE AVENGERS--BENDIS
...BUT THEN AGAIN...PERHAPS I SHOULD SIMPLY BE PATIENT AND LET HIM DIG HIS OWN GRAVE...!
--TELL YOU THAT MAN'S A MENACE! DID YOU SEE THE WAY HE BASHED THROUGH HERE WITHOUT A THOUGHT TO PUBLIC SAFETY?
LIKE A RED-AND-BLUE WRECKING BALL! ALL THAT FLYING GLASS--!
OKAY, THAT WAS THE FATIGUE TALKING. I SHOULDN'T HAVE LET THAT HAPPEN. AND I LOST THE WEB-LINE!
EVEN AS STICKY AS MY FEET CAN BE, VULTURE'S STILL STRONG ENOUGH TO GRAB ME UP AND GET THE TACTICAL ADVANTAGE--
--UNLESS-- HERE'S A NEW ONE--
--UNLESS I KEEP THE FIGHT ON MY TURF!
GATE
Bank

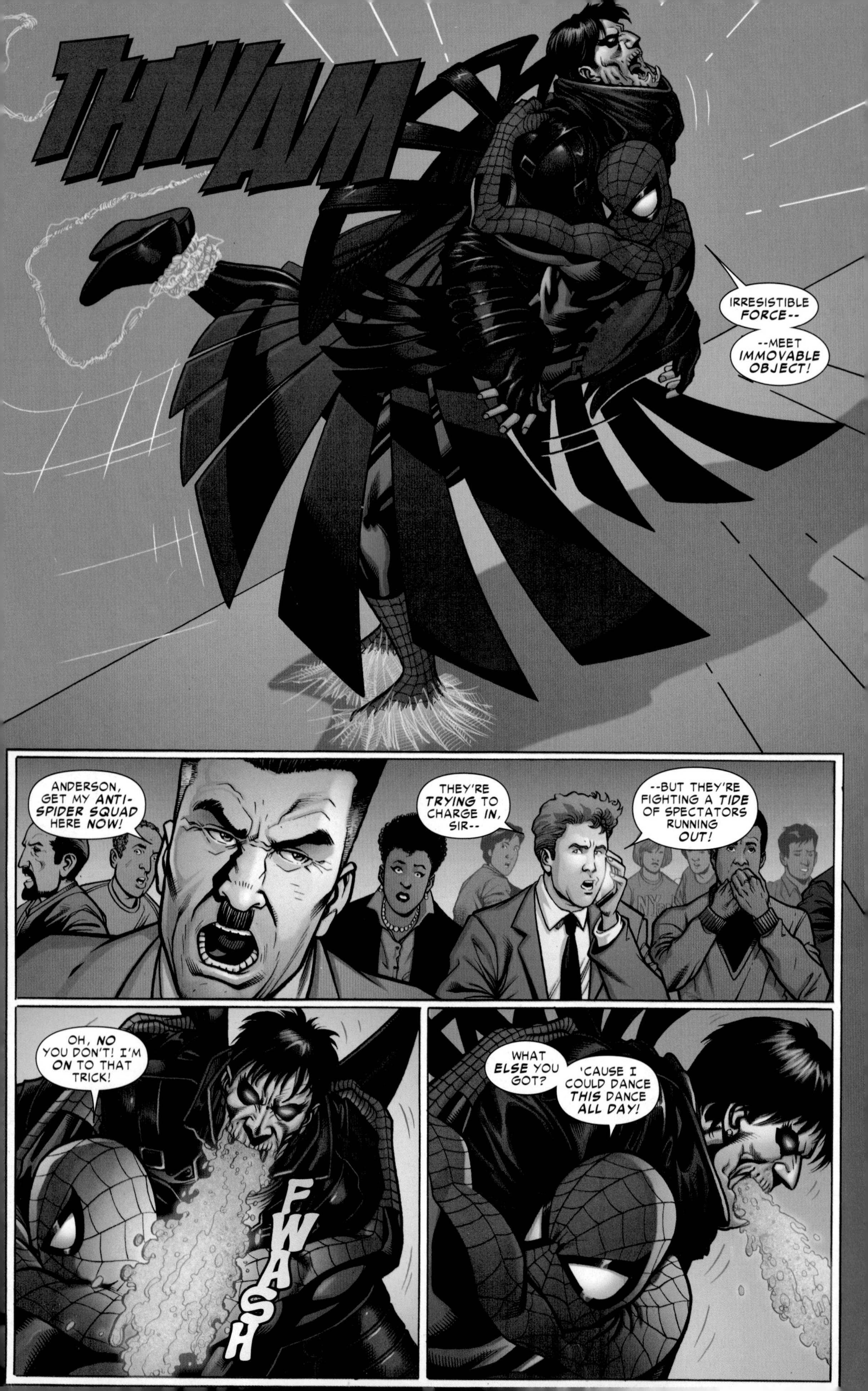
THWAM
IRRESISTIBLE FORCE--
--MEET IMMOVABLE OBJECT!
ANDERSON, GET MY ANTI-SPIDER SQUAD HERE NOW!
THEY'RE TRYING TO CHARGE IN, SIR--
--BUT THEY'RE FIGHTING A TIDE OF SPECTATORS RUNNING OUT!
OH, NO YOU DON'T! I'M ON TO THAT TRICK!
FWASH
WHAT ELSE YOU GOT?
'CAUSE I COULD DANCE THIS DANCE ALL DAY!

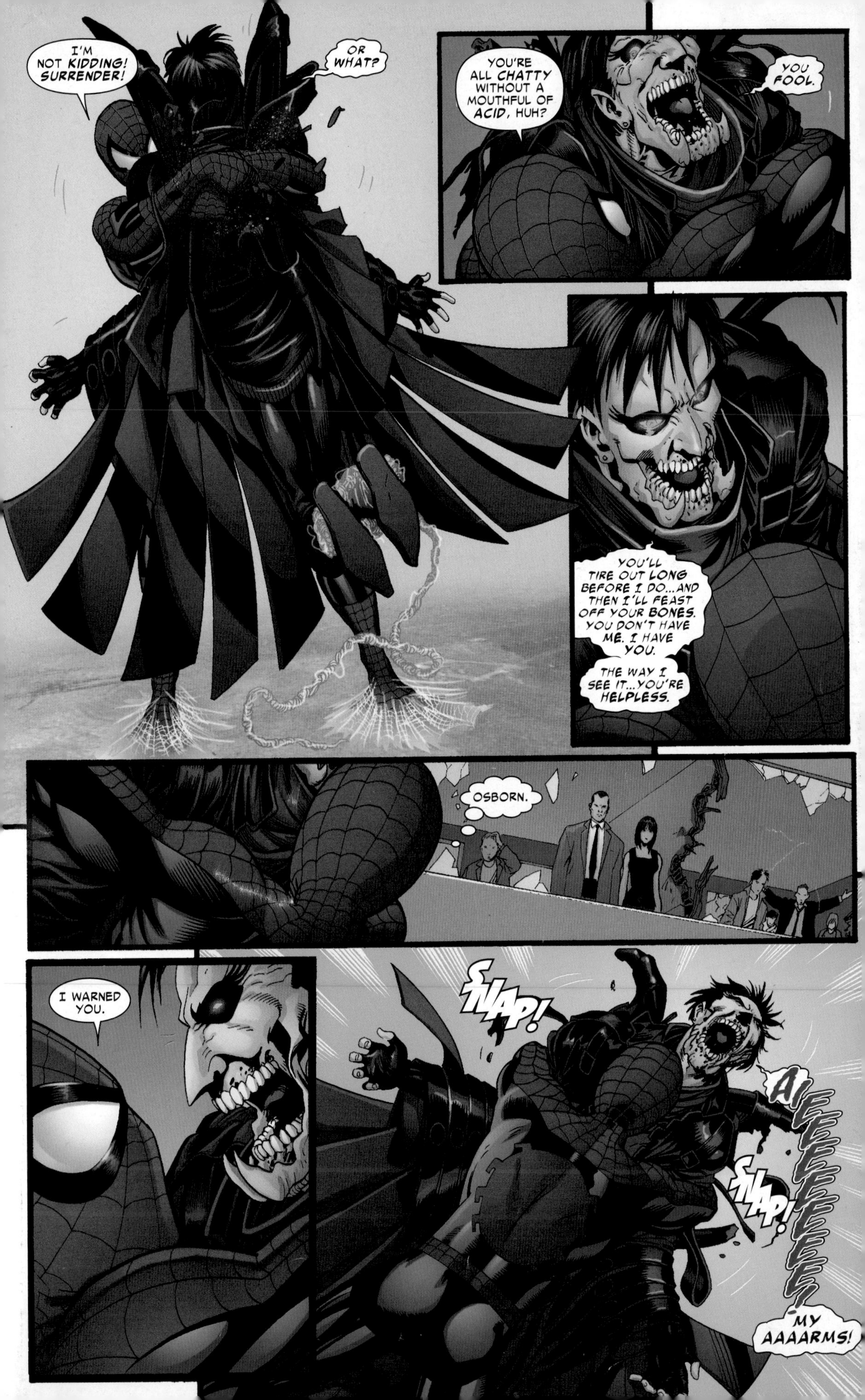
I'M NOT KIDDING! SURRENDER!
OR WHAT?
YOU'RE ALL CHATTY WITHOUT A MOUTHFUL OF ACID, HUH?
YOU FOOL.
YOU'LL TIRE OUT LONG BEFORE I DO...AND THEN I'LL FEAST OFF YOUR BONES. YOU DON'T HAVE ME. I HAVE YOU.
THE WAY I SEE IT...YOU'RE HELPLESS.
OSBORN.
I WARNED YOU.
SNAP!
AIEEEEEEEEEE!
SNAP!
MY AAAARMS!

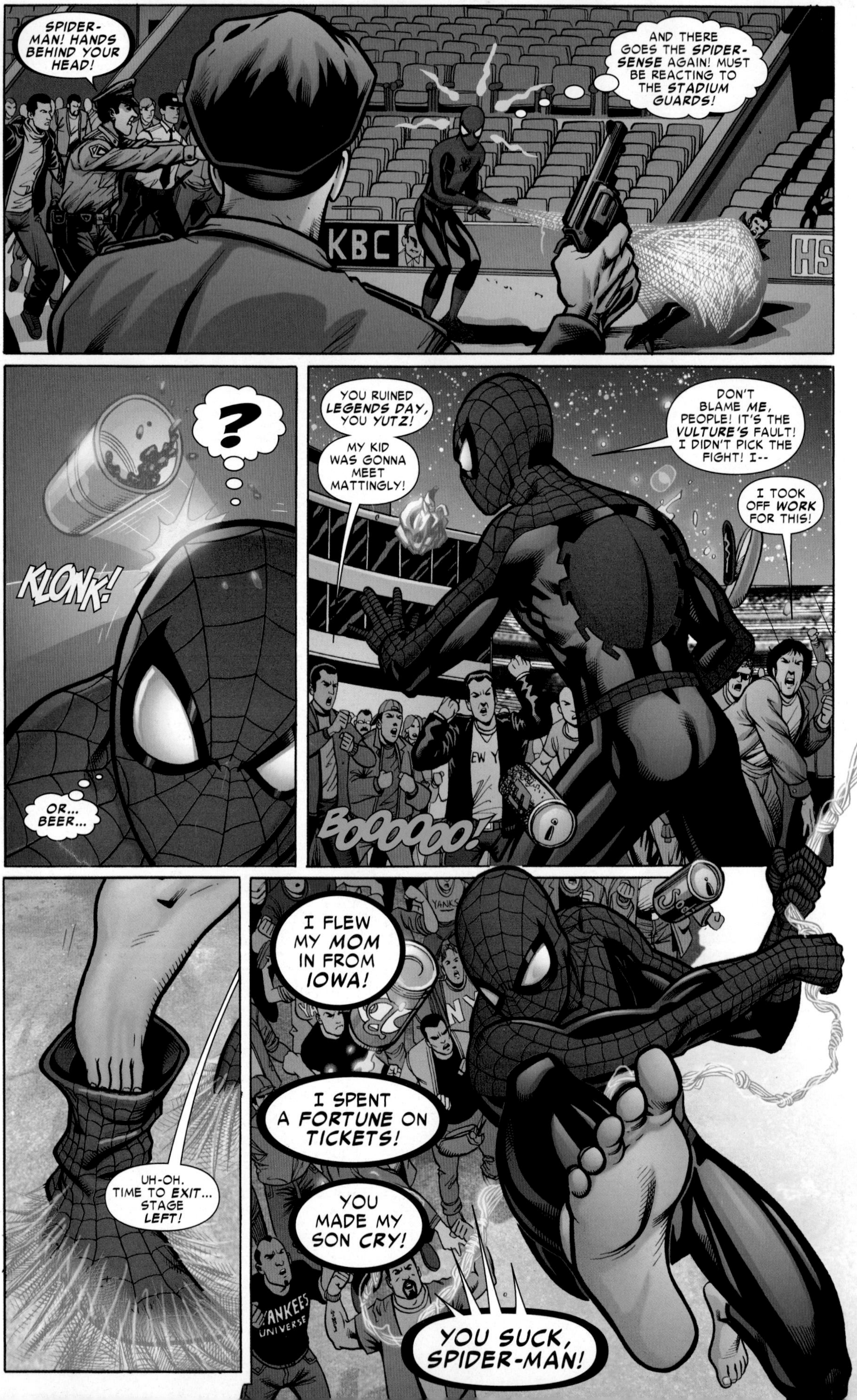
SPIDER-MAN! HANDS BEHIND YOUR HEAD!
AND THERE GOES THE SPIDER-SENSE AGAIN! MUST BE REACTING TO THE STADIUM GUARDS!
KBC
?
KLONK!
OR... BEER...
YOU RUINED LEGENDS DAY, YOU YUTZ!
MY KID WAS GONNA MEET MATTINGLY!
DON'T BLAME ME, PEOPLE! IT'S THE VULTURE'S FAULT! I DIDN'T PICK THE FIGHT! I--
I TOOK OFF WORK FOR THIS!
BOOOOOOO!
UH-OH. TIME TO EXIT... STAGE LEFT!
I FLEW MY MOM IN FROM IOWA!
I SPENT A FORTUNE ON TICKETS!
YOU MADE MY SON CRY!
YOU SUCK, SPIDER-MAN!
YANKEES UNIVERSE

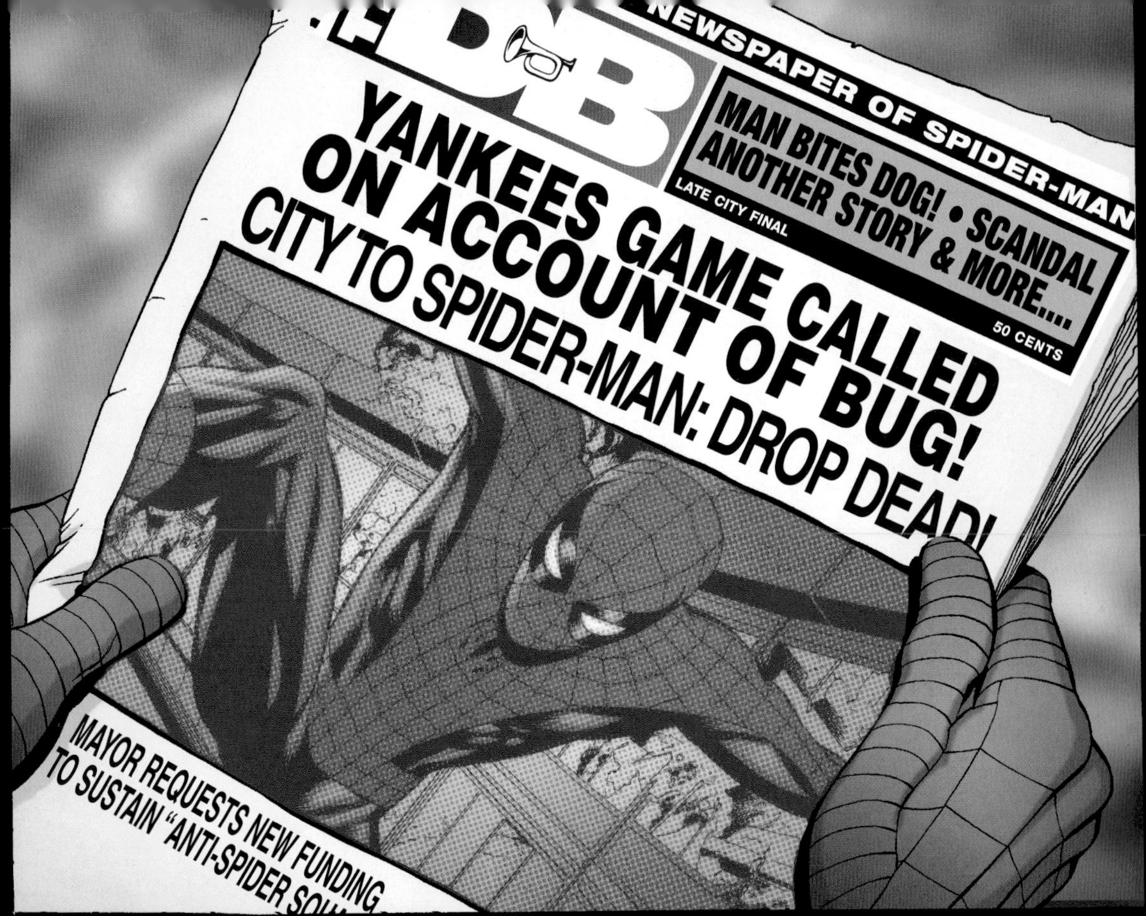

THE DB
NEWSPAPER OF SPIDER-MAN
MAN BITES DOG! • SCANDAL
ANOTHER STORY & MORE...
LATE CITY FINAL
50 CENTS
YANKEES GAME CALLED ON ACCOUNT OF BUG!
CITY TO SPIDER-MAN: DROP DEAD!
MAYOR REQUESTS NEW FUNDING TO SUSTAIN "ANTI-SPIDER SQU

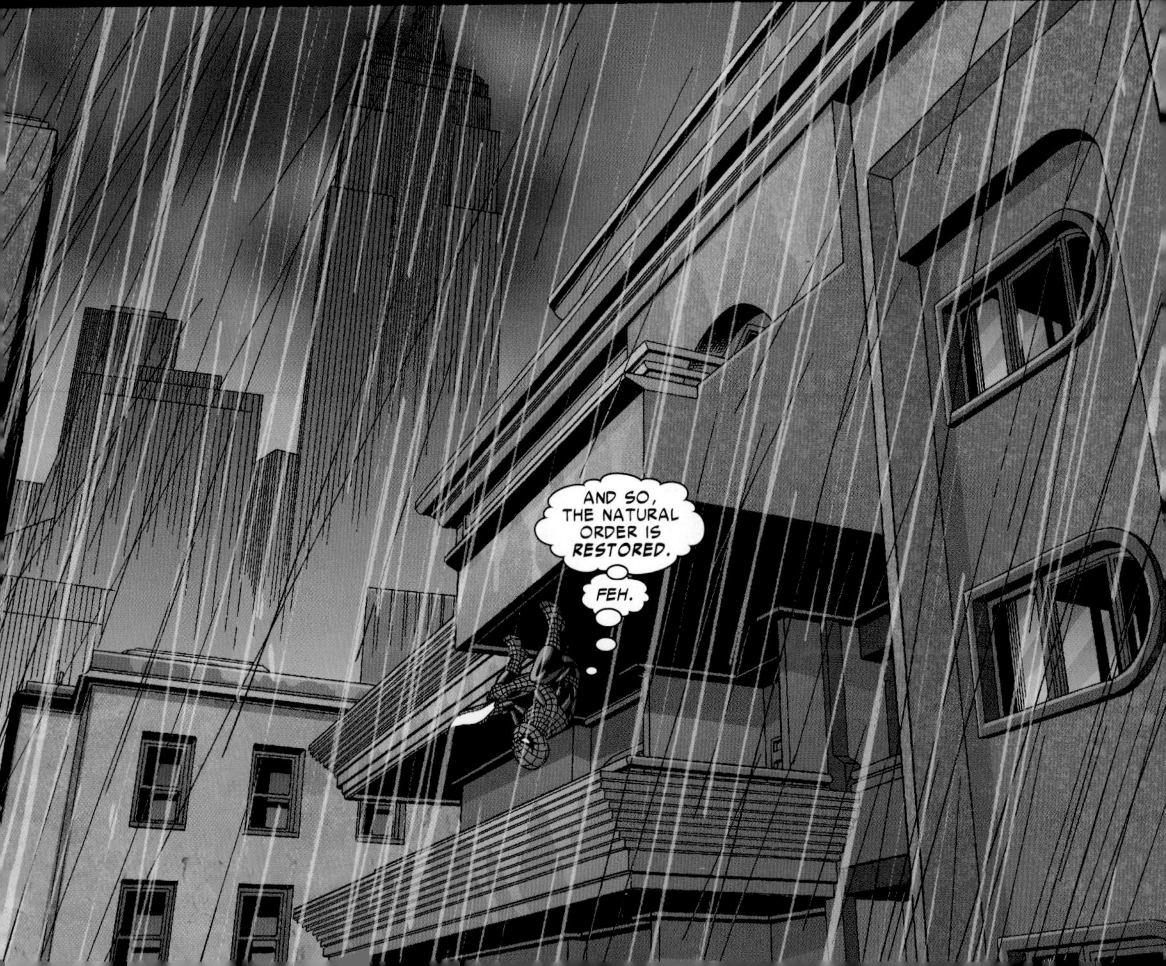

AND SO, THE NATURAL ORDER IS RESTORED.
FEH.

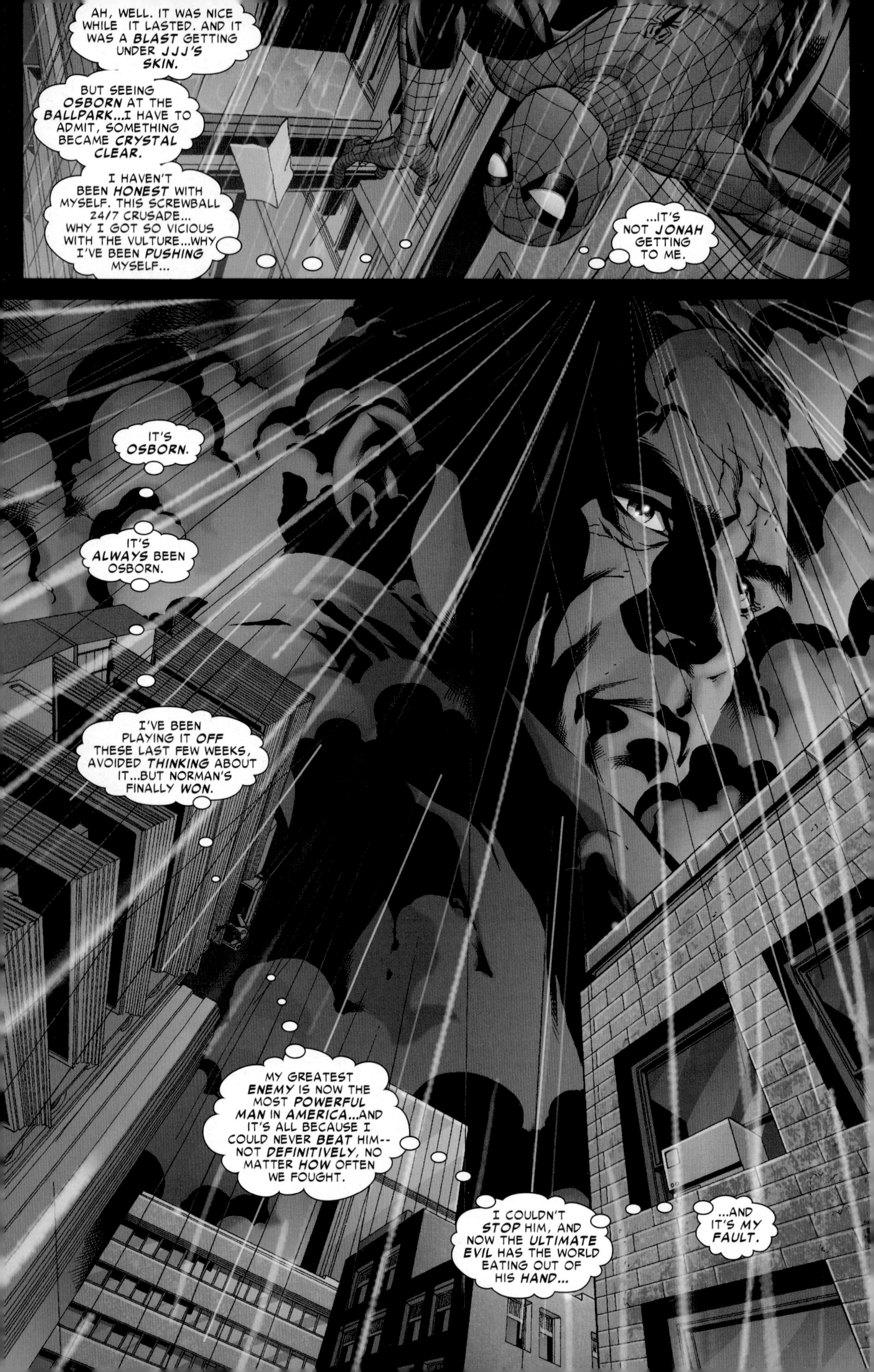
AH, WELL. IT WAS NICE WHILE IT LASTED. AND IT WAS A BLAST GETTING UNDER JJJ'S SKIN.
BUT SEEING OSBORN AT THE BALLPARK...I HAVE TO ADMIT, SOMETHING BECAME CRYSTAL CLEAR.
I HAVEN'T BEEN HONEST WITH MYSELF. THIS SCREWBALL 24/7 CRUSADE... WHY I GOT SO VICIOUS WITH THE VULTURE...WHY I'VE BEEN PUSHING MYSELF...
...IT'S NOT JONAH GETTING TO ME.
IT'S OSBORN.
IT'S ALWAYS BEEN OSBORN.
I'VE BEEN PLAYING IT OFF THESE LAST FEW WEEKS, AVOIDED THINKING ABOUT IT...BUT NORMAN'S FINALLY WON.
MY GREATEST ENEMY IS NOW THE MOST POWERFUL MAN IN AMERICA...AND IT'S ALL BECAUSE I COULD NEVER BEAT HIM--NOT DEFINITIVELY, NO MATTER HOW OFTEN WE FOUGHT.
I COULDN'T STOP HIM, AND NOW THE ULTIMATE EVIL HAS THE WORLD EATING OUT OF HIS HAND...
...AND IT'S MY FAULT.

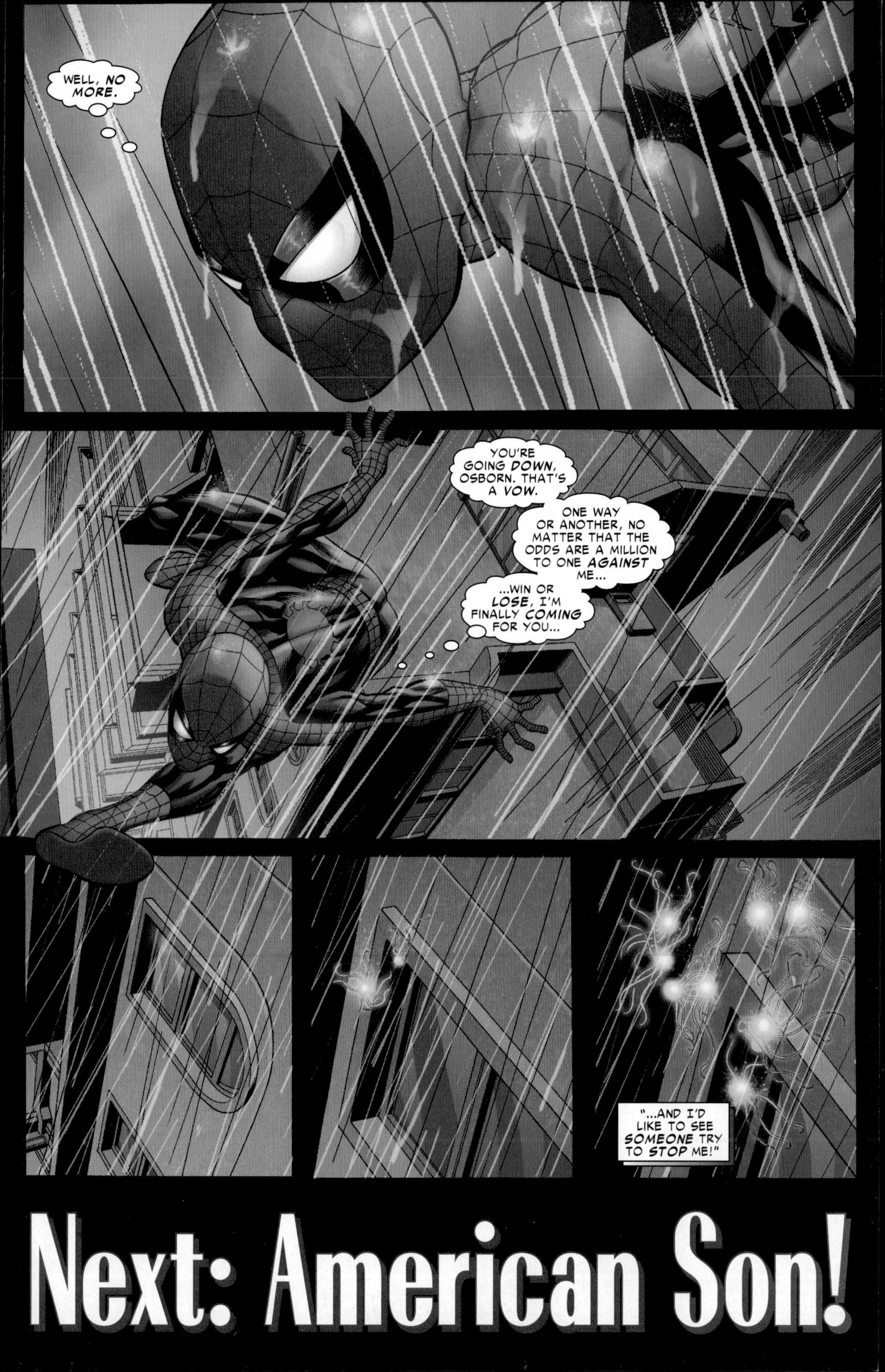
WELL, NO MORE.
YOU'RE GOING DOWN, OSBORN. THAT'S A VOW.
ONE WAY OR ANOTHER, NO MATTER THAT THE ODDS ARE A MILLION TO ONE AGAINST ME...
...WIN OR LOSE, I'M FINALLY COMING FOR YOU...
"...AND I'D LIKE TO SEE SOMEONE TRY TO STOP ME!"

Next: American Son!

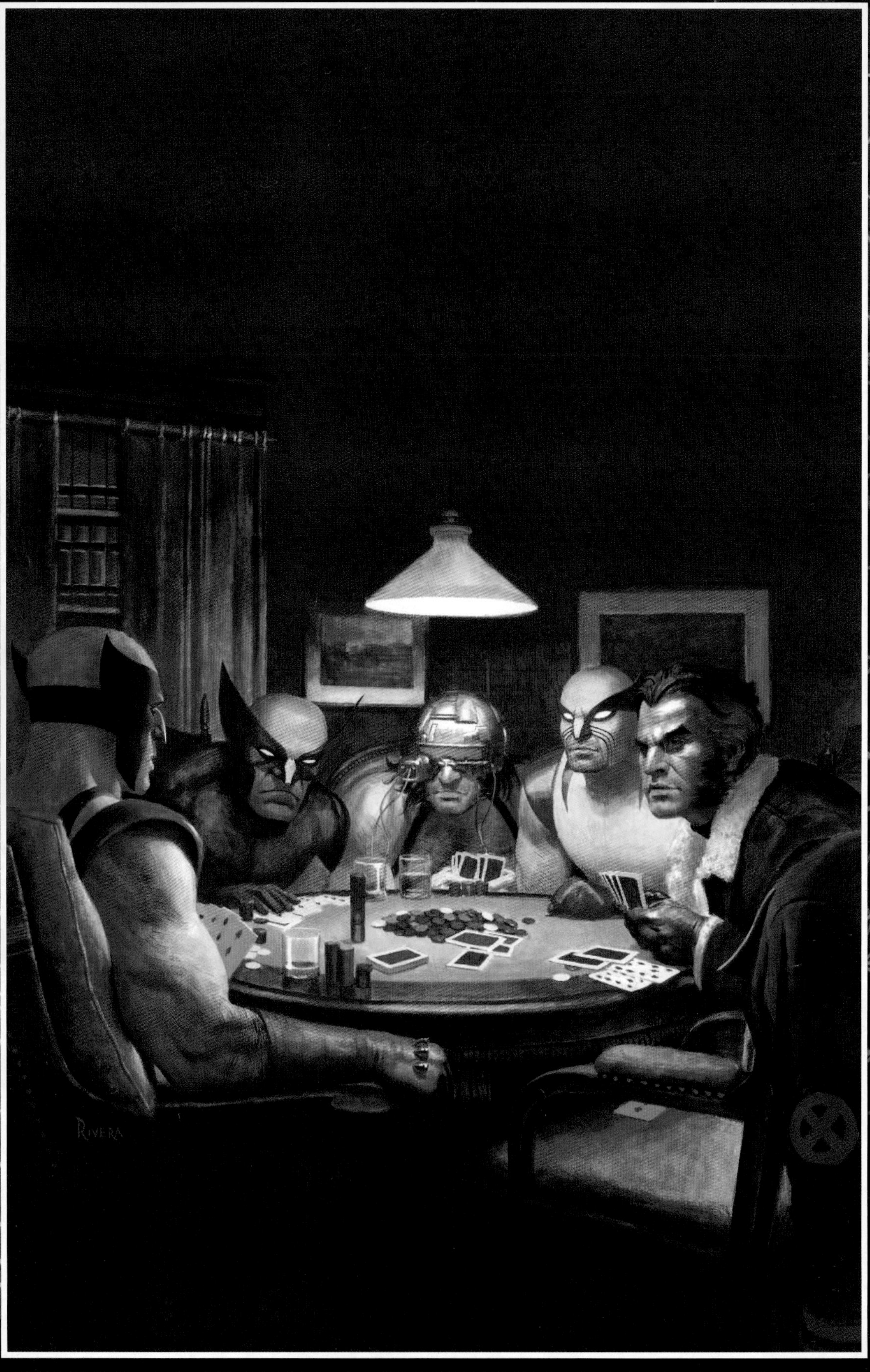
RIVERA

AMAZING SPIDER-MAN #590 WOLVERINE ART APPRECIATION VARIANT BY PAOLO RIVERA

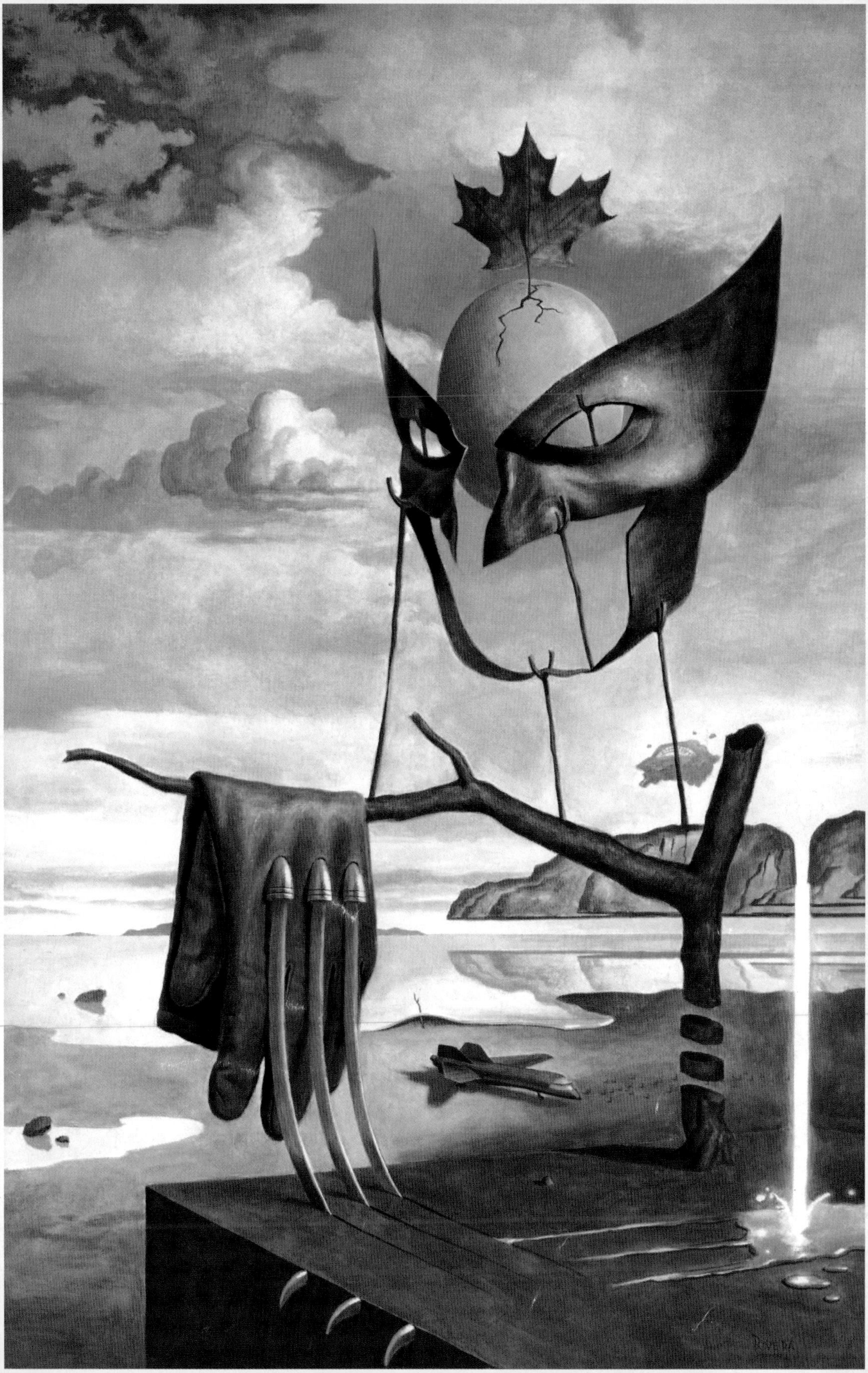

AMAZING SPIDER-MAN #592 WOLVERINE ART APPRECIATION VARIANT BY PAOLO RIVERA

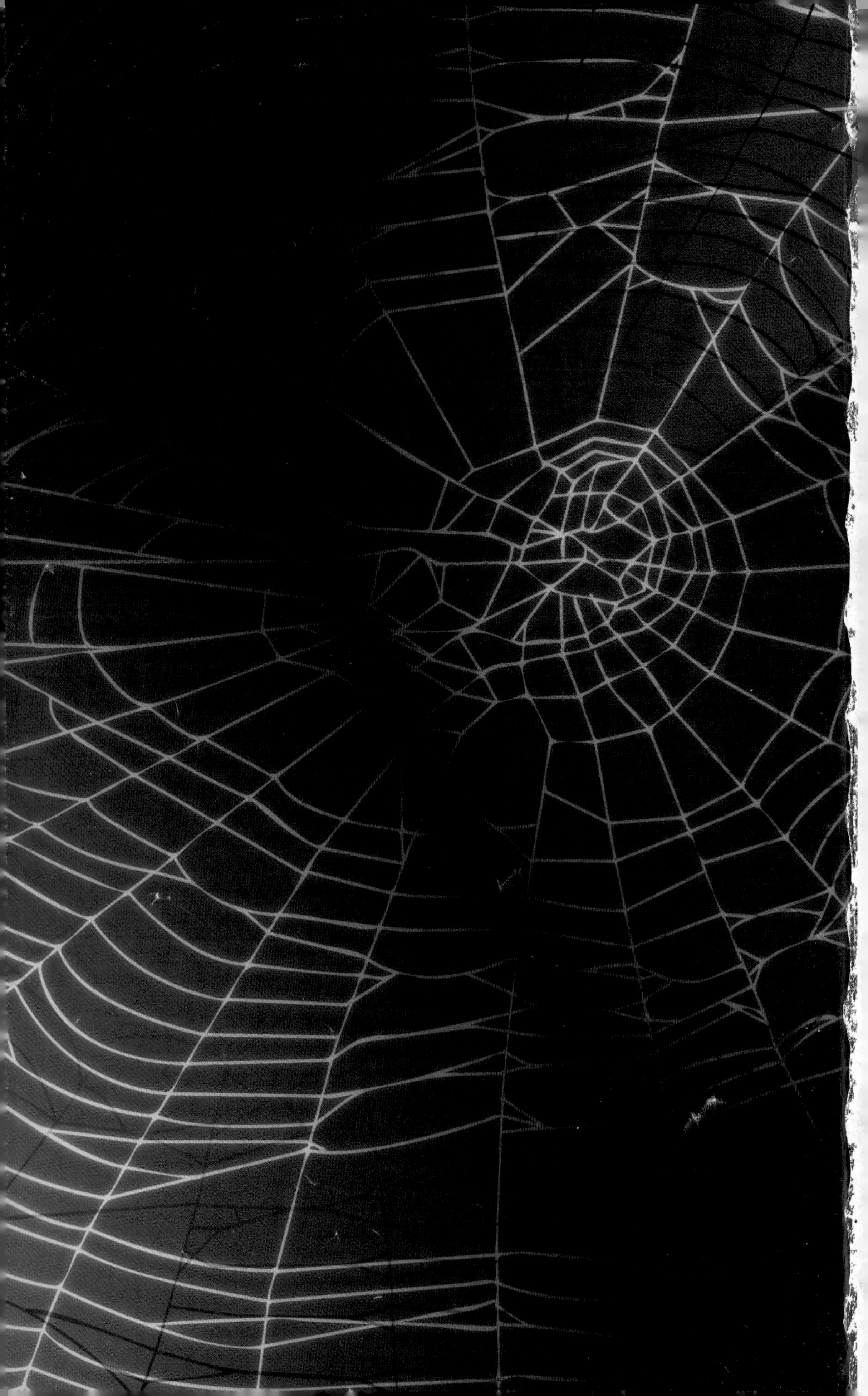